EMPOWERMENT OF SCHEDULED CASTES

EMPOWERMENT OF SCHEDULED CASTES

Dr. R. Vijaya Krishna Naidu

PUBLICATIONS

KALPAZ PUBLICATIONS
DELHI - 110052

EMPOWERMENT OF SCHEDULED CASTES
[*Dalit Studies*]

Rs. 750

ISBN: 81-7835-297-4

Published in 2004 in India by
Kalpaz Publications
C-30, Satyawati Nagar
Delhi-110052
e-mail: kalpaz@hotmail.com

Laser Typeset at: Alphabet, Delhi
Printed at: Mehra Offset Press, Delhi

Dedicated to
My father

Late R. Radha Krishna Naidu

Contents

Preface

In the annals of the Indian history, twentieth century occupies a place of pride for two reasons. For one reason, it was during this century; India attained its independence from the colonial rule and emerged as a Sovereign State. For the other and more socially important reason, it was during this century India and its populace began the determined and relentless efforts and defiance to end the inhuman social inequalities, crusade against the practice of untouchability and to empower the weaker sections to achieve an egalitarian society.

The present book, *Empowerment of Scheduled Castes* clearly reflects the empirical picture of the scenario. It is true that now a number of titles are available and a wide range of studies have been made to reflect different perspectives on development of weaker sections, particularly the Scheduled Castes; yet, this book, I feel is a welcome addition and adds to the existing literature in its own way.

Often the researchers and students of social development studies find it strenuous to locate a source book, which comprehensively covers the basic issues, viz. the genesis of the problem, the constitutional and legal remedies, the process of overcoming social inequalities, the opportunities, attainments and the disappointments and the process of empowerment in one single publication. I tried to address to this problem and made best possible efforts in this direction. The present work is a revised and enlarged version of my doctoral study. The book consists of eight chapters and provides insights into the development and empowerment process of the Scheduled Castes. To explain this social process, I have chosen the important spheres, viz. education, occupation, political participation and social status and tried to explain the changes taking place in these spheres. The study, in a lucid form explains the achievements, limitations and the enduring process of attaining social equality and social empowerment.

Further, I have taken enough care to provide necessary basic and latest information and useful references for the benefit of students interested in the studies of weaker sections and their empowerment.

I am sure that this book will earn the appreciation of both critics as well as the students of social development studies.

R. Vijaya Krishna Naidu

One

The Theoretical Framework

The Concept of Social Stratification

The tendency of people to differentiate among themselves according to specific criteria results in human societies that are stratified or differentiated into a number of layers or segments. People rank themselves according to wealth, prestige and power. Differential distribution of power, prestige, privileges and resources result in differential ranking of status in the hierarchy. As rank in the hierarchy increases, so does the share in the rewards - wealth, power and prestige. MacIver and Page (1967) identified hierarchy of status groups, the recognition of inferior and superior stratification and some degree of permanence of structure as the features of social stratification. As explained by William (1960), stratification denotes some way, whereby some kinds of units are arranged in some kind of strata. He further said that stratification is the ranking of individuals on a scale of superiority - inferiority - equality according to some commonly accepted basis of valuation.

The conflict and functional schools, which are the two main schools of thought, dominated explaining social stratification.

The foremost of the conflict theorists was Karl Marx, who said that the social classes, the dimension of social stratification, are defined by their relationship to the means of production. This provided the basis for his view that in every society there are conflicting classes on the basis of their control of the means of production. Marxian theory visualised the struggle between the competing economic groups as the lever for social change. Max Weber, another classical thinker on stratification, agreed with Marx about the role of economic factor in stratification, but added two more dimensions viz. power and prestige, as the two separate factors, which are but interacting bases of social hierarchy. Dahrendorf (1966) another conflict theorist tried to explain stratification based on authority relationship.

Davis and Moore proposed the functional theory of stratification, (1945) which clearly stated that stratification is a ubiquitous system and is a functional necessity of the society. They opined that social inequality is an unconsciously evolved universal device by which societies ensure that most important positions in the society are conscientiously filled by the most qualified in the society. They felt the necessity to motivate the members with differential rewards not only for the sustenance of comforts but also for their self-respect and ego satisfaction.

Parsons (1954), the other thinker of functional perspective, contended that there are three factors that are evaluated in relation to the central core value of each society. These, as he explained, are possession of those attributes which people own, qualities belonging to individuals, and performances. As the men differ in terms of these factors, inequality naturally follows. To sum up Parsons, stratification is the result of the two social processes, role differentiation and ranking in terms of dominant values.

Lenski (1966) attempts a synthetic approach, which combines the elements of the functional and conflict approach. To him the degree of inequality varies with technical development. His argument is based on the assumption that man is guided by his self-interest in relation to the appropriation of surplus. For Kemper (1976) the viewpoints of stratification have in common two analytical elements, which are social power and evaluation of contribution as determinants of distribution of rewards.

Besides the above, Veblen's (1953) theory of Leisure class explains about stratification. Velbens theory does not have much concern with economic theory. He said two institutions are prominent viz. private property associated with pecuniary element and technology of production. The proportion of society having monopoly of the above two is the leisure class. With the rise in leisure class comes complexity and private ownership, differential employment becoming the main criterion for social differentiation.

It is difficult to find common elements in the approaches that tried to analyse stratification. Taking into consideration the two important approaches, the conflict and functional, it can be said that they are incompatible. Yogendra Singh (1977) agrees with this opinion and to quote him " neither the conflict nor the consensus model is itself sufficient to explain fully all sociological process of social stratification. (Leach, 1967; Allardt, 1968; Jackson, 1968 etc). The proponents of both the theoretical views are non-emphasising convergence or similarity in the two approaches. (Parsons, 1940 and 1953; Davis and Moore 1954; Moore, 1953; Tumin, 1953; 1955; 1963 and 1967; Buckley, 1959; Wrong, 1959; Stinch Combe, 1963; Weslowski, 1966 etc.)

It can be concluded that the thinkers on social stratification have found its dimensions different. They have identified different determinants of stratum such as wealth, income, occupation, education etc. Sociologists have in general distinguished four main types of stratification viz. slavery, estate, class and caste.

The important categorisation of social stratification system is that of open and closed stratification system. Whether a particular society has open or closed social stratification system depends on the ways and means the members of the society employ for acquiring wealth, prestige and power. In an open society, theoretically speaking, each member of the society has equal access to material resources, power and prestige. Every member of the society is free to compete for them and can acquire them by putting his personal efforts. On the other hand in closed societies class, status, power and privileges are ascribed and determined on the basis of the family and inheritance rather than the personal effort. In such societies the individual born in a specific social status group inherits that status and remains in that status group. As this social system is extremely rigid, the individuals have no opportunity to move into or out of the stratum and this type of closed stratum is called the caste system.

The Caste System

The English word 'Caste' rather corresponds more or less closely to what is locally referred to as 'Jati' or 'Kulam'. Besides Jati or Kulam everyone is familiar with concept of 'Varna', which refers to one of the four main categories into which the Hindu society is traditionally divided; Jati refers generally to a much smaller group (Srinivas, 1962). The English word caste is used to denote both, not only by foreigners but also by others who are familiar with English. 'Caste' and 'Sub caste' are the other terms, which refer to primary division and sub division. This is not altogether satisfactory because the caste system is characterised by segmentation of several orders (Beteille, 1965).

Caste is the very complex social institution deeply entrenched in Indian society from immemorial past. The earliest Vedas do not reveal the existence of caste. Careful analysis of the sacred books of India indicates that the caste system developed in the latest phase of decline of the Vedic culture as a result of Aryan invasion and conquest of the original inhabitants. For centuries it remained more or less fluid. But later on it acquired rigidity and exclusiveness. Caste became a complete system encompassing every aspect of the life of the Hindus (Abraham, 1979).

Hutton (1946) laid down the following criteria for castes.

(i) Caste is endogamous.
(ii) There is restriction on mobility between members of different castes.
(iii) There is hierarchical grading of castes.
(iv) In various kinds of contact especially those concerned with food, sex and ritual a member of a higher caste is liable to be polluted by either direct or indirect contact with a member of lower caste.
(v) Caste is very commonly associated with a traditional occupation.
(vi) A man's status is determined by the circumstances of his birth (i.e. the caste in which he is born) unless he is expelled from his caste for some ritual offence.

Several writers who worked on the caste and the caste like groups are of the opinion that the caste or the caste like groups is found even outside India, in areas such as Arabia, Polynesia, Africa, Guatemala, Japan and United States, particularly in the south. (Bailey 1959, Carstairs 1961, Krober 1930, Thompson, 1939, Davis et al., 1941, Ghurye 1932, Ketkar 1909, Dollard 1957; Davis 1941, Harper, 1968; Bereman, 1960; Chappell and Coon, 1947; Nadel, 1954; Tumin, 1952; Donghue, 1957; Gallagher, 1938). But some sociologists and social anthropologists with Indian experience differ with the above viewpoint. To them, the caste system is a unique feature of Indian social structure and the characters that the caste exhibits and it shares with rigid systems of social stratification are not to be found elsewhere in the world. (Johnson, 1944, Simpson and Yinger, 1953; Con, 1945; 1948; Leach, 1959; Myrdal, 1944; Ryan, 1953; Sorokin, 1947). What ever is the case, caste is the first and foremost feature of Indian Society and most rigid form of caste system appear in Indian Society.

Due to complexity and existence of different facets for caste system, it is very difficult to give a precise definition to caste. Risley (1891) defines caste as 'a collection of families bearing a common name, claiming a common descent from a mythical ancestors human or divine; professing to follow the same hereditary calling; and regarded by those who are competent to give an opinion of forming a single homogenous community'.

Ketkar (1909) defines caste as a "Social group having two characteristics: 1) membership is confined to those who are born as members, and includes all persons so born. 2) The members are forbidden by an inexorable social law to marry outside the group. Each one of these groups has a special name by which it is called, several of such small aggregates are grouped together under a common name, while these large groups are but sub divisions of groups still larger which have independent names.

Structural aspect of the caste system is explained accepting it as a general principle of stratification (Barth, 1967). Caste as a cultural system is understood in terms of prominence of ideas of purity and pollution and notions of hierarchy, segregation and carporateness (Dumont, 1970). Caste is also viewed as 'closed system' of stratification (Bailey F.G, 1963). On the other hand Beteille (1966) considers caste systems both 'closed' and 'open'. These analytical variations hinder arriving at a common definition of caste. But at the same time these variations explain the fact that caste is like all other systems of stratification in some way and it is unique in some other respects.

Srinivas (1962) writes "a sociologist would define caste as a hereditary, endogamous, usually localised group, having a traditional association with an occupation and a particular position in the local hierarchy of castes. Relations between castes are governed among other things, by the concept of pollution and purity and generally maximum commensality occurs within the caste (1962).

Ainapur (1986) giving a comprehensive definition of Caste describes, "Caste is a system incorporating within it a structure and organization, and is based on endogamy, hierarchy, and commensal restrictions. It also prescribes the pattern of group relations that may bind the interacting individuals in routine life. The groups in caste system are exhaustive, exclusive, and discrete, i.e. every person is a member of such a group and of only one. Membership in-group influences the members in their roles and activities; there is a high degree of 'role summation'. The groups are interdependent; each needs the services or goods provided by others".

In the modern period, since the early 19th century various efforts have been made to redefine Hinduism with a view to reform it, so as to meet the challenges of the new era on the one hand, and counter Christianity and Islam on the other. Hindu reformers rejected Caste system based on birth. They viewed it as a system of division of labour in society in which mobility by skill and virtue permitted. In order to serve their vested interests and to perpetuate their dominance, the Brahmins, in the course of time, converted the Caste system into a rigid, closed and hereditary one. For the reformers untouchability was a blot on humanity, a disgrace on Hinduism. Untouchability arose out of an aberration of the Varna-Dharma. What was needed was: to reform Hinduism (Vable, 1983; Jones, 1976; Weber, 1958). Even as they rejected the Jati system, Hindu reformers continued to subscribe to the Varna system and Mahatma Gandhi was one of them. In recent times a prominent proponent of anti-untouchability, yet a champion of the Chaturvarna system, recipient of several international awards for his "new social movement", is Pandurang Athavale. According to him the Chaturvarna system created by Sri Krishna has no hierarchical differences of low and high. It is a materialist arrangement for distribution of occupations in society so that people need not have to worry about bread and shelter. Rigid status differentiation of touchability and untouchability is a degeneration of the system. Athavale emphasises like many Bhakti saints "no man born on this earth is lowly and degraded" (Shah, 1994). All are the children of the same Lord. (Ghanshyam Shah, 2002)

Each Varna had many castes and each caste consisted of

many sub-castes. Occupation was basic factor in caste division, for example the Brahmins were engaged in priestly occupations, the Kshatrias were warriors, the Visyas were engaged in trading and the Sudras pursued low occupations. The Untouchables pursued defiling occupations and denied social, religious and political and economic right. (Mahar, Michael, J. (ed.) (1972): *Untouchables in Contemporary India,* University of Arizona Press, Arizona, p. 167. (Mahar, Michael, J. (ed.) 1972)

Many other sociologists and social anthropologists have given their opinion about the castes and caste system. Senart (1930) Hutton (1946) Frunivell (1909) Ghurye (1950). Shevnining (1974) and others have enumerated the features and functions of the caste systems and tried to analyse the caste system. Caste has been explained as a positive and functional system in the writings of quite a few British and Indian ethnographers and writers. Srinivas (1979) is of the opinion that even now the agricultural production requires the co-operation of several castes. Dumont (1970) and Bougle (1971) thought of caste as an ideological system of unique nature. Hocart (1950) earlier held such a view. Max Weber considered caste as a system of status stratification. All the above explain caste as basically a cultural system implying that significant structural changes have not occurred in Indian society due to its stable character and cultural dictum.

To conclude the discussion on caste system, it can be said that birth is the only criterion of membership in the caste. Occupational attributes of the caste system are clearly pronounced and carried values of rank and status. Some occupations carried higher status and rank and other occupations lower status and rank. Occupations enjoy social position commensurate with caste occupation. Classification of sub castes as well as occupations has resulted in social hierarchy. The social hierarchy and implicit inequality of status and rank in religious, economic educational and political relationships among caste groups exist, and placed at the top of the hierarchy are Brahmins and at the bottom are the Untouchables. Ritual purity and pollution have pervaded all walks of life. A gradation hierarchy of values has been given to most mundane things not necessarily based on their utility. Practices that are initiated with such elaborate value system associated with them in course of time ceased to be voluntary. They have become part of tradition customarily enforced and later supported by public opinion and ruling power. (Khan, 1980)

It can be said that higher the status of the caste, greater were the rank and privileges and share in ritual, educational, economic and political powers. The lower ranks were reduced to subordination devoid of privileges. Hinduism and caste systems have become so much intertwined with one another that together they cover all the temporal and spiritual aspects of life (Parvathamma, 1981).

If one were to analyse the caste system one could see a number of lines that separate the castes by their rank. Some of these lines are clear and distinct and some are blurred. But there is one line that stands thick and clear the line that divided the Untouchables from the rest of the society (Agarwal 1976). Bailey (1958) called it the ***pollution barrier***.

Hinduism assured a cultural unity for Hindus within the framework of Varnas, and the caste system has parcelled them into layers of groups and subgroups. The hierarchical constitution of caste system fortified by the religious sanctions gave rise to two types of broad groupings in the Hindu community - the higher ritual order and the lower ritual order. The style of life of higher ritual order is more homogeneous and distinctive than that of lower order. The lower order constituted the depressed sections of the society and they included the Untouchables and other impure castes. (Mathew, Joseph 1987). It is these depressed sections of society that were subjected to various forms of disabilities and discrimination through ages.

The depressed sections of Indian society do not constitute a homogenous group. Uma Ramaswamy (1984) writes that the Untouchables are not a homogenous category. Benjamin (1989) is of the opinion that they belong to different cultural and ethnic groups. Sachidananda (1977) says that these sections are concentrated not in one area but are widely dispersed in the country. But at the same time all these sections were segregated together on the basis of untouchability. However, Benjamin (1989) points out that the quantum and manner of untouchability is not uniform in the case of all Scheduled Castes.

The Scheduled Castes

Several castes in Hindu society (most of them were later recognised as the Scheduled Castes) have been associated with unclean occupations and social restrictions, and suffered from socio-economic, educational and cultural disabilities. Various names have been used to refer to these sections. The names that one comes across for these people are 'Untouchable', 'Chandala', 'Avarna', 'Antyaja', 'Mritipa', 'Svapaha', 'Panchama', 'Untouchable', 'Harijan', 'Out castes', 'Depressed class', 'Exterior caste', 'Scheduled Castes', 'Ex Untouchables' and 'Dalit'.

The people belonging to the castes, to which the elite of Hindu society has ascribed 'untouchability' are Untouchables. Krishnan (2002) argued that Dr. Ambedkar insisted that they be called 'Untouchables' so that there is no obfuscation of reality. Dr. Ambedkar was particular about using the name 'Untouchable' apparently for two related reasons- to rouse the self-respect of the victims of untouchability and to sting the conscience of those individuals of upper castes, who were capable to feeling the qualms of a social conscience, and in any case deprive the practitioners of untouchability of the luxury of an easy slave for their conscience. (Krishnan, 2002)

In the Gupta times (335-570 A.D) these have been described as living apart from village settlements and were known as 'Chandalas' (Sachidananda 1977). The Untouchables were known by various names such as 'Chandalas', 'Svapahas' and 'Mritipas' (Ghurye 1950). As these people were outside the Varna system they were known as 'Avarna', 'Panchamas', or 'Antyaja'. (Kamble, 1981). These people were out castes and as such were socially ostracised by caste Hindus (The words 'caste Hindus' (savarna Hindu) is rather a strange expression. All the Hindus come under the Varna and Caste system and as such there was/is no one like non Varna or non-caste Hindu. The term caste Hindu is especially used when we try to make a distinction between the higher caste Hindus and Untouchable castes). As the lower strata in the society, the Untouchables (***the word 'untouchable' is no longer acceptable in any context. Hence, the use of the word "Untouchable". The use of capital 'U' clearly denotes that the expression 'untouchable' is a thing of past***) were outside the four Varna fold and formed the fifth Varna and as such were 'Panchamas'. Ambedkar (1948) called them 'Broken men' and said, it is because they were broken men that they lived outside the villages. Census Superintendent for Assam in 1931 suggested the term 'Exterior castes' for these sections (Sachidananda 1977). Whereas Issacs (1965) said the Untouchable castes were officially defined as 'Depressed castes'. In 1932, Hutton called them 'Exterior castes' and 'Outcastes'. Jose (1986) writes during the British rule different terms such as 'Depressed castes', 'Exterior castes'; 'Untouchables', 'outcasts', and 'Backward classes' were used to refer to the disabled classes of people in India, including tribal people. Gradually in the official documents the use of the term 'depressed classes ' came to be restricted to those who were subjected to 'untouchability'. However at the second round table conference held in London in 1931 Ambedkar objected to the use of the term 'depressed classes' as it is degrading and contemptuous and suggested other terms such as 'Protestant Hindus' and 'Non Conformist Hindus'. (Jose 1986)

A Gujarathi saint Narasimha Meheta first used the term 'Harijan'. Later Mahatma Gandhi adopted the term for Untouchables. Instead of calling them 'Untouchables' he called them' Harijans', 'the men of God'. However, these communities especially in western India have resented this term. The word has been translated as children of God, means a child whose father's identity is not known. (Issacs, 1965; Sachidananda 1977). As such this term was not only disliked but also hated by some of these sections. Ambedkar followers resented the term 'Harijan', and being challenged to suggest a better name failed to do so (D.Keer 1962). Despite controversy, the term 'Harijan' is popular and widely used for these sections of people. Issacs (1965) called these sections 'Ex-Untouchables' as he felt that their past names are no longer accepted.

The expression 'Scheduled Castes' was first coined by Simon Commission and was embodied in the Government of India Act of 1935. The 'Scheduled' of Scheduled Caste' refers to official lists of caste names, schedules attached to legislation. These lists were drawn up in order to establish entitlements to benefits. Each state of the Indian union has a list, containing on average fifty to sixty names. Each in principle represents a group the membership of which is hereditary and exclusive; no one can belong to more than one. The term was introduced by the Government of India Act, 1935 establishing a scheme for the reservation of seats in legislatures. It remains the official legal category, and it has become an integral part of the set of terms through which identities are allocated and claimed and the structure of contemporary Indian society is understood. To claim benefits— of special legal protection, under welfare schemes specifically for Scheduled Castes, of reserved seats in higher education and in representative assemblies, of reserved jobs in government employment, and special financial assistance for enterprise— a person must obtain official certification as belonging to a group listed in a schedule to the relevant legislation. (Charsley and Karanth, 1998)

Later the term 'Scheduled Castes' was adopted while drafting the Constitution. But the term Scheduled Castes was not defined anywhere in the Constitution. Article 366 (2) (24) reads, "Scheduled Castes means such castes, races or tribes as are deemed under Article 341, to be Scheduled Castes for the purpose of Constitution of India " (Manju Kumar 1982). Article 341 (1) of the Constitution reads " the President of India may with respect to any State (or Union Territories), and where it is a State after consultation with Government thereof, by public notification, specify the castes, races or tribes or parts of or groups within castes, races or tribes which shall, for the purpose of this Constitution be deemed to be Scheduled Castes in relation to that State (or Union Territory) or as the case may be."

Article 341 (2) reads " Parliament may by law include or exclude from the list of Scheduled Castes specified in a notification issued under clause (1), any caste, race, or tribe or part of or group within any caste, race or tribe".

Of late the term '**Dalit**' has gained popularity and is generally used, more often than not, to refer to the Scheduled Castes. The term Dalit is inclusive of all the oppressed and exploited sections of the society. Etymologically the term is inclusive of meanings such as: downtrodden, disadvantaged, underprivileged, dispossessed, deprived, handicapped, abused, humble, prostrate etc. It does not, however, confine merely to exploitation in terms of appropriation of surplus but also relates to suppression of culture — ways of life and value system— and more importantly the denial of dignity. (Das and Massey, 1995). Generally the term 'Dalit' includes, what is called in administrative parlance: Scheduled Castes, Scheduled Tribes and Other Backward Castes. (Ghanshyam Shah, 2002)

The vocal and activist sections of the former 'Untouchables' in preference to 'Harijan' and 'Scheduled Caste' are today increasingly using the term 'Dalit'. Joshi note that the term 'Dalit' was popularised by Untouchable protest movements since the early 1970s. The term 'Dalit' has become a 'positive, assertive expression of pride in Untouchable heritage and a rejection of oppression' (Geetha, 2002)

Various terms that have been used from time to time about these sections may give an impression that all these terms are synonymous. But it is not so. It can be added here that all the Harijans are Scheduled Castes. Besides them all the castes that receive Protective Discrimination under Constitution of India are Scheduled Castes. However all the Scheduled Castes are not subjected to untouchability, as there may be castes that receive Protective Discrimination to be branded as Scheduled Castes, still do not suffer from the stigma of untouchability. To sum up it may be said all the Harijans and Untouchables are Scheduled Castes. But all the Scheduled Castes are not Untouchables (Khan, 1980).

The Scheduled Castes in Indian Caste System

The Scheduled Castes were kept apart from the rest of the Society due to the prevalent practice of untouchability. The Indian caste system based on the notion of purity and pollution believed that the Scheduled Castes were impure and polluted. As a result they were forced to live outside the village \ town proper and suffered from discrimination in all walks of life.

The Census of India 1931 had listed out the disabilities of the 'Harijans' as follows:

(i) Inability to be served by clean Brahmins;
(ii) Inability to be served by barbers, water carriers, tailors etc., who serve the caste Hindus;
(iii) Inability to enter Hindu temples;
(iv) Inability to use public conveniences such as roads, ferries, wells or schools and

(v) Inability to disassociate oneself from depressed occupation.

On account of the restrictions listed above the Scheduled Castes were placed low in social hierarchy and suffered from disabilities and discrimination. These disabilities can be categorized as (a) occupational disabilities (b) educational disabilities (c) Social, cultural and religious disabilities and (d) political disabilities. These disabilities are discussed here under in detail.

Occupational Disabilities: The nature of ones occupation has a direct reference to one's status. Blunt (1969) rightly observed that "at all times and in all countries the Social status of an individual is affected and even determined by the nature of occupation from which he derived his livelihood". The Scheduled Castes were known for their long association with so-called impure, unclean, degrading, socially looked down and least preferred occupations. Many Untouchables followed the hereditary occupations such as scavenging, carcass recovery and flaying and hide tanning, leatherwork, drum beating and grave digging. These occupations that was associated with the Untouchables with permanent ritual pollution, barred social intercourse between them and higher caste Hindus, in the framework of traditional Indian Society. Besides these traditional occupations, they are also involved in 'clean' occupations with a majority of them being agricultural labourers.

Looking into occupations of the Scheduled Castes it can be said that the Scheduled Castes were economically poor and generally were dependent on agricultural labour and other low-income occupations besides their caste occupation. In fact, the greatest majority of Scheduled Caste occupational force, which amounts to 72.20 per cent, is engaged in agricultural labour. (Glen and Sipra Bose, 1978). Besides this all the primary leather workers, scavengers, and who deal with carcass recovery and flaying were almost the Scheduled Castes. In urban areas a large proportion of cart pullers, hamalis, and the like manual workers and other unorganised non-agricultural wages labourers and civic sanitation workers belong to the Scheduled Castes. (Report of the Working Group on the Development of the Scheduled Castes, 1980-85, Government of India)

An important point to be noted here is that even those Scheduled Castes who do follow the 'clean' occupations were also subjected to discrimination. It can be argued here that it is not the polluting occupation alone, which is the reason for discrimination of the Scheduled Castes, but the very birth in the caste seems to be the reason for low status imposed on the Scheduled Castes, as the Scheduled Castes who follow the clean occupations were equally ill treated. The emergent issue here is whether the low status of the Scheduled Castes is due to degrading nature of their occupation or they were condemned to follow these occupations because of their low status. Similar observations were made by Beteille (1969) and Sharma (1969).

One of the important factors that are associated with the occupation is economic condition. Because of their lowly placed occupations, Scheduled Castes had depressed economic conditions. The Scheduled Castes were virtually denied of the right to own land for cultivation, were paid low wages as manual workers and always were in debts far beyond their capacities to repay (Khan, 1980). Although outside the rigid Varna system the Scheduled Castes constituted a vital segment of population and performed mostly unskilled and manual labour and unclean occupations without which the smooth running of traditional system would have been impossible (Oomen, 1977). Their earnings were meagre and were primarily indebted and were forced to work as bonded labour to the upper caste on low wages. Scheduled Castes were also under obligation to perform forced labour.

Educational Disabilities: The Scheduled Castes also suffered from educational disabilities for centuries. Historically they had been most uneducated and illiterate group. (Glen and Sipra Bose 1978) The mass illiteracy among the Scheduled Castes was in turn was due to the social and religious sanctions imposed on them. The sacred books, Brihaspathi and Manusmrithi have prohibited any attempt on the part of Sudras, leave alone Scheduled Castes, to recite Hindu religious slokas and if they ventured to do so, the smrithi ordained that the tongue of such person be cut off.

Besides the religious and social sanctions imposed on the Scheduled Castes against taking up formal education the poverty among the Scheduled Castes is the main obstacle for them to take up formal education. (Pimpley and Sharma 1985). In addition to this ignorance of use of education (Shanta Kumari, 1977) feeling that education is not useful (Dube, 1955) adverse economic conditions (Patwardhan, 1973), concentration of Scheduled Castes in rural areas where educational facilities are absent to some extent (Revankar 1971) lack of knowledge of educational facilities and traditional apathy towards education, home environment (Thekkamalai 1989) were other reasons of educational backwardness among Scheduled Castes. More over for the Scheduled Castes it was felt that children were assets to their families. The older children in the family by helping the mother in domestic chores and looking after the younger siblings make it possible for her to remain in labour market. Apart from their indirect economic contribution a substantial portion of them were wage earners in their own right. (Chouhan 1967, Jaiswal and Jha 1970 and Khan 1980). With all these reasons the Scheduled Castes have remained educationally backward.

Socio Cultural and Religious Disabilities: Untouchability was the major social disability of the Scheduled Castes. Definitions of untouchability are manifold, depending upon context, but there is a common premise that untouchability is a stigma attached to certain people because of their polluted status. Specifically, untouchability refers to the set of practices followed by the rest of the society to protect itself from pollution conveyed by the Untouchables. (Dushkin, Lela. quoted in Mahar, Michael, J. (ed.) 1972)

The theories of Manu, Hutton, C.Von Furer – Haimendorf, Ambedkar and Stephen Fuchs explain the origin of untouchability. For Manu, the ancient Indian lawgiver, untouchability is the result and punishment for miscegenation, between the member of a higher caste and a lower caste or outcaste. As explained by Manu, greater the social gap between the parents, lower the status of their progeny. The consequences are more severe if the mother is from higher caste and thus the children of the Brahmin mother and Sudra father was 'Chandala' the most degraded of all mortals. Hutton said, " the origin of the position of the exterior castes is partly racial, partly religious, and partly a matter of social custom.

There can be little doubt but the idea of untouchability originates in taboo." According to him untouchability was the consequence of ritual impurity. Haimendorf maintained that untouchability is the result of unclean and ritually impure occupations in the urban areas and semi urban areas and gradually it spread to villages. Ambedkar argued that the distinction between the caste Hindus and Untouchables in its original form, before the advent of untouchability, was the distinction between tribes' man and broken men from alien tribes. It was later the broken men who came to be considered as Untouchables. The reason for untouchability for him was because of 1. Contempt and hatred for broken man as of Buddhism by Brahmins and 2. The continued beef eating by the broken man even after the others had given it up. According to Stephen Fuchs, animal-breeding societies that lived on the steppes of Inner Asia developed a hierarchical structure. When a tribe was defeated and conquered the survivors often were sold into slavery. Those who managed to escape had to seek the protection of the other tribes and being powerless they had often to content themselves with menial jobs such as tending horses and cattle. As these societies despised menial and manual work, the contempt was also extended to those who had to perform it and the result was untouchability.

Untouchability, a unique pan Indian phenomenon, as Ghanshyam (2002) argued three schools of thought explain the origin of Untouchability. They are (a) racial and/or conquerors vis-à-vis natives; (b) religious; and (c) economic. According to the racial theory the touchables (Caste Hindus) and Untouchables (Ati-Sudras) belong to two different races; differentiated by colour (Dutt, 1931). The lineage of the former can be traced to the Aryans who invaded India, while the latter have descended from the natives called the Dasa or Dasyus. The Aryans, a white race conquered the Dasas, dark skinned inhabitants, and enslaved them (Risley, 1908, Dutt, 1931).

The practice of untouchability developed in the course of time, some argued as the conflict between the Aryans and the indigenous people became sharp (Bose, 1942; Fick, 1920; Oppert, 1972; Sharma, 1980; Mukherji, 1988, quoted by Ghanshyam, 2002). It was argued that the practice of untouchability was preceded by a long history of social and cultural prejudice of the Vedic Aryans towards some groups of the indigenous population who posed threat to their way of life, based on pastoral wealth and performance of religious rituals and sacrifices. In the early phase, the Aryans made peace with groups, which cooperated with them and allowed them to function at the peripheries of their social organization. But those who continued to be hostile such as Dasa, Rakshaha, Asura, and Pani were identified as enemies. With the exception of the Dasas who probably were less aggressive than the others, they were constantly being driven out of their homes and hearths. They were hated because they spoke a different language and did not follow the religion of the Aryans. (Mukherjee, 1988) Cultural segregation increased as time passed by and the habitational segregation and cultural religious prejudice practiced by the Aryans vis-à-vis certain other groups identified as hostile and unassailable, resulted in the practice of untouchability. The Aryans could not bring them under their control and these groups continued to rebel against the hegemony of the Aryan in economic and cultural spheres.

The Scheduled Castes were said to be carried with them the stigma of their low and impure birth. The caste system was said to be founded on the concept of 'purity and pollution'. As the very positions in the caste hierarchy are based on the ideas of 'purity and pollution', the caste at the top have greater 'purity' in that their food, dress and occupation are regarded as more pure than those of the other castes. Castes at the bottom are regarded as 'impure' and their food, occupations, clothes, customs and myths are regarded as either inferior or impure. Finding themselves at the bottom of the caste hierarchy is such a value system the Untouchable suffered most. Economically completely dependent on the superior castes and much exploited by them, educationally backward, socially degraded and treated with contempt, deliberately deprived of the higher religious and cultural values of the Hindu society, all the Scheduled Castes were attributed with varying degrees of ritual impurity. Close contact with them was polluting; hence they were 'Untouchables'. To be an Untouchable in the Indian Caste system was to be very low, and more or less excluded form the social mainstream.

In essence the Untouchables were excluded from the society of Hindu castes. They were rejected by Hindu society. Ancient Hindu Law has forbidden all social contacts with them. Most of them lived in the outskirts of the villages and slums in the towns, in Kutcha houses that were made of mud and thatched roof.

The life of these sections of people had been miserable and unhygienic. The environment of these people was in no way conducive to the achievement of better standards (Selvanathan 1989). No member of a Hindu caste did accept cooked food, salt, milk or water from an Untouchable. Their touch was polluting and even their nearness was often sufficient to defile a man of high caste. In some cases even their sight was polluting. Kamble (1981) reports that the lower castes in hierarchy were required to keep a respectable physical distance from higher castes ranging from 24 feet to 64 feet. There was no commensal relationship between Untouchables and all others. The services of barbers, water carriers, washer men, tailors who serve caste Hindus were denied to them. They were debarred from using all public conveniences, roads, vehicles, ferries, wells, schools, restaurants and teashops. (Fuchs 1981). They were not allowed to enter the houses of caste Hindus and for that matter was not allowed to enter the streets where higher castes live.

Their dress pattern was also different from those of clean castes. The male Scheduled Castes used only loincloth and females in some part of the country were not allowed to cover their breasts. Gold ornaments were prohibited to them and at the same time they could not afford them either (Oomen 1977). Practices such as meat eating and in particular beef and carrion eating, consumption of alcohol, use of shamans and animal sacrifices, the practice of divorce and remarriages of widows and a less lineally and age-status oriented family structure tend to distinguish low status groups such as Untouchables their cultural traits. (Glen and Sipra Bose, 1978) The religious disabilities took the form that they were debarred from Hindu temples and places of worship, from the celebrations of feasts, offerings and sacrifices. Brahmins did not perform marriages and religious rites for them.

The disabilities of the Scheduled Castes affected the women among them with double intensity. The Scheduled Caste Women suffered from twin disadvantage, one because of their caste and the other because of their gender. They were under-privileged among the under-privileged and discriminated among the discriminated. The Scheduled Caste woman was perceived to be the essence and epitome of ignorance, illiteracy, poverty and pollution not long ago (Kalpana, 2001). As Desai (1993) puts it, the Scheduled Caste women were mere instruments to quench the sexual hunger of the higher castes. Different works in the history have reported the Scheduled Caste woman working for a landlord (usually rich and from a dominant caste) had to submit to the sexual desires of her master. The untouchable status of Scheduled Caste women never came in the way of the gratification of the sexual desires of the higher castes. Violence against Scheduled Caste women is not a new phenomenon and their vulnerability arose partly from their utter dependence on their masters. Women were easy sexual prey, either in return for some inducement or through sheer force. Continuing cases of abuse of Untouchable women have fuelled the campaigns for social respectability waged by radical groups in some regions. (Oliver Mendelsohn and Marika Vicziany, 1998)

The caste and gender of the Scheduled Caste women made her to perform menial tasks that were considered to be impure and defiling such as disposal of human waste, looking after cleanliness at the times of birth, menstruation and death. Even today many of the indigenous 'Dai' and 'Midwife' in the rural areas are from Scheduled Castes only. In some parts of the country the Scheduled Caste woman was a 'Rudali", the professional mourner, specially summoned to weep and wail over the mortal remains of the higher caste person. The disabilities, disadvantages and dishonour afflicted on the Scheduled Caste women in the past continued to hurt and undermine their status and position, until recently. The attitude of the higher castes towards the Scheduled Caste woman as defiling and polluting continued till not long ago. (Kalpana, K, 2001)

The plight of the Untouchables was clear from the following few lines:

"The term untouchability denotes the socio religious practice of which Hindus keep a large number of lower castes from touching or coming near their persons, houses, temples, tanks, and some times even public roads". (Aiyappan 1965)

"The Untouchables are also known as out castes. They are not allowed to live with others in the society. Out castes are tending to separate themselves from the rest of the village and try to order their relationship with their castes groups in the village not in terms of village structure but within the frame work of administration" (Bailey, 1958).

"Untouchables were held as entirely impure and therefore, they were compelled to erect their challas or huts at a great distance from all other habitations. They were allowed approach, except within certain limits, the houses of persons of any other castes" (Borale, 1968).

The places where the Untouchables live shows Fords definition of slums which reads "the slum is residential area, in which the housing is so deteriorated, so substandard or so unwholesome as to be menace to health, safety, morality or welfare of the occupants (Quoted in D.R. Hunter 1964).

The severity of untouchability could be understood by quoting a few references from different studies. "They should not wear clothes upon the shoulders. They must not wear gold or silver ornaments" (Soundarajan; 1973). In some places of south India, the Untouchables even in the early decades of twentieth century subjected to such inhuman treatment as being obliged to carry warning bells so that the high caste people would not come into contact with them or forced to go half clothed for fear high caste people may not be touched by blowing of their clothes". (Bougle 1971)

"They could neither ride bullock carts not wear shoes, nor handle umbrellas and walk in the stress of Brahmins. In roads or in foot paths if they happen to see a priestly caste man they should run away and hide until the Brahmin passes away" (British paramountacy)

"They are prohibited to wear shoes while they happen to walk in the locality of Rajputs and Brahmins. As soon as an Untouchable approaches such locality he has to take out his shoes from his feet and carrying these in hands walks bare footed irrespective of the severity of the weather. They were not only prohibited to enter the temples but even to touch the walls of temples " (Indian council of Social Science, 1976)

Gnana Prakasam, (1998) discussed two main models for studying the culture of Untouchables given by different scholars in his book 'Social Separatism'. Moffatt (1979) calls them models of unity and models of diversity. According to the first, there is basic underlying unity between the cultures of Untouchable and touchable caste. One view is that the village society is a structural whole comprising all castes in that the village with Brahmins and Untouchables at the extremes, contributing to the whole in a complementary hierarchical relationship based on purity and impurity (Dumont 1980; Moffatt 1975, 1979, 1979). Another view is that all castes, both touchable, high and low, share in varying degrees the separable (Barnett 1975; 1977) or non-separable coded-substance (Inden 1976; Davis 1976; Marriott and Inden 1977; Inden and Nicholas 1977). Thus there is fundamental cultural consensus between touchable and Untouchables. In the second perspective, it is argued that the Untouchables have their own cultural system distinct from that of other caste, and that there are significant differences between the cultures of touchable and Untouchable castes (Lynch 1969, 1972; Khare 1984; Lorenzen 1987; Vincentnathan 1993). The Untouchables have liberated themselves from the oppressive elements of high caste culture and have developed a positive outlook on life (Gough 1960; Berreman 1971; Mencher 1974). For example, the Chamars of Madhopur in Uttar Pradesh, according to Cohn, have the culture of a Little tradition which is pre-Aryan or non-Brahmanic (1955). According to Miller (1966), the Mahars of Maharastra have developed a parallel, alternate, or counter-Great tradition separate from the Brahmanic Great tradition (Kamble 1983). The Jatavas of Garvpur in Uttar Pradesh are culturally distinct in their social and ritual pattern, and maintain a cultural identity separate from those of the higher castes (Lapoint and Lapoint 1985.)

It is interesting to note that there exists untouchability among Untouchables.

Fuchs (1951:90) has reported that among the Mehtar caste of Nimar district in Madhya Pradesh, the gurus neither accept food nor intermarry with ordinary Mehtar. The Chamars and the

Bhangis of Chhatera village near Delhi, according to Gangrade (1975) practice untouchability among themselves with regard to food and contact. And for Moffatt (1975: 114-117; 1979: 153,216), the five Untouchable castes of Endavur village in Tamil Nadu replicate caste hierarchy between and within themselves, based on the principles of purity-impurity. These instances show the practice of untouchability by the Untouchables. (Quoted by Gnana Prakasam, 1998). So is the case in Andhra Pradesh, wherein two main sub castes among the Scheduled Castes the Malas and the Madigas do observe untouchability between them. The Malas consider the Madigas inferior. It is because the Madigas predominantly follow the defiling occupations including scavenging, whereas the Malas are predominantly agricultural labour. The super-ordination and subordination at times depend on the numerical strength of each of the subcastes in a particular geographical area.

Political Disabilities: Caste has been most important locus of power in traditional India. The power structure in such a society is characterised as tradition oriented and ascriptive. A largely feudal society emphasised, the rule of elders and tradition, and the dominance of higher castes. In such society power is generally linked with economic religious factors besides education (Khan; 1980). Brahmins held power in Indian society for a long time because of the importance given to the ritual status and knowledge in the past. (Khan 1980, Beteille 1969). Later the economically dominant castes wrested power from Brahmins. This was made possible because of the shift in the importance from the ritual status and knowledge to number land holdings and economic power. (Water 1965, Khan 1980). The Scheduled Castes had absolutely no access to power in the past not only because of the absence of any of the factors that contributed for political participation which the caste Hindus had, but also due to their low social status and economic dependence on the caste Hindus. For reasons such as illiteracy and ignorance, traditional values and customs, lack of hopes and aspirations, the Scheduled Castes have generally accepted the lowest rank tagged on to them with many social disabilities.

Caste associations play a vital role in political campaigns

and are important for backward castes and classes as they strive for the betterment of the group. It serves the common interests of the groups. (Bailey, 1963). It is particularly so in case of Scheduled Castes. (Khan, 1980). But in the past there was no room for entertaining caste associations among Scheduled Castes. They had neither the required capacity nor the courage to do so. (Khan, 1980). Therefore practically no caste association was found, in the earlier times, among the Scheduled Castes.

It can be concluded here that the earlier times the Scheduled Castes absolutely had no access to power due to their low status and economic dependence on caste Hindus. There was no representation for Scheduled Castes in the village councils in the traditional political set-up. (Vanaja 1991) As Oomen (1977) points out their economic subservience was reflected in their political impotence. The Scheduled Castes had little voice in decision-making and in fact disputes among them were being settled by upper castes. As revealed by Ranga Rao (1980) Scheduled Castes still remain in the periphery of power.

The power structure underwent dramatic changes after India attained independence. The adult franchise and democratic decentralization down to village level, based on formal rules, opened new power avenues for the backward sections in the India society. The Panchayati Raj system had emerged as a sequel to the Balwanth Rai Mehta committee recommendations and was considered a political and administrative innovation of far-reaching importance. (Narayana, 1998) The Panchayati Raj has minimized the influence of all pervading caste system in the rural political scenario wherein the lower castes and weaker sections seldom received any share in the power. It all changed as the Community Development and Panchayati Raj institution have given a new thrust to the development of different kind of local leadership. The age-old leadership in the villages based on ascription and caste has given way to secular leadership based on election. To conceive someone from Scheduled Caste, as a leader is strange predicament for the traditional and caste ridden rural set up. Nevertheless, empowerment of the Scheduled Castes has come to stay, reservations being an important facilitator.

Upliftment of Scheduled Castes

Thus the traditional Indian society remained for ages, as hierarchically frozen and segmented into differentially ranked caste groups on the notions of purity and pollution. Inspite of foreign invasions, the social fabric of India remained intact. However, there were attempts by the reformers to abolish or at least mitigate the rigorous of untouchability. Some of the movements were led by the Scheduled Castes leaders themselves and some other by the Caste Hindus. Some of the movements were peaceful and some others had been violent. Some movements were confined to a particular region only and others had national ramifications. Jothirao Phule, who founded Satya Shodhak Samaj in 1873, strived for a caste less society and attacked Brahmanism uncompromisingly. Gandhiji maintained that 'Varnashram' was for the preservation of harmony and growth of soul and Untouchability was the violation of the basic sprit of the Hinduism. He started Harijan Sevak Sangh and strived for removal of untouchability. E.V. Ramaswamy Naicker (popularly known as Periyar) said that the casteism and Hinduism were one and the same and wanted Hinduism be removed altogether. His movement took the shape of Dravidian movement seeking to defend the rights of Dravidians against the Aryans. He organised the Self Respect Movement in 1925, to expose the tyranny and the deceptive methods by which the Brahmins controlled all the spheres of Hindu life and attacked Hindu religion as tool of Brahmin domination. Ambedkar, undoubtedly the hero of the revolt of the Dalits attacked two central features of the Indian order that enforced inequality and economic inequality and sought a cultural revolution that shall destroy the culture of the past and usher the socio economic transformation in India. He led fight against untouchability, Hinduism and Brahmanism. He did not quite agree with Gandhi on many issues and launched his revolutionary movement for the liberation and advancement of the Dalits in 1942.

Ambedkar was the first highly educated and active leader from within the community. He represented all the sufferings through his own bitter experiences of untouchability. His philosophy was such as would facilitate the social revolution in India. He tried to unite the Untouchables and created a semblance of unity. In 1924, he formed "Bhiskrit Hitkarini Sabha", an educational and cultural organisation which aimed at improving the social conditions of the Untouchables. Through "Scheduled Caste Federation" he taught his caste men to struggle for their rights. The Federation, however, could not become a powerful organisation throughout the country. In 1935 he announced his decision to leave Hinduism and join other religion. His book 'Annihilation of Caste' puts forward the various reasons why he rejected Hinduism. He believed that Hinduism was based on the caste system, and the real method of breaking up the caste system is "to destroy the religious notions on which caste system is founded. In a speech, which Ambedkar made on 18 March 1955, he outlined three objectives of his life: (1) to spread education, (2) to give more representation to the Untouchables, and (3) to improve the condition of Untouchables in villages. (Mahar, Michael, J. (ed.) 1972)

The emancipation of the depressed started with the British, who tried to alleviate the Scheduled Castes and other backward sections through introduction of western secular education and provision of job opportunities. As some authors have argued the British did this partly with their selfish motive of weakening the freedom movement and to strengthen their rule in India.

The real emancipation of the depressed masses through provision of equality of opportunity became the preamble of planning in the Independent India. To ensure the welfare of all sections and upliftment of the depressed sections particularly the Scheduled Castes and Scheduled Tribes became the priorities of the new government. This has necessitated in enshrining in the Constitution certain Constitutional safeguards against exploitation and discrimination, and through 'Protective Discrimination' a blue print was launched for educational, economic, social and political amelioration. The society, which was divided into unequal groupings with differential access to opportunities and privileges, was sought to be transformed into an egalitarian society through a master plan of social change aimed through planned development.

After India attained independence the plight of the Scheduled Castes was the primary concern of the social reformers and planners and their efforts shaped into a formidable action.

Independent India's commitment to equality, socialism and welfare led to the launching of multi pronged welfare measures for the development of the Scheduled Castes who constitute a formidable section of the population in the country. The planners of Independent India visualised social change among the Scheduled Castes by bringing about social mobility among them.

Constitutional protection was provided to the Scheduled Castes to undo the social injustice and all forms of exploitation and to bring them into the main stream of development. Broadly, from the point of their objectives, the provisions in the Constitution may be classified into two categories: (Gaikwad, S.L, 1999)

1. The measures, which are mandatory, are the provisions laid down in Part III of the Constitution under the heading of 'Fundamental Rights' protecting these people from a variety of social disabilities to secure equality along with all other citizens. The Articles 14, 15, 16, 19, 25, 29, 30, 44 are some of the important Articles that are aimed at 'equality'.
2. The Article and clauses which safeguard the interests of these communities by providing certain measures, which may be considered under the category of 'welfare measures'

Nandu Ram (2002) categorises the constitutional provisions and related legislative measures in bringing gradual socio economic change among the Dalits in to three different types. In the first type are a number of Constitutional provisions safeguarding representation of Dalits in educational institutions (Article 46) in both central and State Government jobs (Article 335) and in Parliament and State Assemblies (Articles 330 and 332 respectively). The above provisions have been made in a way for their educational, economic and political welfare and are commonly known as reservation policy. In the second type are certain protective measures like prohibition of discriminations, or social and religious disabilities (Article 15) Abolition of Untouchability (Article 17), ban on forced are bonded labour (Article 23) or *begar*, and throwing open public palaces such as temples, roads, tea stalls etc. (Article15-2). Based on Article 17 and other relevant Articles of the Constitution, two special Acts – Untouchability

(Offences) Act, 1955, amended later in 1976 as Protection of Civil Rights Act, 1955 and the Scheduled Castes and Scheduled Tribes (Prevention of Atrocities) Act, 1989 have also been promugulated to protect their life, honour and property. These provisions in essence protect physical, social, and cultural or religious interests of the Dalits. In the third category are developmental measures – mostly legislative and administrative measures like, providing grants in aid and other facilities for construction houses, digging wells for drinking and irrigation purposes, starting small enterprises etc. These measures have been enacted under Article 15 (4) and Article 46 of Constitution and are meant on one hand to lessen the excessive dependence on the reservation policy, and on the other, to enable them to achieve socio economic development in their own geographical location, if they do not fulfil even the minimum prerequisites for deriving benefits of the said policy. (Nanduram, 2002)

The Constitutional Provisions that have a bearing on welfare of the Scheduled Castes are as follows:

Article 14: Equality before law

The State shall not deny to any person equality before the law or the equal protection of the laws within the territory of India

Article 15: Prohibition of discrimination on grounds of religion, race, caste, sex or place of birth

1. The state shall not discriminate against any citizen on grounds only of religion, race, caste, sex, place of birth or any of them.

2. No citizen shall on grounds only of religion, race, caste, sex, place of birth or any of them be subject to any disability, liability, restriction or condition with regard to:

   a. access to shops, public restaurants, hotels and places of public entertainment; or
   b. the use of wells, tanks, bathing ghats, roads and places of public resort maintained wholly or partially out of State funds or dedicated to the use of the general public.

3. Nothing in this Article shall prevent the State from making any special provision for women and children.

4. Nothing in this Article or in clause (2) of Article 29 shall prevent the State from making any special provision for the

advancement of any socially and educationally backward classes of citizens or for the Scheduled Castes and the Scheduled Tribes.

Clause (4) in Article 15 was added in 1951 by the Constitution (First) Amendment Act 1951. The purpose was to bring Articles 15 and 29 in line with Article 16 (4), 46 and 340 and to enable the State to reserve seats for the backward classes of people and the Scheduled Castes and the Scheduled Tribes in educational institutions as also to undertake special measures by the State for their advancement.

Article 16: Equality of opportunity in matters of public employment

1. There shall be equality of opportunity for all citizens in matters relating to employment or appointment to any office under the State.

2. No citizen shall, on grounds only of religion, race, caste, sex, descent, place of birth, residence or any of them, be ineligible for, or discriminated against in respect of any employment or office under the State.

4. Nothing in this Article shall prevent the State from making any provision for the reservation of appointments or posts in favour of any backward class of citizens, which, in the opinion of the State is not adequately represented in the services under the State.

It has been held that two conditions are necessary to attract clause (4) of Article 16. These are 1. A class of citizens who are backward socially and educationally 2. The said class in not adequately represented in the services under the State.

Article 17: Abolition of Untouchability

Untouchability is abolished and its practice in any form is forbidden. The enforcement of any disability arising out of "Untouchability" shall be an offence punishable in accordance with law.

Parliament enacted the Untouchability (Offences) Act, 1955, later amended and renamed it in 1976 as the Protection of Civil Rights Act, 1955.

The word 'untouchability' has not been defied either in the Constitution or in the Act. It is assumed that the expression has a well-known and widely prevalent connotation.

Article 19: Protection of certain rights regarding freedom of speech, etc.

All citizens shall have the right to practice any profession, or to carry on any occupation, trade or business.

Article 29: Protection of the interests of the minorities

No citizen shall be denied admission into any educational institution maintained by the State or receiving aid out of State funds on grounds of religion, race, caste, language or any of them.

Article 46: Promotion of educational and economic interests of Scheduled Castes, Scheduled Tribes and other weaker sections.

The State shall promote with special care the educational and economic interests of the weaker sections of the people, and, in particular, of the Scheduled Castes and the Scheduled Tribes, and shall protect them from social injustice and all forms of exploitation.

Article 330: Reservations of seats for Scheduled Castes and Scheduled Tribes in the House of the People.

1. Seats shall be reserved in the House of the people for Scheduled Castes and Scheduled Tribes

2. The number of seats reserved in any State or Union territory for the Scheduled Castes or the Scheduled Tribes under clause (1) shall bear, as nearly as may be, the same proportion to the total number of seats allotted to that State or Union territory in the House of people as the population of the Scheduled Castes in the State or Union territory or of the Scheduled Tribes in the State or Union territory or part of the State or Union territory, as the case may be, in respect of which seats are so reserved, bears to the total population of the State or Union territory.

Article 332: Reservation of the seats in the Legislative Assemblies of the States

Article 335: Claims of Scheduled Castes and Scheduled Tribes to services and posts

The claims of the members of the Scheduled Castes and the Scheduled Tribes shall be taken into consideration, consistently with the maintenance of efficiency of administration, in the making of appointments to services and post in connection with the affairs of the Union or of a State.

Article 338: National Commission for Scheduled Castes and Scheduled Tribes

The Commission shall consist of a Chairperson, Vice Chairperson and five other Members. It shall be the duty of the commission to investigate and monitor all matters relating to the safeguards provided for the Scheduled Castes and Scheduled Tribes under the Constitution or under any order of the Government and to evaluate the working of such safeguards.

Article 341: Scheduled Castes

1. The President may with respect to any State or Union territory and where it is a State, after consultation with Governor thereof, by public notification, specify the castes, races, or tribes or parts of or groups within castes, races or tribes which shall for the purposes of this Constitution be deemed to be Scheduled Castes in relation to that State or Union territory, as the case may be.

2. Parliament may by law include in or exclude from the list of Scheduled Castes specified in a notification issued under clause (1) any caste, race or tribe or part of or group within any caste, race or tribe, but save as aforesaid a notification issued under the said clauses shall not be varied by any subsequent notification.

The Indian Constitution gives cognisance to the problem of untouchability. The Constitution has made a number of provisions under various Articles- 15(2), 17, 29(2)-considering the practice of untouchability as an offence. Article 35 provides that "Parliament shall have, and the legislature of a State shall not have, power to make laws... prescribing punishment for those acts which are declared to be offences under this part" (i.e. the fundamental rights section of the Constitution). The Parliament exercised its exclusive powers and passed the Untouchability (Offences) Act 1955. The Act outlaws the enforcement of disabilities "on the ground of untouchability" in public. In practice it had very little teeth to take punitive action against the offenders. Due to the pressures built by various Dalit groups over several years, a bill aimed at amending the Untouchability (Offences) Act, 1955, was passed and the renamed, Protection of Civil Rights (Amendment) Act, 1976 came in to force on 19 November 1976. The Act provides for enhanced and stringent punishment including collective fines for offences related to untouchability. (Ghanshyam Shah, 2002).

To stem the increase in the rate of atrocities on the Scheduled Castes the Government of India has enacted THE SCHEDULED CASTES AND SCHEDULED TRIBES (PREVENTION OF ATROCITIES) ACT 1989.The Act has come into force on 30th January 1990. The Act intends to prevent the commission of offences of atrocities against the members of Scheduled Castes and Scheduled Tribes, to provide for special courts for the trial of such offences and for the relief and rehabilitation of the victims of such offences and for the matters connected therewith.

Protective discrimination discussed above in the forms of reservations and economic upliftment has benefited the Scheduled Castes in a significant manner. More than five decades since independence have gone by. The developmental inputs did ensure some change in the line of emancipation of the depressed sections. These inputs were meant to ensure equality of opportunity, thereby to throw open the doors of social mobility, which were hitherto slammed and remained blocked to the deprived sections who remained at the lower rungs of the caste hierarchy.

The Scheduled Castes population that was 14.6 per cent of total population in 1951 increased to 16.5 percent by 1991. According to the 1991 census, there were 138 million persons belonging to the Scheduled Castes. Though Scheduled Castes are found in most states, they are largely concentrated in Uttar Pradesh and Bihar in the north West Bengal in the east, Andhra Pradesh and Tamil Nadu in the south, Rajasthan and Maharastra in western India. Nearly 81 per cent of Scheduled Castes live in rural areas and 19 per cent live in urban areas while the corresponding percentages are 74 per cent and 26 percent in the case of general population.

The efforts of the Government according to some studies have yielded favourable results among the Scheduled Castes and there is perceptible change among them. (Rao and Rao, 1951; Kuppuswamy, 1956; Gupta, 1958; Sinha and Sinha, 1960; Patwardhan, 1965,1968,1973; Beteille, 1969; Lynch, 1969; Bhatt, 1975; Abbasayulu, 1978; Malik, 1979; Khan, 1980; Khan, 1980; Pimpley and Sharma, 1985; Joseph Mathew, 1986; Ramashray Roy and V.B.Singh, 1987; Parmar, 1987; Nanduram, 1988; Selvanathan, 1989; Pandey, 1991; and Venkateswarulu, 1991.) Given below are a few important recent accounts that explain change among the Scheduled Castes.

As far as the Scheduled Castes are concerned two striking positive changes have taken place. First, crude and blatant forms of social discrimination at least in the public sphere are practised far less frequently than before. Yet, they certainly have not disappeared. Second, a middle class within the community has emerged. Besides self-assertion by the Dalits, the following four factors have contributed in bringing about the changes. (Ghanshyam, 2002) First, there is an overall acceptance of equality as a desirable norm, thanks to the permeation of the liberal and radical philosophical discourse, capitalist development, and technological, including communications, changes in society. Second, capitalist development nonetheless sluggish has weakened the traditional functioning of the caste system. Though caste remains, its form and content are different from what prevailed in earlier times. Third, protective discrimination through reservations in government jobs and admission to educational institutions have paved the way for Dalits to enter the middle class. Upward mobility has created hope and given them confidence that there is scope for improving their condition and be at par with others. Fourth, various Legislations prescribing punitive action against the practice of untouchability, though not implemented very effectively, have checked to some extent, blatant discrimination against the Dalits. It is more so in public than private spheres.

The most important contribution the welfare measures have made to the Dalits is that these have enabled them to become socially and politically more conscious of their exploitation and social degradation. These measures, along with an over all change in the existing social political scenario in the country, have made them confident of retaining in some contexts their traditional social identity with a new outlook and/or claiming for new social identity of their choice in other contexts. In the latter case, they have partially succeeded in internalising the new identity and convinced others to recognise that. The examples of Jatavas of Agra (Lynch, 1974) and of Mahars – Buddhists, Dalits of Maharastra (Zelliot, 1996). (Quoted by Nandu Ram, 2002)

Growth of higher education among a section of the Dalits on

the one hand and reservation of 15 percent of the jobs, under Article 16 (4) and 333 of the Constitution at all levels in the Union as well as state governments and public sector undertaking, have facilitated their entry into middle class in general and government white collar jobs in particular. The formation of this 'new middle class' among the Dalits, Nandu Ram argues is "vivisected in its role of acting as catalytic agent of bringing social change and mobility among the Dalit masses and its efforts for getting structurally accommodated in the Indian middle class or classes as such" (quoted by Ghanshyam, 2002).

Whereas majority of the studies explained the positive change among the Scheduled Castes some other studies have given limited or no change among them. Charsley and Karanth (1998) is of the opinion that the Dalith status in the current Indian scenario is quite paradoxical. On one hand there is great positive change, including the political sphere and in contrast to this activism and assertion, across the subcontinent the mass of Scheduled Castes, whether in rural settings or in slums of urban areas, remain cruelly poor.

Krishnan (2002) mentions certain facts that are essential features of Dalit existence of today. According to him the most of the numerically large Dalit castes of each region of India and in each of its regions (except the North Eastern state of India) are agricultural labourers and as such a majority of the bonded labourers of India were from Dalit Castes. Despite their close link with agriculture their share in India's land holdings is poor, and still poorer in irrigated land holdings. Another feature of the Dalits is that, mainly their womenfolk and girl children have been left out to 'enjoy' a near monopoly of civic sanitation work or safai work, usually referred to as sanitation work or safai work, and usually referred to as 'scavenging'. Another occupation, left by force almost entirely to Dalits in most parts of India, is leatherwork, consisting of flaying and country tanning and manufacture of footwear in the unorganized sector. Dalit women are forced to work as traditional dais and attend on cases of childbirth in other communities as a matter of social obligation. Severe educational lag of the Dalits, expressed even at the entry point of the educational ladder, in comparison with the literacy of non-Scheduled Caste and Scheduled Tribe population. The disparity increases as one goes up the educational ladder. Residential segregation of Dalits in localities known in different parts of the country by different names is another essential feature of the Dalit existence today.

The overall review of literature on Scheduled Castes by and large points out that the educational, economic, political and social inequalities are deep-rooted in Indian tradition, and Independent India is determined to alleviate these inequalities. To pursue this aim 'protective discrimination' was offered to the Scheduled Castes. The studies so far undertaken to analyse the changes in the status of the Scheduled Castes reveal that there is perceptible change among the Scheduled Castes because of the protective discrimination.

Further, the studies also reveal that the pace of change is rapid in urban areas, (Jain, 1966; Dube, 1963, Kassembaum and Vidyasagar, 1974; Corwin, 1975; Siva Kumar, 1977; Berreman, 1972; Kolenda, 1984) whereas the change is slow or absent in rural areas. (Bailey, 1956; Desai, 1976; Elayaperumal, 1969; National Commission on Scheduled Castes and Scheduled Tribes, 1989). However, there are hardly any studies on the status of the Scheduled Castes in the semi urban research setting.

Need for the Present Study

The present study is conceived and designed as a more or less comprehensive study of social change among the Scheduled Castes. Most of the sociological studies on Scheduled castes are characterised by two prominent features: 1. Predominance of research focus narrowly on social mobility aspects; and 2. Predominance of either urban or rural research settings. This points out that research studies are lacking which make a comprehensive analysis of social change among the Scheduled Castes and studies on semi-urban settings.

The relative shortage of semi urban-settings in research studies on Scheduled Castes was considered a lacunae not for the simple reason that semi urbanism is a phase of transition between the rural and the urban. Semi-urban locales represent distinctive social life settings, not always partaking of the features of both rural and urban areas in partial and transitional modes.

The present study is undertaken, in view of the above two limitations of the most of the afore mentioned studies and with a view to directing the attention to a more or less comprehensive analysis of social change among the Scheduled Castes located in a semi-urban research setting. Semi-urban communities may be like rural communities in some respects and may be like urban communities in some other respects and they may be unlike both rural and urban settlement in significant respects. In simple terms they may stand apart as community category by itself. In India there are many such places, and many more such places are emerging due to urbanisation, and a study in such a research setting shall fill in the research gap.

In view of the above reflections the overall aim of the present study is to address as comprehensively as feasible the question of trends of development and empowerment occurring among the Scheduled Castes in the semi urban research setting of Gooty in Anantapur District of Andhra Pradesh.

Method of Study

In pursuit of this aim the following dimensions of change and development were specified for the study:

1. To examine the intergenerational disparities in educational attainment of the Scheduled Castes in Gooty.
2. To examine intergenerational occupation change and persistence among the Scheduled Castes in Gooty.
3. To find out trends and patterns of political participation and leadership emergence among Scheduled Castes in Gooty.
4. To analyse change in social status in terms of inter caste relations within the present generation of respondents.

Selection of research Setting: There are 11 towns in Anantapur district as per 2001 census and they are:

1. Anantapur (M)
2. Dharmavaram (M)
3. Guntakal (M)
4. Hindupur (M)
5. Kadiri (M)
6. Rayadurg (M)
7. Tadipatri (M)
8. Gooty (P)
9. Kalyandurg (P)
10. Penukonda (P)
11. Uravakonda (P)

All the above places had been treated as towns from 1901 onwards except Guntakal, which was classified as a town 1921 onwards. Whereas the towns with suffix (M) are the towns that are Municipalities, the towns with suffix (P) are the towns that are Panchayats.

As there is no clear cut definition for semi urban areas for the purpose of the study, the towns with municipalities are considered the urban centre's and the remaining towns with Panchayats have been considered semi urban places, which are considered for the selection of the research setting. The Scheduled Castes population in the semi urban areas is:

1. Gooty	4,700
2. Uravakonda	2,234
3. Kalyanadurg	951
4. Penukonda	542

The study has been carried out in Gooty for the reason that it has not only the maximum number of the Scheduled Castes population, but also it is such a geographical setting which has most of the urban traits conducive for mobility and at the same time where the continuity of the tradition and rural social structure are still prevalent. The overall mobility resultant of the developmental inputs employed for the emancipation of Scheduled Castes is examined in a semi urban context, for semi urban is a phase in the rapid urbanisation process necessitated by industrialisation and the administrative reorganisation. It is against this transitional semi urban scenario that the overall mobility of the Scheduled Castes is traced and analysed.

The universe of the study consists of all of the 320 Scheduled caste households in Gooty proper only. The total number of households of Scheduled Castes in Gooty is 320. Two main sub castes, the Mala and Madiga, form almost all the 320 households. Because of the manageable size of the universe the data were collected from all the 320 households.

The study is based more, if not exclusively on the primary data. The primary data were collected by interviewing the male heads of households. The data were collected by using a standardised interview scheduled that was framed to elicit information for the objective framed earlier. The secondary data were also collected wherever necessary through official sources such as Government records at the Mandal and District level.

In the analysis of data, education, occupation, political participation and social status have been identified as the variables. While education, occupation, and political participation were considered as independent variables, status change has been reckoned as dependent variable.

The collected data is analysed and inferences are drawn by the use of appropriate statistical tools. The data with regard to intergenerational mobility is analysed by the use of Matrices.

Two

The Setting

The present study **The empowerment of Scheduled Castes** was carried out in Gooty, a semi-urban place in Anantapur district of Andhra Pradesh. The discussion hereunder presents the setting of the study.

Andhra Pradesh: The State at a Glance

1. Area	2,75,069 Sq. Km.
2. No. of Revenue Mandals	1125
3. No. of Inhabited Village	28,123
4. No. of Towns	210
5. Density	275 per Sq. Km
6. POPULATION	*2001(Provisional)*
a) Males	3,82,86,811
b) Females	3,74,40,730
Total	7,57,27,541
c) Rural	5,52,23,944
Urban	2,05,03,597
Total	7,57,27,541
7. Sex Ratio 2001	978
8. Growth Rate 1991-2001	13.86
9. Scheduled Castes (1991)	
Males	53,79,654
Females	52,12,412
Total	1,05,92,066
10. Scheduled Tribes (1991)	41,99,481
11. Literacy Rate (percentage)	61.11%

The District: Anantapur district is a part of Rayalaseema region in the State of Andhra Pradesh, South India. This region was once ruled by the most famous king Sri Krishnadevaraya of Vijayanagara dynasty and was named after him. The present districts in the region namely, Cuddapah, Kurnool, and Chittoor in Andhra Pradesh, and Bellary in Karnataka were later ceded by the Nizam of Hyderabad to the British, and were formed into a single district with its headquarters at Anantapur under Madras Presidency. Anantapur district was separately formed in the year 1882 from Bellary district of Karnataka State. Later on it was expanded with the addition of erstwhile Kadiri taluk from Cuddapah district of Andhra Pradesh in the year 1910. In the year 1956, Rayadrug taluk of Bellary district was added to Anantapur district.

Topography and the Boundaries: The district lies between 13°40′ and 15°15′ northern latitude and 76°53′ and 78°30′ eastern Longitude. It is bounded by Bellary district of Karnataka and Kurnool district of Andhra Pradesh on the North, Cuddapah district of Andhra Pradesh and Kolar district of Karnataka on the south and East respectively. The district is more or less oblong in shape, the longer side running north to south with a portion of Chitradurg district of Karnataka state intruding into it from the west.

Rivers: The important river in the district is Pennar. It has its origin in Nandi hills of Karnataka and enters the district in the south of Hindupur and flows through Anantapur district before entering the adjoining Cuddapah district. Jayamangala, Chitravathi, and Vedhavathi or Hagiri, having their origin in Karnataka State, are the other important rivers in the district. Apart from these rivers streams like Kushawathi, Swarnamukhi, Pandameru, Tadakaleru and Papagni are important water supply sources to various large and medium irrigation tanks in the district.

Climate: Anantapur district has a fairly good elevation that provides tolerable climate throughout the year. The geographical position of the district in the middle of the peninsula renders it the driest part of the State and hence the agricultural conditions are more often precarious. Generally monsoon evades this part due to its unfortunate location and the district is subjected to severe droughts. The normal rainfall of the district is 544 millimetres by which it secures the least rainfall in the making, when compared to Rayalaseema region and other parts of Andhra Pradesh.

Soils: The soils in Anantapur district are predominantly red except in Kanekal, Uravakonda, Gooty and Tadipatri areas. These areas occur with red and black soils almost in equal proportion. Thus 80 per cent of the soils are red soils and 20 per cent are black soils in the district.

Population: Anantapur district has a population of 36.89 lakhs as per the provisional figures of 2001 census, with 192 per square mile density of population. Of the total population of the district only 8.67 lakhs (23.5%) are living in urban areas and the number of persons living in rural areas is as high as 28.22 lakhs (76.5%). About 56.99 per cent of people in the district are returned as literates with their number being 21.02 lakhs.

Villages: There are 964 villages in Anantapur district of which 30 are uninhabited. Among the inhabited villages, 117(12.53) have a population of less than 500. 164 (17.56) villages have a population of 500 to 999. 268 (28.69) villages have a population of 1000 to 1999. 318 (34.05%) villages have a population ranging in between 2000 - 4999 and 62 (6.64%) of villages have a population of 5000 - 9999. 5 villages (0.53%) villages in the district have more than 10,000 population.

The total geographical area of the district is 42,28,334 acres. The net area cultivated is 19,67,540 acres. The important crops grown in the district are paddy, jowar, bajra, groundnut and mulberry. The groundnut crop alone accounted for 60 per cent of the total of the cropped areas in the district.

Anantapur district forms southern most part of Andhra Pradesh. The district can roughly be divided into three natural regions namely 1. The northern 2. The central and 3. The southern. The main drawback of the district is that most of the soils are so poor that cannot bear constant cultivation and as a result of which it has to be left as shallows for short periods. This is one of the factors that contribute to the poverty stricken appearance of the district.

The District at a Glance

PARTICULARS	*UNIT*		
GENERAL			
A. GEOGRAPHICAL AREA	SQ.KM	19130	
B. CULTIVABLE LAND	LAKH.HCT.	10.15	
C. REVENUE MANDALS	NO.	63	
D. MUNICPALITIES AND TOWNS	NO.	11	
E. GRAM PANCHAYATS	NO.	1005	
F. REVENUE VILLAGES	NO.	964	
G. ASSEMBLY CONSTITUENCIES	NO.	14	
H. PARLIAMENTARY CONSTITUENCIES	NO.	2	
CLIMATE			
A. RAINFALL	M.Ms.	552.0	
B. TEMPERATURES			
MEAN MAXIMUM	°C	38.4 D	
MEAN MIMIMUM	°C	17.2 D	
POPULATION (2001 Provisional Census)			*% to the total population*
A. TOTAL POPULATION	LAKHS	36.89	
B. URBAN POPULATION	LAKHS	8.67	23.5
C. RURAL POPULATION	LAKHS	28.22	76.5
D. SCHEDULED CASTES	LAKHS	5.24	14.2
E. SCHEDULED TRIBES	LAKHS	1.29	3.5
F. LITERATES	LAKHS	21. 02	56.99
G. TOTAL MAIN WORKERS	LAKHS	16.01	43.4
H. CULTIVATORS	LAKHS	5.68	15.4
I. AGRICULATURAL LABOUR	LAKHS	6.27	17.0
J. DENCITY OF POPULATION (PER SQ.K.M)	NO.	192	

The Locale: The present study **The empowerment of Scheduled Castes** is carried out in Gooty, the head quarters of Gooty Mandal in Anantapur district. This semi-urban place is situated 52 kilometres away from Anantapur on the Bangalore - Hyderabad National highway. It lies between latitude 15°7′ north and longitude 77°39′ east. It can be reached by both bus and rail. The geographical area of the town is 29.919 hectares. With the increase in the population, rise in the Panchayat revenues, a separate Gram Panchayat was started on 15-4-1979 in railway station area, which is popularly called Gooty R.S and also known as Chetnepally Gram Panchayat. Thus Gooty consists of two parts, Gooty Railway station (Gooty R.S) and native Gooty. The later is the locale of the study.

As per the 2001 census the total population of Gooty town is 26,665 of which 13,451 are males and 13,214 are females. The number of literates in the town is 16,122. The Scheduled Castes number to 3,907 of which 1,971 are males and 1,936 are females. Of the total population of Gooty 14.65 per cent are Scheduled Castes.

The Gooty fort is on the east of the town, the township was around the fort originally and gradually extended in all the other directions.

The National Highway number 7 that links north and south of the country passes through Gooty. Gooty is 28 kilometres away from Guntakal division of South Central Railway. The main broad gauge railway lines that link Bombay, Madras and Hyderabad pass through the town making Gooty a Railway junction.

Scheduled Castes of Gooty - The Respondents

As explained earlier there are two parts in Gooty namely Gooty R.S and native Gooty. In native Gooty, there are 320 Scheduled Castes households. All these 320 households were considered for collection of data. The information presented hereunder deals with the demographic and socio-economic particulars of the Scheduled Castes of native Gooty.

In this chapter emphasis is made to understand the demographic, socio-economic characteristics of the respondents, which will by and large influence the mobility. By understanding this, it is expected to gain greater insight into understanding the mobility process of the respondents. These particulars include the age, marital status, education, occupation, and monthly income of the respondents and also of the family members of the respondents, who constitute population. Besides this land possession, place or origin and stay during childhood, size and type of family of the respondents have also been collected. Some of these particulars have been used as a variable in the subsequent chapters to explain the process of mobility among the Scheduled Castes.

Demographic and Socioeconomic Profile of Respondents

All the respondents belong to two sub castes of Mala and Madiga only. The Mala respondents are 130 (40.62%) in number, whereas the Madiga respondents are 190 (59.38%) in number. The other particulars are as follows.

The age distribution of the respondents is presented in Table 2.1. As the table reveals, the Malas and Madigas are distributed among various age groups without much variation. In both the sub castes the last age group namely **55 and above** has a maximum number of respondents with the percentages being 20.8 and 18.4 for Malas and Madigas respectively.

TABLE - 2.1
DISTRIBUTION OF RESPONDENTS BY AGE

Age	*Sub-caste*		*Total*
	Mala	*Madiga*	
Up to 24	3 (2.3)	5 (2.6)	8 (2.5)
25 – 29	9 (6.9)	27 (14.2)	36 (11.3)
30 - 34	18 (13.8)	31 (16.3)	49 (15.3)
35 – 39	21 (16.2)	33 (17.4)	54 (16.9)
40 – 44	17 (13.1)	17 (9.0)	34 (10.6)
45 – 49	17 (13.1)	27 (14.2)	44 (13.7)
50 – 54	18 (13.8)	15 (7.9)	33 (10.3)
55 and above	27 (20.8)	35 (18.4)	62 (19.4)
Total	130	190	320

Table 2.2 presents the marital status of the respondents. Less than 8 per cent of the respondents from each sub caste fall in the categories of other than the category **Married** and the remaining respondents who constitute more than 90 per cent returned as married. The fact that the average age of the respondents is more than 40 explain the very meagre figure in the category **Unmarried.**

TABLE - 2.2
DISTRIBUTION OF RESPONDENTS BY MARITAL STATUS

Category	*Sub-caste*		*Total*
	Mala	*Madiga*	
Unmarried	2 (1.50)	4 (2.10)	6 (1.90)
Married	122 (93.90)	175 (92.10)	297 (92.80)
Divorced	2 (1.50)	2 (1.10)	4 (1.30)
Separated	0 (0.00)	1 (0.50)	1 (0.30)
Widowed	4 (3.10)	8 (4.20)	12 (3.70)
Total	130	190	320

The educational achievement of the respondents has been presented in Table 2.3. As it is clear from the table almost 60 per cent of the respondents are **illiterate**, which reflects the educational backwardness of the respondents. Even among the literates nearly half of them in either of the sub caste have only minimum level of education i.e. the **primary education**. Only about one per cent of the Scheduled Caste respondents could achieve the highest educational qualifications, namely **post graduation**. Taking into consideration the relative percentage, ignoring the level of achievement, the Malas have slight edge over the Madigas in achieving education.

TABLE - 2.3
DISTRIBUTION OF RESPONDENTS BY EDUCATION

Category	*Sub-caste*		*Total*
	Mala	*Madiga*	
Illiterate	75 (57.70)	119 (62.60)	194 (60.60)
Primary	27 (20.80)	35 (18.40)	62 (19.40)
Upper-primary	16 (12.30)	16 (8.40)	32 (10.00)
Secondary School	5 (3.80)	9 (4.70)	14 (4.40)
Intermediate	5 (3.80)	2 (1.10)	7 (2.20)
Graduate	1 (0.80)	7 (3.70)	8 (2.50)
Post-graduate	1 (0.80)	2 (1.10)	3 (0.90)
Total	130	190	320

Table 2.4 presents the occupational categories and the number of respondents in each occupational category. There are more than 60 occupations in which the respondents are engaged. These occupations have been classified into nine different occupational categories. A detailed discussion on this categorization is presented in the Chapter **Occupation**. From the table it is clear that a majority of the respondents are still engaged in the lower occupational categories, namely the **manual labour** and **menial services,** and their percentage is more than 70 per cent. This holds good for both the sub castes. Only a limited number of the respondents (18 in all) could reach the higher occupational categories of Professional and Executive and **White collar**. It is also clear from the table that about a negligible one per cent of the Malas are involved in **Menial Services.** Relatively a substantial 11 per cent of the Madigas are still in this occupational category.

TABLE - 2.4
DISTRIBUTION OF RESPONDENTS BY OCCUPATION

Category	*Sub-caste*		*Total*
	Mala	*Madiga*	
Professional and Executive	2 (1.50)	8 (4.20)	10 (3.10)
White Collar	2 (1.50)	6 (3.20)	8 (2.5)
Para-professional and Para-Executive	3 (2.30)	3 (1.60)	6 (1.90)
Skilled Worker	8 (6.20)	4 (2.10)	12 (3.80)
Service	8 (6.20)	2 (1.10)	10 (3.10)
Business	3 (2.30)	3 (1.6)	6 (1.90)
Semi-skilled and Self-employed	10 (7.70)	8 (4.2)	18 (5.60)
Manual Worker	92 (70.80)	135 (71.00)	227 (70.90)
Menial Service	2 (1.50)	21 (11.00)	23 (7.20)
Total	130	190	320

In Table 2.5 the income levels of the respondents per month have been presented. The income levels clearly show that most of the respondents in either of the sub castes are earning only a minimum income. Majority (about 65 per cent) of the respondents are getting **less than Rs.500** income per month. Only a little more than five per cent of the respondents are earning **more than Rs.2000** income per month. The average income of the respondents works out to Rs.733 per month.

TABLE - 2.5
DISTRIBUTION OF RESPONDENT BY LEVELS OF INCOME

Income Range (Rs.)	*Sub-caste*		*Total*
	Mala	*Madiga*	
Up to 500	87 (66.90)	106 (55.80)	193 (60.30)
501 – 1000	19 (14.60)	43 (22.60)	62 (19.40)
1001 –1500	18 (13.80)	22 (11.60)	40 (12.50)
1501 – 2000	0 (0.00)	6 (3.20)	6 (1.90)
More than 2000	6 (4.70)	13 (6.80)	19 (5.90)
Total	130	190	320

In this study, data pertaining to the place of origin and the place of residence during the childhood (up to 15 years) have been collected from the respondents. The earlier studies have proved that, in case of the Scheduled Castes, the chances of getting better education and employment are more in case they are from an urban area rather than from a rural area. It has also been proved by these studies that the discrimination and forcing of disabilities on Scheduled Castes is more pronounced in the rural areas than in the urban areas. By collecting data about the place of birth and place of residence during the childhood of the respondents it is thought that the researcher would be in a position at least to some extent to say whether the backwardness of the Scheduled Castes is forced on them or not. If a majority of the respondents are from the rural areas in respect of place of birth and place of residence during childhood, and happened to be backward in education and occupation, it can be argued that the backwardness is forced on them. As the tables 2.6 and 2.7 reveal, as many as 95 per cent of the respondents have replied to the point that their place of origin and place of residence during childhood is semi-urban area and that too Gooty only. This shows that at least to some extent they were free in pursuing education and choosing occupations compared to their Scheduled Castes brethren in the rural areas.

TABLE - 2.6
DISTRIBUTION OF RESPONDENTS BY PLACE OF ORIGIN

Place of Origin	*Sub-caste*		*Total*
	Mala	*Madiga*	
Rural	4 (3.10)	16 (8.40)	20 (6.30)
Semi-Urban	126 (96.90)	174 (91.60)	300 (93.70)
Total	130	190	320

TABLE - 2.7
DISTRIBUTION OF RESPONDENTS BY PLACE OF RESIDENCE DURING CHILDHOOD

Place of Residence during Childhood	*Sub-caste*		*Total*
	Mala	*Madiga*	
Rural	4 (3.10)	14 (7.40)	18 (5.60)
Semi-Urban	126 (96.90)	176 (92.60)	302 (94.40)
Total	130	190	320

The Population: Data were also collected with regard to the age, marital status, education, occupation, income and the like of the family members of the respondents who form the **population** excluding the respondents. These particulars will give the family conditions of the respondents that have a bearing in bringing about change among the Scheduled Castes.

The total number of members of all the 320 Scheduled Castes households from which the data were collected is 1345. (excluding the respondents) Of this population 518 persons are returned as belonging to the sub caste Mala, and the remaining 827 have been returned as Madigas, the other sub caste. Including the respondents the population from each sub caste is 648 for Mala and 1017 for Madiga, making the total population 1665. Thus the average size of family works out to 5.20

Table 2.8 presents the sex distribution of the population. The **females** outnumber the **males** in each sub- caste and this is contrary to the All India census, which shows the sex ratio in favour of males. In the present population there are 1303 females per every 1000 males.

TABLE - 2.8
DISTRIBUTION OF POPULATION BY SEX

Particulars	*Sub-caste*		*Total*
	Mala	*Madiga*	
Male	222 (42.90)	362 (43.80)	584 (43.40)
Female	296 (57.10)	465 (56.30)	761 (56,60)
Total	518	827	1345

The age distribution of the population is being presented in Table 2.9. The table reveals that of the total population almost 75 per cent of the population is in the category of less than 30 years age group and this holds good for both the sub castes. Of the total 884 persons in the first age group that is **up to 24**, 138 are less than five years of age and 698 are in the age group of more than five but less than 15 years and below —the school going age group.15 years and less age group put together works out to a total of 836. 28 persons are in the age group of **above 60 years**. Thus theoretically speaking 864 persons are in economically unproductive age group and hence can be termed **dependents**.

TABLE - 2.9
DISTRIBUTION OF POPULATION BY AGE

Age	*Sub-caste*		*Total*
	Mala	*Madiga*	
Up to 24	340 (65.60)	544 (65.80)	884 (65.70)
25 –29	62 (12.00)	78 (9.40)	140 (10.40)
30 – 34	24 (4.70)	58 (7.10)	82 (6.10)
35 – 39	27 (5.20)	35 (4.20)	62 (4.60)
40 – 44	17 (3.30)	30 (3.60)	47 (3.57)
45 – 49	10 (1.90)	23 (2.80)	33 (2.50)
50 – 54	13 (2.50)	21 (2.50)	34 (2.50)
55 and above	25 (4.80)	38 (4.60)	63 (4.70)
Total	518	827	1345

Table 2.10 presents the literacy and educational attainment of the population. As the figures reveal, in both the sub castes put together almost 60 per cent of the population are **illiterates**. Compared to the Madigas the Malas are better in educational attainment as eight per cent more of them are literates. Of the total **literates** again a majority have only **primary education** and this holds good for both the sub castes. Less than one per cent could only achieve the highest level of education, the **post graduation**, among the population of the Scheduled Castes.

TABLE - 2.10
DISTRIBUTION OF POPULATION BY EDUCATIONAL ACHIEVEMENT

Particulars	*Sub-caste*		*Total*
	Mala	*Madiga*	
Illiterate	280 (54.10)	519 (62.80)	799 (59.40)
Primary	90 (17.40)	134 (16.20)	224 (16.70)
Middle	58 (11.20)	65 (7.90)	123 (9.10)
High-school	51 (9.80)	64 (7.80)	115 (8.60)
Intermediate	27 (5.2)	25 (3.0)	52 (3.90)
Graduate	11 (2.10)	18 (2.10)	29 (2.10)
Post-graduate	1 (0.20)	2 (0.20)	3 (0.20)
Total	518	827	1345

The marital status of the population is presented in Table 2.11. About 60 per cent of the population have been returned as **unmarried** and this is because the presence of almost 60 per cent of young population who are below the age of 15 years. It is found that a substantial number in the populations are returned as **widowers** and most of them happen to be the aged widowed parents of the respondents.

The workforce among the Scheduled Castes population is presented in Table 2.12. It is clear form the table that as much as 70 per cent of the population are **non-workers** and are dependents on the workers. The high incidence of non-workers in the population is mainly due to the presence of children who are in the age group of less than 15 years and also due to the female favourable sex ratio.

TABLE - 2.11
DISTRIBUTION OF POPULATION BY MARITAL STATUS

Particulars	*Sub-caste*		*Total*
	Mala	*Madiga*	
Unmarried	302 (58.30)	497 (60.20)	799 (59.40)
Married	205 (39.60)	302 (36.50)	507 (37.70)
Divorced	3 (0.60)	2 (0.20)	5 (0.40)
Separated	0 (0.00)	2 (0.20)	2 (0.10)
Widowed	8 (1.50)	24 (2.90)	32 (2.40)
Total	518	827	1345

TABLE - 2.12
DISTRIBUTION POPULATION BY WORK FORCE

Particulars	*Sub-caste*		*Total*
	Mala	*Madiga*	
Workers	130 (25.10)	287 (34.70)	417 (31.00)
Non-workers	388 (74.90)	540 (65.30)	928 (69.00)
Total	518	827	1345

Table 2.13 shows the occupational categories of the Scheduled Castes population. From the table it is clear that majority of the workers are engaged in occupational categories of **manual workers** and **menial services,** just like respondents. Only about 4 per cent of the population could reach the first two occupational categories i.e. **Professional and Executive** and **White collar**. At the same time a substantial population that is about 10 per cent are in the occupational category **Para Professional and Para Executive**.

TABLE - 2.13

DISTRIBUTION OF POPULATION BY OCCUPATIONAL CATEGORY

Category	*Sub-caste* *Mala*		*Madiga*		*Total*	
Professional and Executive	3	(2.30)	5	(1.70)	8	(1.90)
White Collar	3	(2.30)	6	(2.10)	9	(2.20)
Para-professional & Para-Executive	14	(10.80)	30	(10.50)	44	(10.60)
Skilled Worker	1	(0.80)	1	(0.30)	2	(0.50)
Service	7	(5.40)	6	(2.10)	13	(3.10)
Business	2	(1.60)	6	(2.10)	8	(1.90)
Semi-skilled and Self-employed	4	(3.10)	6	(2.10)	10	(2.40)
Manual Worker	94	(72.30)	221	(77.00)	315	(75.50)
Menial Service	2	(1.50)	6	(2.10)	8	(1.90)
Total	130		287		417	

Table 2.14 presents the income levels of the workers among the population. From the table it is clear that a majority of the working population is getting an income of **less than Rs.500** only per month. Only one person of the total working population is getting **more than Rs.2,000** per month, which shows the low level of earnings of the Scheduled Castes population.

TABLE - 2.14

DISTRIBUTION OF POPULATION BY INCOME LEVELS

Income Range (Rs.)	*Sub-caste* *Mala*		*Madiga*		*Total*	
Up to 500	101	(77.70)	241	(83.90)	342	(82.00)
501 – 1000	18	(13.80)	28	(9.80)	46	(11.00)
1001 –1500	10	(7.70)	11	(3.80)	21	(5.00)
1501 – 2000	1	(0.80)	6	(2.10)	7	(1.80)
More than 2000	0	(0.00)	1	(0.40)	1	(0.2)
Total	130		287		417	

Data were also collected about the type of family, the type of house, ownership of the house and the number of members in the family of the respondent. These particulars are presented hereunder.

Table 2.15 presents the type of family. A little more than 20 per cent of the families are **joint families** in either sub caste. The **nuclear families** are in majority in both the sub castes of the Scheduled Castes and they work out to as much as 78.5 per cent which is identical for both the sub castes.

TABLE - 2.15
DISTRIBUTION OF POPULATION BY TYPE OF FAMILY

Type of Family	*Sub-caste*		*Total*
	Mala	*Madiga*	
Joint Family	28 (21.50)	41 (21.50)	69 (21.50)
Nuclear Family	102 (78.50)	149 (78.50)	251 (78.50)
Total	130	190	320

In the Table 2.16 the type of House the Scheduled Castes live in is presented. About 60 per cent of the Scheduled Castes are living in the **thatched houses**. However taking into consideration the sub castes the Malas are living in better houses than the Madigas and this is clear from the table with 50 per cent of Malas living in **tiled** and **terraced** houses. In either case, only a little more than 10 per cent of respondents are living in terraced houses.

TABLE - 2.16
DISTRIBUTION OF POPULATION BY TYPE OF HOUSE

Type of House	*Sub-caste*		*Total*
	Mala	*Madiga*	
Thatched House	66 (50.80)	122 (64.20)	188 (58.70)
Tiled House	46 (35.40)	48 (25.30)	94 (29.40)
Terraced House	18 (13.80)	20 (10.50)	38 (11.80)
Total	130	190	320

In the Table 2.17 the ownership of the house of the respondent living is presented. About 90 per cent of the Scheduled Caste respondents are living in their **own houses**. The high incidence of ownership of house is due to distribution of free house sites to the Scheduled Castes and providing financial assistance for the constructions of the houses. Inheritance and low cost of construction as most of the houses being thatched are the other reasons for owning the houses by a substantial number of the respondents.

TABLE - 2.17
DISTRIBUTION OF POPULATION BY OWNERSHIP OF HOUSE

Type of House	*Sub-caste*		*Total*
	Mala	*Madiga*	
Own House	107 (82.30)	175 (92.10)	282 (88.10)
Rented House	23 (17.70)	15 (7.90)	38 (1.90)
Total	130	190	320

Lastly Table 2.18 presents the number of members in each family and this includes the respondents also. Families that have four and less than four members can be called **small families** and there are about 40 per cent of such families among the Scheduled Castes of Gooty. About 55 per cent of the Scheduled Castes families have more than four members but less than 8, and these can be called **middle size families**, and about 5 per cent of families have more than eight members and these can be called **big families**.

TABLE - 2.18
DISTRIBUTION OF POPULATION BY FAMILY SIZE

Particulars	*Sub-caste*		*Total*
	Mala	*Madiga*	
Only 2	9 (6.90)	13 (6.90)	22 (6.80)
3 - 4	46 (35.40)	60 (31.60)	106 (33.10)
4 – 6	52 (40.00)	65 (34.20)	117 (36.60)
7 – 8	19 (14.60)	38 (20.00)	57 (17.80)
More than 8	4 (3.10)	14 (7.40)	18 (5.70)
Total	130	190	320

Conclusions

The foregoing analysis of the demographic and socio-economic profile of the Scheduled Castes of Gooty tends to indicate:

1. that there is no significant difference between the Mala and Madiga respondents, with respect to their distribution in various age groups. In both the sub castes the respondents in the age group of 55 and above are in majority;
2. that in both the sub castes the married respondents are very high in number and their percentage is more than 90 in each case;
3. that the illiterates are more in number than the literates and the illiteracy is as much as 60 per cent in each sub caste;
    b. even among the literates from both sub castes almost half of them have just the minimum level of education;
4. that more than 70 per cent of the respondents from each sub caste are engaged in manual work and menial services that are their traditional occupations, with 10 per cent more Madigas engaged in these occupations compared to Malas;
    b. only 3 per cent of Scheduled Castes could reach the professional and executive and white collar jobs, the so called higher occupations and in this aspect also the Madigas outnumber the Malas;
5. that a majority of respondents from both the sub castes are earning an income of less than Rs.500 per month which shows the low level of earning by respondents;
6. that an overwhelming majority of respondents are born and brought up in Gooty only and their percentage works out to as high as 90;
   (When the population excluding the respondents is taken into consideration)
7. that of the Scheduled Caste population in both the sub castes the females outnumber the males;
8. that of the Scheduled Castes population the young population, i.e. less than 30 years age group is in

majority in both the sub castes, which is as high as 65.7 per cent. Of this group again the children who are in the age group of less than 15 years are in majority;

9. that in the population, majority of the Scheduled Castes are illiterates and their percentage is more than 50 in both the sub castes;
    b. of those who are literates again a majority of them have only the minimum level of education;
    c. not even one per cent of the Scheduled Castes population could achieve the highest educational attainment and this holds good for both the sub castes;
10. that about 60 per cent of population are returned as married, and about a significant 38 per cent of population is returned as unmarried, owing to the majority of population being in the age group of less than 15 years;
11. that the dependency ratio is more than 65 per cent in each sub caste and the dependency ratio among the Malas is comparatively more which is about 75 per cent;
12. that taking into consideration the number of workers distributed in different occupational categories in each sub caste more than 70 per cent of workers in the population are from the occupational categories of manual workers and menial services which are their traditional occupations;
    b. only about four per cent of workers in population could achieve the two higher occupational categories namely Professional and Executive and White collar;
    c. about 18 per cent of workers in population are in mediocre occupation such as Para Professional and Para Executive and Skilled workers and the like;
13. that an overwhelming 82 per cent of workers in the population are earning only less than Rs.500 per month income and only one person who is from sub caste Madiga finds place in the income category of more than Rs.2,000;

14. that only 21.5 per cent of the Scheduled Castes families are joint families and the remaining families are nuclear;
15. that the majority of Scheduled Castes families live only in thatched houses and compared the Madigas are more in the thatched houses and comparatively the number of the Madigas living in thatched houses is more than that of the Malas;
16. that as much as 90 per cent of Scheduled Castes respondents are residing in their own house and only about 10 per cent are residing in the rented houses;
17. that about 70 per cent of Scheduled castes families have a family size, where a minimum number of members is 3 and maximum number of members is 6;

The Anantapur district is backward and chronically drought prone. The district is rich neither in agriculture nor in industry. The general backwardness of the district is bound to have its impact on the population in general and backward classes like Scheduled Caste in particular, and this has been examined in terms of education and occupation in the ensuing chapters.

[illegible] Scheduled Castes [illegible] 240 villages. [illegible] that the [illegible] to enter into the village [illegible] use the temples. [illegible] raised platform [illegible] inside a [illegible] sufficient to allow anyone inside [illegible]

[illegible] many village [illegible] a Scheduled Caste person. The Scheduled Castes shave and cut their hair themselves [illegible] into barbers to serve [illegible] that came as a shock in the team was the fact that [illegible] of the 240 villages visited, [illegible] Scheduled Castes are not allowed to walk through the streets with any type of [illegible] (Hindu, 1987 quoted by Harsh Mander, 2002). The problem of untouchability, as a concept [illegible] is basically a social issue, though its economic dimension [illegible] traditionally was related to economic [illegible] occupation. In course of time, religious ideology and [illegible] value system, life style, inter personal relationship etc. not only did reinforce the economic and social divisions, but have formed the material base of segregation of residence, economic dependence, rituals camouflaging economic returns ([illegible] and Shah, 2002).

Untouchability from which the majority of the Scheduled Castes suffer proved to be a great curse to this section. This practice has thrown millions of this section of people into despair and disgrace. Gandhiji who fought against the evil of untouchability said, "I do not want to be reborn. But if I have to be reborn, I should be born an Untouchable so that I share their sorrows, sufferings and atrocities levelled at them, in order that I may endeavor to free myself and them from that miserable condition". The practice of untouchability which unfortunately had received the support and backing of the religious and social sanctions had been deep rooted in the society. The legislative moves for improving the conditions of the Scheduled Castes can be traced way back to the year 1938, the year in which Madras Removal of Social Disabilities Act 1938 was enacted. This Act has made discrimination against the Untouchables, an offence. Again in the same year

Three

Education

The Scheduled Castes and Education

The Scheduled Castes suffered not only economic dispossession and geographical segregation, but were also denied access to education. The closed system of stratification received religious sanction and social inequality was accepted as a religious value. (M.N. Srinivas, 1962; Chouhan, 1967). In line with the factors of religion and values, education too in traditional India was towards perpetuation of the closed system of stratification in which Brahmins were trained to be as priests and scholars, Kshatrias as rules and warriors, Vysyas as businessmen. Under the pretext of the services to the above castes the Sudras and the Scheduled Castes were denied access to education.

The review of literature clearly reveals the educational backwardness of the Scheduled Castes.

Gough observed that " it was seen as improper, even ungodly for Adi Dravidas (local Scheduled Castes) to read or write, and it was traditionally forbidden for both Adi Dradiva and non Brahmin castes even to hear the recitation of the Vedas".(Gough, 1981 in Ghanshyam Shah, 2002)

The Scheduled Castes absolutely had no access to education in traditional India. Early efforts towards the education of the Untouchables were usually associated with British rule and the efforts of the Christian missionaries in India. (Geetha, 2002) Under the British rule, the introduction of western secular education opened new vistas for varied forms of mobility only to those castes, which had access to education. Even the new education did not alleviate the Scheduled Castes from their illiteracy and backwardness. The western education was also monopolised by the upper castes, while the Scheduled Castes were excluded from western education until the first decade of the twentieth century.

They were confined to menial occupations for which formal education was felt to have little relevance and the schools in the rural areas came very late. (Beteille, 1977).

As early as in 1830, the missionaries, for the first time in the history of India, started giving formal education to the Untouchables. Apart from them the British were the first to expose the Untouchables to western education on a large scale. The policy pursued by the British government in India of giving preference to the low castes for education was in accordance with its humanitarian sentiments, and it also had the effect of making lower castes look up to the British for protection. (Mahar, Michael, J. (ed.) 1972)

Schooling was 'formally' open to all communities since 1850s; the education of the Untouchable castes proceeded with snails pace. Reports and studies have documented the social opposition to the early schooling of the 'Untouchables' as well as the social and economic constraints impede their education even today. (Geetha, 2002)

The singular role that Ambedkar played in the upliftment of the Untouchables in the early twentieth century and the importance that he gave to modern education for their betterment deserves special emphasis. In conferences, lectures and meeting, Ambedkar exhorted Untouchables youth to acquire education in order to raise their social status and image. As early as 1924, he established the 'Bahiskrit Hitkarini Sabha', which has among its objectives the opening of hostels, libraries, social centers and classrooms where the Untouchables could study. In 1928, Ambedkar established the Depressed Classes Education Society, 'to organise school education on a sound basis' (Keer, 1971). The People's Education Society that Ambedkar established in 1945 was in tune with his conviction regarding the role that education could play in the social and economic advancement of the Untouchables. As Thakkar observes, economics advancement of the Untouchables was 'to raise their educational standards so that they may know their own condition, have aspirations to rise to the level of the highest Hindu and be in a position to use political power as a means to that end' (Zelliot, 1972: 77). This is best reflected in Ambedkar's famous slogan 'Educate, Agitate and Organise'. (Quoted by Geetha, 2002)

Education of Scheduled Castes received attention in a more precise manner only after Independence. (Whankade, 1987). After Independence realising the importance of education in uplifting the Scheduled Castes the following measures have been taken.

Article 15 of Constitution of India prohibits any discrimination on the ground of religion, caste, race, sex place of birth or any one of them. The clause (4) of the Article 15 states "nothing in this article or in clause (2) of Article 29 shall prevent the state from making special provisions for the advancement of any socially and educationally backward classes of citizen or for the Scheduled Castes and Scheduled tribes"

Article 29(2) reads, " no citizen shall be denied admission into any educational institutions maintained by the State or receiving aid out of State funds on grounds only of religion, race, caste, language or any of them".

Article 46 makes it clear that the "State shall promote with special care the educational and economic interests of the weaker sections of the people, and in particular, of the Scheduled Castes and Scheduled Tribes and shall protect them from social injustice and all forms of exploitation. Both the provisions "any special provision" under Article 15(4) and the "State shall promote with special care the educational interests of Scheduled Castes" are quite comprehensive.

Clause (4) of the Article 15 is an enabling provision. It does not impose any obligation, but leaves it to the discretion of the appropriate State government to take suitable action. In this respect the union Government has asked the State Governments and Union territories in 1954, to provide 15 per cent reservations for Scheduled Castes in educational institutions.

Both the Articles 15(4) and 46 are comprehensive enough, and taking advantage of these provisions, steps have been taken to provide facilities such as reservations, hostels, fee reimbursement, scholarships, special coaching, free text books, free uniforms, stipends etc for the Scheduled Castes to pursue education.

Planning in Independent India emphasised protective discrimination to Scheduled Castes in the form of reservation of seats, provision of scholarships etc. to ensure their educational emancipation. After provision of these inputs the third All India

Educational Survey, (1973) and the studies by a host of scholars viz. Chowdary, 1970; Naik, 1971; Chitnis and Aikara, 1971; Das and Singh, 1975, Bhatia, 1982; Dube and Sachdeva, 1985 etc. pointed out to the continued backwardness of the Scheduled Castes in education. The socio-economic variance of home environment was identified as a factor responsible for their lagging progress. To remedy this lacuna Victor D'Souza (1980) suggested creation of institutional structures to take care of Scheduled Caste students so that they can pursue their education without dropping out in the middle. In sequel to this, hostel programme was taken up vigorously by the State and Central Governments, particularly in Andhra Pradesh where it underwent tremendous expansion.

The education among the Scheduled Castes was limited by any means and the dropouts among them further curtailed literacy rate among them. To stem the alarming rates of dropouts among the Scheduled Castes, Andhra Pradesh has been at the fore front in the provision of educational inputs such as hostels, text books, note books, carpets, bed sheets, boxes, plates, tumblers, pocket money, besides counselling classes and remedial coaching etc. These inputs have curtailed the dropout rates among the Scheduled Castes and enabled them to be in the school system. (Amarnath Das, 1990)

According to the 1991 Census of India, Scheduled Castes communities are among the least literate social groups in the country. Barely 37.41 per cent of the population had acquired the most elementary skills in reading and writing and in 1981 less than 30 per cent of rural Scheduled Caste children (5-14 years) were found to attend schools. (Geetha, 2002) Poverty and immiserization of Scheduled Caste population, their denigrated social status, illiterate home environment and apathetic attitudes towards education are seen to the largely responsible for the poor response to schooling from these communities.

The need of education, especially for the Scheduled Castes is quite obvious. Education is an important vehicle for social mobility among the Scheduled Castes. The studies made on the Scheduled Castes realised the importance of the education in improving the status of the Scheduled Castes. The studies of Singh (1958), Beteille, (1965) Alexander (1966), Jha (1973), Abbasayulu (1978), and

Pimpley (1981) have seen that education as an important factor has contributed positively to uplift the status of the Scheduled Castes. They have argued that with the spread of education there is greater economic independence for the Scheduled Castes and the political participation showed positive trend. With education they have occupied elite position in the society and their socio-economic conditions improved.

Commenting on the need for education among Scheduled Castes, Banks (1954) said, education is needed to them as it provides for social mobility. Centres (1944) opined education promotes occupational mobility. Fuchs (1968) said education reduces the social distance between the Scheduled Castes and the Caste Hindus. Khan (1980) felt that education is important for Scheduled Castes, as it is a dynamic agent of social change and social mobility. Sunila Malik (1979) is of the opinion that education is the major vehicle to secure and maintain prospective occupational gains. Lannoy (1971) observed that the greatest source of hope for the Scheduled Castes is modern education, which acts as a solvent of caste barriers. It is in the belief that education is a great mobility multiplier that special incentives in various forms were provided to Scheduled Castes.

Despite the importance of education to the Scheduled Castes and efforts taken by the Government, they have remained educationally backward.

Many a reason prevented the Scheduled Castes from taking up education. The major handicap in the way of educational development of Scheduled Castes is their economic backwardness on account of untouchability and poverty.

Studies have established that access to and performance in education continue strongly to be a function of social background – caste, class race and sex are the major factors that operate. In India, it is a well documented fact that though access has been formally democratized at all levels of education, three is a successive decrease in enrolment as one moves up from the primary to university education. Studies have shown that higher education is restricted, by and large, to the urban upper and middle strata. (For example, studies done by Taylor (1976), Jayaraman (1977) Sharma (1978) quoted by Mahar, Michael, J. (ed.) 1972)

Education in India has not filtered down to the lower strata except marginally. Their enrolment ratio to the non-Scheduled castes is very low and of those who enroll, few pass the examinations. (Mahar, Michael, J. (ed.) 1972)

Quite a few studies agreed that poverty is the root cause for the educational backwardness of the Scheduled Castes. The studies made by Shah, Patel and Swell (1971), Omparakash and Patwardhan (1971), Parvathamma (1973), Sunila Malik (1979) and Sen, (1985) have pointed out poverty and poor socio-economic conditions of the Scheduled Castes as the main reason for their low educational levels. Besides this studies have also revealed, low ascribed status of the caste, lack of knowledge of educational facilities, lack of appreciation for the value of education, poor home and school environment etc. as the reasons for educational backwardness of the Scheduled Castes.

According to the 1991 census, India has a literacy rate of 52 per cent, but among the Scheduled Castes only 37 per cent are literate. Every second enrolled child from the Scheduled Castes drop out before completing primary education and is forced to sell his/her labour. The obvious reasons for non-attendance and high dropout rate are poverty inadequate schooling facility and the social discrimination.

Jalaludin reported in the Times of India (January 14, 1991) that 47.9 percent of Schedule Caste and Scheduled Tribes children surveyed by Rusia in the Tikamgarh block of Jhansi district did not even enrol in school because they feared that 'they will not be allowed to sit with upper castes or the elite'. The report also mentions factors such as poverty, migration and so on as being serious deterrents to the schooling of Scheduled Caste children. (Quoted by Geetha, 2002)

The findings of the NSS (42nd round) regarding reasons why Dalit children discontinue their studies are of interest. While around 46 percent of Dalit dropout in rural areas is attributed to 'economic reasons' (including participation in domestic work), a significant 30 percent of children discontinue their education because of lack interest in studies/further studies. A further 16 per cent leave the educational mainstream as result of failure (NSSO, 1989). While lack of interest in studies and failure are often seen as a consequence of parental and community attitudes as well as poor academic abilities, the qualities of education that children (especially first generation learners) are exposed to, surely needs critical attention. (Geetha, 2002)

Usual stereotypes against Dalits such as they are mentally weak, dirty etc. are openly or subtly expressed by teachers and non-Dalit students. (Geetha, 2002)

Highlighting the effects of socio-economic backwardness and poverty, Shah, Patel, and Swell (1971) making study on a sample of 5000 cases have reported significant positive correlation between social economic status and educational aspirations. Bennur and Abraham (1973) studied 522 school students and found high academic achievement were associated with high socio-economic status which most of the Scheduled Castes were deprived of. Omparakash (1986) opined that poverty is the single most important reason for Scheduled Castes not attending the school. Non-school going children are assets to the family. Older children help the mother in domestic chores; look after their young siblings, thereby making it possible for the mother to remain in labour market. Besides these indirect contributions a substantial proportion of them are earning in their own right. (Chouhan, 1967, Jaiswal and Jha, 1970). Santa Kumari (1976) also said besides poverty the ignorance about the uses of education is the reasons for the low percentage of the Scheduled Castes children in the schools. Besides this, lower caste children are generally undernourished. (Majumdar, 1958) Malnutrition and ill health as explained by Bose (1969) lead to waning of interest of child in school.

Parvathamma (1973) opined that besides poverty, lack of knowledge of educational facilities, absence of the compulsory education at lower level, the traditional apathy towards education due to socio-economic and environmental factors are found to be reasons for education not reaching the bulk of the Scheduled Castes.

Giving other reasons for low levels of education, Joshy and Rao explained the proportion of the educated among the communities are associated not only with economic positions but also with caste position and it is clear that Scheduled Castes stand low in this regard. Deprivation has adverse effects on the personality adjustment of the deprived. Rangari (1984) explaining his study takes the support of Brody and Brody (1976) and says that because of the lowest status ascribed to the Scheduled Castes for centuries in the caste ridden Indian society, the Scheduled Caste subjects might not have got better genetic potential, adequate biological environment, nutritious food and proper health care and stimulating cultural and learning experiences.

Dube (1955) in his study said that some low castes also felt that education would not in any way help their children in their profession. A low level of aspiration for children's education among Scheduled Castes was to be seen, as there is lack of appreciation of the values of education as a means of social mobility.

Bansal (1973) found that the Scheduled Caste students were poor in the areas of home, school, social and emotional adjustments compared to the higher caste students. That the Scheduled Castes who are mostly concentrated in villages, where post primary schools are hard to find is said to be another reason for low level of education. The incidence of stagnation and wastage is high among Scheduled Caste students because most of them are the first in their respective families to see the school and as such encouragement and paternal help are lacking for them. As the educational status of the parents is generally low the pressure on the children is also low among Scheduled Castes.

Discussing the educational backwardness of the Scheduled Castes Chowdary (1971) says that the majority of non-school going age group in the rural areas belongs to Scheduled Castes. Selvanathan (1989) also is of the same opinion that the percentage of illiterates is substantial among the Scheduled Castes than that among the non-Scheduled Castes. Sharma (1972) also expressed the same opinion and added that academic achievement of Scheduled Caste students is significantly lower than those of upper castes. Naik (1971) concluded that a number of Scheduled Caste children going beyond the matric level are extremely small. Chitnis and Aikara (1977) in a study of the dropouts and stagnation on Scheduled Caste college students of Bombay found a very high incidence of stagnation and dropouts among Scheduled Castes and that they were found to be very inferior in almost every aspect of socio-economic background, in performance as well as progress.

An overall review of the literature on the progress of Scheduled Caste people shows that the progress made by them is quite unsatisfactory in education, employment and overall socio-economic fields. The main hurdles in their progress could be that the means of education is out of their reach as education itself is expensive and urban biased. Their poor family background plays a crucial role in poor performance in education, which is directly linked to occupational and economic status. Although the special provisions have been useful, their implementation has been poor. Those who get educated suffer from stigma of caste and untouchability both at social and psychological level and hence they continue to lag behind the general population. (Mahar, Michael, J. (ed.) 1972)

Many a study concluded that education has helped Scheduled castes. However, some other studies have observed little impact of education on the Scheduled Castes. To them though there is change, the overall impact of change on social mobility and literacy is not much. Mention may be made to studies of Isaacs (1965), Patwardhan (1965), Bhattacharya, Yadav and Pandey (1966), Sagar (1975), D'Souza (1980), Usha Rao (1981) Kamble (1982) in this regard. The study of Suma Chitins of 15 states indicated that though the caste discrimination is not much pronounced, the Scheduled Caste subjects are not altogether free from caste discrimination practices and many of them are yet to escape from their low caste identity. The studies of Isaacs (1965), Singh (1968), Malik (1970), Chitnis (1972) and Singhi (1979) have found that the education has negative effect on Scheduled Castes with education causing alienation of the educated Scheduled castes elite from their own community. It is also reported that in spite of the Government's constant endeavour the level of improvement of literacy level in the case of Scheduled Castes has not caught up with the level of other communities in the society. (Chouhan 1969; Kamat, 1972)

Education has helped the Scheduled Castes at least to some extent. At the same time Sachidananda (1968) and Sunanda Patwardhan (1973), speak of the widening gulf between educated and uneducated youth among the Scheduled Castes. The study of Mohinder Singh (1947) study reveals education accompanied by improvement in economic position through job reservation has resulted in the creation of a middle class among the Scheduled Castes with their attitudes, practices and social standards being more or less close to those of higher castes. The educated Scheduled Caste individuals act as a reference group for the individuals and groups among the Scheduled Castes and they in the attempt of upward mobility are accepting Sanskritization process. (Chanana, 1961; Patwardhan, 1973;) Agreeing with disparity among various Scheduled Castes, Chowdary (1970) is of the opinion that there are considerable variations among the different Scheduled Castes in utilising the educational facilities and opines that certain advanced Scheduled Castes are the real beneficiaries of the educational and economical privileges given by the Government. Sharma and Saxena (1968), Patrudu (1971) also express the same opinion. Certain Scheduled Caste communities, which are better among them, were able to get more benefits of the schemes of Government than the really disadvantaged. (Amir Hassan, 1972)

The Dalits has certainly benefited by the educational facilities. Few belonging to relatively upper strata of Dalits have taken higher education (Chalam, 1988, Shah and Patel, 1977), Agarwal, 1983, Viswanadham and Reddy, 1985). Though seats were reserved for Scheduled Castes in national level institutions, particularly in medicine and engineering have not been fully utilized. All those who got admission are not able to complete the course in time. In order to improve the situation, various Committees and Commissions for the Scheduled Castes have suggested that intensive coaching be provided for Scheduled Castes students in medical colleges and various Indian Institutes of Technology. Coaching seems to have made some difference to their performance. (Geetha, 2002)

Having established education as an important vehicle of mobility, the discussion hereunder traces the educational mobility among the Scheduled Castes in Gooty. For assessing the educational mobility among the Scheduled Castes data were collected from the respondent for three generations. Though the data were collected for three generations, it is only the respondents who have answered for the two earlier generations also. The three generations taken into consideration in the study are the respondents' grandfather, respondents' father, and the respondents' themselves. (The three different generations taken in the present study are the respondent's grandfather, respondents' father and the respondent. Data were also collected of the educational attainment of the Children of the respondent. They are referred in the study, unless otherwise mentioned as Grandfather, Father, Respondent and Children. By children here we mean the children of the respondents.) Data were collected with regard to the education of the wives of the respondents also. It should be remembered here that for ascertaining educational mobility through matrix only the basic educational qualifications have been taken into consideration although the other educational particulars such as degree or diploma were also collected.

ANALYSIS

The educational attainments of the Scheduled Castes over three generations have been presented in Table 3.1. From the table it can be inferred that the majority of the Scheduled Castes are illiterates throughout all the three generations. From the table it can be learnt that in Grand fathers' time there were only 13 (4%) literates out of 311. Even among this 13 more than 75 per cent of them have only primary education, the minimum. In the fathers' time there was some improvement with 45 (14%) out of 320 were literates. Among the 45 literates at the fathers' time at least seven (15.5%) of them had secondary school or more education. However even among the fathers 32 (71.1%) literates had only primary education. At the respondents' time illiteracy has further come down with 126 (39.4%) respondents out of 320 being returned as literates. Even in terms of quality of education there is improvement with 32 (25.4%) of the literates having high school or more than that education, and at least three respondents could achieve the highest educational level, the post graduation.

TABLE - 3.1
EDUCATIONAL ATTAINMENT OF SCHEDULED CASTES OVER THREE GENERATIONS

Level of Education	*Grandfather*		*Father*		*Respondent*		*Total*	
Illiterate	298	(93.10)	275	(86.00)	194	(60.60)	767	(79.90)
Primary	10	(3.10)	32	(10.00)	62	(19.40)	104	(10.80)
Middle	0	(0.00)	6	(1.90)	32	(10.00)	38	(4.00)
High-school	2	(0.60)	1	(0.30)	14	(4.40)	17	(1.80)
Intermediate	0	(0.00)	3	(0.90)	7	(2.20)	10	(1.10)
Graduate	1	(0.30)	2	(0.60)	8	(2.50)	11	(1.10)
Post-graduate	0	(0.00)	1	(0.30)	3	(0.90)	4	(0.40)
Don't know	9	(2.90)	0	(0.00)	0	(0.00)	9	(0.90)
Total	320		320		320		960	

Thus the table makes clear that the illiteracy has come down over generations. This, to some extent, can be attributed to "protective discrimination" offered by the Government to the Scheduled Castes. It is only after India attained freedom that the protective discrimination was provided and the Scheduled Castes were encouraged to take up formal education through reservations and special privileges. Almost all the Scheduled Castes in Grand fathers generation belong to the pre independence time and one can expect only little or no education among them at that time. Most of the Fathers were also from pre independence time or early independence time, which is an early transition period where there is little scope for positive change, in a place like Gooty. Even among the respondents, about 50 percent of them are in the age group of 40 and above, which indicates that half of the respondents were born in and were in school going age group in pre independence period only, and this explains the low level of literacy throughout the three generations.

Educational Mobility

Educational mobility among the Scheduled Castes over three generations has been analysed by the use of mobility tables. The mobility tables consist of same number of rows and columns of educational categories. The frequencies in rows indicate the educational category of one generation; the frequencies in columns indicate the educational category of the other generation. With the help of this mobility tables the changes in education have been compared and examined, cell-by-cell by taking into consideration two generations at a time. As the educational categories are arranged in the same order in rows and columns the diagonal cells indicate immobility. The total of frequencies in the diagonal cells indicate the volume of educational immobility. In the same way the frequencies in other than diagonal cells indicate the educational mobility and the total of these frequencies will give us the volume of educational mobility which can be both positive and negative.

Educational mobility among the Scheduled Castes has been analysed by taking into consideration two generations at a time viz. 1.respondents' grandfather and respondents' father, 2.respondents' father and respondent and 3. respondents' grandfather and respondent and presenting the data in mobility tables.

In Table 3.2 the educational mobility between respondents' grandfather and respondents' father have been analysed. It should be noted here that nine respondents could not furnish the educational particulars of their grandfathers, hence educational mobility for respondents' grandfather and respondents' father generation has been considered only for 311 cases.

As the table indicates compared to the respondents' grandfathers 267 respondents' fathers (85.86%) are educationally immobile whereas 44 (14.14%) are mobile.

Of the 267 immobile respondents' fathers compared to the grandfathers 261 (97.75%) are illiterates, and six each in grandfather and respondents' father generation had primary education.

Of the 44 mobile respondents' fathers compared to respondents' grandfathers 39 (88.64%) have moved up in terms of educational achievement whereas five (11.36%) went down.

Of the 39 respondents' fathers who moved up compared to the respondents' grandfathers; who were illiterates, 26 respondents' fathers have achieved primary education, five respondents' fathers have achieved upper primary education, one father has achieved secondary school education, three fathers have achieved intermediate education and two fathers could become graduates. One grandfather had primary education and compared to him one father could achieve upper primary education. One grandfather has graduation and compared to him one father could become a postgraduate and he is the only postgraduate in respondents' fathers' generation.

Taking into consideration downward mobility, five fathers went down in terms of educational attainment compared to their respondents' grandfathers. Whereas three grandfathers were having primary education and compared to them as many number of fathers were returned as illiterates. Two grand fathers had secondary school education and compared to them two fathers were returned as illiterates. As such downward mobility is from literacy to illiteracy in all the five cases despite the differences in the level of literacy of the grandfathers.

TABLE - 3.2

EDUCATION MOBILITY: GRANDFATHER – FATHER

Grandfather → *Father ↓*	*Post-graduate*	*Graduate*	*Intermediate*	*Secondary School*	*Upper-Primary*	*Primary*	*Illiterate*	*Total ↓*
Post-graduate								0
Graduate	1							1
Intermediate								0
Secondary School							2	2
Upper-primary								0
Primary					1	6	3	10
Illiterate		2	3	1	5	26	261	298
Total →	1	2	3	1	6	32	266	311

Note: As educational particulars of 9 grandfathers' were not available N= 311 in the above mobility table and not 320.

Educational mobility has been analysed for respondents' fathers' and respondents' generation in Table 3.3 and the analysis is for all the 320 cases. As the table makes it clear compared to the respondents' fathers 194 (60.62%) respondents were returned as immobile in terms of educational attainment, whereas the remaining 126 (39.38%) have different educational attainment than that of the respondents' fathers.

Of the 194 immobile respondents, 183 (94.36%) are illiterates, nine (4.64%) have primary education one (0.54%) each has middle and postgraduate education. So is the case with their fathers and hence they are immobile.

Of the 126 respondents who achieved different educational qualifications compared to the respondents' fathers, 107 (84.92%) have moved up whereas 19 (15.08%) went down in terms of educational attainment.

Taking into consideration the upward mobility, compared to the illiterate fathers, 49 respondents have achieved primary education, 22 respondents have achieved secondary education, 10 respondents have achieved secondary school education, four respondents have achieved intermediate education, six respondents could achieve graduate education, and one could achieve post graduate education, the highest degree of positive mobility in terms of steps taken. Compared to the respondents' fathers with primary education, the respondents who could achieve upward mobility number to 13; with seven respondents have achieved upper primary education, two respondents have achieved secondary school education, and only one respondent have achieved graduate education. Similarly one father had upper primary education, and compared to him the respondent could achieve graduate education. One father who had intermediate education and compared to him one respondent could achieve postgraduate education.

Of the 19 respondents who moved down in case of achievement of education compared to their fathers the particulars are as follows: Whereas 10 fathers had primary education; compared to them the respondents were returned as illiterates. Of the fathers who had upper primary education three respondents were returned as having only primary education, and one is returned as illiterate. Of one father having secondary school education, compared to his educational attainment the respondent was returned as having upper primary education, Of the father having intermediate education compared one respondent was returned as having secondary school education and the other as having primary education only. Of the fathers who were graduates, compared, one respondent was returned as having secondary school education and one as having upper primary education.

TABLE - 3.3
EDUCATION MOBILITY: FATHER – RESPONDENT

Father → *Respondent ↓*	*Post-graduate*	*Graduate*	*Intermediate*	*Secondary School*	*Upper-Primary*	*Primary*	*Illiterate*	*Total ↓*
Post-graduate	1							1
Graduate				1	1			2
Intermediate	1			1		1		3
Secondary School					1			1
Upper-primary		1			1	3	1	6
Primary		1	3	2	7	9	10	32
Illiterate	1	6	4	10	22	49	183	275
Total →	3	8	7	14	32	62	194	320

The educational mobility between respondents' grandfathers and respondents have been analysed in Table 3.4. As mentioned earlier nine respondents could not give the education of their grandfathers and as such here also the mobility analysis was done only with regard to 311 cases.

The table 3.4 reveals that of the 311 cases reported in terms of educational attainment, 187 (60.13%) respondents have been reported as immobile and the remaining 124 (39.87%) have been reported as mobile.

Of the 187 immobile respondents; compared to their grandfathers 184 (98.40%) respondents are illiterate and three (1.60%) have primary education and so were the respondents' grandfathers.

Of the 124 mobile respondents compared to their respondents' grandfathers, speaking in terms of educational attainment, 122 (98.39%) respondents moved up and two (1.61%) have went down.

The upward mobility in case of 122 respondents when compared to their grandfathers the particulars are as follows. Compared to their illiterate respondents' grandfathers fifty nine respondents could achieve primary education, 26 respondents have attained upper primary education, 13 respondents could attain secondary school education, seven respondents each could achieve intermediate and graduate education respectively and two respondents are returned as having achieved post graduation, the maximum upward mobility. Of the grandfathers with primary education, compared five respondents could achieve upper primary education, and one respondent each could achieve secondary school and graduate education respectively. One case was reported where the grandfather was graduate and the respondent is a postgraduate.

Only two cases of downward mobility were reported of the respondents when compared to their grandfathers. Compared to the respondents' grandfather with secondary school education, one respondent could achieve upper primary education and the other was returned as illiterate.

TABLE - 3.4

EDUCATION MOBILITY: GRANDFATHER – RESPONDENT

Grandfather → *Respondent ↓*	*Post-graduate*	*Graduate*	*Intermediate*	*Secondary School*	*Upper-Primary*	*Primary*	*Illiterate*	*Total ↓*
Post-graduate								0
Graduate	1							1
Intermediate								0
Secondary School					1		1	2
Upper-primary								0
Primary		1		1	5	3		10
Illiterate	2	7	7	13	26	59	184	298
Total	3	8	7	14	32	62	185	311

Note: As educational partuculars of 9 grandfathers' were not available N= 311 in the above mobility table and not 320.

A few measures have been worked out to compare the educational mobility by considering the educational mobility between respondents' grandfather and respondents' father, respondents' father and respondent and respondents' grandfather and respondent. The measures are presented in Table 3.5.

The first two measures in Table 3.5 are percentages, which speak of mobility or immobility taking into consideration the number of cases reported in either way. (Upward and downward) As the first measure suggests, lowest per cent of mobility (both the ways) is in the case of the mobility between the respondents' grandfather and respondents' father generation, which is only 14.14 per cent. In the other two cases viz. the mobility between respondents' father and respondent generation and respondents' grandfather and respondent generation, more or less an identical percentage of about 40 was reported. (However, as said earlier, there is difference in number of persons considered for mobility analysis; whereas in mobility analysis between respondents' father and respondent, the number of cases considered are 320, in case of mobility analysis of between respondents' grandfather and respondent and respondents' grandfather and respondents' father the number of cases considered are 311 only). It can be concluded here that compared to the mobility between respondents' grandfather and respondents' father generation, the mobility is considerably high in case of mobility between respondents' father and respondents' generation and respondents' grandfather and respondent generation.

The second measure which is per cent immobility, and it reads 85.86, 60.62, and 60.13 between the generations of respondents' grandfather and respondents' father, respondents' father and respondent, and respondents' grandfather and respondent respectively. This clearly indicates that immobility is more pronounced than mobility in terms of education.

For working out other four measures viz, the total mobility, positive mobility, negative mobility and net mobility, the " steps " taken have been considered. By step the author means movement from one cell to another. There are six cells in the education mobility table and the movement from one cell to the other is called **step**. The step can be taken in a positive (upward) or in a negative (downward) direction. Movement into the next immediate cell is taking of one step and it can vary as the case may be. One can, compared to the earlier generation, take a maximum of six steps either way. (From illiteracy to Post graduation or vice versa.)

The measure of total mobility tells us about the total mobility that has taken place between two different generations in each case. In this measure the direction of the mobility is not considered. The total steps taken divided by the total number of mobile persons will give us this measure. The total of mobility or the volume of mobility in each case can be said by using this measure. As the table indicates the total mobility is more in the case of the mobility between respondents' grandfather and respondent generation which is 1.94 steps, a little less in the case of mobility between respondents' father and respondent generation, and is the least in the case of mobility between respondents' grandfather and respondents' father, where it is 1.63.

The upward mobility and the steps taken are considered for working of positive mobility. This measure shall tell us about the quantum of upward mobility. This measure is arrived at my taking into consideration the total steps taken by the upwardly mobile people divided by their number. It is evident from the table that the average positive steps taken are fewer than two in all the cases, which indicates that positive mobility is not more than two steps in no case. The maximum number of upwardly mobile persons could be seen in the case of mobility between respondents' grandfather to respondent generation where it is 122, and the minimum in case of mobility between respondents' grandfather and respondents' father, where it is only 39. Though there is not much difference of positive mobility in all the three cases as shown in the table, there is significant difference of the number of cases of upwardly mobile persons that make difference. It can be concluded that both in terms of quality and quantity of education, the mobility between respondents' grandfather and respondent generation is high compared to the two other cases.

Negative mobility is another measure used in the study. Using the total steps taken by the Scheduled Castes showing downward mobility and dividing it by their number this measure was arrived at. The highest number of persons showing downward mobility which is 19, is noticed in case of mobility between respondents' father and respondent generations and the least which is only two is noticed between respondents' grandfather and respondent generation. From the table it can be learnt that though the highest negative mobility which is 2.0 is noticed in case of grandfather and respondent generation followed by 1.80 in case of respondents' grandfather and respondents' father generation, substantial downward mobility took place in case of respondents' father to respondent generation in terms of number of persons though the negative mobility is least which is only 1.32.

The net mobility is the final measure, which gives us in a way the quality of educational attainment over generation. In calculating this measure we have taken into consideration the net steps, which is arrived at by subtracting the total negative steps from total positive steps and dividing it by number of respondents. Greater net mobility is the outcome of lesser downward mobility and higher upward mobility. From the table it is clear that the highest net mobility is in the case of respondents' grandfather and respondent generation where the measure is 1.88 and this says that about a net 233 positive steps have been taken in this case. The lowest net mobility was reported in the case of grandfather to respondents' father where it is 1.23, which is about 54 net positive steps.

TABLE - 3.5
EDUCATIONAL MOBILITY OVER THREE GENERATIONS A FEW MEASURES

The Measure	*Grandfather & Father*	*Father & Respondent*	*Grandfather & Respondent*
Percentage Mobile	14.14 (44)	39.38 (126)	39.87 (124)
Percentage Immobile	85.86 (267)	60.62 (194)	60.13 (187)
Total Mobility	1.63 (44)	1.82 (126)	1.94 (124)
Positive Mobility	1.62 (39)	1.90 (107)	1.94 (122)
Negative Mobility	1.80 (5)	1.32 (19)	2.00 (2)
Net Mobility	1.23 (44)	1.42 (126)	1.88 (124)

Note: (a) S.No. 3,4,5 & 6 are expressed in terms of steps taken
(b) Figure in parentheses indicates number of cases

Education of women is an important variable. It is important for two reasons. It speaks about the literacy rate among the women. It is equally important because the women being the house wives (being the wives of the respondents in this case) have a role to play in the education of children in terms of making them to take to education and in motivating them to perform.

Table 3.6 shows the educational attainment of the wives of the respondents. The table reveals very disappointing state of affairs. A staggering 281 out of 320 women who are wives of respondents accounting for almost 90 per cent are illiterates. Of the 39 literates nearly half of them (17) have only minimum level of education, the primary education. Only each of the two per cent of the wives of the respondents has upper primary and secondary school education. Even less number of them, which is, 1.6 per cent of them have intermediate education. Of the total 320, only one wife of respondents is a graduate and none of them have attained the highest level of education, the post graduation. The poor literacy and low levels of educational attainment among the women of the Scheduled Castes can be attributed to early marriages, and lack of encouragement to women education among the Scheduled Castes.

TABLE - 3.6
EDUCATIONAL ATTAINMENT OF THE WIVES OF THE RESPONDENTS

Particulars	*Frequency*	*Percentage*
Illiterate	281	87.8
Primary	17	5.30
Middle	7	2.20
High-school	9	2.80
Intermediate	5	1.60
Graduate	1	0.30
Post-graduate	0	0.00
Total	320	100.00

In the present study data were also collected about the children of the respondent, the fourth generation. By children it is meant the progeny of the respondents only. This means the children need not be less than 15 years of age and also not necessarily be living with respondent or vice versa.

Of the 320 families about whom data were collected as the Table 3.7 reveals that 36 (11.25%) families have no children, 29 (9.06%) families have one or more than one, but who are not in school going age group. 55 (17.19%) families have one or more than one child who are /were in school going age group but are not going to/did not attend school. In case of the remaining 200 (62.50%) families that have one or more than one child the children are attending/attended school.

It is clear from the table that of the 320 families, 255 families have/had school going age group children. Of this 255 eligible families as many as 200 (78.43%) families are pursuing/pursued the education of their children, which is a good turn out of families of the Scheduled Castes for education. Only about 20 per cent of families are not pursuing/pursued the education of their children. This shows educational advancement and awareness of the Scheduled Castes of the importance of the education in uplifting themselves.

TABLE - 3.7
DISTRIBUTION OF FAMILIES TO ASCERTAIN EDUCATIONAL ATTAINMENT

Particulars	*Frequency*	*Percentage*
1. No. of families with no children	36	11.25
2. No. of families with children but not in school going age group	29	9.06
3. No. of families with child/children in school going age group/ and more but or not going/did not go to school	55	17.19
4. No. of families with child or children who are going to school/went school	200	62.50
Total	320	100.00

TABLE - 3.7 (A)
EDUCATIONAL ATTAINMENT OF CHILDREN (NUMBER OF FAMILIES)

Particulars	*Frequency*	*Percentage*
No. of families with illiterate children	55	21.56
No. of families with literate children	200	78.44
Total	255	100.00

Note: Out of 320 families 65 families were not included, as 36 families do not have children and in other 29 families have children but the children are not in school going age group.

Speaking in terms of number of children and education___ the total number of children of the respondents is 836. (Table 3.8). Of this total, 138 (16.50%) are not in school going age group and the remaining 698 (83.50%) are in school going age group or were in school going age group. Of this total of 698, 419 (60.03%) are boys/men, and the remaining 279 (39.98%) are girls/women. Of the 698 eligible children, 437 (62.60%) children pursued and pursuing education and in this total 298 (68.19%) are boys/men and 139 (31.80%) are girls / women. Of the total 698 eligible children 261 (37.40%) did not pursue /are not pursuing education. Out of this 261 uneducated children 121 (46.36%) are boys/men, and the girls/women account a little more and are 140 (53.64%) in number.

Of the 255 families with children who are eligible to pursue education, 143 (56.07%) families have children who are of the age of fifteen years and more and these children are 234 in number. Of the above 143 families that have the children of the age of fifteen years and more, in 74 (51.74%) families all the children are of the age of fifteen years and more and they number to 151 in all these 74 families. The number of children who are in school going age group but who are less than fifteen years of age number to 424 (60.74%) out of the total of 698.

Besides finding out whether the children are educated or not, an effort is made to find out the highest and lowest achievement of education of the children in each family. As said earlier, of the total 320 families there were only 255 families which have/had children in school going age group. Of these 255 families; in 55 families the children are uneducated. In the remaining 200 families the highest level of educational attainment is presented in Table 3.9.

TABLE - 3.8
EDUCATIONAL ATTAINMENT OF CHILDREN OF RESPONDENTS

Particulars	*Frequency*
1. Total No. of children	836
2. Non-school going age group	138
3. No. of children who are/were in school age group (Boys 419) — (Girls 279)	698
4. Educated children (Boys 298) — (Girls 139)	437
5. Uneducated children (Boys 121) — (Girls 140)	261
6. No. of families with children who are in age group of 15+	143
7. No. of children in age group 15+ in the above 143 families	274
8. No. of families with all the children in 15+ age group	74
9. Total No. of the children in the above 74 families	151
10. No. of children who are less than 15 years of age but more than 5 year and more age (school going age group)	424

Note: 1. Children mean the progeny of the respondent despite their age (need not be less than 15 year of age)
2. Children may not be living with the respondent or vice versa

Table - 3.9
HIGHEST EDUCATED CHILD IN THE FAMILY

Level of Education	*Still Pursuing*	*Completed*	*Total*
Primary	61	3	64
Upper-primary	36	12	48
Secondary School	36	10	46
Intermediate	16	7	23
Graduate	8	9	17
Post-graduate	0	2	2
Total	157	43	200

Note: No. of families with educated children 200

It is clear from the table that in a majority of families' (64) highest level of achievement is primary education. But at the same time in 61 families children are still pursuing the education whereas only in three families the children have reported of completing education, which means that the children in these 61 are likely to improve their educational levels. Post graduation is the highest level of achievement of the children in case of two families and in both the cases they have completed education. In a good number of families, that is in 86 out of 200 the children are/were in their upper primary, secondary school, intermediate and graduation education with the number of families being 36,36, 16 and 8 respectively. Of these 86 families the children in 38 families have reported of having completed their education, with the children in the remaining 48 families still pursuing the education. It is also clear from the table that of the total 200 families, in 157 families the children who have attained highest educational attainment in the family are still pursuing the education, and as such better educational attainment can be expected. Only in 43 families the children are reported to have completed education.

In the same 200 families where children are pursuing education, the lowest level of educational attainment of the child in the family is also ascertained. However it should be noted here if there is only one child in the family pursuing/pursued education, the child's education is taken as highest. In the families where there are two are more children and still only one child pursued/is pursuing education, in such cases also the education of the child is taken as the highest but not lowest. In 82 families one-child is/was educated and as such only 118 families have been taken into consideration where there are two are more children and where comparison can be made.

As presented in the Table 3.10 in case of 84 families primary education is the lowest educational attainment in family and at the same time in 71 families children are still pursuing education and are expected to cross that level. There are seven families where intermediate education is the lowest education and of this four children are still pursuing their education. Of the total 118 families that have been taken into consideration for ascertaining the lowest level of education the children in 92 (77.97%) families are still pursuing education which means that the levels of education are likely to improve, and only in case of 26 families the lowest level reported is static as they dropped their education.

TABLE - 3.10
LOWEST EDUCATED CHILD IN THE FAMILY

Level of Education	*Still Pursuing*	*Dropped*	*Total*
Primary	71	13	84
Upper-primary	11	5	16
Secondary School	6	5	11
Intermediate	4	3	7
Total	92	26	118

Note: In the following cases caparison could not be made as—

- 31 families have only one child who is/was studying
- 37 families have 2 or more children in school going age group but only one is/was studying.
- 14 families have 2 or more children but only one is in school going age group and is/was studying in all the above 82 cases where only child is/was studying his/her education is taken as 'Highest' and not as 'Lowest' hence could not be compared.

CONCLUSIONS

From the foregoing discussion on education among the Scheduled Castes it can be observed:

1. that the illiteracy among the Scheduled castes is very high and this holds good throughout the three generations considered for the study, the semi-urban area of Gooty;
2. that at the same time, the illiteracy over generations is on decline and this is clear from the figures of illiteracy that stand 93.1, 86 and 60.6 per cent for respondents' grandfather, respondents' father and respondent generations respectively in semi-urban place of Gooty;
3. that the levels of achievement in terms of education are low among the Scheduled Castes as about 50 per cent of them have only the lowest level of achievement, the primary education, and this holds good for all the three generations. At the same time less than one per cent of the Scheduled Castes only could achieve the highest level of educational attainment, the post graduation;

4. that among the literate respondents about 50 per cent of them could achieve more than primary education and they are distributed in all the levels of education;
5. that compared to the grand father as many as 267 fathers have remained immobile, with a staggering majority of them being illiterate;
6. that compared to the respondents' grandfathers 30, fathers have shown upward mobility whereas only five fathers have shown downward mobility;
   b. of the upwardly mobile respondents' fathers a majority have shown only minimal upward mobility;
   c. all the five fathers who have shown downward mobility had been returned as illiterates;
7. that compared to respondents' fathers, 194 (60.62%) of respondents have remained immobile with as much as 183 (94.32%) have returned as illiterates;
8. that compared to the respondents' fathers, 126(39.38%) respondents have different educational attainment, with 107 (84.92%) of them moving upward and 19 (15.08%) of them moving down;
   b. of the 126 upwardly mobile respondents as many as 92 respondents have illiterate fathers; and again a majority of them moved only one step ahead which is from illiteracy to primary even though there are others distributed in other educational attainment categories also;
   c. of the 19 respondents showing downward mobility again, majority of them have been returned as illiterates;
9. that compared to the respondents' grandfathers, 187 (60.13) respondents have remained immobile with as much as 98.39 per cent of them returned as illiterates;
10. that compared to the respondents' grandfathers, 124 respondents have shown mobility with 122 (98.38%) of them moved up, whereas only two moved down;
    b. of the 122 upwardly mobile respondents, 114 (93.44%) respondents have grandfathers who were

illiterates and a majority of them (51.75%) moved only one step ahead i.e. from illiteracy to primary education though there are respondents distributed in other educational attainment categories;

c. only two cases of downward mobility were reported; of which is a mere 0.64 per cent and can be said insignificant;

11. that the per cent mobility is more in the mobility analysis between the respondents' grandfather and respondent generations than the two other cases;
12. that the per cent of immobility is more in the mobility analysis between respondents' grandfather and respondents' father generations than the two other cases;
13. that maximum number of steps taken (either way) in terms of educational attainment is more in the mobility analysis between respondents' father and respondent generations than the two other cases;
14. that the number of positive steps taken in terms of educational attainment is more in the mobility analysis between the respondents' grandfather generation and respondent generation;
15. that maximum number of negative steps in terms of educational attainment taken is more in mobility analysis between the respondents' father and respondent;
16. that the net mobility, which indicates real achievement of education in terms of steps taken, is more in the mobility analysis between the respondents' grandfather and respondent generations than the two other cases;
17. that a staggering 87.8 per cent of the wives of the respondents are illiterates, which reflects poor women literacy among Scheduled Castes;
18. that of the children of Scheduled Castes more than 60 per cent are educated and are in different levels of education is an encouraging phenomena;
19. that of the children of the respondents more boys are taking to education than girls;

20. that speaking in terms of families, as many as 78.43 percent of families that have school going age group children are perusing the education of their children;
21. that of the 200 families where the highest educated child's education was collected, in 78.5 percent of families the children are still pursuing their education which shows the education levels of the children are still to improve;
22. that of the 118 families considered for collecting lowest educated child's education, only in 22 per cent of the families the children have dropped education is comparatively a small figure and again in majority of children in the families and are likely to improve their educational qualifications.

The above discussion on education of the Scheduled Castes under study reveals that the pace of educational attainment while slow, yet is impressively steady. The steady pace is due to the initial voluntary efforts by the missionaries in this area, later compounded by the planned efforts through protective discrimination. This is reflected in low literacy attainments during fathers and respondents generation (initial efforts of missionaries) and a relatively substantial rise in the case of children of respondents. Yet what is to be noted here is that these efforts are being brought under the overall influence of socio-economic and cultural forces, which are against the group under study, and hence is the slow pace of educational progress. It addition the relatively disadvantageous locale in terms of not being a major industrial, urban centre which can give a motive for higher educational attainments for the majority is the other reason. What is to be noted and recognised in this context is that even this relatively minimal and low educational attainment is significant enough to usher mobility and change.

The relative low educational attainment in earlier generations and the minimum attainment at the time of respondent generation has a bearing on the continuity and discontinuity of the traditional occupational practices. This has been examined in the next chapter **Occupation.**

Four

Occupation

Caste and Occupation

One of the features of the caste system has been the close association between caste and occupation (Dumont 1966). This close relationship between caste and occupation eventually contributed to the stability of caste system, a closed and static society, and blocked any possibility of social mobility (Khan, 1980). The caste system has prescribed certain occupations for each caste and these occupations are hereditary. However, there are a few studies, which have thrown some light on changes in the traditional occupational structure, which have occurred throughout Indian history. They have brought to light instance, which were not only possible theoretically, but they have actually occurred. According to Hazara (1940) occupational mobility was allowed among the lower castes even during the classical Hindu period.

The studies on occupation change and deviation in the Indian context, has revealed that the occupational structure has been experiencing basic changes. The major contention of these investigations is that not only the traditional occupation structure is gradually becoming more and more flexible but also a certain number of new occupations have come into existence. Further, the fact that people from different castes are able to move into them is an indication that the relationship between caste and occupation is slowly disintegrating (Blunt, 1931; Davis, 1951; Umamohan, 1983).

This declining relationship between caste and occupation is also noticeable even in the rural areas and the studies conducted in rural areas after independence reveal the practice of occupation other than their own caste occupation. (Mayer, 1960; Reddy, 1968; Kantowsky, 1970; Baum, 1974.) This view is also supported by Beals, (1965) Beteille (1965). At the same time the studies undertaken in urban areas on occupational change and social mobility reveal the continuance of the above trend and occupational deviation is tending to be more pronounced and frequent in the urban areas than the rural areas. Gist (1954) who made research on occupational mobility in urban areas of Karnataka reported occupational change and occupational deviation is tending to be more pronounced in urban areas than in the rural areas. He found that a large proportion of the heads of households and their sons had broken away from their parental occupations. His data shows that the deviation among the Brahmins is more than the deviation among backward castes. The study also reveals as much as 44.8 per cent of the Scheduled Castes have shown deviation. His data also revealed that the Brahmins moved mainly into professional, technical, managerial and clerical posts, the backward castes be represented mainly in skilled, semi-skilled and unskilled occupations. Gist concluded that caste system, as a determinant in occupational choice is still a dynamic force.

The study of Lambart, (1963) in an industrial urban setting reveals that the industrial labour is drawn from all castes, high and low. He writes the general ranking of the castes does not seem to be reflected in significant differences in hierarchical positions within the factory. The studies made by Chirde 1949; Makharia, 1959; Myers, 1960; Morris, 1960; also support the view that industrial labour force is drawn from all castes. A few more studies have thrown some light on certain interesting aspects of occupational change. While some of these studies reported the abandonment of defiling caste occupations by the lower castes, a few others have pointed out that these castes tend to retain them as their subsidiary occupations. Though, it is not liked by the upper castes, abandoning the defiling occupations by the lower castes is not new. Basing himself on the study of a village in Uttar Pradesh, Hitchcock (1959) writes that though the high caste Rajputs did not like it, they could do nothing about the local low castes abandoning their traditional defiling occupations. Srivatsava's study (1973) in a village near Jaipur city shows that about 94 per cent of the main earners are engaged in occupations other than their caste occupations. However, Uma Ramaswamy (1974) has come out with a different conclusion in her study of Scheduled Castes in Andhra Pradesh. She found that by and large Scheduled Castes continue to predominate in their traditional occupations; and she further writes that even in case where there is a change, the actual variation between the former and present occupation in terms of nature of work and economic prospects has been minimal. Shyamalal (1975) also supported the view that Scheduled Castes still continue to dominate in their traditional occupation. However, Mandal (1975) and Abbasayulu, (1979) found evidence of intergenerational occupational mobility among Scheduled Castes in their studies.

Reddy (1966), Jaiswal and Ambastha (1972), Sarkar (1973) Mandal (1975) Umamohan (1983) and a few others have reported retention of traditional caste occupations as subsidiary occupation by the occupationally deviant members. The studies of Sovani (1956) Dhenkney (1959) Jorapur (1971) Garg (1973) have proved certain individuals tend to continue their parental occupations, for example those who are associated with skills, unskilled manual work and business activities have shown this tendency.

There is a general tendency among untouchable castes to renounce their traditional occupation and economic ties associated with those occupations. For instance, the Boad-outcastes of Bissipara in Orissa (Bailey 1957: 227), the Mochis of West Bengal (Sharma 1963: 39) and the Chamars of Rajpur in Uttar Pradesh (Elder 1970:106) have abandoned their caste-linked occupations. In order to improve their status, a change from polluting occupation is necessary, in turn it depends on their economic betterment. But to what extent renouncing untouchable occupation leads to change in their status is difficult to access.

The studies on occupational change and deviation have shown various reasons for the change or deviation. Favourable open economic opportunities (Mandelbaum, 1972), opportunity, scarcity, economic benefits, (Freeman, 1974), decrease in demand for caste oriented goods and services, (Shekar, 1973), increased communication with urban centres, (Kapadia, 1964), proximity to town encouraging migration, (Sharma, 1971) have been pointed out by the researchers as the reasons for occupational mobility. Besides this number of years of formal education completed (Bhowmick, 1968; Jetly, 1969; Jorapur, 1971; Kassembaum and Vidyasagar, 1974; Shyamalal, 1975; Soran Singh, 1976; Umamohan, 1976; Vyas and Chowdary, 1978) has been pointed out by various studies as an important reason for occupational mobility. Apart from this the land reforms, the abolition of Zamindari, Jagirdari and Imandari systems (Sharma, 1974; Viswanatham, 1975), Planned development programs, (Reddy,1966; Bhowmick,1968) social reform movements led by caste organizations and social workers encouraging the abandonment of inferior and defiling occupations (Sunanda Patwardhan, 1967; Srivatsava, 1975; Parmar, 1978) have also led to the change and deviation of occupations.

The foregoing discussion on occupational mobility of the different castes in general proves that the occupational change and deviation is not only present in urban areas, but also in the rural areas. Whereas the rate of occupations change and deviation is much pronounced in the urban areas it is relatively less in the rural areas. The above discussion also reveals that caste system, as a determinant in occupational choice is still a dynamic force, with varying degree based on the context of the situation. As M.N.Srinivas (1972) rightly emphasised that the higher castes are more mobile and tend to dominate white-collar occupations of higher rank while the lower castes are moving into lower level occupations providing a wide variety of essential services to the society.

The Scheduled Castes and Occupation

Taking into consideration the continuation, deviation and change of occupations of Scheduled Castes, the occupations associated with them were removal of night soil, carcass recovery and flaying, hide tanning, drum beating at funeral, grave digging etc. which were considered unclean and degrading.

The scavengers, who clean roads, remove carcass of animals from roads and carry night soil from the toilets, occupy the lowest position among the Scheduled Castes. Studies on scavengers show that their condition has not much improved and their occupation is still looked down upon as polluting. Susan Chaplin (2002) observes that scavengers on the whole are "still marginalised" and even today have to carry night soil on their heads and "the situation continues today". However according to her compared to rural area, scavengers of the cities employed in municipalities, are somewhat better off. Takashi Shinoda (2002) study of the sweepers in Ahmedabad district shows, that their occupational mobility remains extremely limited.

In India today, scavengers and sweepers still carry out the basic sanitary services in cities and towns. While many are employed by local urban authorities to clean the sewers and sweep the streets, a significant number still work in their traditional occupation. This means that scavengers are still cleaning latrines by hand and carrying night soil in baskets on their heads. As their occupation renders them permanently polluted, according to Hindu society, scavengers are treated as Untouchable, even by other Untouchable castes. This discrimination also means that scavengers have extremely limited job opportunities other than sanitary work, which they live in acute of literacy and job mobility. Such socio economic conditions for scavengers still persist despite various articles in the Indian Constitution, which stipulate that the state should promote the economic and educational interest of Scheduled Caste and protect them from discrimination and exploitation.

In 1992, Prime Minister Narasimha Rao, during his Independence Day address, promised to abolish scavenging by the end of the Eight Plan. This intent was finally formalised in the Employment of Manual Scavengers and Construction of Dry Latrines (Prohibition) Act, 1993. (Susan, 20002)

Besides being engaged in the unclean occupations the Scheduled Castes were also employed as agricultural labourers, with 52 per cent of them being landless agricultural labourers. (Working report on Scheduled Castes, 1985). As such only certain occupations followed by the Scheduled Castes are psychologically associated with social stigma. Some other occupations with which the Scheduled Castes are associated do not carry any social stigma. However their position in these occupations does represent their economic weakness. Releasing the importance of the occupation, which directly influences the economic position, the Government embarked upon a package of programme to meet the desired goal of uplifting the Scheduled Castes economically.

The Constitution of India under Article 16 (1) envisages equality of opportunity for all citizens in matters relating to employment or appointments to any office under the State irrespective of their religion, race, caste, sex, descent, place of birth or residence. However, to ameliorate the socio-economic conditions of the backward classes including the Scheduled Castes the Constitution provides for reservation in the services.

Article 16 (4) states "nothing in this Article shall prevent the State from making any provision for the reservation of appointments or posts in favour of any backward class of citizens which in the opinion of the State is not adequately represented in the services under the state."

Article 335 states that "the claims of the members of Scheduled Castes and Scheduled Tribes shall be taken into consideration, consistently with the maintenance of efficiency of administration, in making of appointments to services and posts in connection with the affairs of the Union or of the State"

The Article 16 (4) enables the state to make any provision for reservation in the employment in favour of the backward classes including Scheduled Castes provided that in the opinion of State such communities are not adequately represented in the services.

The words employment or appointment is wide enough to include the matters of promotions, including the selection of posts. (A.I.R. 1962, SC36)

At present the percentage of Scheduled Castes in case of direct recruitment by open competition is fifteen per cent. Where as it is 16 2/3 per cent in case of recruitment other wise than by open competition, vide M.H.A Resolution No 27/25/68 Est. (SCT) dated 25-3-1970. In case recruitment is to be made by promotion the reservation is 15 per cent of the vacancies to be filled.

Besides reservations in employment, the Constitution also made provisions for their economic development. Article 38 states that "the State shall strive to promote the welfare of the people securing and protecting as effectively as it may a social order in which justice, social, economic and political, shall inform all the institutions of the national life."

In addition to Article 39, the constitution specifically states under Article 46 that "the state shall promote with special care the educational and economic interests of the weaker sections of the people and in particular of the Scheduled Castes and the Scheduled Tribes, and shall protect them from social injustice and all forms of exploitation".

According to the above said provisions, steps are being taken to promote economic interests of Scheduled Castes and the Planning commission, in the Five-Year Plans, earmarked certain amount. Finding the results unsatisfactory in the Sixth Five-Year Plan (1980-85) a new strategy was evolved, which comprises 1. the Special Component Plans of the States and Central ministries 2. the Special Central Assistance and 3. the Scheduled Castes Development Corporations in the States.

The Special Component Plan was envisaged to help poor Scheduled Caste families through composite income generation programs for which certain amount was to be earmarked in the plan outlays for the utilisation in appropriate sectors. Whereas the Special Central Assistance is given to the States for income generating schemes launched by them in respect of the Scheduled Castes. The Scheduled Castes Development Corporations are formed by various states in order to mobilise institutional credit for the development schemes to be submitted by Scheduled Castes entrepreneurs.

Though Government has provided for reservations and lot of occupational change has been noticed among the Scheduled Castes, distinction should be made between the shift from traditional to non-traditional occupations and to blue collar and white-collar occupations. Whereas the former shift may not ask for any formal education the later insists on formal education of different levels. If the vertical mobility with some impact be achieved by means of modern employment, besides Governments help, the Scheduled Castes are to equip themselves with needed educational qualifications. Occupations in the past did not pose any problems for the Scheduled Castes with the caste system offering them hereditary traditional occupations. In order to improve the economic portion of Scheduled Castes the Government has offered Special privileges to them, by providing a variety of economic opportunities. Besides providing various concessions and facilities to the Scheduled Castes in pursuing to take up formal education it also made special provisions for them to take up modern employment.

Ownership of land is closely associated with social stratification is India. An important historical characteristic of the Indian social and economic milieu is the overlap between the caste and class. (Thangaraj, 2002) After independence, the Government took measures to distribute the surplus land through land reforms and assignment of cultivable wasteland. These measures were considered crucial for economic development and empowerment of the Scheduled Caste, as most of them worked as agricultural labour. Quite a few studies that studied in this area show that the hitherto landless Scheduled Castes beginning to acquire control over land and the village tenurial relations have started showing changes. At the same time despite the introduction of several welfare programmes there has been no marked change in their socio economic condition due to poor implementation of law and lack of political will. (Thangaraj, 2002)

There were changes in the tenurial relationships. It is important to note that the Brahmins were interested in leasing out their land to the Untouchable castes due to their submissive nature. Beteille's study (1971) indicates that in the south Indian villages, Brahmin landowners were replacing the non-Brahmin tenants with Adi Dravidars, the native Scheduled Castes as the non-Brahmin tenants have become more aggressive. The Brahmin landowners preferred the Scheduled Caste tenants, as they were less militant.

Occupational Mobility among Scheduled Castes

The occupational mobility among Scheduled Castes has been studied in two different contexts. Some studies attempted to study the occupational mobility with reference to Scheduled Castes only and some other in the context of multi caste situation. The studies made by Cohn 1961, Sarkar, 1966; Barber, 1968; Bhowmick, 1968; Bose and Majumdar, 1968; Harper, 1968; Dushkin, 1972; Issacs, 1972: Mahar, 1972, Mencher, 1972; Lal, 1973; Sarkar, 1973; Freeman, 1974; Uma Rama Swami, 1974; Gangrade, 1975; Trosi, 1976; Bhoite and Bhoite, 1977; Laxmanna, 1977; Abbasayulu, 1978; Bada, 1978; Miller, 1978; Parmar, 1978; Malik, 1979, Singh and Sharma, 1980; Usha Rao, 1981; Mathew, 1986, Nandu Ram, 1986; Shantakumari, 1987; Mathew, 1989 and Rao, 1989 were exclusive and in the context of both rural and urban areas.

The exclusive studies made on occupational mobility of the Scheduled Castes reveal divergent opinions. The studies of Cohn, 1961, Sarkar 1966; Barber, 1968; Bhowmick, 1968; Harper, 1968; Bose and Majumdar, 1970; Mahar, 1972; Mencher, 1972; Freeman, 1974; Uma Rama Swami, 1974; Bada, 1975; Gangrade, 1975; Miller, 1975; Bhoite and Bhoite, 1977; Parmar, 1978; Jayaram, 1979; Mankidy, 1979; Mohapatra and Mohapatra, 1979; Singh and Sharma, 1980; have made clear the permissibility of mobility. Where as the studies conducted by Alexander, 1967; Ramu, 1968; Singh, 1968, 1969; Beteille, 1972; Weibe and Peter, 1972; Parvathamma, 1973; Rath, 1974; Nandi, 1976; Kochole, 1980 indicated the non-permissibility of occupational and social mobility, in full or partial as the case was. The studies of Alexander (1967), Weibe and Peter (1972), Nandi (1976), Kochole (1980) point out even the conversion into Christianity by the Scheduled Castes did not help them in improving their position in economic and social spheres.

The exclusive studies on occupational mobility in urban context on Scheduled Castes in various parts of the country reveals a gradual shift from traditional and unclean occupations to non-conventional and clean occupations with no or little resistance. However the Study of Vanaja and Venkateswarulu (1980) found even in urban areas there was no upward mobility for Scheduled Castes.

Some other studies have examined the Scheduled Castes mobility in the context of multi caste relations. Mention may be made to the studies of Driver, 1962, Rao, 1966; Dube, 1967; Jain, 1967; Monga, 1967; Sahay, 1967; Sharma, 1967, 1968 and 1971; Ambastha and Jaiswal, 1972; Bopegamage, and Kulakarni, 1972; Kassembaum and Vidya Sagar, 1974; Shakir, 1974; Corwin, 1976; Siva Kumar, 1977; Atal, 1979; Philips, 1979, 1980.

While analysing the caste and occupational mobility, the studies that included Scheduled Castes in different parts of the country reveal that there is considerable upward occupational mobility among the Scheduled Castes over a period of time. These studies identified education, migration to urban areas, occupational shift, land reforms, modernisation, political participation and strong desire to raise one's social status as the factors for mobility in general. With regard to the unit of the mobility the above studies have taken into consideration mobility at two levels namely individual and family. Barber however argues that mobility in Hindu India is group mobility even though there is incidental individual mobility.

The study of Bopegamage and Kulahali (1972) explains how the occupational structure and structural factors affect the occupational mobility. Atal (1968) and Sharma (1968) also explain how structural factors helped the Scheduled Castes to move up in occupational ladder. The studies of Dube, 1963; Jain, 1966; Kassembaum and Vidya Sagar, 1974; Corwin, 1975; and Siva Kumar, 1977; conducted in urban areas show from all sections a considerable amount of mobility in educational and occupational fields. Philips (1979) study explores the inverse relationship of caste and upward mobility.

The studies that enquired into the changes in occupational structure and mobility among Scheduled Castes give variety of opinions.

Sharma (1971) opined that though traditional caste and occupational inter-relatedness is slowly but steadily breaking down, caste still plays a dominant role in determining the choice of one's new occupations. Atal (1968) also agrees with this and said while open occupations are taken up more and more gradually, but at the same time the traditional occupations are not being given up entirely.

Limited occupational chances are open to the Scheduled Castes who wish to shift from their traditional occupations. They are in skilled and semi-skilled occupations and thus concentration is more and more in small trade and household industries. (Patwardhan, 1973). The lower occupations such as watchman, gardener and the like are entirely followed by the low caste groups (Singh, 1967). To some extent even the abandoning of the traditional occupation does not involve in any major changes in the status of Scheduled Castes and mobility achieved was little and horizontal. G.P. Reddy, 1968; K.L. Sharma, 1969; and Patwardhan, 1973, supported this view. Amir Hassan (1969) reveals that the tendency to stay in traditional occupations is found most in those castes where the occupations requires high skill. The castes whose occupation does not call for high skill and general service in nature, there is shift to other occupations. Srinivas (1962) and Beteille (1969) have also agreed that in a situation of expanding opportunities, it is the upper castes that benefit more and not the lower castes such as Scheduled Castes. D'Souza (1962) in the study of urbanisation in Punjab says the proportion of the Scheduled Castes declined with the increasing occupational complexity and says where better employment opportunities exist; the Scheduled Castes have little scope. D'Souza, 1962; Upreti, 1967 have concluded that the Scheduled Castes are still sticking to their traditional occupations.

Though the relationship between caste and occupation has changed, the studies of Mukharje, 1965; Bopegamage and Veera Raghavan, 1967; Nanda, 1969; Jetley, 1969, concluded that the current occupations the Scheduled Castes are holding to a large degree are evaluated as being equal to their traditional caste occupations at rural areas.

Suma Chitnis (1981) reports that the Scheduled Castes lack confidence to compete openly for employment, they are diffident about venturing into private sector employment and are inclined to confine themselves to the security of reserved positions in Government.

Commenting on the development of Scheduled Castes Visaria (1974) reports that in terms of economic indicators, size of land holding, employment, occupation, income and savings, it is found that the position of the Scheduled Castes has progressively worsened between 1950 and 70. The results of the survey conducted by Vageswari (1972) indicate that the income levels of Scheduled Castes have worsened and did not keep pace with price rise. Further the gap between the Scheduled Castes and non-Scheduled Castes with regard to their incomes widened. Hanumantha Rao (1977) who made a study of Scheduled Castes in a village of Andhra says even the land legislation did not help the Scheduled Castes and ownership of land by these groups are extremely negligible. The Scheduled Caste cultivators do not have any significant place in the village. He reports even the structural changes in economy of the village did not help to strengthen the economic base of the Scheduled Castes. They continue to be land less poor.

The Scheduled Castes are endeavouring to forsake all those occupations, which are considered degrading. They do not want their children to follow these occupations, which degrade their social status. (Chitnis, 1981)

The Scheduled Castes have been know for their association with the unclean occupations and are placed low in the society. (Gough, 1960; Dumont, 1966; Beteille, 1969; Hardgrave, 1969; and Sharma, 1969). Explaining the changes taking place in the occupations of Scheduled Castes, Jyotirmayee Sharma (1958) says the Scheduled Castes have association with cultivation besides their caste occupations, and may have forsaken their caste occupations altogether. Saberwal (1972) has reported that the Balmikis decided to give up safai to improve their status. Elder (1970) expressed the same opinion and said the Chamers had recognised that if they wanted to rise in the social hierarchy they have to abandon their polluting leatherwork. Danda (1968) observed that acquisition of education makes it possible for the Scheduled Castes to give up their defiling professions.

Troisi (1976) reported that the Noniyas exploited the economic resources to attain the status of Kshatriyas caste and the Santhals improved their status by acquiring land by use of violence. The study of Selvanathan (1989) also reveals that there is shift of occupation among the Scheduled Castes from cultivation and agricultural labour to non-agricultural workers.

The study of Rao (1989) concluded the higher the occupational prestige grade of father, the smaller is the proportion of sons in lower occupational prestige grades. The study also observed that education has a direct positive bearing on the upward occupational mobility both on inter and intra generation lines. The study of Joseph (1989) concludes in the fields of education and occupation the Scheduled Castes have been able to fare better and they are quite optimistic about their bright future even if the present conditions continue to prevail over a long time. Factors behind their limited but impressive social mobility are education, rural development programmes, government jobs and cultivable land holdings. The study of Malik (1979) reveals that primarily through educational attainment only the Scheduled Castes could change their occupations. Nanduram (1988) concluded that all the respondents of his study were upwardly mobile and says the trend of mobility among Scheduled Castes is upward and the degree of mobility is increasing steadily. Shantakumari (1976) said in her study compared to the respondents' fathers' generation more number of respondents are having non-traditional occupations. Mathew (1986) said education has enabled the Mahars to move up in the occupational ladder. He also said their occupational development is due to the factors such as conversion to Christianity, state action and protest activities of the people in the villages.

Scheduled Castes, who number 13.82 Crores, constitute about one-sixth of the population of the country. A large majority of them are agricultural labourers living below the poverty line and their conditions of life are worse than that of other poverty groups. The literacy rate among the Scheduled Castes in 1991 was only 37.41 per cent against the national average of 52.21 per cent. There is a clear nexus between the economic plight of Scheduled Castes and the atrocities and social disabilities, which they are subjected to. In the early seventies, during the Fourth Five-year plan a direct attack on poverty was initiated and anti poverty measures or Poverty Alleviation Programmes directly and exclusively aimed at the poor were introduced. This has been continued in one form or other in the successive plans. A great majority of the Scheduled Castes being from below poverty line have utilised the schemes and benefited from them. Special care was taken to include the Scheduled Castes in all these Schemes so that they could get their due in the development. The various schemes that helped the Scheduled Castes in the poverty alleviation are quite a few. Some of them are as follows:

The Small Farmers Development Agency (SFDA) and the Marginal Farmers and Landless Labour (MFAL) schemes were considered to be the earliest of the poverty alleviation programmes, were started in the year 1970-71. The Integrated Rural Development Programme (IRDP) replaced these schemes in 1978 and was extended to the entire country in 1980. To provide greater thrust to self-employment the programme Training of Rural Youth in Self-Employment (TRYSEM) and Development of Women and Children in Rural Areas (DWCRA) were introduced as part of the IRDP. Different wage employment schemes or public works programmes such as Rural Manpower Programme, 1960-61, Crash Scheme of Rural Employment (CSRE) in 1971, Rural Works Programme in 1970-71, and Pilot Intensive Rural Employment Programme (PIREP) in 1972 was also introduced. The Drought Prone Area Programme

(DPAP) was also started as an employment programme in 1973-74. The Food for Work Programme emerged in 1977 and the National Rural Employment Programme (NREP) commenced in 1980. The Rural Landless Employment Guarantee Programme (RLEGP) was introduced in 1983. In 1989-90, Jawahar Rozgar Yojana (JRY) replaced the earlier schemes. The Employment Assurance Scheme was started on October 1993 to provide a minimum of 100 days of assured unskilled manual work to the rural poor. The Prime Minister's Rozgar Yojana (PMRY) is another scheme to provide employment to one million youth in urban and rural areas during the period 1993 to 1997. In order to cater to the urban areas, programme such as Scheme for Urban Micro Enterprises (SUME), Scheme for Urban Wage Employment (SUWE) were evolved. A programme of development of land and irrigation wells in the landholdings of the rural poor was taken up under the Million Wells Programme. The construction of houses for Scheduled Castes, Scheduled Tribes, freed bonded labours, and other poor was also initiated under the Indira Awas Yojana. More than a million wells and about three million houses have been constructed under these programmes since theirs inception. All these schemes have helped the Scheduled Castes in their own way by giving them their due share.

Traditionally the Scheduled Castes were in disadvantageous position occupationally and were confined to though essential but least preferred occupations. Only during the last few decades due to the influence of several forces, the Scheduled Castes have been venturing into other occupations, both caste-oriented and caste free. However it may be stressed here that the vast majority could only enter lower level occupations which requires lesser levels of achievement in terms of education or vocational skills or occupations which are particularly associated with manual labour or entrepreneurial activity which require lesser levels of investment and managerial abilities.

Occupational Mobility of Respondents

Considering the above factors and also keeping in view the overall social conditions with regard to hierarchy in occupational structure the following classification of occupations has been adopted to understand the mobility process. The considerations for upward occupational mobility is if there is deviation of the occupation which is:

1. Caste to Caste free occupations.
2. Manual to partially manual or non-manual occupations.
3. Unskilled to skilled occupations.
4. The occupations with no educational attainment to minimal educational attainment and higher educational attainment.
5. The occupations with lower aesthetic values to higher.
6. Insecure to secure occupations - both in terms of income as well as days of employment.
7. Occupations with lower to higher incomes.

By taking into account the above considerations the occupations of the Scheduled Castes have been classified into nine categories. The occupations in the respondent's generation are 61 in number and alphabetically they are:

Bank clerk, Bus driver, Butcher, Conductor, Check post Inspector, Compounder, Cinema operator, Construction worker, Coolie, Cool drink shop Worker, Cobbler, Electrician, Excise Constable, Fruit vendor, Gateman, Gang man, Hostel Warden, Health worker, Hamali, (porter in bus stand and market place) Hostel worker, Jail warden, Jatkawala, Lecturer, Lorry cleaner, Male nurse, Mechanic, Municipal worker, Marginal farmer, Mason, Milk vendor, Police Constable, Peon, Painter, Physical Education Teacher, Post Office clerk, Record sorter, Railway driver, Railway Electrician, Railway Fitter, Railway Shunter, Rickshaw Puller, Station Master, Signal Man, Sub contractor, Shoe Shop owner, Saw mill worker, Stone crusher, Sweeper, Scavenger, Teacher, Typist, Telephone operator, Tractor mechanic, Petty tea Bunk owner, Tailor and Petty work Shop owner.

Besides the above said occupations in the respondents' time, in respondents' fathers' generation and respondents' grandfathers' generation, the common occupations were Bonded Labour, Talari, Sepoy and Woodcutter. In respondents' fathers' generation the occupations such as Butler (with British), Village Development Officer, Compost man, Mason and Post man, and in respondents' grandfathers' generation Weaver, Grass vendor, Court peon were exclusively found. It is to be noted here all the above occupations are the primary occupations, and these were alone considered for analysing the mobility.

THE OCCUPATIONAL CATEGORIES

For analysing the occupational mobility all the above occupations have been classified into nine hierarchical categories. The nine categories are (1) Professional and Executive (2) White Collar (3) Para Professional and Para Executive (4) Skilled Workers (5) Services (6) Business (7) Semiskilled and Self employed manual workers (8) Manual workers and (9) Menial services.

The Occupational Categories:

Sl. No.	*Occupational category*	*Base for category*	*Occupations in the category*
1.	Professional and Executive	Definite formal educational qualifications and training- carry power and authority- professional skills- higher prestige, aesthetic value and income- non hereditary	Lecturer, Teacher, Physical education teacher, Jail warden, Station master,
2.	White-Collar	Definite formal educational qualifications-non hereditary- higher income and prestige	Bank clerk, Postal clerk, Postal inspector, Typist, Conductor and Record sorter
3.	Para Professional and Para Executive	Low order professional executive who function at lower levels of hierarchy- require definite educational qualifications and training-generally subordinate to professional and executive and carry power and authority to some extent	Village development office, Compounder, Health officer, Police constable, Excise constable, Male nurse, Sepoy
4.	Skilled Workers	Formal training skills- non hereditary- functionally essential-caste free- salary earners (usually)	Railway driver, Bus driver, Telephone operator, Electrician, Tractor mechanic, Railway fitter, Mechanic and Cinema operator

5. Services	Lower order of subordinate service- salaried employees – carry minimum authority and power – require minimal or no educational qualifications – caste free (except Talari)	Attender, Peon, Shunter, Gate man, Signal man, Talari, Butler, Postman, Municipality worker and Court peon.
6. Business	Self employed-not much of investment- minimum returns and are not regularly guaranteed-	Beedi bunk owner, Petty Hotel owner, Petty workshop owner, Brick making, Shoe shop, Sub contractor
7. Semi Skilled and Self Employed Manual workers	Skills acquired more by job experience- without formal training or hereditary skills– manual work is a pre condition- self employed manual labour	Painter, Tailor, mason, Saw mill worker, Weaver, Milk vendor, Marginal farmer, Grass vendor, Fire wood vendor, Rickshaw puller, Jatkawala
8. Manual workers	Wage earners either weekly or daily- subjected to exploitation and suppression- days of employment not guaranteed- wholly manual work- not on regular pay role	Agriculture labour, Hamali, Stone crusher, Gang man, Hostel worker, Lorry cleaner, construction worker, Cooley, Cool drink shop worker
9. Menial services	Essential but least preferred services- usually caste oriented- considered to be polluting- employment by regular salary or traditional	Scavenger, Sweeper, Cobbler, Butcher, Compost man

In the study we come across both traditional and modern occupations. Of the traditional occupations, some are ritually polluting and some others are clean. The first four categories namely, the Professional and Executive, the White collar, the Para Professional and Para Executive and Skilled workers are completely modern occupations and at the same time clean occupations. In the fifth category i.e. the Services, we find mostly the modern occupations (except the Talari) and at the same time subordinate services. The sixth category consists of the Scheduled Castes who are involved in business, that are generally small in investment and returns. Here we find a shoe shop owner, who makes and sells shoes, which is a modern form of traditional caste occupation, the leatherwork. The next category of Semi skilled and self-employed manual workers mostly consists of traditional occupations and the occupations that are not hereditary caste occupations of the Scheduled Castes. In the course of time they have moved into these occupations. Most of these occupations require skills but at the same time are not that respectable positions. The eighth category consists of manual workers who are wage earners and include both traditional and modern occupations. The last and the ninth category is the only category where we find traditional and at the same time ritually polluting occupations that are traditional and hereditary caste occupations of the Scheduled Castes.

For arriving at this occupational classification the occupational conditions of the Scheduled Castes of Gooty were alone considered. For example the category of 'Business' in general can be placed comparatively high, but here, has been placed in a comparatively low position, because of the low level of investment and low levels of incomes in this particular context. So are placed the other occupations also in different categories and it may or may not agree with general classification of occupations. In the classification the occupations of all the three generations are considered. Under each category are given the requirements and/or characteristics for arriving at it along with the names of the occupations.

Occupational Mobility Analysis

For construction the occupational mobility tables the above nine categories have been considered and movement from one occupational category to another is considered mobility.

The occupations of Scheduled Castes by occupational category over three generations have been presented in Table 4.1. It is clear from the table that throughout all the three generations maximum number of Scheduled Castes is placed in the low occupational categories of Manual worker and Menial services. Heavy concentration of Scheduled Castes over three generations could be seen around the category of Manual workers, which worked out to nearly 80 per cent or more. Though the category of Menial services is another category where concentration of the

Scheduled Castes could be seen, the number of persons in this category has gradually come down over generations.

The only other category where there is at least little concentration over three generations is the category of Semi Skilled and Self-Employed Manual Workers. However there is marked difference with most of the persons in that category in respondents' grandfathers' generations who were engaged in more or less traditional occupations, it is not so in the respondents generation throughout all the three generations. In all the other occupational categories the frequency is low.

TABLE - 4.1
DISTRIBUTION OF SCHEDULED CASTES BY OCCUPATIONAL CATEGORY OVER THREE GENERATIONS

Occupational Category		*Grandfather*	*Father*	*Respondent*
Professional & Executive	(1)	1	5	10
White Collar	(2)	0	0	8
Para Professional & Para Executive	(3)	1	4	6
Skilled Workers	(4)	0	0	12
Services	(5)	4	4	10
Business	(6)	0	4	6
Semi-skilled and Self employed Workers	(7)	15	10	18
Manual Workers	(8)	221	244	227
Menial Services	(9)	70	49	23
Don't Know		8	—	—
Total		320	320	320

In the collection of data, eight respondents could not give the occupations of their grandfathers. Hence in preparing occupational mobility tables, in respondents' grandfathers' generation the total number of cases is only 312, whereas it is 320 each in fathers' all respondents generation and the tables have been worked out accordingly.

The occupational mobility among various occupational categories between respondents' fathers' and respondents' grandfathers' generation has been presented in the Table 4.2. It is clear from the table that as many as 243 (77.88%) fathers have remained immobile compared to the respondents' grandfathers.

Of the 243 fathers who are immobile two are placed in occupational category of Services, six in occupational category of Semi Skilled and Self Employed Manual workers, and as many as two hundreds in occupational category of Manual workers and thirty five in occupational category of Menial Workers, and so are the grandfathers.

Among the fathers of respondents' considered here, only 69 (21.12) have shown mobility compared to grandfather. Of this 69 mobile fathers 49 (71.01%) moved up where as 20 (28.99%) went down.

Of the upwardly mobile fathers compared to grandfathers, who were Semi Skilled and Self Employed Manual Workers, one father could achieve occupational category of Services and two could achieve occupational category of Professional and Executive. While the grandfathers were in the occupational category of Manual Workers, three fathers each could achieve occupational categories of business and Semi-skilled Self employed manual labour respectively, two fathers could achieve occupational category of Para professional and Para Executive and three could acquire occupational Professional and Executive. Compared to the grandfathers in occupational category of Menial Workers, 30 fathers could reach the occupational category of Manual workers, one father each could achieve the occupational category of Services, Business and Semi-skilled and Self employed manual workers, respectively and two could achieve the occupational category of Para Professional and Para Executive.

With regard to the downward mobility, compared to the grandfather who was in occupational category of Professional and Executive, one father went down to the occupational category of Manual Workers, which is considerable downward mobility. One more father went down to the occupational category of Manual Workers compared to the grandfather who was placed in occupational category of Para professional and Para Executive. With grandfather placed in occupational category of Services two fathers went down to the Occupational Category of Manual Workers. With grandfather occupational category being Semi-skilled and Self-employed manual labour, four fathers reached occupational category of Manual Workers and two fathers occupational category of Menial Services. 50 per cent of downward mobility recorded was from occupational category of Manual workers to Menial Services, with ten fathers placed in occupational category of Menial service compared to the grandfather who were Manual workers.

TABLE - 4.2

OCCUPATIONAL MOBILITY – GRANDFATHER AND FATHER

Grandfather → Father ↓	1	2	3	4	5	6	7	8	9	Total ↓
1								1		1
2										0
3								1		1
4										0
5					2			2		4
6										0
7	2				1		6	4	2	15
8	3		2			3	3	200	10	221
9			2		1	1	1	30	35	70
Total →	5	0	4	0	4	4	10	238	47	312

1. Professional & Executive; 2. White Collar; 3. Para Professional & Para Executive; 4. Skilled Workers; 5. Services; 6. Business; 7. Semi-skilled and Self employed workers; 8. Manual Workers; 9. Menial Services

Table 4.3 presents occupational mobility between the respondents' fathers' and respondents'. As the table reveals, of the total 320 cases, 206 (64.38%) respondents have remained immobile compared to their fathers. Of these immobile respondents, one is placed in occupational category of Professional and Executive, four in occupational category of Semi-skilled and Self employed manual workers, 188 (91.26%) the majority in occupational category of Manual Workers, and 13 in occupational category of Menial Services, and so were the fathers.

Of the total of 320 cases, 114 (35.62%) respondents have moved out of their father's occupational category. Of the 114 mobile respondents, 88 (77.19%) have moved up whereas 26 (22.81%) have moved down in occupational categories.

Of the 88 upwardly mobile fathers, compared to the father in occupational category of Business, one respondent each have moved to occupational category of Para Professional and Para Executive and Services respectively. Compared to the fathers in occupational category of Semi-skilled and Self-employed manual workers, two respondents each have moved to occupational categories of Professional and Executive and White-Collar respectively. Maximum number of upward mobility could be seen in respect of the respondents compared to their fathers who were in occupational category of Manual Workers. Compared to the fathers in this category six, five, four, ten, eight, four and nine respondents moved to the occupational categories, Professional and Executive, White-Collar, Para professional and Para Executive, Skilled Workers, Services, Business and Semi-skilled and Self Employed manual workers respectively. Compared to the fathers who were in Menial services, the respondents have also moved significantly out of this category, but predominantly only to the next occupational category of the Manual workers and their number works out to 31.

Of the mobile respondents compared to their fathers, 26 (22.81%) have moved down in occupational categories. Whereas the father was in the occupational category of Professional and Executive, one respondent each have moved down to the occupational categories of White Collar, Skilled worker, Services and Manual Workers respectively. Compared to the father in occupational category of Para Professional and Para executive, two respondents each have moved down to the occupational categories of Semi-skilled and Self employed manual workers and Manual workers respectively. With the fathers placed in occupational category of Services, one each respondent went down to the occupational categories of Business and Semi-skilled and Self employed manual workers whereas two went down to the occupational category of Manual workers. Compared to fathers' occupational category of Business, one respondent each moved down to occupational category of Semi-skilled and Self employed manual workers and Manual workers. Two respondents went down by getting them placed in occupational category of Manual workers, while their fathers were in occupational category of Semi-skilled and Self employed manual workers. 10 respondents compared to their fathers in the occupational category of Manual workers went down to the occupational category of Menial services.

TABLE - 4.3

OCCUPATIONAL MOBILITY – FATHER AND RESPONDENT

Father → Respondent ↓	1	2	3	4	5	6	7	8	9	Total ↓
1	1	1		1				1		5
2										0
3							2	2		4
4										0
5						1	1	2		4
6			1		1		1	1		4
7	2	2					4	2		10
8	6	5	4	10	8	4	9	188	10	244
9	1		1	1		1	1	31	13	49
Total →	10	8	6	12	10	6	18	227	23	320

1. Professional & Executive; 2. White Collar; 3. Para Professional & Para Executive; 4. Skilled Workers; 5. Services; 6. Business; 7. Semi-skilled and Self employed workers; 8. Manual Workers; 9. Menial Services

The occupational mobility between the respondents' grandfathers' and respondents' generations was presented in Table 4.4. As the table reveals compared to the grandfather 175 (56.08%) of respondents remained in the same occupational category, whereas the remaining 137 (43.92%) have moved out of their grandfathers' occupations.

Taking into consideration the immobility, four grandfathers were in occupational category of Semi-skilled and Self employed manual workers, 161 in occupational category of Manual workers, and ten in occupational category of Menial services and so are the respondents.

Of the 312 cases considered for the occupational mobility between grandfathers' and respondents' generation, 137 (43.92%) respondents compared to their grandfathers have moved away from the occupational categories of the grandfather. Whereas 114 (83.21%) have moved up, 23 (16.79%) have moved down in the occupational categories.

Compared to the grandfathers who were in occupational category of Semi-skilled and self-employed manual workers, two and three respondents have achieved the occupational categories of Professional and Executive and White Collar respectively. Much of upward mobility could be seen compared to the grandfathers who were in occupational category of Manual workers, seven, five, six, ten, eight, four and nine respondents have moved up by achieving the occupational categories of Professional and Executive, White collar, Para Professional and Para Executive, Skilled workers, Services, Business and Semi-skilled and self employed manual workers. Substantial mobility is also to be seen, compared to the grandfather in occupational category of Menial Services, with as many as 54 respondents moving up, but could only reach the next occupational category of the Manual workers. However one could reach occupational category of Professional and Executive, the maximum possible mobility and one respondent each could achieve occupational categories of Services and Business, and three occupational category of Semi-skilled and self employed manual workers.

Compared to the grandfathers, 23 respondents have moved down in occupational categories. Whereas the grandfather was in occupational category of Professional and Executive and compared to him one respondent could reach the occupational category of Services, and with the grandfather placed in occupational category of Para professional and Para executive another respondent went down and was placed in occupational category of Menial services. With grandfather in occupational category of Services, one respondent each went down to occupational category of Business and Semi-skilled and Self employed manual workers and two to occupational category of Manual workers. Compared to the grandfather in occupational category of Semi-skilled and Self-employed manual workers, five respondents showed downward mobility by reaching occupational category of Manual workers, and one by reaching occupational category of Menial services. 11 respondents compared to the grandfathers who were Manual workers went down and were engaged in Menial services.

TABLE - 4.4

OCCUPATIONAL MOBILITY – GRANDFATHER AND RESPONDENT

Father → Respondent ↓	1	2	3	4	5	6	7	8	9	Total ↓
1					1					1
2				-						0
3									1	1
4										0
5						1	1	2		4
6										0
7	2	3					4	5	1	15
8	7	5	6	10	8	4	9	161	11	221
9	1				1	1	3	54	10	70
Total →	10	8	6	10	10	6	17	222	23	312

1. Professional & Executive; 2. White Collar; 3. Para Professional & Para Executive; 4. Skilled Workers; 5. Services; 6. Business; 7. Semi-skilled and Self employed workers; 8. Manual Workers; 9. Menial Services

The occupational categories, the number of grandfather in each occupational category, and the comparison of father whether they are in the same or different occupational category were given in Table 4.5. From the table it is clear that heavy concentration of Scheduled Castes was in occupational categories of Manual workers and of Menial Services, with no frequencies at all in occupational categories of White-Collar, Skilled Workers and Business.

As the table presents, put together almost 78 per cent of the fathers remained immobile. In occupational category of Manual workers as many as 200 (90.5%) out of 221 remained in the parental occupational category only. However in the occupational category of Menial services compared to the grandfather, a substantial 50 per cent have moved in to different occupational categories. On the whole while about 78 per cent remained in parental occupational categories, only about 12 per cent have different occupational categories.

TABLE - 4.5
FATHERS WHOSE OCCUPATIONAL CATEGORIES ARE THE SAME OR DIFFERENT TO THOSE OF GRANDFATHER

Occupational Category of Grandfather	*Occupational Category of father*			*Same as % of Total*
	Same	*Different*	*Total*	
1	0	1	1	—
2	0	0	0	—
3	0	1	1	—
4	0	0	0	—
5	2	2	4	50.00
6	0	0	0	—
7	6	9	15	40.00
8	200	21	221	90.0
9	35	35	70	50.00
Total	243	69	312	77.9

Particulars	*Frequency*	*Percent*
Same occupational category	243	77.90
Different occupational category	69	22.10
Total	312	100.00

Table 4.6 presents the respondents' fathers who have achieved lower or higher occupational categories compared to the grandfathers'. It is clear from the table that in the occupational

categories of White collar, Para professional and Para executive, Skilled workers, Services, and Business, none of the fathers could achieve higher occupational category compared to the grandfathers. Only in the last three occupational categories, could the fathers achieve the higher occupational category, where as more than 50 per cent of the fathers achieved higher occupational category, compared to the grandfathers in occupational category of Manual Workers, 100 per cent of the fathers, compared to the grandfathers in Menial services, could achieve higher occupational category. As the latter part of the table shows, of the mobile fathers compared to those of grandfathers, whereas about 71 per cent are upwardly mobile about 29 per cent have shown downward mobility.

TABLE 4.6
FATHERS WHOSE OCCUPATIONAL CATEGORIES THAT ARE HIGHER OR LOWER TO THAT OF GRANDFATHER

Occupational Category of Grandfather	*Occupational Category of father*			*% of the higher to Total*
	Higher	*Lower*	*Total*	
1	NA	1	1	0.00
2	—	—	—	—
3	0	1	1	0.00
4	—	—	—	—
5	0	2	2	0.00
6	—	—	—	—
7	3	6	9	33.30
8	11	10	21	52.40
9	35	NA	35	100.00

Particulars	*Frequency*	*Percent*
Higher occupational category	49	71.00
Lower occupational category	20	29.00
Total	69	100.00

N.A. (Not applicable) as one can not move higher or lower than occupational categories 1 and 9 respectively.

Table 4.7 shows occupational categories of respondents' father and occupational categories of respondents comparing whether they are in the same or different occupational category. Here also heavy concentration of the Scheduled Castes is in occupational category of Manual workers, followed by occupational category of Menial Services. As the table reveals 20 per cent, 40 per cent, 70 per cent and about 27 per cent of respondents have retained their parental occupational category, which is Professional and Executive, Semi-skilled and Self employed manual workers, Manual Workers and Menial services respectively. Put together about 64 per cent of the respondents remained in occupational categories of their fathers, whereas about 36 per cent have moved away from their fathers' occupational categories.

TABLE - 4.7
RESPONDENTS WHOSE OCCUPATIONAL CATEGORIES ARE THE SAME OR DIFFERENT TO THOSE OF FATHERS

Occupational Category of Father	*Occupational Category of Respondent*			*Same as % of Total*
	Same	*Different*	*Total*	
1	1	4	5	20.00
2	0	0	0	—
3	0	4	4	0.00
4	0	0	0	—
5	0	4	4	0.00
6	0	4	4	0.00
7	4	6	10	40.00
8	188	56	244	77.00
9	13	35	49	26.50
Total	206	114	320	64.40

Particulars	*Frequency*	*Percent*
Same occupational category	206	64.40
Different occupational category	114	35.40
Total	320	100.00

Table No. 4.8 examines whether mobile respondents have achieved higher or lower occupational category compared to their fathers. It is clear from the table that in none of the respondents in occupational categories of White collar, Para professional and Para executive, Skilled workers and Services could achieve higher occupational category compared to their fathers. 50 per cent of respondents compared to the fathers in occupational categories of Business, Semi-skilled and Self employed manual workers, Manual workers and Menial services, 50 per cent about 67 per cent, about 82 per cent and 100 per cent or respondents moved to higher occupational categories. From the latter part of the table it is clear that this put together about 77 per cent of the mobile respondents moved up and the remaining about 23 per cent moved down in occupational categories compared to their fathers.

TABLE - 4.8
OCCUPATIONAL CATEGORIES OF THE RESPONDENTS THAT ARE HIGHER OF LOWER TO THOSE OF FATHER

Occupational Category of Father	*Occupational Category of Respondent*			*% of the higher to Total*
	Higher	*Lower*	*Total*	
1	NA	4	4	0.00
2	—	—	—	—
3	NA	4	4	0.00
4	—	—	—	—
5	NA	4	4	0.00
6	2	2	4	50.00
7	4	2	6	66.60
8	46	10	56	82.10
9	36	NA	36	100.00

Particulars	*Frequency*	*Percent*
Higher occupational category	88	77.20
Lower occupational category	26	22.80
Total	114	100.00

N.A. (Not applicable) as one can not move higher or lower than occupational categories 1 and 9 respectively.

Table No 4.9 analyses the occupational categories of respondents' grandfathers' and makes a comparison of the respondents whose occupational category is same or different to those of respondents' grandfather. As the table reveals there are no respondents in the first six occupational categories who have the same occupational categories compared to the grandfather. Only in occupational category of Manual workers and Menial services where there is high concentration in both the generations, about 73 per cent of the respondents and 14 per cent of the respondent in occupational category of Menial services, have been returned as the respondents having similar occupational category compared to the grandfather. As the later part of the table reveals put together about 56 per cent of the respondents have retained the occupational categories of their grandfathers, where as about 44 per cent have moved away to different occupational categories.

TABLE - 4.9
RESPONDENTS WHOSE OCCUPATIONAL CATEGORIES THAT ARE SAME OR DIFFERENT TO THOSE OF GRANDFATHER

Occupational Category of Grandfather	*Occupational Category of Respondent*			*Same as % of Total*
	Same	*Different*	*Total*	
1	0	1	1	0.00
2	0	0	0	—
3	0	1	1	0.00
4	0	0	0	—
5	0	4	4	0.00
6	0	0	0	—
7	4	11	15	26.70
8	161	60	221	72.90
9	10	16	70	14.30
Total	175	137	312	56.10

Particulars	*Frequency*	*Percent*
Same occupational category	175	56.1
Different occupational category	137	43.9
Total	312	100.0

Table No 4.10 explains the occupational categories of the respondents that are higher or lower to that of respondents' grandfather. Of the mobile respondents compared to their grandfathers in occupational categories of White collar, Para professional and Para Executive, Skilled workers, Services and Business, no respondent has moved into higher occupational category. Compared to the grandfather in occupational category of Semi Skilled and Self employed manual labour, five respondents moved into higher occupational categories, whereas six into the lower occupational categories. Compared to the grandfathers who were Manual Workers 49 respondents have moved up and 11 moved down in occupational categories and compared to the grandfathers in occupational category of Menial services, all the mobile respondents moved up. On the whole about 83 per cent of the mobile respondent compared to the grandfather have moved up and about 17 per cent have went down.

TABLE - 4.10
OCCUPATIONAL CATEGORIES OF RESPONDENTS THAT ARE HIGHER OR LOWER TO THOSE OF GRANDFATHER.

Occupational Category of Grandfather	*Occupational Category of Respondent*			*% of Higher to the Total*
	Higher	*Lower*	*Total*	
1	NA	1	1	0.00
2	—	—	—	—
3	NA	1	1	0.00
4	—	—	—	—
5	NA	4	4	0.00
6	—	—	—	—
7	5	6	11	45.50
8	49	11	60	81.70
9	60	NA	60	100.00

Particulars	*Frequency*	*Percent*
Higher occupational category	114	83.20
Lower occupational category	23	16.80
Total	137	100.00

N.A. (Not applicable) as one can not move higher or lower than occupational categories 1 and 9 respectively.

To measure the occupational mobility, two occupational mobility measures have been worked out viz., the Gross Intergenerational Occupational Mobility Rate and the Intergenerational Upward Occupational Mobility Rate. The measure Gross Intergenerational Occupational Mobility Rate (GIOMR) is arrived at by dividing the number of persons with occupational category different from that of those of their fathers and grandfathers by the total number of persons. The other measure Gross Upward Intergenerational Occupational Mobility Rate (GUOIMR) is arrived at by dividing the number of persons with occupational categories higher than those of their father or grandfather by the total number of persons. If either of the measures is more than value of .50, it indicates higher mobility rate, and less than .50 indicates lower mobility rate. (Rao, 1989)

As the Table 4.11 reveals that GIOMR is more in the case of mobility analysis of the respondents' grandfather and respondents generation. However even this is low as it works out to less than .50 and hence is lower mobility. Taking into consideration the GUIOMR the maximum of GUIOMR could be seen while comparing the respondents' grandfather and respondents' generation and the lowest compared to respondents' grandfather and respondents' fathers' generations. It can be concluded in all the cases the mobility is low, since in all the cases that the value is less than 0.50.

TABLE - 4.11
INTERGENERATIONAL MOBILITY RATES

Mobility Rate	*Grandfather/ father*	*Father-Respondent*	*Grandfather-Respondent*
Gross Intergenerational Occupational Mobility Rate (GIOMR)	0.22	0.36	0.43
Gross Upward Intergenerational Occupational Mobility Rate (GUIMOR)	0.16	0.28	0.37

An attempt is made to find out the occupations of the fourth generation, i.e. the employed male children of the respondents. For this purpose data were collected, analysed and is presented hereunder.

Of the 320 respondents, only 84 respondents have employed male children. Of these 84 respondents who have employed male children, 59 respondents have only one employed son, 15 respondents have two employed sons, 10 respondents have three employed sons.

The occupational category distribution of the children of respondents is as follows taking the best of the employed son. 74 (90%) among the male employed children of respondents are in the occupational category of Manual workers, four in the occupational category of Menial services, two in the occupational category of Semi-skilled and Self employed manual workers, one each in the occupational categories of Semi-skilled and Self employed manual worker and Business and two in the occupational category of Professional and Executive. 90 per cent of them being in occupational category of Manual workers should not be considered a disappointing trend for that a majority of them have minimum or no educational attainment.

When we take into consideration the 74 respondents in occupational category of Manual Workers and compare them to their employed male children, in 55 cases there is no mobility and the remaining 19 sons have shown mobility compared to the respondents. Of the immobile 55 respondents, 42 have one son, five have two sons, eight have three sons with all their sons, in the same occupational category of Manual workers. The mobile male employed sons, compared to the respondents who have one son, and who is in occupational category of Manual workers, three have moved to occupational category of White collar, one each to occupational category of Para Professional and Para executive and Skilled workers, two each to occupational categories of Services, Semi-skilled and Self employed manual workers and Menial services.

Taking into consideration seven respondents who have two sons, and who are in occupational category of Manual workers, and taken the best of the two employed sons, two have moved into occupational category of Skilled workers, whereas one each into occupational categories of White collar, Services, Business and Semi-skilled and Self employed Manual Workers. Taking into consideration the son with lower occupational category of the two, one each moved into occupational category of Skilled workers and Business and five have remained in occupational category of Manual workers. There is no downward mobility in case of respondents having two employed sons. There is only one respondent who is in occupational category of Manual worker, and has got three employed children, and compared to the respondent the best of the employed sons has moved into occupational category of Semi-skilled and Self employed manual workers, and the other two have remained in occupational category of Manual workers.

Four respondents who are in occupational category of Menial Services have employed sons and all these respondents have only one son each. Compared to these four respondents, two employed sons remained in occupation category of Menial services, where as each of the other two have moved into other occupational categories of Services and Manual workers respectively.

Two respondents in occupational category of Menial services, have employed sons, one has two sons and the other three sons. In case of the respondent with two employed sons taking into consideration the best, one son has remained in occupational category of Semi-skilled and Self employed manual labour, and taking the least occupational category of the two, the other son went down into the occupational category of Manual workers. In case of the respondent having three sons it is downward mobility as in all the cases with all of the four having went down to occupational category of Manual workers.

One respondent, who is in the occupational category of Business, has two employed sons and it is immobility in the case of both the sons. Each of them retained their fathers' occupation category, which is Business.

One respondent in occupational category of Para professional and Para executive have two employed sons and it is downward mobility for the sons as they could achieve only occupational categories of Services and Semi-skilled and Self employed manual workers compared to the respondents' occupational category of Para professional and Para Executive.

Two respondents in occupational category of Professional and Executive have one employed son each. In the first case it is immobility as the son retained the father's occupational category of Professional and Executive. In the other's case it is downward mobility as the son went down to the occupational category of Para professional and Para Executive.

The above discussion reveals that the occupational structure among the Scheduled Castes is undergoing change. The trends indicate that in majority of the cases the changes are independent of education but are related to development process namely urbanisation and whatever possible little industrialisation. The Scheduled Castes are moving into caste free as well as the caste occupations of the other lower castes. The few who have benefited by education are mostly in the services stratum because of their lower educational attainments and even this could be achieved mostly due to the protective discrimination. These trends are evident from the following summarisation.

Conclusions

From the foregoing analysis on Occupations on the Scheduled Castes it can be concluded:

1. that in all the three generations more than 75 per cent of the Scheduled Castes are engaged in the occupational categories of Manual workers and Menial services, which are supposed to be their traditional agricultural and non agricultural occupations;
2. that the number of Scheduled Castes remained in occupational categories of Manual worker and Menial services are more or less the same in the two generations of respondents' grandfathers and respondents' fathers, however it has come down in respondents generations substantially;
3. that there is substantial decrease in the number of Scheduled Castes engaged in Menial services over generations;
4. that compared to the grandfathers, about 80 per cent of the fathers had remained in the same occupations, whereas only 20 per cent of them have moved away from the occupations of grandfather;

5. that majority of the fathers who moved away from the occupations of the grandfather, and here the occupational categories of grandfathers were Manual workers and Menial services;
6. that majority of fathers, who changed occupations compared to the grandfathers, have moved up in occupational categories, and they amount to as much as 71 per cent. As many as 35 of the fathers have given up Menial services compared to the grandfathers;
7. that compared to the fathers about 64 per cent of the respondents have remained in the occupations of their fathers. Only about 36 per cent of the respondents have moved into different occupations;
8. that again the majority of the respondents who have moved into other occupations have their fathers in the occupational categories of Manual workers and Menial services;
9. that compared to the fathers, the respondents who moved into other occupations, a majority— which is about 77 per cent have moved into higher occupational categories;
10. that compared to the grandfathers about 56 percent of the respondents have remained in the occupations of the grandfathers, which is a small per cent compared to the two other cases (grand father to father, father to respondent) and about 44 per cent of them have moved into different occupations;
11. that even in this case the majority of the mobile respondents have their grandfathers in the occupational categories of Manual workers and Menial services;
12. that of the respondents who have moved into different occupations compared to the grandfathers as much as 83 per cent of them moved into higher occupational categories;
13. that Gross intergenerational occupational mobility rate is higher compared between the two generations of respondents' grandfather and respondent than the two other cases;

14. that the Gross Upward Intergenerational Occupational Mobility rate is also higher compared between respondents' grandfather and respondent than that of the two other cases;
15. that 26 per cent of the respondents alone have employed male children;
16. that most of this employed children have no or minimal educational attainment and as such more than 90 per cent of them are in occupational category of Manual workers,
17. that in case of male employed children compared to the respondents immobility is more pronounced than mobility;

The entry into caste free and caste occupations of other lower castes, which are essentially service oriented and yet linked with processes such as urbanisation, industrialisation has prompted mobilisation of the Scheduled Castes for political action. Emergence of leadership and group organization among them has been discussed in the next chapter the **Political Participation.**

Five

Political Participation

Political Power in Traditional India

Gooty, the semi-urban place was only a village hitherto for all practical purposes. The political status of Gooty is now that of a major Panchayat. An attempt is made to examine the power structure in the villages in general in these parts of the region, which will give us insight, to understand the political participation, organization, and leadership among the Scheduled castes of Gooty.

A few studies have paid attention on the political process at grassroots' level in the rural India. (Vanaja, 1991) Mention may be made to the studies of Beteille (1965) in a village of Tamilnadu, Ranga Rao (1980) in a village of Telengana, and Murali (1982), in a village of Rayalaseema region of Andhra Pradesh.

In traditional India, especially before independence there was no formal political system governing the rural people in the villages. However, a few studies that were conducted have indicated the existence of informal political system organising more efficiently at the level of family, caste and village. (Ranga Rao, 1968; Khare, 1974; Mukhopadhyay, 1974; Murali, 1981).

In traditional India, the caste councils acted as informal political system and governed the members of the respective castes. (Dube, 1970). The functions of the Caste Councils were concerned with the preservations of the caste (Rudolf, 1967), enforcement of the rules and regulations pertaining to the caste and settlement of the disputes (Srinivas, 1954), and management of the affairs of the caste. (Mayer, 1960).

The caste Panchayats wielded power mainly concerning the social and cultural aspects of social life. (Hutton, 1946) These Panchayats were meant for the welfare and upliftment of the members of the respective castes. They maintained customary law and order, rules and regulations pertaining to matters like marriage, eating, contacts, and purity and pollution etc. A defiler of these rules and regulations had to face the caste Panchayat to account for his conduct. If he could not satisfy the caste Panchayat, the latter used to penalise him for his defaults by imposing upon him obligations of purification performances etc. or outcaste him for a specific period (Sharma, 1980).

Blunt (1931) giving details of the different caste Panchayats explain that in each of the caste Panchayat the system and the practices of individual castes differ. He also explains each Panchayat has a headman, and the headmanship is sometimes hereditary, some times elected, and the same principle was applied to the members of the caste Panchayat, who may also include vice chairman and executive officers, who may likewise be hereditary or elected. Election may be for life or for each meeting. Often two systems are combined the headman being hereditary and the members elected or vice versa.

The functioning of village as a political and social entity brought together members of different castes. The villages used to have the traditional village Panchayat which, though run by the locally dominant castes usually included representatives of the other castes. The available historical evidence points to the existence of village councils in India in which members of every caste took part. (Murali, 1982)

Thus at the village level the heads of the different castes formed into an informal organization called the Village Council. However the village council does not include the head of the Scheduled Caste. (Murali, 1982) The village council exerted authority in conformity with tradition and regulated moral, jural and pragmatic actions (Somers, 1978) of the village people. The head of the highest caste in the village by and large headed the village council and at times the headman used to be from the dominant caste of the village. The heads of the higher castes had major say in the affairs of the village and Rudolph (1967) argued that the village councillors derived their legitimacy from the comprehensive sacred ideology. The Village council performed a variety of tasks including the maintenance of law and order, settling of disputes, celebration of festivals constructions of roads, bridges, tanks etc. (Srinivas, 1982)

The principle of hereditary and traditional legitimacy thus confined the leadership positions to a few rich and higher caste individuals in traditional India (Murali, 1990). As such the Scheduled Castes in traditional India were completely ignored who were rich neither in wealth nor in ritual hierarchy. It can be concluded here that higher status of caste, landed wealth, male sex and age seniority were prominent political resources in traditional India, however, the later two factors worked favourably with the presence of the former two only.

Notable changes came in the power structure of the Indian society with the advent of British rule. The then Government appointed officials like 'Village Munsif' and 'Village Karanam' in the villages who exercised considerable authority. These officials again used to be generally from higher castes started playing vital role in village affairs and emerged as village leaders. (Ranga Rao, 1980)

With India attaining Independence the political system underwent significant changes. The adaptation of Constitution based upon the principles of equality, liberty, freedom and sovereignty by Independent India resulted in bringing out a change in the socio-political structures of the country. Introduction of universal adult franchise and right to contest elections on democratic lines has opened avenues for mass participation in politics. The system of reservation of seats in political bodies and central and state levels for backward classes like Scheduled Castes and Scheduled Tribes for the first time put forth new elements in political structure.

Democratisation of the country envisages equitable distribution of power. (D Souza, 1976) However there was a wide gap between the envisaged norms and the practices resulting in the presence of a peculiar situation, what Beteille (1972) referred to as 'disharmonic social condition' and difference in wealth and power persisted as a legacy of the past. (Gough, 1963).

The studies of village political system after Independence in India by Bailey, 1963; Orenstein, 1965; Ramu and Weibe, 1970; and others reveal that the caste councils regulated the members of the respective castes and the village councils enforced control over the people., The political resources were distributed among a limited number of people, (Leach and Mukherji, 1970). The traditional leaders (Dhillon, 1955, Harper, 1958) and the hereditary village officials (Bailey, 1963) remained the most influential persons in the villages even after independence. However, the achievement has come to attain some significance to some extent. The achieved factors like external contacts (Dube, 1955,) education (Hitchcock, 1960) and individual merit (Opler, 1959; Orenstein, 1960) started to gain recognition among leadership circles.

The change that took place at the micro level on account of democratisation and opportunities for development thus has some effect on traditional political system especially on the caste councils.

After 12 years of independence the policy makers of India recognised the need for creating a political organization for the rural people. Based on the recommendations of Balwanth Rai Mehta committee, a system of local self-government in India was introduced in the Year 1959. The new political system, which came to be known as 'Panchayati Raj' was, organised at three different levels viz. the village, the taluk, (Mandal in Andhra Pradesh) and the District. The Panchayati Raj institution at the village level is the "Village Panchayat" and each village was divided into wards taking into consideration the size of the population. The voters from each ward elected their representative to the Village Panchayat. Such elected members were designated as the executive members of the Panchayat. All the voters in the village elected the Sarpanch and Upa Sarpanch of the Village Panchayat in the direct election. The Village Panchayat has been given powers to provide civic amenities to the village and to plan and execute programs for the development of the village. The Village Panchayat gained revenue by levying and collecting taxes.

In creation of second tier, all the Panchayati presidents were given membership in the next level of Panchayat Raj Organization, namely the Panchayath Samithi. The members of the Panchayati Samithi elect the President of the Panchayati Samithi. This Panchayati Samithi was made responsible for the development of villages in its jurisdiction. The Panchayati Samithi Presidents in turn are the members of the next tier of Panchayati Raj Organization, the Zilla Parishad. The Chairman represented the Zilla Parishad and it is responsible for the rural development programs in the entire district.

Thus the introduction of Panchayati Raj Organization took democracy to the doorsteps of the villages and the rural people. It gave a legal status to the elected representatives. The political system in village at this time presented a condition in which the formal and informal structures exist side by side. Sharma (1977), making comment on this situation said that the informal Panchayats and their leaders continued to be more influential than the formal Panchayat. However, at the same time the studies of John (1963) and Benarjee (1974) concluded that the informal leaders shifted themselves to the modern democratic offices in the Panchayati Raj Organization.

It can be emphatically said that the Panchayati Raj Organisation, especially the village panchayats has created additional opportunities for the leaders in the villages and power was transferred from the ritually superior castes to numerically and economically strong dominant castes. (Franda, 1979; Ranga Rao,1980 and Murali, 1982) The studies on the political process in Indian villages in the later Panchayati Raj phase revealed the continued control of the upper strata even under democratic set up. (Neale, 1965; Singh, 1969; Narain, 1976; Seshadri, 1976; Kulke, 1983). Mukhopadhyay (1974) opined that the lower castes failed to take part in the politics despite the reservations provided to them. The reasons for the non-participations of the lower castes in the political process can be attributed to their economic handicaps. Explaining this Yogendra Singh (1973), writes, "the new democratic rights and the legal safeguards provided to the less powerful classes motivated them to aspire for power, but their economic handicaps thwarted their desires.' Mehta (1969) reports that the Panchayati Raj has failed in benefiting the weaker sections of the rural society and concludes that the Scheduled Castes and Tribes have no effective choice in Panchayat Smithies, the real governing body.

It can be concluded here that the political scenario in rural India presents the existence of the traditional and modern political systems in the earlier phases of Panchayati Raj and the replacement of the traditional system by modern village Panchayati system in the recent past. The change from convention and tradition to democracy is said to have taken place either by consensus or by conflict.

Political system in the villages of Anantapur District:
(Source: The Anantapur District Gazetteer)

The political system in Anantapur underwent changes in the structure and functions over years. During the pre Vijayanagara days the villages in the district were managed by the local assemblies, which were called 'Urs' or 'Sabhas'. All the adult members of the villages constituted these local assemblies. This local assembly had an executive body called 'Panchayat'. This Panchayat looked after the defence, economy, justice, worship and other functions of the village. (Venkata Rangaiah and Ram Reddy, 1967). Later in the post Vijayanagara period, a system called 'Ayagars System' which functioned as a link among the caste, economy and polity in the villages of this region. An 'Ayagar' is an expert and usually an elder used to head the caste that represents his profession. There used to be Ayagars from each caste. (Venkata Rangaiah and Ram Reddy, 1967) Along with the village officials like 'Gowd' and 'Karanam' the Ayagars served the villages. During the British rule this Ayagars system was affected. Whereas the lands in the village in pre British rule were considered common property of the village, in British period in the year 1801 rights on land were conferred to the farmers. However, this did not last long and in 1809 the individual rights were cancelled and the land was leased to 'Mirasidars'. As this caused discontent among the farmers 'Riotwary system' of the individual ownership of land to the farmers was reintroduced in 1820. The British have at this time appointed the Karanam and Village Munsif to maintain ledgers and collect taxes. Being the servants of the government these officials had gained social prominence and authority. The Karanams' were mostly from the literate Brahmin families and the Munsif from the locally dominant castes such as Reddy and Kamma.

Traditional village Panchayats, also known as the 'Gram Panchayats', governed the villages in Anantapur district. Each of these Panchayats was headed by Village Head man and was assisted by the village elders. The village headman was known as 'Grama Pedda' and in managing the affairs of the village he was assisted by the village elders and the Karanam and Village Munsif. Usually the village head was from the Brahmin caste and at times from any other dominant caste. The village elders were generally the heads of the other castes that resided in that village. The village council looked after the maintenance of law and order in the village and settled the disputes among the villages.

An attempt was made in 1884 to formalise the Panchayati system. The Madras Local Boards Act, 1884 made a legal provision for constituting boards at village, taluk and district levels leading to the formation of 18 Union boards by 1919. In 1920 individual formal Panchayats came into existence in Anantapur district, due to enactment of Village Panchayats Act of 1920 in Madras province. Under the Act each village can have a formal Panchayat of it own, with seven to fifteen members elected by adults depending on the size of the village. By 1946 there were 20 major Panchayats and 128 minor Panchayats in the district. Again in the year 1956, the Panchayats in a formal form was introduced with the enactment of a new legislation called the Madras Village Panchayat Act of 1950. As per the act all the villages that have a population of more than 500 could have Panchayats and the villages with less population were to be clubbed with the adjacent villages for formation of Panchayats. In 1956 all the villages were bought under the formal Panchayats.

On the recommendations of the Balwanth Rai Mehta Committee, Government of India introduced 'Panchayati Raj' the three-tier system of democratic decentralisation throughout the country. In Andhra Pradesh the Panchayat Raj came into existence in the year 1959 with enactment of "Andhra Pradesh Panchayati Samithi and Zilla Parishad Act."

So far the villages in the district went to the polls in the years 1959, 1964, 1970, 1981, 1988, 1995 and 2002. Until 1970 there was indirect election to the post of the President later it was direct election. Now as per the statistics of the Panchayat Office, there are 865 Village Panchayats in the district and of which the elections were conducted for 860 village Panchayats.

The rural leadership was given a Constitutional and legal recognition in the framework of Panchayati Raj. It has carved out a share of political power for the weaker section. This received further momentum and consolidation through 73rd Amendment Act in 1992, which accorded a Constitutional status to Panchayati

Raj, elaborating the composition, constitution and duration, powers and responsibilities elections and auditing of the panchayats at the village, intermediate and district level. (Asha Koushik, 1998) The most significant part of 73rd Amendment deals with reservation for the Scheduled Castes, Scheduled Tribes in proportion to their population at each level and not less than one third of membership and office of chairperson to women. Legislations were followed by elections to the lakhs of Grampanchayats in the country, which saw emergence of new breed of leaders, who included weaker sections and women, endowed with zeal and enthusiasm.

Andhra Pradesh has introduced reservations to the Scheduled Castes and Scheduled Tribes in proportion to their population and direct election to the post of the Sarpanch even before the 73rd Amendment.

In a study on the 225 Scheduled Caste Sarpanches drawn from all the three natural regions of Andhra Pradesh, namely Rayalaseema, Telangana and Costal Andhra, Naidu (2002) concluded that reservations to the Scheduled Castes were proposed in the Panchayati Raj to pave way for their political empowerment. However, at the village level, the reservations have served the purpose only in terms of quantity but not quality. The Scheduled Castes leaders are by and large educationally and economically backward. Given their socio, economic, educational and political backwardness, at the very outset, one cannot straight away expect effective leadership from Scheduled Castes leaders. The Scheduled Castes leaders, as the study indicates are not assertive, confident, enthusiastic and without any perception of their position and power. According to them, the higher castes continue to hold sway in the village and dominate them. The higher castes act 'hand in glove' and in many of the instances the Scheduled Caste leader is only a 'sponsored leader'. The respondents were asked to give their opinion on whether they have freedom to take decisions in discharging their duties. Only 12 (5.33%) respondents have said they have complete freedom to take independent decisions. All the respondents have said being a Scheduled Caste leader they get influenced by the dominant castes in the village. According to the study of Naidu (2002) the political empowerment of the Scheduled Castes has led to the emergence of first generation of leaders. This would certainly inspire more of the Scheduled Castes to take a plunge into the political process. The first generation leaders may be unassuming, diffident and dependent, but with continued patronage, participation and passage of time it is hoped that effective leadership may emerge among the Scheduled Caste.

In the background of the above the power structure, the caste associations, political participation, organization and mobilisation and leadership among the Scheduled Castes are discussed hereunder.

The Caste Association: It is the tendency of the people to organise themselves into a group and then try to achieve their goals and objectives through collective strength. Thus caste association plays a vital role in protecting and uplifting the interests of the backward classes such as Scheduled Castes. Water (1965) reported that several castes have organised their own associations to take care of the educational, economic and cultural problems of them. Lynch (1968) also made a mention of the effective role of the castes association while discussing the case of the Jatavas, who are the Scheduled Castes, in sharing and acquiring power.

As explained earlier, there are two sub castes among the Scheduled Castes of Gooty, the Madigas and the Malas. The Madigas are in majority compared to the Malas. Both the sub castes do not mix up for any practical purpose. Hence there was and even now has no single caste association for both the sub castes. The Madigas who are in majority in Gooty and they are better organised than that of Malas.

The Scheduled Caste respondents were asked about the caste association. They were asked about the existence of caste association at grandfather's, father's and their time and also their involvement.

Not all but majority respondents from each sub caste said that there was caste association in their grand fathers time, (taking into consideration the present generation, the average age of the respondent and the life expectancy the approximate time period of the three generations are calculated. It was arrived at that up to 1920, was the grand father's generation time period from then up to 1960 was the father's generation time period and after 1960 is the respondent's generation time period) separately for both the

Malas and the Madigas. Most of the respondents did recall that the then caste associations were useless and ineffective for all practical purposes dealing with the other castes. However the caste association of the Scheduled Castes had influence over its own members. It this part of the region the Madigas traditionally had different jajmani system called 'udyogam' and the caste association is responsible to allot clients to the patrons for rendering services on rotation basis, so that each client will have the advantage of a generous patron or vice versa. Naturally such power of caste association makes it popular and strong. In matters other than this allocation of clients, the respondents who could tell something about the caste association at grandfathers' time said that there used to be some elders who used to take collective decision in accordance with what the higher castes wanted them to do. Only during the fathers time the caste association started functioning a little more independently. In father's time there used to be fourteen elders who were the executive members and two heads for the Madiga caste association, eight elders and one head for the Mala caste association. At this time as far as the matters of Scheduled Castes were concerned, the Caste associations used to take their own decisions. In case of matters of involvement of the other castes also both the Mala and Madiga associations used to depend heavily on the higher castes and took decisions in compliance with the wishes of the higher castes.

Now, in respondents' time, the Caste association of the Madigas does exist, but at the same time the Caste association of the Malas has disintegrated for all practical purposes. The Malas are relatively better placed than the Madigas in the fields of education and employment and it is reported that they used to pay little attention to their caste association, and at times ignored the decisions of the Caste association. Of late the caste association of Malas lost its grip over its members and now, it is reported that none of the Malas approach their caste association for any thing.

However, the Caste association of the Madiga sub caste is still going strong. This Caste association is formed with all the Madigas as its members. There are fourteen elders who are the executive members and are called 'Kula Peddalu'. Seven each of them elect 'Panchayati Pedda' the heads of the caste association.

Thus this caste association has two heads and fourteen executive members. This caste association has jurisdiction over the Madigas of surrounding villages. The Madigas of all these villages approach the Madiga Caste Association for settlement of disputes. This caste association still has more or less firm grip over its members and seldom the parties to disputes from this sub caste approach the police and court for settlement of disputes. Even if some one from this sub caste were to go to police, it was reported that the police advise the parties to settle the issue in the caste association itself. If the parties still insist that the police do register cases, but at the same time record the statement of the head of the caste association, which is given due weight. Only one such instance of a Madiga person ignoring the caste association verdict and approaching the police and court in case of settlement of dispute over property is reported over the years.

The Caste association takes cognisance of all the matters relating to the Madigas and settles the disputes or offences involving sex, breach of marriage, distribution of property, ill treatment of the wife by husband, widow remarriage etc. The most familiar punishment imposed by the caste association is exaction of fines, feasts to the caste members, and in extreme cases excommunication, which may be a temporary penalty for a given period or for an indefinite time subject to the performance of some required expiation for the offence punished. It can be said that the caste association of the Madigas is also losing prominence as a formal association by name 'Harijana Seva Sangam' coming into existence to serve the Madigas.

With regard to the Caste association, the respondents were asked whether there was caste association at their grand father's time. Only 231 respondents out of the 320 have said there was Caste association at their grand father's time. The remaining 89 respondents did not reply in negative but said they do not have idea of the existence of the Caste association at the time of their grand fathers. The respondents who replied positive to the above question were again asked whether their grand father held any official position in the caste association. To this question only 19 of the respondents said that their grand fathers were the 'Kula Peddalu' and two said that their grand fathers were the heads of the caste association.

The respondents were again asked about the existence of Caste association at the time of their fathers. As many as 302 respondents out of 320 have replied in positive to this question. When this question was followed up by the question did their fathers held any position in the caste association twenty-three respondents have said that their fathers were 'Kula Peddalu' the executive members, and three have said that their fathers were the heads of the Caste association.

Now in the respondent's generation there is no Caste association for the Malas. There is Caste association for the Madigas and fourteen respondents are 'Kula Peddalu' the executive members and two are 'Panchayati Peddalu' the heads of the Caste association.

THE MOBILISATION OF THE SCHEDULED CASTES

The Scheduled Castes of Gooty are mobilising themselves into organisations and unions to fight for their rights and causes. These unions or associations work for the attainment of common goal or to fight against the discrimination, suppression and atrocities. Some of the important unions or associations of the Scheduled Castes are discussed here under.

Harijana Seva Sangam: The Harijana Seva Sangam came into existence in the year 1984 with an aim to serve the Madiga sub caste exclusively. It is a registered association. The association has 151 members. The association has three office positions namely, President, Secretary, and Treasurer. The members of the association elect the office bearers. Every member pays a membership fee of Rs. 2/- every month. At present one of the heads of the Caste association of the Madigas, is the President of the Harijana Seva Sangam. This association meets once in every month to consider the matters put forth by the members of the association. They discuss matters to find solutions agreeable to all the members of the association.

Though the Harijana Seva Sangam and the Caste Association of the Madigas serve only the Madigas, there is some difference between the two associations. While the Caste association has a jurisdiction over ten villages and settles the disputes of the Madigas in all these ten villages, the Harijana Seva Sangam's jurisdiction is limited and it serves only the members of the association, who are the Madigas of Gooty only. After Harijana Seva Sangam has come into existence the number of Madigas of Gooty approaching the Caste Association has gone down considerably, as now that they approach the Harijana Seva Sangam. However the Caste association looks after the interests of the Madigas of the nearby villages.

The Harijana Seva Sangam like the Caste Panchayat settles the disputes of the members in the matters of marriage, distribution of property, adultery, divorce, and the like. Besides these the members also discuss the day-to-day problems, and how to face them collectively. For example, the fair price shop dealer in their locality for some time was hoarding the stocks and was not selling ration to all of them. The Harijana Seva Sangam that made petition against this fair price shop dealer to the authorities to set things right. This association educates its members about the privileges and plans and schemes meant for them and help them in availing these facilities. It also educates the members in the fields of personal hygiene and food habits. The Harijana Seva Sangam secretary has told this researcher that it is because of the continuous persuasion of this association that most of its members gave up carcass eating altogether, and a majority gave up beef eating and alcohol. This association has sought and received a grant of Rs.20,000/- from the Endowment Department of the Government of Andhra Pradesh to construct a temple to Lord Rama in their locality. The Scheduled Castes were allowed in all but one temple in the town. This association has fought against the higher castes that resisted their entry into that particular temple and succeeded in gaining entry into the temple for all the Scheduled Castes. It was also reported that this association has persuaded landlords to secure freedom to five Madiga bonded labourers. The Harijana Seva Sangam also made it clear to all the concerned that it is not compulsory for them to remove carcass, and they will remove carcass only if they are paid to do the job.

Ambedkar Sangam: The Ambedkar Sangam came into existence in 1980 to serve the Malas only. It was started with about 100 members and functioned effectively for about five years. However this association could not continue because of factions among the members and rift over leadership issue of the association. Now the Ambedkar Sangam exists only on the records and for all other practical purposes it is a disintegrated association. Now one educated unemployed youth looks after the interest of the Mala people. He educates the Malas about the privileges and plans that are meant for them and meets authorities to get things done on behalf of the Malas.

The government has launched many schemes to uplift the Scheduled Castes economically. To avail these schemes the Scheduled Castes have to approach various banks and funding agencies to get loans and also the district authorities to get subsidies. Realising the strength of collective bargaining the Scheduled Castes who are making use of these economic schemes and also who wish to avail these schemes have formed themselves into an association called **The Scheduled Castes Beneficiaries Association.** There are more than 50 members in this association. The members of the association contribute for the running of the association, and the Secretary along with the executive members make travels and meet the concerned authorities to get things done. The members of these associations have expressed satisfaction with the working and results of this association. A few of them reported that when they approached the banks and authorities to avail facilities that are meant for them, they used to be indifferent or were demanding bribes. Now because of their collective strength, they say there are no such problems.

Most of the Scheduled Castes who are manual labourers are working in quarry as stone crushers and some more as the workers in a slab polishing industry. These workers have formed an Association called **Slab Polishing Workers Association.** This association works for the betterment of conditions in terms of both work and monetary benefits. Most of the members of this association are the Scheduled Castes, though there are a few members from other castes also. This association looks after the interest of the workers by protecting them from the exploitation of the contractors in quarry and the management of the slab polishing industry.

The Scheduled Castes of Gooty to fight against the atrocities have formed **'The Scheduled Castes United Front'**. This association has more than 100 members and works against discrimination and atrocities against the Scheduled Castes. If discrimination and atrocities against the Scheduled Castes are reported to this association, the Office bearers meet the concerned persons and take steps to see such practices are stopped and not repeated. It was reported that this association has succeeded in fighting against discrimination in the nearby villages where the Scheduled Castes are still discriminated.

POLITICAL PARTICIPATION

The Scheduled Castes absolutely had no access to political power and political activity throughout, not only because of the educational and occupational backwardness but also due to their low social status and complete dependence on the higher caste Hindus. Khan (1980) reports that in traditional India the Scheduled Castes were completely out of the purview of political power and political participation. After India attained independence and with the introduction of adult franchise, community development programme and Panchayati Raj, there was radical change in the power structure where the Scheduled Castes also found a crucial role to play.

The Panchayati Raj organization has come into existence with the principle objective of giving institutionalised format to the local leadership. By introducing the Panchayati Raj system the Government envisages the democracy to reach the doorsteps of the rural people and replacement of the age-old leadership based on ascription. This has led to the replacement of the traditional social structure, which has neglected Scheduled Castes completely to the modern power structure where every caste received due importance particularly in the villages. Murali (1982) reports that the election to the Panchayats has forced the leaders to depend upon various castes in order to gain political strength. Jayaram (1981) also observed that the numerical strength of a caste has gained new significance in politics, in the sense that a group, which is large in size, has greater chance of electing its candidates to representative bodies, than a group, which is smaller in size, of course, irrespective of the caste rank in social hierarchy. For the Scheduled Castes who are living in substantial number in villages, this provided a real chance to participate in the political activity.

Besides this, in order to secure political participation and to ensure adequate representation of the Scheduled Castes, reservations in political bodies are made for them in the Constitution. Besides reservations of seats in the House of People and Legislative Assembly (Art.330 (1) and 332(1)) reservations are provided in Panchayati Raj. Special care has been taken for the representation of the Scheduled Castes in all the three tiers of the Panchayati Raj. This has enable and ensured not only the participation of Scheduled Castes but also development of leader ship among them. Several studies made thereafter, by the researchers on the aspects of political participation, leadership among the Scheduled Castes have agreed with the opinion that there is marked change in the political scenario, where the Scheduled Castes also have due role to play unlike the traditional system. The positive relation between political participation, leadership and social status was also explored in these studies.

The study of Beteille (1969) in a village of Tamilnadu reveals that with regard to power structure, a new element of political power independent of caste and class has emerged. He points out that it is through participation in village Panchayat, political parties and political networks that mobility takes place among the lower caste people of the village. Lynch (1969) concludes in his study that in modern independent India, political participation is functional alternative to Sanskritization. The work of Hardgrave (1969) on the Nadars of Tamilnadu clearly refers the caste mobility my means of political participation. He finds as the Nadar caste rose in wealth and political power, there was rise in ritual and social status. Harper (1968) study also reveals that political participation was used as a weapon to rise in status in the social ladder. The study on the Jatavas of Agra City by Lynch (1969) is also a proof of Scheduled Castes using political participation as one of the modern avenues to rise in the social hierarchy of the society. The Jatavas who were traditional leather workers had abandoned this, and besides political participation used Sanskritization and have now become a political entity. Aiyappan (1966) reports how the Iravas of Kerala who are Scheduled Castes fought against untouchability and occupied important position as in the then Kerala Ministry. The Mahars of Maharastra used political means in an extensive way to attain higher status in a consistent way. (Zelliot, 1969) Parmar (1987) also gives the same opinion on the rise of status of the Mahyavanshis by making use of political means.

The Study of Singh (1985) that looked into the leadership among the Scheduled Castes concludes that the majority of the Scheduled Castes are gaining entry to formal power structure of the village through the reserved seats. The leaders among the Scheduled Castes are drawn mainly from the young, literate and numerically dominant group. They hail from families that have registered tremendous education and occupation mobility over generations. At the same time he opines that through achievement of power and authority in village power structure is significant variable in the social mobility and assimilation of the Scheduled Castes in the larger society they still continue to experience untouchability from the co-leaders and village people.

The Scheduled Castes respondents in Gooty were asked a few questions about their political participation. In Gooty the political parties, Congress (I) and Telugu Desam Party has hold on the majority of the Scheduled Castes. Interestingly no Scheduled Caste respondent has said that he is supporter or member of the Communist party, which is having substantial following in this region. Inquired about this, some of the respondents have said that they want to solve their problems amicably with out any confrontation and for them, Communist party means achieving of goals through confrontations.

The respondents were asked whether they are members or supporters of any political party. Out of the 320 respondents only 52 have said that they are the members of political parties and of this 52, as many as 29 have said that they are the members of the Congress (I) party, and the other 23 have said that they are members of Telugu Desam party. Besides the above 52 members, another 113 respondents have reported that they are supporters of political parties. Of this 113, as many as 57 respondents have said that they are supporters of the Congress (I) party and the remaining 56 have said that they are supporters of the Telugu Desam Party. These supporters have said they always work and vote for their parties only irrespective of the candidate.

The respondents who said that they are members of the political party have been again asked if they hold any position. For this only three respondents have replied in the positive, and all these three are from the Congress (I) party. The positions held by these three respondents are the Town Congress Organising Secretary, the Town Congress Secretary and Member, District Congress Committee. None of the respondents who said that they are members of the Telugu Desam Party are holding any position in the party.

The respondents who are members of the political parties are asked about their activities for the sake of the party. The members have replied that they actively participate in fund collection for the party, enrol new members, propagate the ideals of the party, organise processions and participate in them and at the time of the election work and canvass for the party candidate. The members are also asked about on whose instance they have joined the party and are participating in the activities of the party, they have said that the political leaders of the higher castes, friends and relatives in the party and their own caste leaders are responsible for them joining in their respective parties.

LEADERSHIP AMONG THE SCHEDULED CASTES

For uplifting of the lower castes especially the Scheduled Castes who were at the lowest rung of the society depends by and large upon the leadership and the quality of leadership made available to them. Ambedkar, who was from the Scheduled Castes could provide efficient leadership and could organise, mobilise and inspire the Mahars of Maharastra. The contribution of Ambedkar goes a long way in the success of the Mahars in uplifting themselves. For social reasons such as traditional values, and customs the Scheduled Castes were looked down, and very little was to be expected of them in the matter of effective leadership. Khan (1980) in his study on Scheduled Castes makes clear that the Scheduled Castes have no recognised leader at all.

Speaking of the leaders, they could be divided into two kinds, the formal and informal leaders. The formal leaders consist of Legislators, Panchayat Members, and Political Party leaders. The informal leaders consist of the Caste Panchayat head and executive members, educated youth, and the elders.

Before discussing the role of the leadership among the Scheduled Castes the role of the non-Scheduled Castes leaders in uplifting the Scheduled Castes is also of importance, and is discussed hereunder. The Studies of Lewis,(1958) Gangrade, (1961) Punit, (1969) have also made a mention of the non Scheduled Caste leaders who worked for the welfare of the Scheduled Castes. The Gooty Town Congress President, who is from a twice-born caste, it is reported that one such non Scheduled Caste leader who is working for the welfare of the Scheduled Castes. The Town Congress Organizing Secretary and the Town Congress Secretary have told this researcher that because of him only, they took part in political activity and could become leaders. They have also revealed that because of the persuasion of this leader considerable change could be brought about among the Scheduled Castes, in the matters of food habits and personal hygiene. If the matters of discrimination are bought to his notice, it was reported that he on behalf of the Scheduled Castes meets the concerned higher castes, to put an end to such practices. It is reported that he played a vital role in getting their entry into one temple which resisted the entry of the Scheduled Castes for quite some time even after the other temples in the town were thrown open to them.

Taking into consideration the Scheduled Castes of Gooty, two leaders of Scheduled Castes could become the members of the Legislative Assembly. However, they are not the respondents. One woman Legislator who hails from Gooty, contested and won election to the Legislative Assembly from the reserved Singanamala Constituency of Anantapur District. She was Minister for Women and Child Welfare in the cabinet of erstwhile Chenna Reddy ministry. The other leader who was Member of Legislative Assembly from Gooty constituency of course hails from the nearby town Guntakal. However both Gooty and Guntakal form a single constituency.

Taking into consideration the political parties, the Scheduled Castes respondents are more or less equally inclined towards the major political parties in the State the Congress (I) party and the Telugu Desam Party. The legislators referred to above are however, from the Congress (I) party. There are three leaders among the Scheduled Castes, who are also, respondents, holding positions in

Congress (I) party. One respondent is the member of the District Congress Committee, and two other respondents are the Town Organising Secretary and Town Secretary of the Congress (I) party respectively. One respondent is also Town Youth Congress Leader.

Leadership is also made available to the Scheduled Castes from the Village Panchayat members. The introduction of Panchayat Raj and reservation of seats for the Scheduled Castes has helped the Scheduled Castes of Gooty. Gooty was a major Panchayat and was having ten wards, with two of them being reserved for the Scheduled Castes. The Scheduled Castes of Gooty because of this are getting exposed to the power structure and leadership. The seventh and eighth wards of Gooty are reserved for the Scheduled Castes, and in all the elections candidates from Madiga sub caste only contested and won these wards. None of the Malas contested from these wards, because of their numerical inferiority. The Scheduled Castes did not contest in the wards other than those reserved for them. In the last election two respondents were elected for these reserved wards.

Taking into consideration the informal leaders, as reported earlier there is caste association only for the Madigas and not for the Malas. There are 14 elders (Kula Peddalu) who are the executive members and two heads (Panchayati Peddalu) who constitute the informal leaders. This caste association exercises its power over the Madigas. These leaders by and large are elders in age. By virtue of their age and experience they have become leaders of the Caste association, but by and large they are ignorant and not helpful to the Scheduled Castes in the matters of making use of the privileges, incentives, schemes that are meant for them.

The informal leadership to the Scheduled Castes is also available to the younger generation of the Scheduled Castes through the educated youth and educated employees among the Scheduled Castes.

Among the Malas there is one educated unemployed youth who takes care of the problems of the Malas. The Malas in case of any problem or in case they want any advice with regard to the privileges and schemes that are meant for them they approach this youth. He on behalf of them meets the authorities and gets things done. The respondents also reported that some of the

Scheduled Caste who are well educated and are in good positions (for example, a lecturer) would also provide informal leadership to them. They advise the other Scheduled Castes to send their youngsters to the schools, and advise the youngsters to go to school and college regularly and get into Government services. They act as reference group for the other Scheduled Castes, and help and advice them when asked for.

Conclusions

From the foregoing discussion on political participation it can be concluded:

1. that there were Caste associations for the Scheduled Castes both in the grandfathers' and fathers' generation and in either of the generations they were reported to be ineffective;
2. that the Caste association is losing its grip over the Scheduled Castes, and this holds good in case of both the sub castes and more so with respect to the Mala sub caste;
3. that more formal association are replacing and taking over the role of the traditional Caste associations;
4. that the Scheduled Castes are organising and mobilising themselves into powerful associations and organizations to achieve the desired goals. This is clear from different organizations that they have started;
5. that the Madiga sub caste is more organised than that of the Mala sub caste in the matters of coming together in achieving their goals;
6. that the Scheduled Castes are actively involved in politics. This is clear as a sizeable number of them are reporting themselves as the members and supporters of one political party or other;
7. that the Scheduled Castes with their substantial numerical strength are acting as pressure groups and are able to get things done by the political parties that approach them for votes;
8. that most of the members who belong to different political parties have reported that they have become members and are taking active part at the instance of

the leaders of higher castes and their own caste, and relatives and friends;

9. that two of the Scheduled Castes from Gooty constituency could rise to the positions of the member of Legislative Assembly and one was Minister in the State Cabinet for some time;
10. that in striving for the welfare of the Scheduled Castes, besides the Scheduled Castes leadership, non Scheduled Castes leadership also is available to the Scheduled Castes of Gooty.
11. that the Scheduled Castes so far have contested only from their reserved seats in the Panchayati elections and have not ventured out;
12. that besides formal leadership informal leadership is also available to the Scheduled Castes of Gooty, in the form of educated youth, educated and well placed employees;

The discussion on education, occupation and political participation of the Scheduled Castes under study proves that the better literacy attainments, occupational mobility, politicisation and sensitisation of Scheduled Castes has been taking place. The analysis so far reveals that there are perceptible changes in the fields of education, occupation, and political participation of the Scheduled Castes. Whether these changes have any bearing on the overall status of the Scheduled Castes is examined in the next chapter the **Social Status**.

Six

SOCIAL STATUS

The Scheduled Castes were subjected to various kinds of social disabilities and discrimination. The conditions of Scheduled Castes, the Untouchables in traditional India were appalling. The Untouchables were socially degraded and were treated with contempt, deliberately deprived of the higher religious and cultural values of Hindu Society. They were debarred from Hindu temples, places of worship and from using roads, vehicles, ferries, wells, schools and public conveniences. Brahmins should not perform religious rites for them; nor should barbers, water carriers, washer men and tailors serve them. (Census of India, 1931, Vol. I, Part I)Their dress pattern also revealed their low status with most of the men using only loin cloth. In Tamilnadu their women were not allowed to cover their breasts. (Upadhay, 1990) They were forced to live in squalor and unhygienic surroundings away from the village main. The segregated neighbourhoods were also reported in towns and cities (Lynch, 1969). There was no commensal relation between them and the higher caste Hindus. No member of higher caste Hindu accepted cooked food, salt or milk from an Untouchable. (Fuchs, 1981) Gold ornaments were prohibited to them, and at the same time they could not afford them. (Oomen, 1977) The social discrimination went to the extent of regarding their very shadows as imminent pollutants (Ghurye, 1969) and hence were branded as Untouchables and was socially and residentially segregated.

With all the above said disabilities life had been miserable for the Scheduled Castes. Many an attempt was made from time to time to uplift these sections by social reformers, and social activists. The reform activities, which were generally confined to one area, saw a great awakening among the Scheduled Castes. In Chattisgarh district of Madhya Pradesh the Chamars once were the most degraded and polluting and now are popularly know as Satnamis. This Sect emerging in the 18th century with the efforts of Jagjivan Ram as its initial founder had ultimately succeeded in enhancing their status. Similarly the Ezhavas of Kerala who were the traditional toddy tapers of Kerala under the leadership of Narayan Guru tried to change their conditions by emphasising on socio-economic reforms, which led to some success. The Mahars of Maharastra, under the leadership of Ambedkar, tried to enhance their status and they could succeed to some extent. Besides Scheduled Castes themselves many higher caste Hindu leaders like Mahatma Gandhi tried to uplift the status of the Scheduled Castes.

Over the years, the Dalits have increasingly felt that they have to depend on the State to get protection and equality in the social and economic spheres. By the turn of 19th century different Dalit groups had started asserting their rights to get education, to enter temples, to dress like others, free movements on the public roads, economic opportunities in the non-traditional sectors etc. They pressurised the British rulers for creating space for them in public spheres, so as to protect their interests. They demanded for special representations in legislatures and governments jobs. A number of struggles, culminated in 1932 in the Ambedkar-Gandhi pact, known as the Communal Award or the Poona Pact, wherein Ambedkar yielded to Gandhi's instance and gave up his demand for a 'separate electorate' and Gandhi on his part conceded reservation of 148 seats for Depressed Classes for ten years. The Government of India Act of 1935 incorporated the agreement and guaranteed reservation to the various legislatures of India and also provided for some safeguards against any discrimination on the basis of caste, religion, race etc. The Poona Pact had far-reaching impact on Dalit politics of post-independent India and in the making of the Indian Constitution. (Ghanshyam Shah, 2002)

On the eve of Independence, pressure from the Dalits-Scheduled Castes and Scheduled Tribes-mounted on the leading liberal members of the Constituent Assembly for providing special protective measures to Scheduled Castes. Dalit leaders asked: "What would be our place in Independent India?" The main challenge before the Constituent Assembly was to assure Dalits of a better deal in Independent India (Shah, 1987). Hence, the constitution directed the State to take positive measures for ameliorating the conditions of the Constitution made certain provisions known as 'protective discrimination'. They are related to political reservation (Articles 330 and 332); reservations of seats in educational institutions (Article, 15(4) and 29) and reservation for government jobs (Articles 15(4), 320((4), 333 and 335). These provisions are variously known as 'protective discrimination', 'affirmative action' or 'reverse discrimination'. From the Dalit perspective, Nadu Ram (2002) observed that the provision "may better be accepted as policies of compensation for discrimination of past as well of present time".

Independent India's commitment to equality and reorientation to socialism and welfare led to the launching of multidimensional welfare measures for the sake of the Scheduled Castes. The welfare of the Scheduled Castes, who constitute over and above 15 per cent of the total population of the country, had been of great concern to the government. When India attained freedom and the Constitution of India was drafted, attempts were made to give a special status to the Scheduled Castes not only to remove their social disabilities but also to uplift their socio-economic, educational and political status. This has been done in order to accelerate the pace of development among the Scheduled Castes so that they can catch up with the rest of the society.

The State condemns discrimination in any form. In fact the Constitution has made a number of provisions under various Articles to categorise the practice of untouchability- the stigma from which the Scheduled Castes suffer- as an offence. Constitutional protection was provided to the Scheduled Castes to undo the social injustice and all forms of exploitation and to bring them into the main stream of development. The Constitutional safeguards that are meant for the Scheduled Castes are as follows:

Article 15 (2): No citizen shall on grounds only of religion, race, caste, sex, place of birth or any of them be subjected to any disability, liability, restriction or condition with regard to:

a. access to shops, public restaurants, hotels and places of public entertainment; or

b. the use of wells, tanks, bathing ghats, roads and places of public resort maintained wholly or partially out of State funds or dedicated to the use of the general public.

Article 17: Untouchability is abolished and its practice in any form is forbidden. The enforcement of any disability arising out of "Untouchability" shall be an offence punishable in accordance with law.

Despite the law the practice of Untouchability continued unabatedly.

Making a study on the practice of Untouchability, the National Commissioner for Scheduled Castes and Scheduled Tribes, in April 1990 undertook a sample study in seven states of Bihar, Madhya Pradesh, Maharastra, Rajastan, Andhra Pradesh, Tamil Nadu, Karnataka and Kerala and founded that untouchability was prevalent in the following forms:

i. Scheduled Castes did not have access to temples and other places of public worship to a large extent in Uttar Pradesh, Tamil Nadu, Kerala, Rajastan and Karnataka.
ii. A sizeable section of Secluded Castes in Tamil Nadu did not have access to drinking water resources. A similar situation existed in Uttar Pradesh, Rajastan and Kerala.
iii. Untouchability in the form of non-access to tea stalls and hotels were still found in Uttar Pradesh, Tamil Nadu, Rajastan and Kerala.
iv. Barber services were not available to a section Scheduled Caste in Tamil Nadu and to a lesser degree in Uttar Pradesh, Rajastan, Maharastra, Karnataka and Kerala.
v. Washerman services were not found to be available to a section of Scheduled Caste in Tamil Nadu. To some extent this disability existed in Uttar Pradesh, as well.
vi. In Tamil Nadu, Bihar, Uttar Pradesh, Kerala and Karnataka Scheduled Castes were found to be discriminated against in the matter of participation in social ceremonies.
vii. Discrimination in matter of participation in sitting at village Chaupals and Gramasabhas existed in Tamil Nadu and Uttar Pradesh and to a lesser extent in Rajasthan.

viii. In Rajasthan a section of Scheduled Caste were discriminated against in educational institutions, public health centres, etc.

ix. Discrimination in respect of use of utensils meant for the general public existed in Uttar Pradesh, Tamil Nadu, Rajasthan and Maharastra.

x. Forced practice of occupations like removal of carcasses, etc, by Scheduled Castes was found prevalent in Tamil Nadu and to a lesser extent in Uttar Pradesh.

xi. Scheduled Castes were discriminated against in the use of public cremation/burial grounds, public passages, etc., in Tamil Nadu, and to a lesser extent in Maharastra and Uttar Pradesh. Scheduled Castes were at a disadvantage in the matter of construction/ acquiring occupational residential premises in Tamil Nadu, and to lesser extent in Uttar Pradesh. This includes access to dharmashalas/sarais.

Similarly, in 1990, the Ambedkar Centenary Celebration Committee of Chittoor District of Andhra Pradesh, the neighbour district of Anantapur where the present study was conducted, an elaborate door-to-door survey over four padayatras to 249 villages to assess the prevalence of untouchability (Frontier, 1991). The findings are as follows:

Through out the district as rule, members of Scheduled Castes were not allowed into the house of the non-Scheduled Castes. Even the major towns like Chittoor, Tirupathi, etc., are exceptions to the extent that the rule does not apply to unknown persons. If a person belongs to a Scheduled Caste community from the same or nearby village as the resident of the house he is visiting, he cannot enter the house. It is also not at all easy for members of Scheduled Castes to get accommodation in areas where non-Scheduled Castes live either in the town or the village.

The team came across 122 teashops in 249 villages including three Mandal headquarters where tea is served in separate glasses for the Scheduled Castes and in most of the cases the Scheduled Caste communities have to wash the tumblers themselves, both before and after drinking tea and hold the glass when teashop owner pours tea from a height.

Members of Scheduled Caste communities are not allowed entry in as many as 80 temples in 249 villages. This does not mean that there is free entry into temples in the rest of the villages. In most cases a wall does not enclose the temples. The deity is either placed on a raised platform or kept inside a small temple with space not sufficient to allow anyone inside. So there is no scope for either entry or preventing people form worshipping. As a rule no barber in any village cuts the hair or shaves a Scheduled Caste person. The Scheduled Castes shave and cut their hair themselves or some of them turn into barbers to serve the rest.

What came as a shock to the team was, the fact that in at least 16 of the 249 villages visited till date Scheduled Castes are not allowed to walk through the streets with any type of footwear (Frontier, 1991) (quoted by Harsh Mander, 2002)

The problem of untouchability is a complex one. It is essentially a social issue, through its economic dimension is not unimportant. Traditionally it was related to economic status and occupation. In course of time, religious ideology and culture-value system, life style, inter personal relationship etc- not only did reinforce the economic and social divisions, but have formed the material base of segregation of residence, economic dependence, rituals camouflaging economic returns. (Ghanshyam Shah, 2002)

Untouchability from which the majority of the Scheduled Castes suffer proved to be a great curse to this section. This practice has thrown millions of this section of people into despair and disgrace. Gandhiji who fought against the evil of untouchability said, "I do not want to be reborn. But if I have to be reborn, I should be born an Untouchable so that I share their sorrows, sufferings and atrocities levelled at them, in order that I may endeavor to free myself and them from that miserable conditions". The practice of untouchability which unfortunately had received the support and backing of the religious and social sanctions had been deep rooted in the society. The legislative moves for improving the conditions of the Scheduled Castes can be traced way back to the year 1938, the year in which Madras Removal of Social Disabilities Act 1938 was enacted. This Act has made discrimination against the Untouchables, an offence. Again in the same year

Temple Entry Acts were passed in the Madras and Bombay presidencies to enable the entry of Scheduled Castes members into temples. The Madras Temple Authorisation Act of 1947 considered it a criminal offence to prevent any Hindu from entering and worshipping at any temple. Almost all provinces of India followed suit, by passing bills on removal of social disabilities as well as Temple Entry Acts in the due course. (Galanter, 1972)

The Independent India with determination to eradicate this evil practice has incorporated Article 17 in its Constitution, which out rightly rejected the practice of untouchability in any form. In order to implement Article 17, Article 35 of the Constitution has empowered the Parliament of India to prescribe the punishment for the offences pronounced under part III of the Indian Constitution. In accordance with Article 35 the Parliament of India enacted "THE UNTOUCHABILITY (OFFENSES) ACT which has come into force from May 8, 1955.

The Act has not defined the term 'Untouchability', however, is fairly a comprehensive legislation. The Act has provided for punishment for enforcing certain religious social and other kinds of disabilities on grounds of untouchability. This Act has laid down penalties for the refusal of rendering services to Scheduled Castes and made provision for the use of Public places by Scheduled Castes without any distinction of caste. The Act provided punishment for enforcing religious disabilities such as preventing a person from entering any place of public worship or from worshiping or offering prayers or performing any religious service in any place of public worship or use of water or any sacred tank, well, spring or watercourse. The offender shall be punishable with imprisonment, which may be extended to six months, or with a fine, which may be extended to five hundred rupees or both.

Under sections 3 to 7 of the Act, who ever practice the Untouchability shall be punishable with imprisonment or with fine or with both. The Act also deals with providing punishments for enforcing the socioeconomic disabilities. However the Act was not found that effective in the eradication of untouchability and therefore was amended in 1976 and is known as the PROTECTION OF CIVIL RIGHTS ACT, 1955.

The Untouchability (Offences) Amendment Bill, 1972, renamed as the Protection of Civil Rights (Amendment) Act, came in force in 1976. The Act provided for enhanced and stringent punishment including collective fines for offences relating to untouchability. Some salient features of the amended Act were:

1. All untouchability offences will continue to be cognisable. Hitherto untouchability offences could be compounded, but they have been made not compoundable under the amended Act.
2. Direct or indirect preaching of Untouchability or its justification on historical, philosophical, religious or traditional grounds has been made an offence under the Act.
3. Compelling of any person out of "Untouchability" to do scavenging, sweeping and the like jobs has been made punishable.
4. The State Governments have been empowered to impose collective fines on the inhabitants of any area where such inhabitants are concerned in commission of untouchability.
5. The punishment of untouchability offences has been considerably enhanced and both imprisonment and fine will now be simultaneously awarded for such offences.

The above said legislation now provides safeguards for the Scheduled Castes against the practice of Untouchability. However it may be stressed the works of Mahatma Gandhi who said, "Untouchability will not be removed by force, even of law. It can be fully removed when the majority of the Hindus realise it is a crime against God and man and ashamed of it." In other words the effectiveness of legislation and the removal of the practice of untouchability can become more a reality when there is a structural change pertaining to change in social attitudes and value orientation.

The State governments were directed to introduce separate measures to fight against untouchability, notably, to appoint officers and special courts to deal with offenders, to provide legal aid to victims, and to take strong steps to identify and remedy problems in areas with a particularly high incidence of untouchability.

In spite of Constitutional safeguards and legal provisions for the Scheduled Castes the cases of atrocities against Scheduled Castes were on the rise. These atrocities have their roots in the socio-economic causes. With the majority of the Scheduled Castes being backward in all spheres of life, they had been mercilessly exploited by the higher castes.

The fact that Government programs have helped the Scheduled Castes to advance in all spheres of life at least to some extent, which in turn enabled them to fight against exploitation and discrimination, has caused anger and heart burn among the other Hindu castes. Their educational, economic and political advancement also caused discontentment among the other sections of the society, which led to increase in the number of atrocities on the Scheduled Castes. The continued atrocities on Scheduled Castes indicate the continued vulnerable status of the Scheduled Castes and the emerging mobility efforts on the part of the Scheduled Castes and resistance of the upper caste Hindus to defy such efforts.

The visible practice of Untouchability has come down over the year, but the atrocities against the Scheduled Castes did not come down as the reports suggested. They continued unabated in the different forms of murder, grievous hurt, arson and rape of Scheduled Caste women. Where as the police records recorded the registered these cases, many a case went unregistered. The Commissioner for Scheduled Castes and Scheduled Tribes has given three important reasons for atrocities. They are (i) unresolved land disputes related to allotment of government land or distribution of surplus land to the land-less Scheduled Castes and Scheduled Tribes (ii) tension or bitterness on non payment of or underpayment of minimum wages prescribed by the Government (iii) resentment against the manifestation of awareness among the Scheduled Castes and the Scheduled Tribes about their rights and privileges as enshrined in the Constitution and various legislative measures and protective discrimination. The Caste prejudices had been another important reason for the atrocities. Resentment against protective discrimination also accentuates conflict between the caste Hindus and the Scheduled Castes and Scheduled Tribes leading to the atrocities against them. (Ghanshyam Shah, 2002)

P.S. Krishnan (quoted by Ghanshyam Shah, 2002) notes two other reasons for atrocities against the Scheduled Castes. One is lack of provisions or access to essential facilities to Dalits and the assertion for the facilities and the second is a new phenomenon in which the atrocities take place for no cause other than ' Dalit assertion of self respect'.

The National Commissioner for Scheduled Castes and Scheduled Tribes (April, 1990) made a detailed study of atrocities such as murder, grievous hurt, rape, arson and crime involving substantial loss of property of Dalits during the period 1983 to 1987, in five states namely Bihar, Rajastan, Madhya Pradesh and Tamil Nadu. The Commission found an alarming increase in the crimes against Scheduled Castes (an 8 percent rise between 1981 and 1986), especially murders and rape. There was an apparent link between atrocities, both of caste prejudice and untouchability and political and economic issue regarding land, wage, indebtedness, bondage, etc. Disputes related to land were identified as the single most important cause, including disputes regarding implementation of land reforms, and allotment of cultivable land and house-sites, other conflicts centred around envy of a good crop raised by Dalits, use of community land, etc. Likewise, any attempt by Dalit agricultural labourers to agitate for reasonable wages were usually met with violence at the hands of the land-owning classes. (Harsh Mander, 2002)

Organised political assertion by Dalits as a separate power group in North India is comparatively recent phenomenon, symbolised most dramatically in the rise to power of the Bahujan Samaj Party, in winter election 1993, to Uttar Pradesh assembly. The new assertion by Dalit, as a separate self-conscious political entity, is based on shared perception of caste discrimination and oppression. This new-found militant and aggressive caste consciousness is in some way parallel to classical Marxist "class consciousness", because it signifies an awareness of oppression and consequent need for organised mass action to fight it. But it simultaneously runs fundamentally counter to Marxian class-consciousness because the basis of the shared identity is not ones position in the mode of production, but in the ritual caste hierarchy of the society. (Harsh Mander, 2002)

After finding steady increase in the cases all over the country an effective step was needed to prevent them. To stem the increase in the rate of atrocities on the Scheduled Castes the Government of India has enacted THE SCHEDULED CASTES AND SCHEDULED TRIBES (PREVENTION OF ATROCITIES) ACT 1989.The Act has come into force on 30th January 1990. The Act intends to prevent the commission of offences of atrocities against the members of Scheduled Castes and Scheduled Tribes, to provide for special courts for the trial of such offences and for the relief and rehabilitation of the victims of such offences and for the matters connected therewith. The salient features of the Act are as follows:

1. The Act has spelled out certain acts atrocities and has pronounced the punishments for such acts. The Act has listed out fourteen acts such as forcing a member of Scheduled Caste or Scheduled Tribe to drink or eat any inedible or obnoxious substance, acts with intent to cause injury, insult or annoyance to any member of the Scheduled Caste or Scheduled Tribe by dumping excreta, waste matter, carcass or any other obnoxious substance in his premises or neighbourhood and the such, the offender shall be punishable with imprisonment of a term which shall not be less than six months but which may be extended to five years and with fine.
2. Severe punishment is to be awarded to those who gives or fabricates false evidence intending thereby to cause, or knowing it to be likely that he will thereby cause any member of Scheduled Caste to be convicted of an offence.
3. Committing mischief by fire or any explosive substance intending to cause or knowing it to be likely that he will thereby cause damage to any property, or place of worship of Scheduled Caste shall be punishable with imprisonment extending to seven years and fine and imprisonment for life and fine respectively.
4. Where a person has been convicted of any offence punishable under this chapter the special court may, in addition to awarding any punishment by order in

writing, declare that any property movable or immovable or both belonging to the person, which has been used for the commission of that offence shall stand forfeited to Government.

For the purpose of speedy trial the State Government shall specify for each district a court of session to be a special court to try offences under this Act, and for every special court the State Government shall specify a public prosecutor or appoint an advocate for the purpose of conducting cases.

P.V. Rathod and Vijay Kumar (2002) critically examined the working of the Scheduled Castes and Schedules Tribes (Prevention of Atrocities) Act, 1989 in Gujarat. They find that the Act is not yet implemented effectively. The authors made several suggestions to provide teeth the act.

Besides all these constitutional and legal safe guards the reservations (discussed is earlier chapters) were made in educational institutions, employment and political bodies.

The above measures are intended to bring the Scheduled Castes into the mainstream of the society. These welfare measures are revised from time to time to make them more useful for these sections. The Scheduled Castes are provided with multidimensional welfare measures in all the aspects of human activity through protective discrimination. Commenting on the Welfare measures of the Government for the Scheduled Castes, Dushkin (1957) observed, "Probably nowhere in the world is so large a lower class minority granted so much favourable special treatment by the Government as are the depressed castes of India".

These welfare measures had made an impact on the Scheduled Castes and there is perceptible change among the Scheduled Castes. The protective discrimination had helped the Scheduled Castes to raise their status in the society.

Analysing the progress due to the protective discrimination among the Scheduled Castes, Chandra Shekar, (1972) Malik (1979) have identified access to religious and other public places, lessening of social and religious distances, integration of all caste groups, which include the Scheduled Castes also in educational institutions, sharing of political power, desegregation of residence and occupational mobility as the five major areas of progress.

The studies that have reported the progress of the Scheduled Castes are sizeable in number.

The study made by Sinha (1986) reveals that the efforts of the Government and non-Government bodies have resulted in improvement of the educational, economic and political status of the Scheduled Castes. He argues that the Scheduled Castes are not social disadvantageous for the lack of opportunities but due to the fact that these benefits have not been equally distributed. Vageswari (1972) reports that the positions of the Scheduled Castes in the use of wells, temples, streets etc had considerably improved. However she agrees that in ritualistic acts the discrimination continues. Beteille (1966) explains that with the creation of new power institutions such as Panchayats, the numerically strong Adidravidas could improve their status by making their presence felt by the other castes.

Sunanda Patwardhan (1973) while accepting the positive trend in the improvement of the status of the Scheduled Castes says that planned development, reservation of posts in public services, and in educational institutions, their political participation have made mobility flexible and greater. The larger system and the micro system are changing in response to external forces in the political economic and bureaucratic systems. She also argued that the notion of purity and pollution is much less in evidence in urban centres and adds that there is change as well as continuity. The coexistence of elements of change and continuity shows structural stability as well as strain, co-operation as well as conflict. The study made by Rao and Rao (1955), have also found that there is positive change and upliftment in the status of the Scheduled Castes and conclude that even the converts tended to return to the fold of Hinduism. Patwardhan (1973) observes that there is a gradual but definite decline in the situation of social inequality of Indian Society and the Constitutional and legal provisions have brought about perceptible change in the conditions of the Scheduled Castes. Beteille (1967) has observed that because of the protective discrimination there is slow but steady erosion in the legitimacy accorded to inequality. Lynch's (1969) study of the Jatavas makes clear that the legal innovations have opened new frontiers of political opportunities to the Scheduled Castes and have brought a positive change in all aspects of Social and economic life. Bhat (1975) has also concluded that there is a considerable progress in the movement of upward vertical mobility due to constitutional and legal provisions. Abbasayulu (1978) found that constitutional provisions have benefited many of Scheduled Caste subjects to obtain elite positions. Malik (1979) has also expressed similar views stating that constitutional and legal provisions have brought about a positive change in education, income and political status among the Scheduled Castes. Growth of higher education among a section of the Dalits on the one hand and reservation of 15 percent of the jobs, under Article 16(4) and 333 of the Constitution at all levels in the Union as well as state governments and public sector undertaking, have facilitated their entry into middle class in general and government white collar jobs in particular. The formation of this 'new middle class' among the Dalits, Nandu Ram (2002) argues is "vivisected in its role of acting as catalytic agent of bringing social change and mobility among the Dalit masses and its efforts for getting structurally accommodated in the Indian middle class or classes as such".

The Chamars of Chavandi Kalan in Rajasthan (Agarwal 1971: 78-79), The Chamars of Dehradun (Bhatt 1961: 232-38), the Chamars of Chhatera village near Delhi (Gandrade 1975: 262) and the Scheduled Castes (for example Patni, Mahara and Namasudra) of Sumar Valley in Assam employ Brahmans for their religious needs. The Harijans (for example Bhogab, Chamar and Ghasis) Bihar are allowed temple entry, draw water from public well, dance together with touchables, accept food from educated Harijans (Vidyarthi and Mishra (1977:84). Well-to-do Pulayas of Kerala exchange food with high caste, and also receive the services of the barber and the Washerman (Alexander 1968a: 1072;73; 1972; 160-61). In Surat city of Gujarat, according to Parmar (1987: 135-136), 196 touchable families live in the rented houses of the Mahyavanshis in the latter's residential area. These examples illustrate the decline in the practice of untouchability in ample in different parts of the country.(quoted by Gnana Prakasam, 1998)

As far as Dalits are concerned two striking positive changes have taken place. First, crude and blatant forms of social discrimination, at least in the pubic sphere are practised far less frequently than before. Yet, they certainly have not disappeared. Second, a middle class within the community has emerged. Four factors according to Ghanshyam Shah (2002) have contributed in bringing about the changes. First, there is an overall acceptance of equality as a desirable norm, thanks to permeation of the liberal and radical philosophical discourse, capitalist development, and technological including communications, changes in society. It is almost an outdated moral value to hold that inequality is desirable and necessary, or is the consequence of one's karma of the past birth. Second, capitalist development, nonetheless sluggish, has weakened the traditional functioning of the caste system. Though caste remains, its form and content are different from what prevailed in earlier societies. Caste is a limiting rather than the determining factor in choice of occupation (Gough, 1960). Occupational diversification, albeit to a limited extent, has taken place within the Dalit community. Those Dalits who have some assets for investment and/or marketable skills, have received university education, and have become professional, entrepreneurs, white collar employees, professional politicians, etc. Third, protective discrimination through reservations in government jobs and admission to educational institutions has paved the way for Dalits to enter the middle class, upward mobility has created hope and given them confidence that there is scope for improving their condition and be at par with others. Fourth, various legislation prescribing punitive action against the practice of untouchability, though not implemented very effectively, have checked to some extent, blatant discrimination against the Dalits. It is more so in public than private spheres.

The reservation policy of the Government has paid dividends in terms of lessening the gap between the Scheduled Castes and non-Scheduled Castes. Khare (1981) writes that the policy of reservations has adequately compensated the centuries of oppression against the Scheduled Castes and helped them in overcoming the psychological educational and economic disadvantages. Sachidananda (1977) work makes it clear that the new educated Scheduled Castes elite has emerged as a result of the policies of the Government in providing the Scheduled Castes reservation in education, which ultimately helped them to improve their status. Pandya (1959) in his study of Ahmedabad concluded that the traditional barriers are breaking down with the new field of employment thrown open to the Scheduled Castes. Cohn (1955) explained how Chamars the Scheduled Castes have raised their status by adopting the practices of orthodox Brahmins. Beteille (1967) points out in his study that the Scheduled Castes are now able to adopt Hindu names, occupations, diet, and social practices. Ainapur (1986) making study of two villages writes that the higher caste members attend the marriage ceremonies of the Scheduled Castes but they do not accept food or water from them. He also reports that in a village where there are teashops which are run by the Lingayaths who are at the top of hierarchy in the village, the Scheduled Castes are allowed to take tea and food from these teashops; but they drink tea or water in cups, which are kept outside the hotel for this purpose. After taking tea they have to wash their own cups and plates and keep them separately.

Harper (1968) explains improvement of status in Untouchables who sanskritized their ways of life by enforcing taboo on beef eating and refusing to do degrading activities. T.R.Singh (1969) who studied the Madigas of Andhra Pradesh also points out that they no longer eat carrion and tan hide and as such could improve their status. Alexander (1968) reports that the Pullayas of Kerala have now adopted Sanskrit gods and stopped offering toddy. There is also change in patterns of living, modes of dress among them, which boosted their status. Sunanda Patwardhan (1973) reports the process of Sanskritization among several Scheduled Castes. She points out that the Mahars have shown maximum degree of mobility due to several factors. Soran Singh (1976) also reports occupational mobility among the Scheduled Castes leading to change in their status.

Beteille (1967), Issacs (1965), Lynch (1969) pointed out how political action helps the Scheduled Castes to better their position in society. The Mahars of Maharastra, the Jatavas of Agra used politics as means to achieve better social status. Parmar (1989) traces the success story of the Mahyavanshis of Surat city explained that at the initial stage the Europeans and the Christian missionaries have helped them in improving their status. Later they put ban on entering into unclean occupations, stopped eating beef. They used educational and political means to improve their status. In economic activity practically all the Mahyavanshis in Surat earn their lively hood through non-conventional and clean occupations. He reports among the Mahyavanshis, 94 per cent are literates who are of the age of 30 years and below.

Sunila Malik (1979 who conducted study in Ambala town explains that the less educated and non-mobile Scheduled Castes are living in the colonies of their own, whereas highly educated Scheduled Castes are living in the larger community which makes clear that the higher castes are accepting the Scheduled Castes as their neighbours. The study also mentions that the educated respondents opined that they have improved a great deal; the illiterate and less educated Scheduled Castes have perceived only a slight improvement in their status. The study of Suma Chitnis explains the Scheduled Castes are making use of facilities and says that the caste among the Scheduled Castes that have a relatively better access to educational facilities in a State happen, more often than not, the caste that form large percentage of Scheduled Castes population of that particular State. The study reveals that overwhelming majority of the respondents have completed school without failure and they do no have any difficulties in comprehending the lessons.

The protective discrimination had made an impact on the Scheduled Castes and there is perceptible change among the Scheduled Castes. The protective discrimination had helped the Scheduled Castes to raise their status in the society.

Analysing the progress due to the protective discrimination among the Scheduled Castes, sociologist have identified access to religious and other public places, lessening of social and religious distances, integration of all caste groups, which include the Scheduled Castes also in educational institutions, sharing of political power, desegregation of residence and occupational mobility as the five major areas of progress.

According to Ghanshyam (2002) the two striking positive changes that have taken place were; the crude and blatant forms of social discrimination has come down and are practised far less at least in the public places and secondly a new middle class has emerged among them.

The studies of Kuppuswamy, 1956, Gupta, 1958, Sinha, 1960; Kothurkar, 1962; Das, 1967; Abraham, 1968; Chibbar, 1968; Laxmanna, 1968; Dutta, 1970; Anant, 1972; Premi, 1974; Bhat, 1975; Desai, 1976; Vidyarthi and Mishra, 1977; Malik, 1979; Khan, 1980; Rao, 1981, Jayaram, 1981; have also shown that the position of Scheduled Castes has improved.

While the majority of the studies have argued that there is positive change some studies revealed that there is little or no change among the Scheduled Castes due to protective discrimination.

Notwithstanding the Constitutional provisions and various Legislations, untouchability continues, as Ghanshyam Shah finds in Gujarat, one of the more developed states of India. I.P. Desai studied the problem in 1972. Shah, in a restudy, visited the same villages to find out what changes have taken place in the practice of untouchability over a period of time. He observes that though untouchability is not visible in schools but it has not yet disappeared in village Panchayats. The elected members belonging to Scheduled Castes experience discrimination in 30 percent of the villages. It is still observed to some extent in public transport and postal services. There is no change in private sphere. It is still very high. In most of the villages they are not allowed to enter temples and private house. On the basis of various studies, Harsh Mander finds that, "There is widest prevalence of untouchability in the cultural and domestic spheres. It is partial in occupational sphere. But in the public sphere, barring in Panchayats and occasional restriction on dress and footwear, it is largely absent". A blatant display of untouchability is not discernible in urban areas but subtle discriminations in most walks of life have persisted. Krishnan (2002) observes "In many metropolitan areas, 'untouchability' has seemingly attenuated, but is practised with sophisticated concealment in variety of ingenious ways, revealing creativity worthy of better cause. In many modern offices, Dalits have to suffer snide remarks and quiet and neat acts of discrimination. Ramesh Kamble (2002) substantiates the above observation in his study on "Untouchability in Urban setting" and according to him even in the cosmopolitan city, several educated middle-class Dalits perceive and experience discrimination and caste prejudice. The intensity of the experience however varies from situation.

Beteille (1969) explaining little change among the Scheduled Castes says that a long tradition of oppression and servitude makes it difficult for the Scheduled Castes to develop the confidence in a short time which they require for the full utilisation of the benefits provided by the Government. He argues that the policies and programs of the Government are ineffective as the stubborn social forces, which are firmly entrenched in the economic and political system of the country, often block the advance of these Scheduled Castes. He concludes that the new legal and political order in India firmly rejected the value of inequality based on the caste. Although Scheduled Castes are legally free to adopt whatever styles of life they chose, there are numerous social and economic constraints, which in practice prevent them from doing so.

Ainapur (1986) studying two villages in Karnataka reports that the Scheduled Castes live in their own colonies; situated in outskirts of the village. They not allowed drawing water from village wells, but in one village they have their own wells and in other village they have to fetch water from the nearby stream. He says the attitude of the high caste Hindus towards the Scheduled Castes is one of arrogance and ill feeling. The Scheduled Castes are not allowed into the Hindu temples situated in the village. They have to offer prayers standing outside the temple.

In village studies and studies of untouchables it is reported that untouchables live at the outskirts of the main village separate from touchable. They have their separate colony. (Fuchs 1950, 1951, 1981; Mayer 1960; Mathur 1964, Beteille 1969; Mandelbaum 1972; Beck 1972; Mencher 1974; Moffatt 1975; 1979, 1979; Khan 1979; Mukherji 1980; Dumont 1980; Parmar 1982; Deshpande 1983; Lapoint and Lapoint 1985; Roy and Singh 1987; Bhaskar 1988). (Quoted by Gnana Prakasam, 1998)

Desai (1976) studied the practice of untouchability with reference to the behavioural situation in 69 villages of Gujarat and found that in 64 per cent of the villages the source of water are separate for the Untouchables and Savarnas, and in 10 per cent of the villages there is no regular sources of water supply for Untouchables. They have to rely on the mercy of the Savarnas. Further he finds that of 69 villages, only in five villages the Untouchables are allowed into temples to worship there and entry into houses and shops owned by Caste Hindus. In 487 of village Panchayats untouchability is observed by the Savarnas. However in state transport bus, village primary school, and post office untouchability is uniformly becoming extinct.

The study of Selvanathan (1987) reveals that the Scheduled Castes are experiencing discrimination in both rural and urban areas. The study also reveals that they are not aware of Constitutional provision intended for them and a majority of them have not benefited through reservation policy. The higher income groups among the Scheduled Castes are the more beneficiaries of the reservations and not the bigger lot. Suma Chitnis (1981) says that the practice of caste discrimination does not seem to be as pronounced as it may have been prior to the declaration of the practice of untouchability an offence. However the respondents are not altogether free from caste discrimination practices.

Galanter (1969) reported a large-scale disregard to the provision of anti untouchability laws passed by the Government. Sachidananda (1977) observed though the untouchability is legally abolished, the practice is still prevalent in society. Parvathamma, 1968; Chitnis, 1977; Vatsa 1977; believed that abolition of untouchability is only a mere legal fiction. Issacs, 1965; Jatava, 1965; Beteille, 1972, Brijmohan, 1972; Sagar, 1975; Goel, 1981; Ghosh, 1980; Jayaraman, 1981; Ram, 1989, have reported the failure of law in protecting the Scheduled Castes.

Bailey (1959) reports that in spite of the considerable economic progress made by the outcastes in a village of Orissa, they had not risen correspondingly in the social hierarchy of the village. Issacs (1965) has found several cases of discrimination existing in schools with Scheduled Castes students not being allowed at hostels where the wards of higher castes reside and are made to eat and sleep separately. Elayaperumal (1969) has observed in the study of 404 villages of Madhya Pradesh, about social discrimination against Scheduled Castes Panchs, who are elected members of goan Panchayats. Anant (1972) found that there is continuing manifestation of untouchability despite constitutional safeguards. The reports of Commissioner of Scheduled Castes also reveal widespread practice of untouchability though rare in urban areas. The studies of Desai and Damle, 1954; La Touche, 1958; Goyal, 1958; Gandhi, 1973; Ramu, 1977; Ghosh, 1977; Ghosh, 1980; Kamble, 1982; have expressed the opinion that instead of integration of the Scheduled Castes into the main stream of the society there is a widening gulf between the Scheduled Castes and non-Scheduled Castes.

The Scheduled Castes of Gooty: The Scheduled Castes lived through ages ecologically segregated and this holds good even now as reported by many studies. To find out whether or not there is any change in this regard, the respondents were asked who are their immediate neighbours. Here immediate neighbours mean the neighbours who reside on either side of the respondents' houses it. The responses given are presented in table 6.1. As the table reveals almost 90 per cent of the respondents have only the Scheduled Castes as their immediate neighbours and that too they belong to their own sub caste more pronouncedly. Whereas only about three per cent of the respondents have the backward castes as their neighbours, and even very insignificant number of respondents have the forward castes as their neighbours. Others who do not fit into the caste structure such as Christians, Muslims and Scheduled Tribes account for a little more than two per cent, which is again is a low percentage. 16(5 per cent) respondents have more than one of the above said categories as their neighbours, whereas in the case of 15 respondents on one side it is again the Scheduled Castes and only in one case there is a neighbour who is from forward caste. On the other hand in the case of two respondents the neighbours belong to other Scheduled Castes, in the case of seven respondents the neighbours being from backward castes, and in the case of three respondents each the neighbour are from forward castes and others respectively.

TABLE - 6.1
TABLE SHOWING IMMEDIATE NEIGHBORS OF THE SCHEDULED CASTE RESPONDENTS

Immediate Neighbors	*Sub-caste*		*Total*
	Mala	*Madiga*	
Same Caste	112 (86.20)	168 (88.40)	280 (87.50)
Other Scheduled Caste	0 (0.00)	5 (2.60)	5 (1.60)
Backward Castes Only	6 (4.60)	3 (1.60)	9 (2.80)
Forward Caste	3 (2.30)	0 (0.00)	3 (0.9)
Others	3 (2.30)	4 (2.10)	7 (2.2)
More than one Category	6 (4.60)	10 (5.3)	16 (5.00)
Total	130	190	320

It is the fact that the majority of the Schedule Castes are living ecologically segregated as they are living in separate colonies that are meant for them. However, it is not the fact that they are forced to live in segregation but they are living separately because they got their houses inherited or allotted by the government in these places. Almost 76 per cent of them who inherited their houses are staying in that house only.

To find out further whether they are free from ecological segregation, the respondents were asked whether they are allowed to construct their houses in areas other than their localities. (Table 6.2A) Of the total 320 respondents, all the 130 Mala respondents and 185 out of 190 Madiga respondents replied in positive to this question. The three who replied in the negative are probed further and it is found that it is more self-imposed restriction than being enforced by the upper castes. All these three are elderly respondents and are traditional in their thinking and outlook. This question has been followed up and again the respondents were asked whether they are free to construct houses even in forward castes locality, besides backward castes locality. (Table 6.2B) To this follow-up question, of the 317 respondents who positively responded to the above question, all the 130 Mala respondents have said they are free to construct houses wherever they like, including forward caste locality. To emphasise this they have quoted the examples of some of their caste people residing in forward castes locality. Out of 187 Madiga respondents who positively replied to the above question 184 have again said that they are free to construct houses in forward castes locality also besides backward castes locality. Only three respondents said, they might not be allowed to construct houses in forward castes locality. When asked about the reasons for this all the three have said they are scavengers and they said because of their occupation they might not be allowed to construct their houses next to the houses of higher castes houses. However the other scavengers in the study did not agree with the opinion.

TABLE - 6.2(A)

RESPONSES OF THE RESPONDENTS TO THE QUESTION "ARE YOU ALLOWED TO CONSTRUCT HOUSE IN OTHER THAN YOUR LOCALITY?"

Response	*Sub-caste*		*Total*
	Mala	*Madiga*	
Yes	130	187	317
No	0	3	3
Total	130	190	320

TABLE - 6.2(B)

LOCALITY OF THE CONSTRUCTION OF HOUSE

Immediate Neighbors	*Sub-caste*		*Total*
	Mala	*Madiga*	
In Backward Castes locality only	0 (0.00)	3 (1.60)	3 (0.90)
In the Forward Castes locality also	130 (100.00)	184 (98.40)	314 (99.10)
Total	130	187	317

Many of the earlier studies have revealed that the Scheduled Castes were not allowed to make use of the civic amenities available in the village or town. They were not allowed to use the village tank at all, or at times not from the side where the villagers use it, not allowed to draw water from common village well, were not allowed to have formal education by making use of the school, and so on. The studies have also revealed change in the situation where Scheduled Castes have been accepted as a part of the main stream, with difference in intensity of change, from place to place.

The respondents in Gooty were asked whether they are allowed to make use of civic amenities. These civic amenities include the use of bore wells and taps, school, village tank, commonplace of toilet, roads and streets. The responses are being presented in Table 6.3. Except in the case of use roads and streets there were at least some negative responses given by the respondents in the case of making use of other civic amenities. However it does not mean that they are not allowed to make use of these amenities but they are not making use of it because they do not have a chance to make use of it.

TABLE - 6.3
MAKING USE OF THE CIVIC AMENITIES

Particulars	*Sub-Caste*				*Total*	
	Mala		*Madiga*			
	Yes	*Not Applicable*	*Yes*	*Not Applicable*	*Yes*	*Not Applicable*
Common Bore Well/Public Tap/Well	18 (13.80)	112 (86.20)	22 (11.50)	168 (88.50)	40 (12.50)	280 (77.50)
Roads and Streets	130 (100.00)	0 (0.00)	190 (100.00)	0 (0.00)	320 (100.00)	0 (0.00)
Schools	37 (28.50)	93 (71.50)	53 (27.90)	137 (62.10)	90 (28.10)	230 (71.90)
Government Hospital	82 (63.10)	48 (36.90)	96 (50.50)	94 (49.50)	178 (55.70)	142 (44.3)
Village Tank	13 (10.00)	117 (90.00)	89 (46.90)	101 (53.10)	102 (31.90)	218 (68.10)
Common Place of Toilet	38 (29.20)	92 (70.80)	51 26.80)	139 (73.20)	89 (27.80)	231 (72.20)

As said earlier most of Scheduled Castes are residing in colonies, which are provided with the bore wells or public taps. As such they are not using the common bore well or public tap along with other castes. Among those who are living outside these colonies, a few are having taps in their own houses and the rest are using the common public tap. It is brought to the notice of the researcher that, few other castes that are residing near Scheduled Castes colonies which have adequate drinking water facility, come there to take water for drinking purpose.

The schools are being used by the Scheduled Castes like any other castes. There are no restrictions imposed on the Scheduled Castes in making use of the school. The Scheduled Castes respondents who have school going age group children, send their children to the school. 29 per cent of the Scheduled Caste respondents have answered positive about making use of school. So is the case with the making use of hospital, as more than 55 per cent of the respondents answering in positive of making use of the hospital.

Comparatively less number of Scheduled Castes respondents have answered in the positive about making use of the tank in Gooty. Only two Scheduled Castes colonies are nearer to the tank, along with other caste those also use the tank. The Scheduled Castes like other castes use the tank for bathing, washing clothes, cleaning the cattle etc. The Scheduled Castes who have replied in the negative about making use of tank said they can use tank, but are not using it only because it is far away from their houses. They said there are no restrictions imposed on them in using the tank and they have quoted of their children swimming in the tank without being restricted by any one.

With regard to making use of commonplace of toilet, the majority of the Scheduled Castes respondents have replied in the negative. A substantial number of respondents' (134) have toilet in their houses and as such the question of the using common place of toilets does not arise for them. In Gooty there is nothing like a common place of toilet. The respondents, who do not have toilet in their own houses, use the common place of toilet, but there are only two places of common toilet, which the Scheduled Castes use along with the other castes. There are hillocks near three colonies of the Scheduled Castes, which the Scheduled Castes use as common places of toilet with other Castes without any objection from the other higher castes. The other Scheduled Castes who have reported of not having toilets in their houses are also using the toilet places, which are generally near to their houses. They are used by them only and not by other castes for being far away from their place of residence. It can be concluded here that the civic amenities in Gooty are being utilised by the Scheduled Castes without any restriction imposed by the higher castes.

Common meal has an extremely important social and structural significance in Hindu Society. The common meal expresses symbolically both the unity of those who eat together and the cleavage between or among those who eat separately. Generally two castes do not interdine unless the structural difference between them is small. (Beteille, 1969). Interdining accepting and offering food as such prove no cleavages between or among the castes. The Untouchables, the so-called polluted castes were never allowed to have commensal relationship with the other higher castes. The lack of commensal relationship is an indicator of social distance. As said earlier, there are two sub castes among the Scheduled Castes in Gooty, viz. the Mala and Madiga. The two sub castes consider each other inferior and there is little or no commensal relationship between the two sub castes of Scheduled Castes and in rural area even now this holds good.

In the present study the responses of the Scheduled Castes were collected about the practice of interdining among themselves and with other higher caste Hindus. Table 6.4 presents the inter dining interactions among Scheduled Castes, Table 6.5 presents the interdining interaction of Scheduled Castes with other upper caste Hindus.

As the table 6.4 reveals the total of 320 Scheduled Caste respondents as high as 95 per cent of them have answered in the affirmative of having commensal relation with other sub caste. However taking into consideration the sub caste and negative responses about commensal relation, the Madigas respondents are more (10%), compared to the Mala respondents (1.54%). Traditionally the Malas are considered to be superior to the other sub caste Madigas. There was even the practice of untouchability among the Malas and Madigas, the Malas enforcing the untouchability. However, in a particular village, if the numerical strength of the Madigas is more, it has a sobering effect on the relations. But when inquired about the disparity and more number of Madiga respondents refusing to have commensal relationship with the Mala the answer is rather interesting. In the present case as the Madigas are more in number in Gooty they feel they are superior and as such more negative responses come from them about the commensal relationship with other sub castes viz the Malas.

TABLE - 6.4

RESPONSES OF SCHEDULED CASTE RESPONDENTS TO THE QUESTION "DO YOU DINE WITH OTHER SCHEDULED CASTES?"

Response	*Sub-caste*		*Total*
	Mala	*Madiga*	
Yes	128 (98.46)	171 (90.00)	299 (93.43)
No	2 (1.54)	19 (10.00)	21 (6.70)
Total	130	190	320

In Table No 6.5 the responses of the Scheduled Castes with regard to their inter dining interaction with the higher castes were analysed. As the table reveals as much as about 93 per cent of the respondents have reported of having inter dining interaction with higher caste Hindus.

TABLE - 6.5(A)

RESPONSES OF THE SCHEDULED CASTE RESPONDENTS TO THE QUESTION "DO YOU DINE ALONG WITH OTHER HIGHER CASTES?"

Response	*Sub-caste*		*Total*
	Mala	*Madiga*	
Yes	121 (93.07)	176 (92.63)	297 (92.81)
No	9 (6.93)	14 (7.37)	23 (7.19)
Total	130	190	320

From the table it is clear that a high percentage of respondents are having inter dining relations with the higher caste Hindus and this holds good in case both the sub castes the Malas and the Madigas, as the percentage of positive responses in both cases is almost 93 per cent. Of those who do not have interdining relations with higher castes, it is reported that the respondents who are scavengers by occupation are not being invited by the upper castes Hindus. Besides the scavengers, some other respondents have said they refuse to have interdining with higher castes for the fear of being discriminated while being served. A few respondents have also reported of not having interdining with the upper castes and the reason is self construed discrimination than imposed.

The respondents who have replied in the positive about being invited to the homes of upper castes and having commensal relationship with them are further asked about the caste of the people who invite them. For this majority of the respondents have replied that they are mostly being invited by the backward castes, and they account to as much as 60 per cent. Only about 40 per cent of the respondents have said that besides being invited by the lower castes, they also are being invited by the forward castes to dine with them. The Madiga respondents are more in number than the Mala respondents who have said of being invited by the forward castes. However, the respondents have clarified that by and large the Scheduled Castes are being invited by the upper castes Hindus, be them forward castes or backward castes. It is the question of the respondent having an intimate friend from upper castes or not that decides the issue. If the respondent is having an intimate friend from upper caste, be it a forward caste or backward caste, he will be invited to have lunch or dinner with them, and it is not the other things that decide the matter.

TABLE - 6.5(B)
"THE CASTES YOU DINE WITH ARE"

Response	*Sub-caste*		*Total*
	Mala	*Madiga*	
Backward caste only	79 (65.28)	102 (57.95)	181 (60.94)
Forward castes also	42 (34.72)	74 (42.05)	116 (39.06)
Total	121	176	297

The respondents who said of having commensal relationship with higher caste Hindus were asked whether they are being served in the common batches or not. A few earlier studies have reported that the Scheduled Castes though invited by upper castes for lunch or dinner are not treated equal and are not being served in the common batches.

As the table 6.5(C) reveals majority of the respondents have said that they are being served in the common batches. They sit in a common row and food is served to them just as to the people from any other castes. However some respondents have answered in the negative of being served in common batches. When probed further it was found that those who have said so are the respondents who by profession are agricultural labour and respondents who are involved in menial occupation and have said that they are not being served in the common batches. The agriculture labourers, who by and large have client and patron relationship with their landlords, are being invited to the ceremonies and marriages in the house of their patrons and landlords and they work in their capacities. They reported that they would be served food outside the house after the other higher castes have taken food. They said that using separate utensils and tumblers, which will not be used for other higher castes, are serving them. They are served in the leaves and after dinner or lunch they have to remove the leaves in which they were served and have to clean the place.

TABLE - 6.5(C)

ARE YOU BEING SERVED IN COMMON BATCHES?

Response	*Sub-caste*					
	Mala			*Madiga*		
	Yes	*No*	*Total*	*Yes*	*No*	*Total*
Who dine with backward caste only	76 (96.20)	3 (3.80)	79	98 (96.07)	4 (3.93)	102
Who dine with Forward castes also	32 (76.19)	10 (23.81)	42	86 (89.19)	8 (10.81)	74
Total	108	13	121	164	12	176

It can be concluded here that the restrictions on commensal relationship between the Scheduled Castes and other higher caste Hindus are fast deteriorating. It is only those Scheduled Castes who are completely depending on the higher castes Hindus are being discriminated to some extent even now.

The Scheduled Castes earlier suffered from discrimination in almost all walks of life. They were discriminated in places such as work place, common gatherings, the marriages and ceremonies of the higher castes and the like places. They were not allowed to enter the tea stalls and hotels which other higher caste Hindus visit. The services of the servicing castes such as washer man, barber tailor and the like were not available for them. To find out whether there is any discrimination in such areas of interaction the respondents were asked to give their responses about feeling discriminated in different contexts of interaction. In Table 6.6 the responses of Scheduled Castes about their feeling discriminated is given.

As the table reveals only to the question pertaining to the interaction in work place, ceremonies and marriages of higher castes, the receiving of the services of the servicing castes few respondents have reported of feeling discriminated and this works out to about six per cent, sixteen per cent and nine per cent in each of these places of interaction respectively. Some of the respondents who work as agriculture labour reported that they are being ill treated by the landlord, and as well as by the other higher castes colleagues. The ill treatment, they said is in the form of calling them by names, practising untouchability etc. Most of the agricultural labourers and some respondents, who are engaged in menial occupations, again reported of being ill-treated by caste Hindus at marriages and ceremonies of the higher caste Hindus. The ill-treatment they reported is in the form of not allowing them to dine along with others in common batch and in some cases not allowing them to enter their houses. About nine per cent of the respondent said they are being discriminated by the servicing castes. It is said that if the Scheduled Caste person is too poor or engaged in menial occupation, the services of the servicing castes are still not available to them.

It is bought to the notice of the researcher that the services of the Brahmins are available to the well-to-do Scheduled Castes, who can afford and wish to engage them. It was reported that, if the marriages of the Scheduled Castes are to be officiated, the Brahmin comes to the temple where the marriage takes place, but not to their houses. It the temple, from a clear physical distance he directs the couple to perform the marriage rites and rituals.

TABLE - 6.6
RESPONSES OF THE SCHEDULED CASTE RESPONDENTS TO THE QUESTION "DO YOU FEEL DISCRIMINATED IN THE FOLLOWING PLACES?

Place of Interaction	*Sub-caste*				*Total*	
	Mala		*Madiga*			
	Yes	*No*	*Yes*	*No*	*Yes*	*No*
Work Place	7 (5.40)	123 (94.60)	12 (6.30)	178 (93.70)	19 (5.90)	301 (94.10)
Common Gathering	2 (1.50)	128 (98.50)	7 (3.70)	183 (96.30)	9 (2.80)	311 (93.20)
Marriages & Ceremonies of Higher Castes	17 (13.10)	113 (86.90)	34 (17.90)	156 (82.10)	51 (15.90)	269 (84.10)
Hotel	0 (0.00)	130 (100.00)	4 (2.10)	186 (97.90)	4 (1.20)	316 (98.80)
Tea shop	0 (0.00)	130 (100.00)	4 (2.10)	186 (97.90)	4 (1.20)	316 (98.80)
Bus/Train	0 (0.00)	130 (100.00)	2 (1.10)	188 (98.90)	2 (0.60)	318 (99.40)
Provision Shop	3 (2.30)	127 (97.70)	8 (4.20)	182 (95.80)	11 (3.40)	309 (96.60)
Govt. fair shop	0 (0.00)	130 (100.00)	0 (0.00)	190 (100.00)	0 (0.00)	320 (100.00)
Services of Servicing Castes	7 (5.40)	123 (94.60)	22 (11.60)	168 (88.40)	29 (9.10)	291 (90.90)

Officiating marriage rites by a Brahmin through not that pronounced, it is indicative of the changing trends and their improving social status which is brought about by the changes in their social occupational and political participation.

With regard to discrimination, places of interaction such as common place of gathering, hotel, tea stall, bus/train, provision shop the respondents who reported of being discriminated is very less in number. A few respondents have reported that at common gathering they cannot sit by the side of the higher caste Hindus, or have to stand all the time in their presence. In case of use of hotel, tea stall, bus/train none of the Malas have said they feel discriminated but only a few Madigas have reported discrimination. However it should be noted here that the some Scheduled Castes who have said of feeling discriminated, the discrimination is more of self-construed discrimination than being enforced by the upper castes. Some Scheduled Castes especially those who are in old age and poor educationally and economically, experience self construed discrimination, than the discrimination enforced by upper castes. When the majority of the Scheduled Castes are making use of all civic amenities and feel not being discriminated, some of them with their traditional out look and for their own reasons, construing discrimination themselves. This type of discrimination is showing itself in the form of not entering the hotels and tea stalls and not sitting by the side of a forward caste Hindus in bus/train. Few Madigas reported that a provision shop run by an old Visya in the Gooty, still show discrimination, for he makes them to collect the groceries dropping them on table in the shop instead of giving it to them and receives money in the same way without coming into physical contact with them. None of the Scheduled Castes respondents have reported of being discriminated by dealer of Government fair price shop.

The Hindu temples were totally inaccessible to the Scheduled Castes in the past. Though the Government has made legislation against obstruction of Scheduled Castes from entering a temple, calling it an offence, still in villages Scheduled Castes were not allowed to enter into the village common temples.

The Scheduled Caste respondents in Gooty were asked about entering into common temples and participating in common village festivals. The Scheduled Castes by and large have their own deities in villages and they worship these deities. In Gooty also the Scheduled Castes have temples for the deities Peddamma, Kuntemma, Gangamma, Sunkulamma and Ankalamma. Besides the temples for these deities there are temples for lord Rama and lord Hanuman and all these temples are in the Scheduled Castes residential locality only. The Scheduled Castes by and large worship in these temples only. However there are no restrictions in Gooty for allowing the Scheduled Castes into common temples. All the Scheduled Castes respondents have admitted that they are allowed in all the temples and they can worship in all the temples. Only in one temple, the Vasavi, the entry of Scheduled Castes was restricted till recently. But now into that temple also the Scheduled Castes are allowed. Some of the respondents have said that in the event of marriage in their houses they visit all the temples in Gooty and offer prayers and coconuts.

In the village common festivals also the Scheduled Castes respondents like any other castes participate and take part. Some of the Scheduled Castes said that they perform certain duties such as beating drum, carrying torches, at the time of these ceremonies, and the other Scheduled Castes said just like any other caste Hindus they also participate in the common village festivals.

Table 6.7 gives the religious interaction of the Scheduled Castes respondents. It is clear from the table that they do not suffer from religious disabilities. All the respondents have replied in the positive of participating in common village festivals. Only two respondents from the sub caste Mala have replied in the negative of visiting common village temples and then said they are converting into Christianity and so are visiting the church but not temples. However, they also said they do participate in common village festivals.

TABLE - 6.7
RELIGIOUS INTERACTION OF THE SCHEDULED CASTE RESPONDENTS

Particulars	*Sub-caste*				*Total*	
	Mala		*Madiga*			
	Yes	*No*	*Yes*	*No*	*Yes*	*No*
Participating in common village festivals	130 (100.00)	0 (0.00)	190 (100.00)	0 (0.00)	320 (100.00)	0 (0.00)
Visiting common village temples	128 (98.50)	2 (1.20)	190 (100.00)	0 (0.00)	318 (100.00)	2 (0.60)

It is a common practice to use one's caste name along with the name as a prefix or suffix. The interaction between two strangers without knowing the others caste may be different compared to the other way. Some studies have reported that the Scheduled Castes for the fact of facing discrimination do not reveal their caste identity to others. It is in this regard that, the Scheduled Caste respondents were asked whether they use their caste name along with their names. It is clear from the Table 6.8 that only about 17 per cent of respondents still use their caste name along with their names. This shows the practice of using the caste name along with names is in decline among the Scheduled Castes.

TABLE - 6.8

RESPONSES OF SCHEDULED CASTE RESPONDENTS FOR THE QUESTION "DO YOU USE CASTE NAME ALONG WITH YOUR NAME?"

Responses	*Sub-caste*		*Total*
	Mala	*Madiga*	
YES	21 (16.10)	32 (16.80)	53 16.60)
NO	109 (83.90)	158 (83.20)	267 (83.40)

The Scheduled Castes respondents were asked whether they feel that they are kept at a distance by the caste Hindus in general. This is an opinion question and with an intention of probing the feelings of the Scheduled Castes about feeling kept at a distance in general despite the specific inquires made above. The responses given by the respondents were given in Table 6.9. As the table reveals, about 18 per cent of the respondents replied that they are looked down by the upper castes. This question has been followed up with a supplementary question and the respondents were asked about the reason or reasons they feel why the Upper castes keep them at a distance. Out of 320 respondents 128 respondents have said still the Scheduled Castes are kept at a distance. The respondents have given more than one reason that they think makes the upper caste Hindus to keep them at distance and these responses are presented in Table 6.10.

TABLE - 6.9
RESPONSES OF THE SCHEDULED CASTE RESPONDENTS TO THE QUESTION "DO YOU FEEL HIGHER CASTES DISCRIMINATE YOU?"

Responses	*Sub-caste*		*Total*
	Mala	*Madiga*	
YES	27 (20.70)	29 (15.30)	56 (17.50)
NO	103 (79.30)	161 (84.70)	264 (82.50)
Total	130	190	320

TABLE - 6.10
RESPONSES OF THE SCHEDULED CASTE RESPONDENTS TO THE QUESTION "WHAT DO YOU THINK ARE REASONS FOR UPPER CASTES TO KEEP YOU AT DISTANCE?"

Reasons given by Respondents	*Sub-caste*		*Total*
	Mala	*Madiga*	
Unclean Occupation	12 (9.23)	26 (13.68)	38 (11.88)
Food Habits	11 (8.46)	25 (13.16)	36 (11.25)
Fear of Pollution	8 (6.15)	24 (12.63)	32 (10.00)
Poor Economic Conditions	11 (8.46)	3 (1.58)	14 (4.38)
Illiteracy/ignorance	14 (10.77)	7 (3.68)	21 (6.56)
Physical Features	0 (0.00)	2 (1.05)	2 (0.63)
Birth in the Caste	9 (6.92)	23 (12.10)	32 (10.00)

From Table 6.10 it is clear that the respondents who answered in the positive being kept at distance, majority of them feel that it is their unclean occupation and food habits which (32 respondents) are the main reasons for upper castes keeping them at a distance. The fear of their causing pollution of the higher caste Hindus, by coming into contact is the other reason (32 respondents) as given by the Scheduled Castes, for upper castes to keep them at a distance. The other important reason given by the respondents are poor economic conditions (14 respondents), illiteracy and ignorance (21 respondents).

Only a couple of respondents said it is their physical features is the reason for the upper castes to keep them at a distance. Another important reason interestingly given by a majority of the respondents, who answered in the affirmative of being looked down by the upper caste Hindus, is the very birth in the caste. They have quoted the incidents of the Scheduled Castes being looked down upon, though they are not in menial occupations, and follow clean food habits and are in respectable positions educationally and economically.

The Scheduled Castes respondents were asked about the measures that they think would reduce the social distance between the Scheduled Castes and upper castes Hindus. The responses given by them are presented in Table 6.11. Majority of the respondents have given more than one measure they think, will reduce the Social distance between them and the upper caste Hindus. Most of them have said if the Scheduled Castes get educated well and get a decent employment the discrimination will come down. A good number of respondents have said the government should take stern measures against untouchability and discrimination and this, they said, will bring down discrimination. The other important reasons given by the respondents are economic development, personal cleanliness, the Scheduled Castes standing united against discrimination and fighting against it in all the possible ways, by changing their food habits and behaviour pattern. There are a few irrelevant answers also, but a majority of the respondents didn't suggest any measures as such.

The respondents were specifically asked about their awareness on the existence and minimum knowledge of the legal provisions that were made against Untouchability and atrocities. As the table 6.12 reveals about eighty percent of the respondents know, without much sub caste variation, the existence of a law that pronounces Untouchability an offence, and minimum knowledge of that Act. But majority of the respondents, again with out much sub caste differences, does not know about the existence of prevention of atrocities Act.

TABLE - 6.11
RESPONSES OF THE SCHEDULED CASTE RESPONDENTS TO THE QUESTION, "WHAT DO YOU THINK THE MEASURES THAT CAN REDUCE THE SOCIAL DISTANCE BETWEEN THE SCHEDULED CASTES AND UPPER CASTES?"

Responses	*Sub-caste* *Mala*	*Madiga*	*Total*
Education	62 (47.7)	41 (21.6)	103 (32.2)
Economic development	5 (3.8)	8 (4.2)	13 (4.1)
Better employment	17 (13.1)	64 (33.7)	81 (25.3)
Steps by Government and political parties	30 (23.1)	17 (8.9)	47 (14.7)
Personal cleanliness	5 (3.9)	9 (4.7)	14 (4.4)
Standing united against upper castes discrimination	9 (6.9)	4 (2.1)	13 (4.1)
Change of food habits	6 (4.6)	3 (1.6)	9 (2.8)
Change of behaviour pattern	6 (4.6)	1 (0.5)	7 (2.2)
Other	7 (5.4)	5 (2.6)	12 (3.8)
Irrelevant	2 (1.5)	2 (1.1)	4 (1.3)
No Answer	57 (43.9)	81 (42.6)	138 (43.1)

TABLE - 6.12
RESPONSES OF THE RESPONDENTS ABOUT THEIR AWARENESS TO THE DIFFERENT LAWS MEANT FOR THEM

Particulars	*Sub-caste* *Mala*		*Madiga*		*Total*	
	Yes	*No*	*Yes*	*No*	*Yes*	*No*
The Untouchability (Offences) Act,1955 (or) Protection of Civil Rights Act, 1955	98 (75.38)	32 (24.62)	152 (80.00)	38 (20.00)	250 (78.13)	70 (21.87)
The Scheduled Castes and Scheduled Tribes (Prevention of Atrocities) Act, 1989	38 (29.23)	92 (70.77)	54 (28.42)	136 (71.58)	92 (28.75)	228 (71.25)

The above discussion reveals that there is perceptible change in the social status of the Scheduled Castes under study compared to that in the past. The changes are observed in the aspects of ecological segregation, use of civic amenities, social interaction and in their attitudes. The study reveals that the Scheduled Castes of Gooty are no longer discriminated in the form of ecological segregation, use of civic amenities and social interaction situation like interdining and common gathering etc. Such changes are largely due to the Scheduled Castes entry into the caste free and secular occupations, occupations of other castes by and large the occupations of the other lower castes slightly higher than the Scheduled Castes and practice of better and clean social practices and political participation. Recognising their community strength as a political pressure group, the Scheduled Castes are trying to ward off discrimination. Further this has been helped by the literacy attainments, however minimal they are.

On the other hand the Scheduled Castes who continued to be involved in poorly paid menial defiling and service occupations, suffer with social inferiority and generally keep out themselves in the social interaction. Their own sub caste members keep such members at a distance too. Further it may be pointed here that in most instances the Scheduled Castes are self reliant in terms of housing colonies, civic amenities and as such they have fewer occasions, either to compete or share with other section of population. These trends are evident from the following findings.

Conclusions

From the foregoing analysis on the social status of the Scheduled Castes in can be concluded:

1. that a majority of the Scheduled Castes are living in separate colonies of their own and as such a majority of them have their castes only as their immediate neighbours;
2. that even though a majority of the Scheduled Castes are living in their own colonies, no ecological segregation is enforced on them. A significant number of Scheduled Castes are living in the residential areas where the upper castes Hindus live;

3. that the absence of enforcing of ecological segregation is further evident from the opinions of the positive responses of respondents, who have said that they are free to construct houses outside their locality, and that too in the localities where forwards castes live;
4. that the Scheduled Castes are free to use all the civic amenities and whoever wishes to make use of these amenities are making use of them;
5. that hitherto there was no commensal relationship between the two major sub castes of Scheduled Castes namely the Malas and the Madigas, but now it is not the case;
6. that the majority of the Scheduled castes have commensal relationship with the upper caste Hindus, however, the majority of them have commensal relations with the backward castes only;
7. that at the same time a significant number of the Scheduled Castes respondents have commensal relation with forward castes also;
8. that the majority respondents who have commensal relation with the higher castes Hindus are getting equal treatment on par with the others, on the occasions of interdining, with a few exceptions. However if they are dining with the backward castes the number of respondents who have reported of getting equal treatment is more in number;
9. that the discrimination of Scheduled Castes is on the wane and in certain cases it is almost absent. Discrimination is meted out on Scheduled Castes to some extent at the marriages and ceremonies of the higher caste Hindus. Still the servicing castes to some extent refuse to render service to some of the Scheduled Castes who are economically and otherwise poor. Other places where discrimination to some extent is noticed is the work place and that too if the respondent is completely dependent on the employer;
10. that there are no religious restrictions imposed on the Scheduled Castes. Almost all of them visit all the

temples in the town and participate in common village festivals;

11. that the practice of using the caste name along with the name is on the wane and about 17 per cent of the respondents only are using the caste name along with their names;
12. that as much as 83 per cent of the Scheduled Casts feel that they are not being discriminated by higher caste Hindus in general;
13. that considerable number of the Scheduled Castes feel unclean occupation, food habits and fear of pollution are the main reasons, for upper castes to keep them at a distance;
14. that the birth in the very caste is another significant reason given by the Scheduled Castes for the upper castes to keep them at distance;
15. that the Scheduled Castes feel better education and better employment are the important remedies to reduce the social distance between them and the upper castes;
16. that the majority of the respondents are aware of the Protection of Civil Rights Act, 1955 and at the same time an almost equal majority of the respondents do not know about the existence of The Scheduled Castes and Scheduled Tribes (Prevention of Atrocities)Act, 1989.

Seven

Empowerment of the Scheduled Castes

The concept of empowerment

The mid-1980s saw the term empowerment becoming popular and widely used in the field of development. In grass root programmes and policy debates alike, empowerment has virtually replaced terms such as welfare, upliftment, community participation, and poverty alleviation to describe the goal of development and intervention. Empowerment has become the key solution to many social, economic, political, educational and environmental problems.

Empowerment means the process by which power is gained, developed, seized, facilitated or given (Webster's Dictionary). An individual or group moves from a condition of relative powerlessness to relative power through the empowerment process.

Empowerment may be broadly defined as control over material assets, intellectual resources and ideology (Batliwala 1995). The process of challenging existing power relations and gaining greater control over the sources of power may be termed as empowerment. Empowerment therefore is a process aimed at changing the nature and direction of systemic forces which marginalise the disadvantaged sections in a given context. (Sharma, 1991) Empowerment is the process of increasing the capacity of individuals or groups to make choices and to transform those choices into desired actions and outcomes. Central to this process are actions that both build individual and collective assets, and improve the efficiency and fairness of the organizational and institutional context which govern the use of these assets (World Bank).

Empowerment is a process and is not, therefore, something that can be given to the people. The process of empowerment is both individual and collective, since it is through involvement in groups that people most often begin to develop their awareness and the ability to organise to take active part to bring about change. It is both a process and the result of the process. It is transformation of the structures or institutions that reinforces and perpetuates discrimination. Empowered people have freedom of choice and action. This in turn enables them to better influence the course of their lives and the decisions which affect them.

Perceptions of being empowered vary across time, culture and domains of a person's life: in India, a low caste woman currently feels empowered when she is given a fair hearing in a public meeting, which is comprised of men and women from different social and economic groups; in Brazil, in Porto Allegre, citizens – both men and women — feel empowered if they are able to engage in decisions on budget allocations; in Ethiopia, citizens and civil society groups report feeling empowered by consultations undertaken during the preparation of the poverty reduction support program; in the USA, immigrant workers feel empowered through unionization which has allowed them to negotiate working conditions with employers; and in the UK, a battered woman feels empowered when she is freed from the threat of violence and becomes able to make decisions about her own life. In essence empowerment speaks to self-determined change. It implies bringing together the supply and demand sides of development – changing the environment within which poor people live and helping them build and capitalize on their own attributes. Empowerment is a crosscutting issue. From education and health care to governance and economic policy, activities, which seek to empower poor people, are expected to increase development opportunities, enhance development outcomes and improve people's quality of life. (World Bank)

The levels of empowerment according to Longwe (1990) are *welfare, access, conscientisation, participation* and *control*. The first level *Welfare* address only the basic needs without recognizing or attempting to solve the underlying structural causes, which necessitate provision of welfare services. At this point the disadvantaged sections are merely passive beneficiaries of welfare benefits. In the Second level of *Access* it is essential for the disadvantaged sections to make meaningful progress. This involves equality of access to resources. The path of empowerment is initiated when the disadvantaged recognise their lack of access to resources as a barrier to their overall growth and take action to address this. In the third level of empowerment, the *conscientisation*, the disadvantaged measure the inequalities and realise that their problems stem from inherent structural and institutional discrimination. They must also recognize the role they can often play in reinforcing the system that restricts their growth. In the level of *participation* the disadvantaged participate in equal terms with others in the society. To reach this level mobilization is necessary. By organising themselves and working collectively, the disadvantaged will be empowered and aim for increased representation which will lead to increased empowerment and ultimately greater control. In the last level of empowerment of *Control* the balance of power between different sections is equal and none of the sections will have dominance over the others.

Empowerment of the disadvantaged in India

India as a welfare State is committed to the welfare and development of its people in general and of vulnerable sections in particular. The Preamble, Directive Principles of State Policy, Fundamental Rights and specific sections in the Constitution of India, stand testimony to the commitment of the State to its people. The Government has special concern and commitment for the well being of the Socially Disadvantaged Groups viz., the Scheduled Castes (SCs), the Scheduled Tribes (STs), the Other Backward Classes (OBCs) and the Minorities. These Groups have passed through the processes of welfare and development during the past half a century.

Welfare programmes in the beginning were directed to provide a few basic curative and rehabilitative services. Over the years, a developmental orientation in contrast to curative and custodial approach was given to welfare programmes. At present these are oriented towards providing social justice and empowerment to the disadvantaged and marginalized sections of the society. Hence, it is no more welfare but empowerment of the disadvantaged sections.

The responsibility for empowerment of the targeted groups in India is being shared between Central and State governments. The Central government is responsible for formulating the related policies and programmes besides coordinating and promoting implementation of different schemes by the States.

The Scheduled Castes undoubtedly have been the most backward among the disadvantaged sections of the Indian population. They constitute a significant size and according to the 1991 Census, the Scheduled Castes account for 138.22 million, representing 16.48 per cent of the country's total population. Of these, 81 per cent live in rural areas. There has been an increase in the percentage of SC population to the total population from 15.28 in 1981 to 16.48 in 1991, with a decadal growth rate of 3.20 per cent during 1981-91. They are dispersed all over the country, except in one State and two UTs viz., Nagaland, Andaman and Nicobar Islands and Lakshadweep. Uttar Pradesh alone, being the largest State, accounts for 21.05 per cent of the total SC population. Nearly 84 per cent of the country's total SC population lives in 10 States viz., Andhra Pradesh (7.66%), Bihar (9.09%), Karnataka (5.33%), Kerala (2.09%), Madhya Pradesh (6.96%), Maharashtra (6.34%), Rajasthan (5.50%), Tamil Nadu (7.75%), Uttar Pradesh (21.18%) and West Bengal (11.63%). In a few States, the Scheduled Castes constitute more than 20 per cent of the total of their respective population. These include - Punjab (28.31%), Himachal Pradesh (25.34%), West Bengal (23.62%) and Uttar Pradesh (21.05%).

The Scheduled Castes account for 179.7 million, representing 17.5 per cent of the population in 2001 (projected on the basis of the trend of their decadal growth rates, in the absence of the data of 2001 Census).

Recognising the relative backwardness of these weaker sections of the society, the Constitution of India guarantees equality before the law (Article 14) and enjoins the State to make special provisions for the advancement of any socially and educationally backward classes or for Scheduled Castes (Article 15(4)). It also empowers the State to make provisions for reservation in appointments or posts in favour of any backward class of citizens (Article (16(4)). The Constitution of India also states categorically that untouchability is abolished and its practice in any form is forbidden (Article 17). Further, it enjoins the State to promote, with special care, the educational and economic interests of the weaker sections of the people and, in particular, of Scheduled Castes and promises to protect them from social injustice and all forms of exploitation (Article 46). Reservation of seats for Scheduled Castes in the democratic institutions (Article 330) and in services (Article 335) is another measure of positive discrimination in favour of these Groups. It empowers the State to appoint a Commission to investigate into the conditions of socially and educationally backward classes (Article 340) and to specify the Castes to be deemed as Scheduled Castes (Article 341).

Five Year plans vis-à-vis empowerment of the Scheduled Castes:

The Constitutional commitments made in favour of the Socially Disadvantaged Groups prompted the policy makers and the planners to accord high priority for the welfare and development of these groups right from the beginning of the country's developmental planning.

The developmental planning launched in 1951 through the First Plan (1951-56) envisaged that the programmes under various sectors of development would benefit all sections of the population including Scheduled Castes, OBCs and Minorities. But, unfortunately, it never happened so. Therefore, special programmes under the Backward Classes Sector were formulated, keeping in view the special requirements of Scheduled Castes. The Second Plan (1956-61) promised to ensure that the benefits of economic development accrue more and more to the relatively less privileged classes of society in order to reduce inequalities. The Third Plan (1961-66) advocated greater 'equality of opportunity' and a reduction in disparities in income and wealth and the even distribution of economic power. The Fourth and Fifth Plans (1969-78) envisaged the 'basic goal as rapid increase in the standard of living of the people through measures which also promote equality and social justice'. One of the important features of the subsequent Annual Plan (1979-80) was the launching of the special mechanism of Special Component Plan (SCP) for Scheduled Castes to ensure that these groups receive their due share of funds/benefits from the other developmental sectors.

The Sixth Plan (1980-85) marked a shift in the approach to the development of Scheduled Castes. Special emphasis was laid on the implementation of the newly launched SCP for Scheduled Castes facilitating easy convergence and pooling of resources from all the other developmental sectors in proportion to the population of Scheduled Castes and monitoring of various developmental programmes for the benefit of Scheduled Castes. In the Seventh Plan (1985-90), SCP for Scheduled Castes was strengthened, while the other schemes for the welfare and development of Scheduled Castes continued. There was a substantial increase in the flow of funds for the development of Scheduled Castes under SCP from State Plans, Central Plans, Special Central Assistance (SCA) and Institutional Finance resulting in the expansion of infrastructural facilities and enlargement of their coverage. Priority in the Seventh Plan was given to the educational development of Scheduled Castes. Another important achievement of this Plan was the setting up of a National Scheduled Castes and Scheduled Tribes Finance and Development Corporation (NSFDC) in 1989 to extend loans-cum-subsidies and thus encourage these Groups to become gainfully engaged in various income-generation activities.

The major objective of the Eighth Plan (1992-97) was to intensify the efforts and to bridge the gap between the development of Scheduled Castes, OBCs and Minorities and other sections of the society, so that by the turn of the century these disadvantaged sections of the population could be brought on par with the rest of the society. It was envisaged that all forms of oppression of Scheduled Castes, suppression of their rights, untouchability, non-payment of minimum wages etc., would be eliminated, so as to enable them to avail of the benefits of all developmental efforts. Although the efforts have paid dividends with regard to improvement of socio-economic status of these groups, the benefits were, however, not evenly distributed among all communities. As such, a lot remains to be done to achieve the goal of bringing these groups on par with the rest of the society. For the economic development of Scheduled Castes, OBCs and Minorities, the following three National level Apex bodies were set up to act as catalytic agents in developing schemes for employment generation and financing pilot projects viz. i) The National Backward Classes

Finance and Development Corporation (1992); ii) The National Minorities Development and Finance Corporation (1994-95); and iii) National Safai Karamchari Finance and Development Corporation (1996-97).

The Ninth Plan (1997-2002)(discussed in detail later in this topic) was committed to empower the Socially Disadvantaged Groups as agents of socio-economic change and development through - creating an enabling environment conducive for Scheduled Castes, OBCs and Minorities to exercise their rights freely, enjoy their privileges and be able to lead a life with confidence and dignity on par with the rest of the society; ensuring removal of disparities; eliminating exploitation and suppression and providing protection to the disadvantaged groups; ensuring developmental benefits to 'reach the un-reached' through equitable distribution and social justice; ensuring participation of these Groups in the process of planning not merely as beneficiaries but also as participants in planning programmes and their implementation; accelerating the on-going process of improving socio-economic status through the effective implementation of various policies and programmes to bring them on par with the rest of the society; and ensuring a certain percentage of funds/ benefits from all the relevant programmes to flow to women belonging to these groups who are the most affected. As most of the Ministries/Departments implement programmes common for both Scheduled Castes and Scheduled Tribes (STs), including earmarking of a percentage of funds/ benefits under SCP for Scheduled Castes and Tribal Sub-Plan (TSP) for STs.

The Status of Scheduled Castes through Five year plans:

As a result of various affirmative actions, pro-active policies and programmatic interventions put into action by the government the status of Scheduled Castes has registered quantifiable improvement during the last five developmental decades. The following pages demonstrate the measures taken for empowerment of the Scheduled Castes through plans and the results these measures have yielded in the fields of education, economy, social status, polity and the like, for the development of the Scheduled Castes through Five-year plans. In the discussion, however, the emphasis is on recently completed Ninth Plan and the ongoing Tenth Plan.

Scheduled Caste population as a percentage of total population has increased from 14.6 in 1971 to 17.5 in 2001. Though the decadal growth rate for Scheduled Castes, estimated to be 30 per cent, was more than the growth rate of 21.3 per cent of the total population in 2001, yet a decline was noticed between 1991 and 2001.

The sex ratio of Scheduled Castes as it stood in 1991 was not only adverse, but also showed a declining trend as it fell from 935 in 1971 to 922 in 1991. In fact, the sex ratio of Scheduled Castes, which held a better status than that of the total population in 1971, suddenly took a turn to worse in 1981 and continued with the same tempo. This, as a gender concern, needs to be looked into. Higher mortality amongst females and their limited access to health and family welfare services could be attributed to the causes of this adverse sex ratio. However, this is not an exception to Scheduled Castes alone, but a common feature in respect of general population also.

Empowerment of Scheduled Castes through Education

Education, being the most important vehicle for empowering weaker sections of the society, sincere efforts have been made to improve the educational status of Scheduled Castes on priority basis.

LITERACY RATES OF SCHEDULED CASTES

Category	*1971*	*1981*	*1991*	*Percentage increase of 1991 over 1971*
General Population (including SC/ST)	29.45	36.23	52.21	77.28
Scheduled Castes	14.67	21.38	37.41	155.01
Gap Between SCs and General Population	14.78	14.85	14.80	0.14

* Excludes 0-6 age group. Source: Educational Development of SCs and STs, Department of Education, 1995.

Between 1971 and 1991, the literacy rate of Scheduled Castes increased by 2.6 times, while that of total population increased by 1.8 times. However, the gap between the literacy rates of Scheduled Castes and of the total population continued during the two decades between 1971 and 1991 almost at the same level of 14 per cent and above, but with slight variations. Although, there has been a visible increase in the literacy rates, the gap between the literacy rates of Scheduled Castes and those of the general population still persists.

Similarly, 'Female Literacy', which is an important indicator in the field of education, has also shown a progressive trend in respect of Scheduled Castes.

FEMALE LITERACY RATES OF SCHEDULED CASTES AND GENERAL POPULATION

Category	*1971*	*1981*	*1991**
Female Literacy Rates (All Communities including SC/ST)	21.97	29.85	39.29
Scheduled Castes	6.44	10.93	23.76
Gap Between Female literacy rate of SCs and of All Communities	15.53	18.92	15.53

* Excludes 0-6 age group. Source: Educational Development of SCs and STs, Department of Education, 1995.

The data reveals that the female literacy rates in respect of Scheduled Castes have increased substantially from 6.44 per cent in 1971 to 23.76 percent in 1991. Besides, the most encouraging sign was the increase in the female literacy rate amongst Scheduled Castes and the reducing gap between the female literacy rates of Scheduled Castes and of the general population during 1981 to 1991. However, the female literacy rates of these communities as a whole continued to be very low requiring focused attention.

The enrolment ratios of Scheduled Caste girls and boys have continued to show a progressive trend along with the rest of the population.

GROSS ENROLMENT RATIOS OF SCHEDULED CASTES AND GENERAL POPULATION

Levels/ Years	*Gen. Population*			*Scheduled Castes*		
	Boys	*Girls*	*Total*	*Boys*	*Girls*	*Total*
1980-81						
I-V (6-11 Years)	95.8	64.1	80.5	105.4	57.8	82.2
VI-VIII (11-14 Years)	54.3	28.6	41.9	41.4	16.2	29.1
1990-91						
I-V (6-11 Years)	114.0	85.5	100.1	122.7	80.6	102.2
VI-VIII (11-14 Years)	76.6	47.0	62.1	61.4	33.3	47.7
1995-96						
I-V (6-11 Years)	114.5	93.3	104.3	127.6	95.1	111.9
VI-VIII (11-14 Years)	79.5	54.9	67.6	74.9	46.8	61.3
Pace of Progress						
I-V (Primary Level)	18.7	29.2	23.8	22.2	37.3	29.7
VI-VIII (Middle Level)	25.2	26.3	25.7	33.5	30.6	32.2

Source: Selected Education Statistics. 1995-96.

The overall progress made by Scheduled Castes in terms of enrolment ratios at primary and middle levels between 1980-81 and 1995-96 has been impressive, as they could prove much better than the general population. The dropout rate, which is a crucial indicator in the field of education, also reveals that there has been a steady decline in the dropout rates of Scheduled Castes.

The figures in 1998-99 are still very high - 44.27 in classes I to V; 63.58 in classes I to VIII; and 76.63 in classes I to X. This indicates clearly that the problem gets worse at the higher levels of schooling. However, an encouraging sign is the reduction in the gap between the dropout rates of the total population and Scheduled Castes at all levels between 1990-91 and 1998-99.

DROPOUT RATES AMONGST SCHEDULED CASTES AT VARIOUS STAGES OF EDUCATION

Category	*(Classes I-V)*		*(Classes I-VIII)*		*(Classes I-X)*	
	1980-81	*1989-90*	*1980-81*	*1989-90*	*1980-81*	*1989-90*
General	58.70	48.08	72.70	63.40	82.46	71.34
SC	60.16	49.03	76.84	72.09	86.91	80.58

Source: Educational Development of SCs and STs (1995) and Unpublished Data of the Department of Education.

Note: 1. Since the latest data on the dropout rates of SCs and STs is available only for 1990-91, data for General Population was also used for the same year for effective comparison.

2. Figures for 1990-91 in respect of SCs and STs are not available for primary level.

The problem of dropouts, as the above data reveal, happens to be a common feature amongst Scheduled Castes and other general category also.

The improvement in terms of literacy rate, female literacy, gross enrolment and decline in the drop out rates can be attributed to the several policies, programmes and schemes that work for the educational development of Scheduled Castes. The importance of education in the empowerment of the Scheduled Castes is well recognised by the policy makers. Scheduled Castes education is a priority and different schemes meant for the Scheduled Castes in the ensuing discussion make that very clear.

Programmes for the Improvement of Education

Pre-Matric Scholarships for the Children of those engaged in unclean Occupations

Begun in 1977-78, this scheme is for education development of those who are engaged in the so-called unclean occupations, viz., scavenging of dry latrines, tanning, flaying and sweeping with traditional links with scavenging. The Scheme aims to motivate the children of scavengers, sweepers, flayers and tanners to pursue education and also to reduce school dropout rates amongst them. The scheme as modified with effect from 1 November 1991 provides scholarship of Rs 25 per month in classes

I to V, Rs 40 per month in classes VI to VIII and Rs 50 per month in classes IX to X, in respect of day-scholars. For hostellers, a scholarship of Rs 200 per month in classes III to VIII and Rs 250 per month in classes IX to X is provided. An ad-hoc grant of Rs.500 per annum is also provided to day-scholars as well as hostellers. The scheme was further modified with effect from 25 February 1994. The income ceiling has been removed. There is no restriction as to the number of children of same parents who would be eligible for scholarship up to class VIII, subject, however, to the condition that if a third or subsequent child is born after 1 April 1993, a total of only two children in the family would be eligible for scholarship. In respect of classes IX and X only two children of the same parents would be eligible for scholarship. The additional provisions for students amongst target groups with disabilities have also been introduced with effect from 1 April 1998, keeping in view the provisions of the persons with disabilities. During 1998-99, Central assistance of Rs 3.95 crore was released up to December 1998 benefiting 4.09 lakh (anticipated) students. An amount of Rs. 7.88 crores was released to the States/UTs during the year 1999-2000 for an anticipated coverage of 4.38 lakhs students. Against the total Ninth Plan outlay of Rs. 30 crore, for the scheme, the expenditure was Rs. 36.25 crore. The scheme covered 19.2 lakh beneficiaries, 2.3 lakh more than the target of 16.9 lakh beneficiaries. An evaluation report on the performance of the scheme has revealed that the programme is instrumental in encouraging many people who are living below the poverty line to send their children to the schools.

Who can apply for the award?

The children of scavengers of dry latrines, tanners, flayers and sweepers who have traditional link with scavenging and pursuing recognised pre matriculation courses in India in recognised institutions, can apply for scholarship. There is no restriction as to the number of children of the same parents who would be eligible for award of scholarship upto class VIII subject, however, to the condition that if a third or subsequent child were born after 1.4.1993 a total of any two children in the family would be eligible for such scholarship awards. In respect of classes IX &

X, only two children of the same parents would be eligible for the award of scholarship. There is no income ceiling under the Scheme.

All eligible students are coverable under the Scheme.

Where, when and how to apply?

Eligible students are required to apply to the head of the educational institution where one is enrolled. A student has to apply for scholarship immediately after he/she has obtained admission in the educational institution.

A student should apply for scholarship in the proforma prescribed by the concerned State Govt./UT Administration for this purpose. The prescribed application forms, which vary from State to State, are available with the concerned Sanctioning and Disbursement Authorities/Educational Institutions.

Quantum of assistance available

The value of scholarship under the Scheme is as under:

Value of Scholarship and Adhoc grant

I Hostlers: The students as hostlers will be covered from class III to X. The rates of scholarships are as under:—

Class III to VIII Rs.200/- per month for 10 months
Class IX to X Rs.250/- per month for 10 months

II Day scholars: The students as day scholars will be covered from Class I to Class X. The rates of scholarships are as under:

Class I to V Rs. 25/-per month for 10 months
Class VI to VIII Rs. 40/-per month for 10 months
Class IX to X Rs. 50/- per month for 10 months

III Ad-hoc grant: An adhoc grant of Rs. 500/- per student per annum to all students i.e. hostlers as well as day scholars.

IV. Additional provisions for students amongst target groups with disabilities.

(a) Reader Allowance of Rs.100 per month for blind students in classes IX and X.

(b) Transport allowance of Rs.50 per month for the disabled students not residing in the hostel located within the premises of educational institution. The disability as per the Persons with Disabilities (Equal Opportunities), Protection of Rights and Full Participation Act, 1955 is defined as blindness, low-vision, leprosy-cured, hearing impairment, locomotor disability, mental retardation and mental illness.

(c) Special pay of Rs.100 per month be admissible to any employee of the hostel willing to extend help to a severely orthopaedically handicapped student residing in a hostel managed by the educational institution or by the State Government/Union Territory Administration who may need the assistance of a helper.

(d) Escort allowance of Rs.50 per month for severely handicapped day scholar students with lower extremity disability.

(e) Allowance of Rs.100 per month towards extra coaching to mentally retarded and mentally ill students in classes IX and X.

The provisions proposed in (b) to (d) above also apply to leprosy-cured students.

Note 1: The students amongst target groups with disabilities covered under this scheme can, however, also get such additional benefits from other schemes, which are not covered in the above provision.

Note 2: The disability as defined under the said Act has to be certified by competent medical authority of the State Government/Union Territory Administration.

Construction of Hostel Buildings for SC Boys and Girls

The objective of the Scheme is to provide hostel facilities to SC Boys & Girls studying in middle schools, higher secondary schools, colleges and Universities. The Scheme provides for release of Central Assistance to State Governments on 50:50 basis, for construction of Hostels for Boys and Girls belonging to Scheduled Castes. The Union Territory Administrations receive 100% Central Assistance. The maintenance of hostels, boarding & lodging of students, however, rests with the respective States/UTs. The Non-Governmental Organisations also get assistance on the basis of 45:45:10 through their States/UTs, for extension of their existing hostels. The Centrally Controlled Universities can receive financial assistance upto 90% under the Scheme and the remaining 10% is required to be contributed by them. Likewise, the other universities can also receive central assistance upto 45% and the remaining amount has to be provided by their respective States (45%) and themselves (10%).

The scheme of 'Hostels for SC Boys and Girls' launched in 1961-62, being one of the major support services to improve enrolment, aims at reducing the present high drop-out rates and increasing retention amongst SC/ST students by providing them hostel facilities in the middle, secondary and higher secondary schools, colleges and universities. The central assistance to the scheme has been declining, as the State Governments are not able to provide the required matching share under this scheme. Evaluation of the scheme carried out by the Ministry reveals that the performance of some states in providing matching grants, maintenance of services and management of hostels is not encouraging. Also, the basic amenities therein are substandard due to poor maintenance of buildings. As against the total Ninth Plan outlay of Rs. 97.05 crore for the scheme, the expenditure was Rs. 118.10 crore for the construction of 354 girls' hostels and 388 boys' hostels benefiting 25,196 SC girls and 17,244 SC boys.

Special Educational Development Programme for Scheduled Castes Girls belonging to Low Literacy Levels

To provide a package of educational inputs through residential schools for Scheduled Castes girls in areas of very low literacy and where traditions and environment are not conducive to learning amongst SC girls. This Scheme is implemented by the Zilla Parishads of the concerned Districts. The scheme of 'Special Educational Development Programmes for SC Girls belonging to Low Literacy Districts', introduced in 1996-97, aims to establish special residential schools for SC Girls who are first generation learners from low literacy pockets where the traditions and environment are not conducive to learning. The scheme covers 48 districts spread over Bihar, Madhya Pradesh, Rajasthan and Uttar Pradesh where the literacy amongst SC girls was less than 2 per cent, as per 1981 Census. Central assistance is given to Zilla Parishads to run the schools by themselves or through credible Non-Government

Organisations (NGOs). Of the Ninth Plan allocation of Rs. 7.70 crore, the expenditure was only Rs. 1.61 crore, and against a target of 140 schools, only 104 schools could be funded.

Book Bank Scheme

The objective of the Scheme is to provide books to deserving SC and ST students pursuing Medical, Engineering, Agriculture, Veterinary, Polytechnics, Law, Chartered Accountancy, MBA and Biosciences courses. The Scheme provides for sharing of textbooks by two students in respect of graduate level courses and separate set of books is provided to individual students at Post-Graduate level and for those pursuing Chartered Accountancy. A set of books costs between Rs.2,400/- to Rs.7,500/-, depending upon the courses. The provision of such sets of books also includes Braille books, talking books/cassettes for visually handicapped students. Towards storage of these books, grant is also provided for almirahs. Respective States/UT's implements the Scheme and the expenditure on the Scheme is co-shared on 50:50 basis between the Centre and the State Governments. The U.T. Administration receives 100% Central assistance. Against the total Ninth Plan outlay of Rs. 12 crore for the scheme, the expenditure was Rs. 10.61 crore for benefiting about 1.15 lakh SC/ST students.

Upgradation of Merit of SC/ST Students

The objective of the Scheme is to upgrade the merit of SC & ST students by providing them remedial and special coaching in classes IX to XII. While the remedial coaching aims at removing deficiencies in various subjects, the special coaching is provided with a view to prepare the students for competitive examinations for seeking entry into professional courses like engineering and medical disciplines. The Scheme provides for 100% central assistance to the States/UT's. A package grant of Rs.15,000/- per student per year is provided and the States/UT's are not required to bear any financial burden. The students with disabilities amongst SCs and STs, receive specified special allowances like readers allowance, transport allowance, escorts allowance etc.

The Ninth Plan allocation of Rs. 5.26 crore was later raised to Rs. 42.50 crore which was earmarked for 2001-02 with a view to assisting 25,000 SC/ST students from Classes VI to Degree/Diploma-level courses. But, unfortunately, the expenditure was Rs. 4.72 crore only for benefiting 3,755 SC students. Despite the Centre's willingness to bear the entire cost, most of the States/UTs failed to respond favourably for implementing the scheme. Therefore, the scheme had very limited impact in achieving its objective.

Coaching and Allied Schemes

The Coaching and Allied Scheme was started in the Fourth Five Year Plan for imparting training to Scheduled Castes/Scheduled Tribes in respect of various competitive examinations held by recruiting bodies such as Union Public Service Commission, State public service commissions, public-sector undertakings, banking service recruitment boards and similar agencies. Grant is given to the Pre-Examination Training Centres (PETCs) which are run either by the State/UT governments or universities or private institutes. Financial assistance is provided to State governments on a matching basis 50:50 over and above their committed liabilities. The UT administrations, universities and private institutes are given cent-percent grants. Some of the coaching centres have made considerable contribution enabling SC/ST candidates to get into IAS and allied services, medical, engineering and banking services. The Scheme provides for stipends upto Rs.500/- per month to the outstation students and Rs.150.00/Rs.85.00 per month for local students for taking coaching at the pre-examination training centres. Such SC and ST candidates, whose own income or of the parents does not exceed Rs.44, 500/- p.a, are eligible for assistance under the scheme.

Coaching and Allied Scheme for SC/ST students which aims to improve the knowledge and aptitude of SC/ST students by providing special coaching to them through Pre-Examination Training Centres (PETCs), was recast during the Ninth Plan by bringing revision in the unit-cost. Universities and private institutions receive 100 per cent Central assistance on a contractual basis, while State owned PETCs receive the Central assistance to the extent of 50 per cent of the contractual amount. The scheme, which was common for both SC and ST students till the year 2000-01, is now exclusively meant for SC students, after a separate

Ministry of Tribal Affairs was set up in 1999. Of the Ninth Plan outlay of Rs. 16.71 crore for the scheme, the expenditure was Rs. 11.09 crore for coaching and training for 48,500 SC/ST students.

The scheme of Pre-Examination Coaching for Weaker Sections, based on economic criteria, is extended to enable them to compete on equal terms with other candidates in competitive examinations for various jobs and it is being implemented through the Institutions of repute. Against a provision of Rs. 12 crore for the Ninth Plan, Rs. 11.29 crore was spent for funding 417 Institutions to train 30,310 students.

Post-Matric Scholarship for SC/ST Students

The nation-wide popular scheme of 'Post-Matric Scholarships (PMS) for SC Students', the largest educational scholarship scheme of its kind in the country, continued to promote higher education amongst Scheduled Castes. The scheme extends scholarships to all eligible SC students who pursue post matriculation courses in recognised institutions. The revision of the scheme in 1997-98 expanded its scope for enhancing the income ceiling of parents of the beneficiaries and for extending some additional benefits to persons with disabilities amongst Scheduled Castes. Scholarships are given to all the eligible SC students based on a Means Test which includes provision of maintenance allowance, reimbursement of compulsory non-refundable fees, thesis typing/printing charges, study tour charges, book allowance for students pursuing correspondence courses etc. An expenditure of Rs. 457.29 crore was incurred benefiting around 21 lakh SC students studying at the Post-Matric and above levels, including the professional/technical courses. An evaluation study on the scheme conducted by the Ministry reveals that SC students in some states are facing hardships due to non-payment of scholarships in time, as the State Governments could not meet the expenditure on committed liability under the scheme.

The scheme of Post-Matric Scholarship to SC/ST was introduced in 1994-95 with the objective of providing financial assistance to students studying at post-matriculation stages in different schools and colleges so as to enable them to complete their education. Beginning with mere 114 students in 1994-95, the scheme is presently covering nearly 21 lakh students. The scheme meets full non-refundable compulsory fees charged by the institution, prescribed allowances towards maintenance for hostellers and day scholars essential books for students pursuing correspondence course, study tour charges, thesis typing/printing charges and additional allowances for SC and ST students with disabilities. Parents/ guardians' income should not exceed Rs.60,965/- per annum, all children of same parents/guardians are eligible. An amount of Rs. 161 crores was released to the States/UTs during the year 1999-2000 for an anticipated coverage of 23 lakh students.

The Government has increased the maintenance allowance rates with effect from 1 April 1998. The income ceilings have also been revised from Rs 33,400 and Rs 44,500 per annum to Rs 38,220 and Rs 50,920 per annum. The revised ceilings account for price index for industrial workers up to October 1997. Now all children of the same parents/guardians are eligible to get the benefit of the scheme, if otherwise eligible. During 1998-99, Central assistance of Rs 99.86 crore was released up to December 1998.

Eligibility to apply for the award

All Scheduled Caste and Scheduled Tribe students pursuing recognised post matriculation courses in India in recognised institutions and satisfying the means test under the scheme can apply for scholarship. The existing means test applicable w.e.f. 1.4.2000 is as under:

Income ceiling limit of parents/ Guardians per annum	*Scholarship eligibility towards maintenance Allowance and fees*
Rs. 45,760/-	Full maintenance allowance and full fees
Rs. 60,965/	(i) Full maintenance allowance and full fees for courses in Group 'A' (ii) half maintenance allowance and full fees for courses in Groups 'B,C,D &E'

All eligible students are coverable under the Scheme.

Eligible students are required to apply to the respective sanctioning and disbursement authority in their respective States/Union Territories i.e. where a candidate is permanently settled. Different States/ Union Territories have designated different authorities viz., Heads of the educational institutions/ District Social Welfare Officers/Directorate of Social Welfare/ District Education Officers etc. for this purpose.

When and how to apply?

A student has to apply for scholarship immediately after he/she has obtained admission in the educational institution.

A student should apply for scholarship in the proforma prescribed by the concerned State Govt./UT Administration for this purpose. The prescribed application forms, which vary from State to State, are available with the concerned Sanctioning and Disbursement Authorities/Educational Institutions. The complete application form as duly forwarded by the head of concerned educational institution should be sent to the concerned sanctioning and disbursement authority within the stipulated time. Students studying out of their State/UT, should send their application to the Director of Social Welfare (or State/UT level sanctioning and disbursement authority) of their State to which they belong i.e. permanently settled.

Quantum of assistance available:

The value of scholarship under the Scheme is as under:

I. Value of Scholarship

The value of scholarship includes maintenance allowance, provision for students with disabilities, reimbursement of compulsory non-refundable fees, Study Tour Charges, Thesis Typing/ Printing Charges and book allowance for students pursuing correspondence courses, for complete duration of the course. The details are given below:

i) Maintenance allowance

Course of study	*Rate of maintenance*	*Allowance (Rs. Per month)*
Group A Medical/Engineering including Degree level courses in Indian Medicine, B.A.M.& S. and comparable courses in Ayurvedic, Unani/Tibia and Homeopathic System of Medicine. B.Sc. (Agriculture/ B.V.Sc./ B.F.Sc. (Fisheries). Higher Technical and all professional studies like Degree And Post-graduate courses in Agricultural and Veterinary Science.	425	190
Group B Diploma level courses in Indian Medicine and comparable Courses in Ayurvedic, Unani/Tibia and Homeopathic System of medicine. Diploma and comparable courses in Engineering, technology, architecture, medicine, diploma level courses in printing technology and courses for overseer draftsman, Surveyor. Commercial Pilot License, Diploma and higher courses in Hotel Management catering technology and applied Nutrition. Degree and post-graduate course in nursing and pharmacy. Wireless and television operators/sound recording and sound engineering motion picture, photography, film direction/ Acting/screenplay/writing. Degree/post-graduate diploma courses in business Management, chartered and Cost/Works Accountancy. Post-graduate courses in science subjects	290	190
Group C Certificate course in Engineering/Technology Architecture And Medicine. Diploma and Certificate courses in Agriculture, Pharmacy, Veterinary Science, Fisheries, Diary Development, Hygiene and Public Health, Sanitary Inspector's Course, Courses for Rural Services, Cooperation and Community		

Course of study	*Rate of mainte-nance*	*Allowance (Rs. Per month)*
Development, Sub-Officer's Course at the National Fire Service College, Nagpur, Library Science. Degree/Post-graduate Diploma and Post Graduate courses In Teachers Training, Library Science and Physical Education, Music Fine Arts and Law, Craft Instructor's Training Course, Certificate Course in Hotel Management/ Catering Technology and Applied Nutrition. Passenger Transport Management, Associate Degree in Pharmacy. Post-graduate courses in Arts and Commerce subjects.	290	190
Group D		
General courses upto Graduate level (2nd year and onwards)	230	150
Group E		
Class XI and XII in 10+2 system, Intermediate courses and first year of general courses upto graduate level		150

(ii) Additional Provision for SC and ST students with disability

(A) Reader Allowance for blind Scholars

Level of Course Reader Allowance (Rs. Per month)

Group A, B, C	150
Group D	125
Group E	100

(B) Provision of transport allowance upto Rs.100 per month for disabled students, if such a student does not reside in the hostel, which is within the premises of educational institution. The disability as per the Persons with Disabilities (Equal Opportunities, Protection of Rights and Full Participation) Act, 1995 is defined as blindness, low-vision, leprosy-cured, hearing impairment, locomotor disability, mental retardation and mental illness.

(C) Escort Allowance of Rs.100/- per month for severally handicapped day scholar students with low extremity disability.

(D) Special Pay of Rs.100/- per month be admissible to any employee of the hostel willing to extend help to a severely orthopaedically handicapped student residing in hostel of an educational institution, who may need the assistance of a helper.

(E) Allowance of Rs.150/- per month towards extra coaching to mentally retarded and mentally ill Students.

The provisions in (B) to (D) will also apply to such leprosy - cured students.

(iii) Fees

Scholars will be paid enrolment/registration, tuition, games, Union, Library, Magazine, Medical Examination and such other fees compulsorily payable by the scholar to the institution or University/Board. Refundable deposit like caution money, security deposit will, however, be excluded.

(iv) Study Tours

Study tour charges upto a maximum of Rs.500 per annum, limited to the actual expenditure incurred by the student on transportation charges etc. will be paid to the scholars studying professional and technical courses, provided that the head of the institution certifies that the study tour is essential for the scholar for completion of his/her course of study.

(v) Thesis Typing/Printing Charges

Thesis typing/printing charges upto a maximum of Rs.600 will be paid to research scholars on the recommendation of the Head of the Institution.

(vi) Correspondence courses including distance and continuing education

The students pursuing such courses are also eligible for an annual allowance of Rs.500/- for essential/prescribed books, as applicable w.e.f. 1.10.1995, besides reimbursement of course fees.

National Overseas Scholarships for Scheduled Castes

The Scheme provides financial assistance to meritorious selected students for pursuing higher studies abroad in specified fields of Masters level courses, Ph.D and Post Doctoral research programmes in Engineering, Technology and Science only.

Eligibility to apply for the award

Students belonging to Scheduled Castes, Denotified, Nomadic and Semi-Nomadic Tribes, Scheduled Caste converts to other religion, Landless Agricultural Labourers and Traditional Artisans who are below 35 years of age, having monthly income (self or that of parents/guardians) not exceeding Rs. 12,000/- and are desirous of pursuing any of the following courses at Masters/ Doctoral/Post Doctoral level in a foreign university/institution:—

1. Automation Robotics including Artificial Intelligence, Mechatronics and Manufacturing Technology 2. Laser Technology 3. Paper Technology 4. Naval Architecture/Offshore structures 5. Information Technology including Computer Engineering, Software, Software Quality Assurance, Networking/Connectivity Engineering, Communication System under Hazardous or Post-disaster conditions, Multi-media Communication 6. Low Temperature Thermal Dynamics 7. Optometry 8. Art Restoration Technology 9. Ceramic & Glass Technology 10. Dock and Harbour Engineering 11. Industrial Safety 12. Bio-technology/Genetic Engineering 13. Petroleum Technology 14. Aircraft/Space Engineering 15. Imaging System Technology 16. Graphic Engineering 17. Composite Materials Engineering including Decentralised Power Distribution (for solar heat) system, Energy Storage Engineering, Energy Conservation, Energy Efficient Habitat Engineering 18. Satellite/Remote Sensing 19. Packaging Engg./Technology 20. Nuclear Engineering.

I. Minimum Qualification

(a) For Post Doctoral: 1st class or 60% marks or equivalent grade in relevant Masters Degree, Ph.D and 5 years Teaching /Professional experience in the concerned field.

(b) For Ph.D.: 1st class or 60% marks or equivalent grade in relevant Masters' degree, and 2 years' Teaching/ Research/Professional experience/M.Phil degree in the concerned field.

(c) For Masters' Degree: 1st Class or 60% marks or equivalent grade in relevant Bachelors' degree and 2 years work experience in the concerned field.

II. One Child in a family and one time award

Not more than one child of the same parents/guardians will be eligible and to this effect a self-certification will be required from the candidate. The awardee cannot be considered for the award for second or subsequent times as the individual can be awarded for once.

Number of awards available

Twenty-one awards per year are available under the existing Scheme, with following distribution:

(i)	Scheduled Castes	17
(ii)	Denotified, Nomadic and Semi-Nomadic Tribes	1
(iii)	Scheduled Caste converts to other religion	2
(iv)	Landless Agl. Labourers and Traditional Artisans	1
	Total	**21**

When, where and how to apply?

Desirous candidates should apply to the Ministry of Social Justice and Empowerment in response to the detailed advertisement when issued by the Ministry. This advertisement is usually published in leading newspapers in Hindi/English and other regional languages and the Employment News.

Candidates should apply in the application form prescribed and made available by this Ministry subsequent to release of advertisement in respect of selection of candidates for awards under the scheme. This application form is provided on request, in person or by post. The application form as filled in by the applicant should be complete in all respects and also accompanied with proofs of caste/ category, income, age, educational qualifications attained, experience acquired etc.

How much financial assistance is available?

Existing financial assistance

I. Value of maintenance allowance

The annual maintenance allowance of US Dollars 7,700/- has been prescribed for all levels of courses covered under the Scheme. The annual maintenance allowance for candidates in United Kingdom will be Pound Sterling 5,000/- for all levels of courses covered under the Scheme.

II. Earnings from research/teaching assistanceship

The awardees are permitted to supplement their prescribed allowances by undertaking Research/Teaching Assistantship upto US Dollars 2400/- per annum and for awardees in United Kingdom, Pound Sterling 1560/- per annum and beyond these prescribed ceilings, their maintenance allowance under the scheme will be correspondingly reduced by the Indian Missions abroad

III. Contingency allowance

Contingency allowance for books/essential apparatus/study tour/typing and binding of thesis etc. will be US Dollars 500/- per annum and for candidates in United Kingdom, it will be Pound Sterling 325/- per annum.

Besides the above Poll Tax, Visa fees, Equipment allowance and incidental journey expenses, Fees and medical insurance premium, Air Passage and Local Travel will be paid.

The prescribed financial assistance is provided upto completion of the course/research or the following period, whichever is earlier:

(a) For Post Doctoral Research	1½ years
(b) Ph.D.	4 years
(c) Master Degree	3 years

Who gives the assistance?

Ministry of Social Justice and Empowerment provides financial assistance for the admissible expenditure incurred in India and the expenditure incurred abroad on the awardees is met by the concerned Indian Missions. Consequent upon final selection of a candidate for award under the scheme, the candidate is issued a provisional award letter by this Ministry, which also includes a certificate giving therein the details of financial entitlements under the scheme.

Seeking admission abroad

Selected candidates are required to themselves arrange for their admission in foreign accredited educational institutions/universities. In this regard the details may, however, be obtainable at embassies, consulates, missions of foreign countries in India.

After a candidate has obtained confirmed admission in a foreign educational institution, the candidate is required to intimate the same to this Ministry which in turn may get it verified through the Indian Missions abroad. After receipt of the confirmation of the admission, this Ministry will issue the 'confirmed award letter' to the concerned candidate, wherein the details of the course; educational institution etc. will be also mentioned.

Other Educational Programmes and Schemes

Besides the above special schemes and programmes, in pursuance of the commitments made by the National Policy on Education, the Department of Education continued to take various steps to reduce dropout rates and increase school enrolment and retention rates amongst the children belonging to Scheduled Castes.

The following special provisions for Scheduled Castes have been incorporated in the existing schemes of the Departments of Elementary Education & Literacy and Secondary Education & Higher Education - relaxed norms for opening of primary schools; a primary school within one km walking distance from habitations of 200 population instead of habitations of 300 population; and abolition of tuition fee in Government schools in all states, at least up to the primary level. Most of the states have already abolished tuition fee for SC students up to the Senior Secondary level, along with incentives like provision of free textbooks, uniforms, stationery, school bags etc. to these students. The other major programmes of the Department of Elementary Education & Literacy having relevance to Scheduled Castes and OBCs include - the District Primary Education Programme (DPEP), Lok Jumbish, Shiksha Karmi, Non-Formal Education (NFE) and National Programme for Nutritional Support to Primary Education (popularly known as Mid-Day Meals).

One of the strategies of the programme of Sarva Shiksha Abhiyan (SSA) is the educational development of children belonging to Scheduled Castes, OBCs and educationally backward Minorities. SSA is a historic stride towards achieving the long cherished goal of Universalisation of Elementary Education (UEE) through a time-bound integrated approach, in partnership with the states. SSA aims to universalise elementary education to cover all children in the 6-14 age-group by 2010 through the community-owned and mission-mode approach. It also envisages bridging of gender and social gaps through a special focus on the children of Scheduled Castes, STs and other disadvantaged groups.

The DPEP aims mainly at providing access to primary education for all children, reducing primary drop-out rates to less than 10 per cent and increasing learning achievement of primary school students by at least 25 per cent. It is also meant to reduce the gap among gender and social groups to less than 5 per cent. The NFE programme lays emphasis on girls, working children and those belonging to Scheduled Castes. At present, there are 2,92,000 NFE centres covering about 7.3 million children in 25 States/UTs. The major thrust of the National Literacy Mission, which aims to attain full literacy, i.e. a sustainable threshold level of 75 per cent by 2005, is on the promotion of literacy among women, Scheduled Castes, STs and OBCs. This is reflected in the fact that a high 61 per cent of learners are females, while 23 per cent belong to Scheduled Castes and 13 per cent to STs. Janshala, yet another community-based primary education programme, aims to make primary education more accessible and effective, especially for girls and children of deprived communities, marginalised groups, Scheduled Castes, STs, Minorities, working children and children with special needs. Janshala is a block-based programme with emphasis on community participation and decentralisation. This is the first ever programme in the world where five United Nations agencies have collaborated and pooled resources to support an initiative in education. The programme now covers 105 blocks in 9 states - Andhra Pradesh, Chhattisgarh, Jharkhand, Karnataka, Madhya Pradesh, Maharashtra, Orissa, Rajasthan and Uttar Pradesh – with a total project outlay of Rs. 98.29 crore. Janshala programme is to run for five years from 1998 to 2002.

To enable SC and ST students to pursue higher technical studies, the following special provisions have been extended by the Department of Secondary & Higher Education : reservation of seats for Scheduled Castes/STs in the Central Government institutions of higher education, including Indian Institutes of Technology (IITs), Indian Institutes of Management (IIMs), Regional Engineering Colleges (RECs), Central Universities,

Kendriya Vidyalayas and Navodaya Vidyalayas, etc.; relaxation in the minimum qualifying cut-off percentages for admission to universities, colleges and technical institutions; remedial and special coaching for SC/ST students to improve academic skills and linguistic proficiency and raise their level of comprehension. The IITs have a scheme to provide one year's preparatory course for SC/ST students who fail marginally in the entrance examination. Out of 43,000 scholarships at the secondary stage for talented children from rural areas, 13,000 are reserved exclusively for SC/ST students. Besides, 70 scholarships are reserved exclusively for SC/ST students under the National Talent Search Scheme. SC/ST candidates are provided relaxation up to 10 per cent of cut-off marks for the Junior Research Fellowship (JRF) test and all SC/ST candidates qualifying for the JRF are awarded fellowships. Around 50 Junior Fellowships are awarded every year in sciences to SC/ST candidates who appear in the National Eligibility Test (NET) and qualify the eligibility test for lectureship. Also, special attention is being paid to 146 districts identified as low female literacy districts.

To enhance skills and linguistic proficiency in various subjects, special coaching is provided to SC students. The scheme is in operation in 26 universities and 449 colleges. Coaching for students belonging to educationally backward minority communities to compete in various competitive examinations is being provided through 77 coaching centres, including 10 coaching centres for women functioning in 22 universities and 55 colleges.

BABA SAHEB DR.AMBEDKAR FOUNDATION

The Foundation was set up on 24 March 1992 as a registered society. The Foundation has been entrusted with the responsibility to manage, administer and carry on the schemes and programmes identified during the centenary celebrations of Bharat Ratna BabaSaheb Dr B.R. Ambedkar. These are:

1. Dr Ambedkar National Public Library in Delhi;
2. Dr Ambedkar Chairs in universities/institutions for research on the thoughts and ideals of BabaSaheb;
3. Dr Ambedkar National Award for social understanding and uplift of weaker sections;

4. Dr Ambedkar International Award for social change, harmony, equity, justice and human dignity for the exploited and the underprivileged.

Empowerment of Scheduled Castes through Economic Development

Poverty alleviation programmes put into action both in rural and urban areas since the 1980s have not only helped the poor people to rise above the poverty line, but also brought down the poverty rates quite effectively. In respect of Scheduled Castes, besides the general population, the percentage of the number of families living below the poverty line has shown a declining trend over the decade 1983-84 to 1993-94.

PERCENTAGE OF POPULATION LIVING BELOW POVERTY LINE

Category	*1983-84*	*1993-94*	*Percentage Decrease*
General	44.48	35.97	(-) 8.51
SCs	57.60	48.37	(-) 9.23

Source: Perspective Planning Division, Planning Commission, New Delhi.

Note: The aggregate poverty ratio of SCs and ST population 1983-84 has been worked out as a weighted average of rural and urban poverty ratio using 1981 census population of the respective Groups in rural and urban areas aa weights. In a similar way, 1991 census population is used to obtain aggregate poverty ratio for these two groups in 1993-94.

Despite a reduction in the percentage of the population living below poverty line, the incidence of poverty amongst Scheduled Castes continues to be very high, when compared to the general population, the reasons being that a majority of the Scheduled Castes (77.11%)are landless with no productive assets and are devoid of sustainable employment and minimum wages, and women belonging to these Groups who live not only below the poverty line, but in abject/extreme poverty, are denied of both minimum and equal wages.

The rate of decline in respect of the percentage of Scheduled Castes living below the poverty line was marginally higher than that of the total population between 1993-94 and 1999-2000. The gap between the total population and the Scheduled Castes also decreased during the same period in both urban and rural areas. However, the incidence of poverty amongst Scheduled Castes still continues to be very high with 36.25 per cent in rural areas and 38.47 per cent in urban areas, when compared to 27.09 and 23.62 per cent respectively, in respect of total population in 1999-2000. This is primarily due to the fact that a large number of Scheduled Castes who are living below the poverty line are landless with no productive assets and with no access to sustainable employment and minimum wages. The women belonging to these groups suffer even worse because of the added disadvantage of being denied of equal and minimum wages.

Implementation of SCP, and SCA to SCP

During 1970's, the Government instituted, three special mechanisms viz., Special Component Plan (SCP) for Scheduled Castes, Tribal Sub-Plan (TSP) for STs and Special Central Assistance (SCA) to SCP and TSP. While the major objective of SCP and TSP is to ensure the much needed flow of funds and benefits for the welfare and development of these two categories in proportion to their population, SCA to SCP and TSP extends financial assistance to States and UTs as an additive to their SCP and TSP for filling up of the critical gaps in the family-based employment-cum-income generation programmes.

Special Central Assistance is an additive to States Special Component Plan intended for development, especially the economic development of Scheduled Castes. This Central scheme is the most important programme of the Ministry of Social Justice and Empowerment for the alleviation of poverty among Scheduled Castes people. The underlying objective behind Special Central Assistance which provides cent-percent grant to States and Union Territories as an additive to their special component plans is that it would be used to give an added thrust to the development programmes for Scheduled Castes people with reference to their occupational pattern and the need for increasing the productivity of and income from their limited assets by taking up family oriented schemes for them. The SCA is used to fill the critical gaps and vital missing inputs in family-oriented income-generating schemes so as to make the schemes more meaningful and effective. This scheme was started in 1979-80 with a token provision of Rs five crore. The State governments and Union Territory administrations are required to disburse Special Central Assistance to various sectors and agencies including SCDCs which are involved in the implementation of economic development programmes for Scheduled Castes.

SCA is released to the States/U.Ts based on SC population of the respective States/U.Ts (40%) relative backwardness of the States/U.Ts (10%) percentage of Scheduled Caste families in the States/U.Ts covered by composite economic development programmes in the Plans to enable them to cross the poverty line (25%) and the flow of funds to Special Component Plan out of the Annual Plan as compared to the Scheduled Caste population percentage in the States/U.Ts (25%). The second installment of SCA is released to the States/U.Ts after the unspent balance from the previous year and 75% of the first installment is utilized.

The flow of funds during the Eighth Plan for SCP under Central and State sectors was to the tune of 27.8 % and 10.8% respectively against the target of 16.8%.

FLOW OF FUNDS THROUGH SCP AND SCA DURING VII AND VIII PLANS

Items	*Seventh Plan (1985-90)*	*Eighth Plan (1992-97)*		
	Flow of funds	*Outlay**	*Flow of funds*	*Percentage*
SCP for SCs				
Flow from Central Plan (in respect of 13 Ministries/Departments)	625.09	37687.00	10471.00	27.78
Flow from State Plan (In respect of 24 State/UTs)	7385.42	202850.19	21921.53	10.81
Special Central Assistance				
SCA to SCP	930.00	—	1125.00	—

Source: Ministry of Social Justice and Empowerment.; *includes the outlays of the eighth plan in respect of only those ministries/departments and states/Uts which were earmarking funds under SCP and TSP.

SCA TO SPECIAL COMPONENT PLAN FOR SCHEDULED CASTES RELEASED TO THE STATES/UTS

(Population in lakhs and amount released in lakhs)

Sl. No.	*States/UT*	*Population*	*1998-1999*	*1999-2000*	*2000-2001*
1	2	3	4	5	6
1	Andhra Pradesh	105.92	3388.78	4134.94	3720.00
2	Assam	16.59	596.66	695.31	1810.69
3	Bihar	99.51	3620.07	3471.49	0.00
4	Chattisgarh	21.48	0.00	0.00	500.00
5	Gujarat	30.60	371.40	682.27	1521.88
6	Goa	0.24	2.72	5.49	8.00
7	Haryana	32.51	741.77	840.36	930.63
8	Himachal Pradesh	13.10	259.56	298.18	440.00
9	Jammu & Kashmir	6.21	132.80	183.44	218.00
10	Jharkhand	26.21	0.00	0.00	500.00
11	Karnataka	73.69	1820.07	2097.36	2643.64
12	Kerala	28.87	724.54	813.24	1251.07
13	Madhya Pradesh	74.79	2237.08	3303.27	1720.00
14	Maharashtra	87.58	1673.92	2067.30	2722.00
15	Manipur	0.37	10.62	12.54	38.96
16	Orissa	51.29	2281.57	1907.72	1884.00
17	Punjab	57.42	1119.74	1280.29	1784.00
18	Rajasthan	76.08	2575.48	2792.68	3738.96
19	Sikkim	0.24	4.03	22.37	23.87
20	Tamil Nadu	107.12	3236.93	4036.92	3558.00
21	Tripura	4.51	108.72	159.14	476.48
22	Uttar Pradesh	280.44	7518.15	9728.65	9398.00
23	Uttaranchal	12.32	0.00	0	500.00
24	West Bengal	160.81	3378.39	4962.00	5450.63
25	Chandigarh	1.06	22.00	25.00	25.00
26	Delhi	17.95	201.71	149.91	149.91
27	Pondicherry	1.31	73.29	30.13	25.18
	Total	1388.22	36100.00	43700.00	45038.90

The implementation of the special strategies of the Special Component Plan (SCP) for Scheduled Castes and the Special Central Assistance (SCA) to SCP, has been receiving special attention, since their inception, as these are effective instruments to ensure proportionate flow of funds for Scheduled Castes from the other general development sectors. In respect of the Special

Plan Component Plan (SCP), the situation at the Central level was not found to be very encouraging as the earmarking of funds was adhered to only by 13 Ministries/Departments viz. Labour, Education, Science & Technology, Industry, Textiles, Petroleum and Natural Gas, Women and Child Development, Health and Family Welfare, Commerce, Fertilisers, Rural Development, Non-conventional Energy Sources and Agriculture and Cooperation. At the State level, 21 States viz., Andhra Pradesh, Bihar, Assam, Goa, Gujarat, Haryana, Himachal Pradesh, Jammu & Kashmir, Karnataka, Kerala, Madhya Pradesh, Maharashtra, Manipur, Orissa, Punjab, Rajasthan, Sikkim, Tamil Nadu, Tripura, Uttar Pradesh, West Bengal; and 3 UTs viz. Chandigarh, Delhi and Pondicherry were earmarking funds for SCP. Of these, 18 States/UTs have been maintaining separate Budget Heads for SCP to ensure proper quantification of funds and their effective utilisation for the purpose they were meant for. The rest were being pursued to emulate the same system as it helps prevent the diversion of funds. During the Eighth Plan, the flow of funds for SCP under the Central and State sectors by the end of 1996-97 was estimated to be 27.8 per cent and 10.8 per cent respectively, against the total SC population proportion of 16.48 per cent. Funds to the extent of Rs. 1,646.00 crore (10.63 per cent) from 14 Ministries/Departments at the Central level and funds to the extent of Rs. 42,308.97 crore (12.20 per cent) from 22 States/UTs are flowing to SCP.

The Special Central Assistance (SCA) to States/UTs, as an additive to SCP and TSP, was enhanced during the Eighth Plan so as to strengthen the efforts of States in filling up the gaps under the family-based income generation projects. The SCA to SCP was enhanced from Rs.930 crore in the Seventh Plan to Rs.1125 crore in the Eighth Plan, indicating 21 per cent increase. Similarly, the SCA to TSP was also enhanced from Rs.756 crore in the Seventh Plan to Rs.1250 crore in the Eighth Plan, showing a rise by 65 per cent. SCA to SCP was enhanced from Rs. 1,125 crore in the Eighth Plan to Rs. 2,092.95 crore in the Ninth Plan, indicating an increase by 86 per cent.

Despite the fact that the strategy of SCP has been in operation for more than fifteen years, it could not influence all those concerned towards the right perspective. Further, lack of effective monitoring to ensure that all these concerned earmark funds under SCP and TSP and that the funds received under SCP, TSP and SCA are utilised both effectively and purposefully is another area of concern in this regard.

National Scheduled Castes and Scheduled Tribes Finance Development Corporation (NSFDC)

The National Scheduled Castes and Scheduled Tribes Finance Development Corporation was set up under Section 25 of Companies Act, 1956 with the objective of financing income generating activities for benefiting SC & ST population living below the poverty line limits (These limits are Rs.32,952 for rural areas and Rs.42,412/- for urban areas at present) The NSFDC provides funds at low interest rates to the target groups through the State Scheduled Castes Development Corporations (SCDCs) and other channelising agencies for implementing various economically feasible and financially viable self employment schemes/projects in sectors such as Agriculture, Horticulture, Animal Husbandry and Dairy Development, Minor irrigation, Small Industries, Trade and Services and Transport. NSFDC is extending concessional financial assistance through the State Channelising Agencies namely State SC and ST Finance and Development Corporation. The State Agencies extend loans to beneficiaries at 7% p.a. interest upto Rs.5 lakh and @ 9% for amounts exceeding Rs.5 lakh. NSFDC provides term loan upto 85% of the project cost. Balance 10% is funded by the State Agencies and 5% by the beneficiaries. Smaller loans are funded on 100% basis without insisting on any contribution by the beneficiary. An amount of Rs. 30 crores was released to the NSFDC during 1999-2000.

STATE SCHEDULED CASTES DEVELOPMENT CORPORATION

The scheme for assistance to the State-level Scheduled Castes Development Corporations (SCDCs) was introduced in 1978-79 to uplift the SC/ST population living below the poverty line. At present SCDCs are functioning in 25 States/Union Territories. The Centre contributes 49 per cent to the authorised share capital of the SCDC against the 51 per cent contributed by the State government. The SCDCs identify eligible beneficiaries from amongst below the poverty line SC families and motivate them to undertake income generating economic development schemes and to improve their vocational skills. Sponsoring schemes to banks and other financial institutions for credit support. In 1998-99 (up to November 1998), an amount of Rs 35.85 crore was released as Government of India contribution. An amount of Rs. 20 crores was released to the States SCDCs during the year 1999-2000.

The National Scheduled Castes and Scheduled Tribes Finance and Development Corporation (NSFDC) continued to function as a catalytic agent for financing, facilitating and mobilising funds from various sources for promoting economic development activities amongst Scheduled Castes living below the poverty line. Financial assistance, at a concessional rate of interest, is extended to the target groups for taking up viable economic activities through the 34 State Channelising Agencies, which include Scheduled Caste Development Corporations (SCDCs) and other recognised financial institutions. Skill and entrepreneurial training is also imparted to unemployed SC youths through reputed training institutions. A micro-credit scheme has also been taken up since 2000-01 for funding Self-Help Groups (SHGs) by which small loans are provided to the target groups through NGOs. The Authorised Share Capital of the Corporation was Rs. 300 crore and it was raised to Rs. 1,000 crore in 1999-2000. Its paid-up share capital is now Rs. 421 crore. The Corporation has so far sanctioned 2,759 projects, which on completion would enable 3.4 lakh SC beneficiaries to take up various employment-cumincome-generating activities. During the last year of the Ninth Plan (2001-02), NSFDC was bifurcated into two separate Corporations - one for Scheduled Castes and the other for STs viz. National Scheduled Castes Finance and Development Corporation for Scheduled Castes and National Scheduled Tribes Finance and Development Corporation for STs.

SCDCs are playing a key role at State level as guarantors, promoters and catalysts for generating credit from financial institutions and providing missing inputs by way of margin money loans and subsidy to Scheduled Castes living below the poverty line. At present, these Corporations are functioning in 25 States/ UTs. This Scheme was revised in 1998-99 with a view to ensuring effective utilisation of central assistance extended to the States. Of the Ninth Plan allocation of Rs. 180 crore, an expenditure of Rs. 173.63 crore was incurred for extending financial assistance to 14.88 lakh Scheduled Castes.

Besides the priority areas of education and economic development, Government has been making conscious efforts to promote welfare measures in various other spheres also for the empowerment of the Scheduled Castes through several Schemes by different ministries.

Health and Family Welfare

The National Health Policy (1983) accorded high priority for extending health services to those residing in the backward rural areas, with a concentration of Scheduled Castes. It laid special emphasis on endemic diseases. National Malaria Eradication Programme including Filarial Control, Japanese Encephalitis Control and Kalaazar Control were implemented by States/UTs with 50 per cent central assistance for spraying insecticides, supply of Anti-Malaria drugs etc. in the areas of SC concentration under SCP. The National Leprosy Eradication Programme is 100 per cent centrally assisted programme for the detection and treatment of leprosy cases. This programme has been in action in all districts of the country and covers the entire SC population. The National Tuberculosis Control Programme (NTCP) implemented with central assistance, supplies anti-TB drugs, equipment etc. to areas with high concentration of Scheduled Castes under SCP. Further, the norms of NTCP were relaxed and the following steps were taken for facilitating effective service delivery in rural/tribal areas for— (i) providing Senior Treatment Supervisors and Senior Tuberculosis Laboratories Supervisors for 2-3 lakh population against the established norms of 5 lakh; (ii) opening of microscopic centres for 50,000 population against the established norms of 1 lakh; (iii) opening of more Direct Observation Therapy (DOT) Centres; and iv) provision to reimburse the travel claims of patients and attendants for taking treatment at DOT Centres. Under the National Programme on Control of Blindness, 100 per cent central assistance is being extended for strengthening of ophthalmic infrastructure, training of personnel, etc. in areas with SC concentration for treatment of eye ailments and control of blindness under SCP. The National AIDS Control Programme is implemented in areas with sizeable SC population, though no separate provision is made for SCP.

Labour & Employment

In the field of Labour and Employment, the Ministry of Labour is implementing special training and rehabilitation programmes for Scheduled Castes to equip them with necessary training in upgradation of skills and, thus, improve their employment opportunities. The scheme of 'Coaching–cum-Guidance Centre for Scheduled Castes/STs' was implemented through 22 Centres in various States/UTs to provide occupational information as well as individual guidance and to conduct confidence-building programmes for the benefit of the SC/ST job seekers. To facilitate the recruitment of SC/ST candidates against reserved vacancies in various Central Government Ministries/Departments, the Directorate-General of Employment and Training (DGET) has launched another scheme, viz. 'Special Coaching Scheme' in 1973 for SC/ST job-seekers registered with the employment exchanges to enable them to appear in Competitive Examinations/Selection Tests conducted for recruitment in Group C and equivalent posts. The scheme was launched on a pilot basis at Delhi and Ghaziabad and so far 17 phases of this programme have been completed and the 18th phase is in progress since January, 2000. Encouraged with the success of the above scheme, the scheme has been extended to 12 more places through the Coaching-cum-Guidance Centres located at Bangalore, Kolkata, Hyderabad, Ranchi, Surat, Kanpur, Guwahati, Imphal, Hissar, Jabalpur, Chennai and Tiruvananthapuram.

Further, a number of welfare schemes for providing medical, housing, educational, recreational and family welfare benefits are being implemented under the Labour Welfare Funds with special dispensation for SC and ST workers engaged in mining. Also, 15 per cent of the houses built by mining managements are reserved for Scheduled Castes/STs. Under the Integrated Housing Scheme for Beedi Workers, the exclusive ownership of land is not insisted upon in respect of Scheduled Castes/STs. Under the Scheme 'Award of Scholarships to the Wards of Miners and Beedi Workers', reservation for SC/ST students is provided on the basis of percentage of SC/ST population in the district, subject to a floor of 15 per cent for Scheduled Castes and 7.5 per cent for STs. The minimum marks for eligibility under the scholarship scheme for Scheduled Castes are 35 per cent, against 45 per cent in case of other students. Thus, education and housing have been identified as the major thrust areas and the tempo of the welfare schemes relating to them have been substantially stepped up with the consequential benefits flowing in greater measure to the Scheduled Castes/ STs.

The rehabilitation of bonded labour has a special significance for Scheduled Castes, as these communities constitute 61.5 per cent of bonded labour in the country as per the Report of the National Commission on Rural Labour, 1991. According to reports received from State Governments of Andhra Pradesh, Arunachal Pradesh, Bihar (including Jharkhand), Gujarat, Haryana, Karnataka, Kerala, Madhya Pradesh (including Chhattisgarh), Maharashtra, Orissa, Rajasthan, Tamil Nadu and Uttar Pradesh (including Uttaranchal) as many as 2.8 lakh bonded labourers have been identified and out of these 2.6 lakh have been rehabilitated up to March 2001. A separate SC Development Planning Cell has been functioning under the Ministry, since 1981 to co-ordinate the policy, planning and monitoring.

Women & Child Development

Programmes for women and children implemented by the Department of Women and Child Development are primarily directed towards the most disadvantaged groups of population like Scheduled Castes, STs and other economically backward classes living in backward rural areas, tribal areas and urban slums. The basic consideration of all the schemes is to ensure that the benefits flow to women and children belonging to the disadvantaged sections of the population. The Department has been implementing one of the largest area-based programme of Integrated Child Development

Services (ICDS). It aims to provide a package of 6 basic services of health, immunisation, supplementary feeding, referral services, nonformal pre-school education and health and nutrition education - for children below 6 years and for expectant and nursing mothers living in the most backward and rural areas and urban slums with high concentration of severely disadvantaged groups. By the end of the Ninth Plan, ICDS is expected to be universalised by covering all the 5,652 Blocks/ Wards to benefit 54.3 million children and 10.9 million mothers. Most of the evaluation studies have indicated that out of the total beneficiaries under the schemes; about 78 per cent belong to Scheduled Castes. Also, under the scheme of Hostels for Working Women implemented by the Department, there are stipulations to reserve 15 per cent of seats for Scheduled Castes.

Rural Development

The Ministry of Rural Development plays a vital role in raising the status of the poor above the poverty line and improving the quality of life in rural areas through the implementation of various poverty alleviation programmes and providing avenues for self/wage employment to the most disadvantaged Groups like Scheduled Castes. Under the Jawahar Gram Samriddhi Yojana (JGSY), which provides wage employment, 22.5 per cent of Plan allocation is earmarked for SC/ST families living 'Below the Poverty Line' (BPL). During the Ninth Plan, 395.6 million man-days were provided for Scheduled Castes, accounting for 28.5 per cent of total employment under this scheme. Under the Employment Assurance Scheme (EAS) which is open to all rural poor who are in need of wage-employment, preference is given to Scheduled Castes/STs and parents of child labour withdrawn from hazardous occupations who are below the poverty line. Around 500 million mandays were provided to Scheduled Castes during the Ninth Plan under EAS, accounting for 33.7 per cent of total employment provided under the scheme. JGSY and EAS have been brought under the purview of the mega scheme of Sampoorna Gramin Rozgar Yojana (SGRY) since September 2001.

For taking up self-employment and income generation

activities, Swarnajayanti Gram Swarozgar Yojana (SGSY) stipulates that at least 50 per cent of the swarozgaris will be from Scheduled Castes/ STs. Under SGSY, 1.8 million Scheduled Caste swarozgaris accounting for 32.5 per cent of the total number of swarozgaris, benefited during the Ninth Plan. In addition to these poverty alleviation programmes, this Ministry also provides basic amenities like housing, drinking water, etc. Indira Awas Yojana (IAY) has the objective of providing dwelling units to BPL rural households belonging primarily to Scheduled Castes. About 1.8 million dwelling units were constructed for Scheduled Castes accounting for 47.4 per cent of total houses under the scheme during the Ninth Plan. Around 60 per cent of the total allocation was earmarked for Scheduled Castes/STs. Under the Credit-cum-Subsidy scheme of rural housing, a minimum of 60 per cent of the funds allocated as subsidy to each state has been earmarked for the construction of houses for Scheduled Castes/STs.

Under the Accelerated Rural Water Supply Programme (ARWSP), States are required to utilise a minimum of 25 per cent of funds for provision of drinking water supply to Scheduled Castes. Around 23.1 million Scheduled Castes have been benefited, accounting for 18.1 per cent of total beneficiaries under ARSWP. Under the Central Rural Sanitation Programme (CRSP), sanitary latrines are provided to rural population with preference to SC/ ST families and people below the poverty line. A minimum of 20 per cent of the total funds is earmarked for providing subsidy to individual BPL households belonging to Scheduled Castes and STs. Where such households are more than 20 per cent of the total population, earmarking is enhanced at least to match the percentage of SC population. During the Ninth Plan, one million (21.2 per cent) sanitary latrines were provided to Scheduled Castes.

The National Social Assistance Programme (NSAP), comprising the National Old Age Pensions Scheme (NOAPS), the National Family Benefit Scheme (NFBS) and the National Maternity Benefit Scheme (NMBS) introduces a national policy for social security assistance to the poor SC/ST families and represents a significant step forward. During the Ninth Plan, 7.8 million Scheduled Castes were covered under NOAPS, accounting for

24.4 per cent of total 32.2 million beneficiaries. Of the total one million beneficiaries of the NFBS, 2 lakh (20.2 per cent) comprised of SC families. NMBS (now transferred to Department of Family Welfare w.e.f. 2001-02) benefited 1.2 million SC women, who accounted for 21.8 per cent of the total 5.6 million beneficiaries.

Urban Development

The special scheme of Urban Self- Employment Programme under Swarna Jayanti Shahari Rozgar Yojana (SJSRY) extends assistance to the urban poor living below the poverty line with special attention to women and persons belonging to Scheduled Castes and STs to set up gainful self-employment ventures. The benefits for Scheduled Castes are granted keeping in view the extent of the proportion of their strength in the local population. The National Agenda for Governance identified 'Housing for All' as a major programme with special emphasis on the needs of the vulnerable groups wherein it was proposed to facilitate construction of 20 lakh additional units every year, with emphasis on the Economically Weaker Sections and Low Income Groups as also the needs of Scheduled Castes/STs. A special Cell in the Ministry of Urban Development and Poverty Alleviation monitors the implementation of the various Government Orders regarding reservation in services for Scheduled Castes/STs through periodical returns. In addition, the Cell also monitors the filling up of the backlog of vacancies reserved for Scheduled Castes, STs and OBCs under the Special Recruitment Drive in respect of the Attached/ Subordinate Offices and the Public Sector Undertakings of this Ministry.

Empowerment of the Scheduled Castes through Participation in Administration and Decision Making

Participation of Scheduled Castes in the administration and decision-making is yet another indicator of the positive impact of developmental planning on the status of Scheduled Castes. The same can be seen from their representation in the Government especially at the senior level of Group A posts, where decisions are taken.

REPRESENTATION OF SCHEDULED CASTES IN SERVICES (1974 TO 1994)

Category	*Group of Service*				*Total*
	A	*B*	C	*D*	
(As on 1.1.1974) Total	33672	52343	1566796	1242548	2895359
SC	1094	24.01	161775	230203	395473
	(3.25)	(4.59)	(10.33)	(18.53)	(13.66)
(As on 1.1.1984) Total	—	—	—	—	3303342
SC	—	—	—	—	527573
					(15.97)
(As on 1.1.1994) Total	59016	103198	2381613	1023285	3567112
SC	6046	12442	374758	209423	602670
	(10.25)	(12.06)	(15.73)	(20.46)	(16.90)

Source: Department of Administrative Reforms & Public Grievances, Annual Report, 1994.

Note: Figures in parenthesis indicate percentage of SCs and ST to the population

The total representation of Scheduled Castes in services covering A to D Groups has risen from 13.66 per cent in 1974 to 16.9 per cent in 1994, which, in fact, is more than their legitimate share of 16.5 per cent. The increasing participation of Scheduled Castes and STs in Group 'A' Services, that is - Scheduled Castes from 3.25 per cent in 1974 to 10.25 per cent in 1994 directly reflects the impact of various affirmative measures taken in bringing them into the mainstream. At the same time, the data also reveal the gaps that need to be bridged with effective interventions, if this group have to be brought on par with the general population, especially in respect of Group A Posts, the level at which the decision-making takes place.

The rise in the total representation of Scheduled Castes in Central Government Services covering A to D Groups from 13.66 per cent in 1974 to 16.70 percent in 1999 is marginally higher than their share in the total population. Although, their representation has shown an increasing trend from 3.25 per cent in 1974 to 11.29 per cent in 1999 in Group A Services, though not the expected level, it does reflect the impact of various affirmative measures taken for bringing them into the mainstream.

Representation of Scheduled Castes in All India Services of

IAS, IPS and IFS is not very encouraging, as they represent 10.6 per cent of the total in the IAS, 12.4 per cent in the IPS and 11.5 per cent in the IFS in 2000 which is still below their expected level. Although, the percentage of Scheduled Castes in IAS and IPS declined between 1996 and 2000, yet the actual number has increased over the same period.

Empowerment of Scheduled Castes through Political representation

Affirmative discrimination through reservation for Scheduled Castes in the Lok Sabha, State Legislative Assemblies and in the Panchayati Raj Institutions (PRIs) has established the growing strength of Scheduled Castes not only in terms of their participation in the democratic processes of the country since independence, but also their increasing representation in the political decision making.

The 73rd and 74th Amendments to the Constitution were made in order to revitalise the Rural and Urban Local Bodies respectively by giving them Constitutional status, allocating powers and functions, making provisions for finances, ensuring regular elections and providing for reservation of seats for SCs, STs and women and weaker sections so as to ensure their participation in the political process at all levels. These Amendments have also provided for reservation of offices of Chairpersons at all levels of Local Bodies to ensure their effective role in decision making.

The representation of Scheduled Castes in the political decision-making institutions at various levels has been quite impressive, though they are yet to receive their due share in PRIs, State Legislative Assemblies and Lok Sabha. In the 1996 elections, their representation in the Lok Sabha accounted for 13.01% per cent. Further, while in the PRIs, the share of Scheduled Castes stood at 14.3 per cent in 2001, their share in State Legislative Assemblies was 13.8 per cent in 2000 and 14.5 per cent in the Lok Sabha in 1999. The representation of Scheduled Castes in the Central Council of Ministers has increased marginally in absolute numbers from 6 to 7 during the period between 1991 and 1999. However, their representation as a percentage to the total has declined from 10.5 per cent to 9.5 per cent over the same period.

Of the 7 Scheduled Castes in the Central Council of Ministers in 1999, 3 are of Cabinet rank and 4 are Ministers of State.

Empowerment of the Scheduled Castes through Legislation

There are a number of laws, both Central and State, which provide for safeguards to Scheduled Castes and Scheduled Tribes. Some of these emanate from the various Constitutional provisions. A list of such laws is given below:

— The Protection of Civil Rights Act, 1955.
— The Scheduled Castes and the Scheduled Tribes (Prevention of Atrocities) Act, 1989.
— The Bonded Labour System (Abolition) Act, 1976.
— The Child Labour (Prohibition and Regulation) Act, 1986.
— The Minimum Wages Act 1948
— The Panchayat (Extension to the Scheduled Areas) Act, 1996
— Acts and regulations in force in different States to prevent alienation of land belonging to SCs/STs. In some States such provision exists in the Land Revenue Code.

Besides the IPC, the Protection of Civil Rights (PCR) Act of 1955 and the Scheduled Castes and Scheduled Tribes (Prevention of Atrocities) Act of 1989, are the two major legal instruments which help prevent/control the atrocities against Scheduled Castes and STs. Under these Acts, as many as 434 Special Courts/Mobile Courts were set up in 7 States. In addition, Special Cells/Squads/ Officers have also been appointed in 19 States to ensure effective implementation of the Act. In accordance with the PCR Act of 1955, special legal aid was also extended to the victims of untouchability and other crimes through Special Officers who ensured effective implementation of the Act, besides extending support for social and economic rehabilitation of the SC/ST victims. The crimes committed against Scheduled Castes and STs vis-à-vis the general population as reported by the National Crimes Record Bureau, New Delhi, reveal that the number of crimes against Scheduled Castes and STs has started declining from 38,927 in 1994 to 36,413 in 1996. However, the share of the crime against Scheduled Castes and STs in the total crime in the country between 1995 and 1996 remained the same. The number of crimes committed which are covered under the Special Laws viz., PCR Act of 1955 and the Prevention of Atrocities Act of 1989, have also shown a declining trend as they have come down from 18,048 in 1994 to 11,863 in 1996. This can no doubt, be attributed to the effective implementation of the two Special Legislations under which Mobile Courts/Special Courts, Special Squads were set up and Special Officers were appointed. Amongst the various types of crimes committed against Scheduled Castes and STs, those covered under PCR Act in respect of Scheduled Castes and those under POA Act in respect of STs continued to be on a high side, besides rape, murder, arson and kidnap and abduction between 1994 and 1996.

What is required to be done in case any practice of Untouchability? What are the provisions of the relevant act?

Person subjected to and affected by the practice of untouchability may approach the Police Station covering the area of such incidence and register First Information Report (FIR) as per provision under Sections 3 to 7 of the Protection of Civil Rights Act, 1955.

Important provisions of the Protection of Civil Rights Act, 1955 relating to Untouchability are as under:

Section 3— Preventing on the ground of untouchability

(a) from entering any place of public worship, which is open to other persons professing the same religion of any section thereof, or

(b) from worshipping or offering prayers or performing any religious service in any place of public worship, or bathing in, or using the waters of, any sacred tank, well, spring or water - course,(river or lake or bathing at any ghat of such tank, water-course, river of lake).

Section 4— Enforcing on the ground of untouchability, any disability with regard to

(i) access to any shop, public restaurant, hotel or place of public entertainment; or

(ii) the use of any utensils and other articles kept in any public restaurant, hotel, dharm shala, sarai or musafirkhana for the use of the general public or

(iii) the practice of any profession or the carrying on of any occupation, trade or business (or employment in any job) or

(iv) the use of, or access to, any river, stream, spring, well, tank, cistern, water-tap or other watering place, or any bathing ghat, burial or cremation ground, any sanitary convenience, any road, or (passage, or any other place of public resort which other members of the public, or, have a right to use or have access to; or

(v) the use of, or access to, any place used for charitable or a public purpose maintained wholly or partly out of State funds or dedicated to the use of general public or

(vi) the enjoyment of any benefit under a charitable trust created for the benefit of the general public ; or

(vii) the use of, or access to, any public conveyance; or

(viii) the construction, acquisition, or occupation of any residential premises in any locality, whatsoever; or

(ix) the use of any dharmshala, sarai or musafirkhana which is open to the general public, or

(x) the observance of any social or religious custom, usage or ceremony or

(xi) the use of jewelry and finery;

Section 5— Refusing on the ground of 'untouchability'

(a) admission to any person to any hospital, dispensary, educational institution or any hostel if such hospital/dispensary, educational institution or hostel is established or maintained for the benefit of the general public or any section thereof; or

(b) discriminates against any such person after admission to any of the aforesaid institutions;

Section 6: Refusing on the ground of 'untouchability' to sell any goods or refuses to render any service to any person at the same time and place and on the same terms and conditions at or which such goods are sold or services are rendered to other persons in the ordinary course of business.

Section 7 (1)

(a) Acting, on the ground of untouchability leading to prevention of any person from exercising any right accruing to him by reason of the abolition of 'untouchability' under Article 17 of the Constitution; or

(b) molests, injures, annoys, obstructs or causes or attempts to cause obstruction to any person in the exercise of any such right or molests, injures, annoys or boycotts any person by reason of his having exercised any such rights; or

(c) by words, either spoken or written, or by signs or by visible representations or otherwise, incites or encourages any person or class of persons or the public generally to practice "untouchability" in any form whatsoever; or

(d) insults or attempts to insult, on the ground of "untouchability" a member of Scheduled Castes.

For enlarging the scope and making penal provisions more stringent, the Untouchability (Offences) Act, 1955 has been comprehensively amended and renamed as the Protection of Civil Rights Act, 1955 which came into force with effect from 19 November 1976. The detailed text of the Protection of Civil Rights Act, 1955 and the Protection of Civil Rights Rules, 1977 are as under:

THE PROTECTION OF CIVIL RIGHTS ACT, 1955

(As on the 1st September 1977)

An Act to prescribe punishment for the preaching and practice of "Untouchability" for the enforcement of any disability arising therefrom and for matters connected therewith.

1. (1) This Act may be called the Protection of Civil Rights Act, 1955.
   (2) It extends to the whole of India.
   (3) It shall come into force on such date as the Central Government may, by notifications in the Official Gazette appoint.
2. In this Act, unless the context otherwise requires:—
   (a) "civil rights" means any right accruing to a person by reason of the abolition of "untouchability" by article 17 of the Constitution;
   (aa) "hotel" includes a refreshment room, a boarding house, a lodging house, a coffee house and a café;
   (b) "place" includes a house, building and other structure and premises; and also includes a tent, vehicle and vessel;)
   (c) "Place of public entertainment" includes any place to

which the public are admitted and in which an entertainment is provided or held.

Explanation— "Entertainment" includes any exhibition, performance, game, sport and other form of amusement;

(d) "place of public worship" means a place, by whatever name known, which is used as a place of public religious worship or which is dedicated generally to, or is used generally by, persons professing any religion or belonging to any religious denomination or any section thereof, for the performance of any religious service, or for offering prayers therein; and includes—

(i) all lands and subsidiary shrines appurtenant attached or to any such place;

(ii) a privately owned place of worship which is, in fact, allowed by the owner thereof to be used as a place of public worship, and

(iii) such land or subsidiary shrine appurtenant to such privately owned place of worship as is allowed by the owner thereof to be used as a place of public religious worship;)

(da) "prescribed" means prescribed by rules made under this Act;

(db) "scheduled castes" has the meaning assigned to it in clause (24) of article 366 of the Constitution;)

(e) "shop" means any premises where goods are sold either wholesale or by retail or both wholesale and by retail and includes—

(i) any place from where goods are sold by a hawker or vendor or from a mobile van or cart,

(ii) a laundry and a hair cutting saloon;

(iii) any other place where services are rendered to customers.

3. Whoever on the ground of "untouchability" prevents any person—

(a) from entering any place of public worship which is open to other persons professing the same religion or any section thereof, as such person; or

(b) from worshipping or offering prayers or performing

any religious service in any place of public worship, or bathing in or using the waters of, any sacred tank, well, spring or water-course (river or lake or bathing at any ghat of such tank, water-course, river or lake) in the same manner and to the same extent as is permissible to other persons professing the same religion or any section thereof, as such person;

shall be punishable with imprisonment for a term of not less than one month and not more than six months and also with fine which shall be not less than one hundred rupees and not more than five hundred rupees

Explanation— For the purpose of this section and section 4 persons professing the Buddhist, Sikh or Jain religion or persons professing the Hindu religion in any of its forms or development including Virashaivas, Lingayats, Adivasis, followers of Brahmo, Prarthana, Arya Samaj and the Swaminarayan Sampraday shall be deemed to be Hindus.

4. Whoever on the ground of "untouchability" enforces against any person any disability with regard to—
   (i) access to any shop, public restaurant, hotel or place of public entertainment; or
   (ii) the use of any utensils, and other articles kept in any public restaurant, hotel, dharmshala, sarai or musafirkhana for the use of the general public or of any section thereof; or
   (iii) the practice of any profession or the carrying on of any occupation, trade or business or employment in any job; or
   (iv) the use of, or access to, any river, stream, spring, well, tank, cistern, water-tap or other watering place, or any bathing ghat, burial or cremation ground, any sanitary convenience, any road, or passage, or any other place of public resort which other members of the public, or any section thereof, have a right to use or have access to; or
   (v) the use of, or access to, any place used for a charitable or a public purpose maintained wholly or partly out of State funds or dedicated to the use of the general public or any section thereof; or

(vi) the enjoyment of any benefit under a charitable trust created for the benefit of the general public or of any section thereof; or

(vii) the use of, or access to, any public conveyance; or

(viii) the construction, acquisition or occupation of any residential premises in any locality, whatsoever; or

(ix) the use of any dharmshala, sarai or musafirkhana which is open to the general public, or to any section thereof; or

(x) the observance of any social or religious custom, usage or ceremony or taking part in, or taking out, any religious, social or cultural procession; or

(xi) the use of jewelry and finery;

shall be punishable with imprisonment for a term of not less than one month and not more than six months and also with fine which shall be not less than one hundred rupees and not more than five hundred rupees

Explanation— For the purposes of this section, "enforcement of any disability" includes any discrimination on the ground of "untouchability"

5. Whoever on the ground of "untouchability"—

(a) refuses admission to any person to any hospital dispensary, educational institution or any hostel, if such hospital, dispensary, educational institution or hostel is established or maintained for the benefit of the general public or any section thereof; or

(b) does any act which discriminates against any such person after admission to any of the aforesaid institution;

shall be punishable with imprisonment for a term of not less than one month and not more than six months and also with fine which shall be not less than one hundred rupees and not more than five hundred rupees

6. Whoever on the ground of "untouchability" refuses to sell any goods or refuses to render any service to any person at the same time and place and on the same terms and conditions at or on which such goods are sold or services are rendered to other persons in the ordinary course of

business shall be punishable with imprisonment for a term of not less than one month and not more than six months and also with fine which shall be not less than one hundred rupees and not more than five hundred rupees.

7. (1) Whoever—

(a) prevents any person from exercising any right accruing to him by reason of the abolition of "untouchability" under article 17 of the Constitution; or

(b) molests, injures, annoys, obstructs or causes or attempts to cause obstruction to any person in the exercise of any such right or molests, injures, annoys or boycotts any person by reason of his having exercised any such right; or

(c) by words, either spoken or written, or by signs or by visible representations or otherwise, incites or encourages any person or class of persons or the public generally to practice "untouchability" in any form whatsoever; or

(d) insults or attempts to insult, on the ground of "untouchability" a member of a Scheduled Caste,

shall be punishable with imprisonment for a term of not less than one month and not more than six months, and also with fine which shall be not less than one hundred rupees and not more than five hundred rupees

Explanation I— A person shall be deemed to boycott another person who—

(a) refuses to let to such other person or refuses to permit such other person, to use or occupy any house or land or refuses to deal with, work for hire for, or do business with, such other person or to render to him or receive from him any customary service, or refuses to do any of the said things on the terms on which such things would be commonly done in the ordinary course of business; or

(b) abstains from such social, professional or business relations as he would ordinarily maintain with such other person.

Explanation II— For the purpose of clause (c) a person shall be deemed to incite or encourage the practice of "untouchability"—

(i) if he, directly or indirectly, preaches "untouchability" or its practice in any form; or

(ii) if he justifies, whether on historical, philosophical or religious grounds or on the ground of any tradition of the caste system or on any other ground, the practice of "untouchability" in any form.

(1A) Whoever commits any offence against the person or property of any individual as a reprisal or revenge for his having exercised any right accruing to him by reason of the abolition of "untouchability" under article 17 of the constitution, shall, where the offence is punishable with imprisonment for a term exceeding two years, be punishable with imprisonment for a term which shall not be less than two years and also with fine.

(2) Whoever—

(i) denies to any person belonging to his community or any section thereof any right or privilege to which such person would be entitled as a member of such community or section, or

(ii) takes any part in the ex-communication of such person, on the ground that such person has refused to practice "untouchability" or that such person has done any act in furtherance of the objects of this Act.

shall be punishable with imprisonment for a terms of not less than one month and not more than six months, and also with fine which shall be not less than one hundred rupees and not more than five hundred rupees

7A. (1) Whoever compels any person, on the ground of "untouchability" to do any scavenging or sweeping or to remove any carcass or to flay any animal or to remove the umbilical cord or to do any other job of a similar nature, shall be deemed to have enforced a disability arising out of "untouchability"

(2) Whoever is deemed under sub-section (1) to have enforced a disability arising out of "untouchability" shall be punishable with imprisonment for a term which shall not be less than three months and not more than six months and also with fine which shall not be less than one hundred rupees and not more than five hundred rupees.

Explanation— For the purposes of this section, "compulsion" includes a threat of social or economic boycott.

8. When a person who is convicted of an offence under section 6 holds any license under any law for the time being in force in respect of any profession, trade, calling or employment in relation to which the offence is committed, the court trying the offence may, without prejudice to any other penalty to which such person may be liable under that section, direct that the license shall stand cancelled or be suspended for such period as the court may deem fit, and every order of the court so canceling or suspending a license shall have effect as if it had been passed by the authority competent to cancel or suspend the license under any such law.

   Explanation— In this section, "license" includes a permit or permission.

9. Where the manager or trustee of a place of public worship or any educational institution or hostel which is in receipt of a grant of land or money from the government is convicted of an offence under this Act and such conviction is not reversed or quashed in any appeal or revision, the Government may, if in its opinion the circumstances of the case warrant such a course, direct the suspension or resumption of the whole or any part of such grant.

10. Whoever abets any offence under this Act shall be punishable with the punishment provided for the offence.

    Explanation— A public servant who willfully neglects the investigation of any offence punishable under this Act shall be deemed to have abetted an offence punishable under this Act.

10A. (1) If, after an inquiry in the prescribed manner, the State Government is satisfied that the inhabitants of an area are concerned in, or abetting the commission of, any offence punishable under this Act, or harboring persons concerned in the commission of such offence or failing to render all the assistance in their power to discover or apprehend the offender or offenders or suppressing material evidence of the commission of such offence, the State Government may, by notification in the Official Gazette, impose a collective fine on such inhabitants and apportion such fine amongst the inhabitants who are liable collectively to pay it, and such apportionment shall be made according to the State Government's judgment of the respective means of such inhabitants and in making any such apportionment the State Government may assign a apportion of such fine to a Hindu undivided family to be payable by it:

Provided that the fine apportioned to an inhabitant shall not be realised until the petition, if any, filed by him under sub-section (3) is disposed of.

(2) The notification made under sub-section (1) shall be proclaimed in the area by beat of drum or in such other manner as the State Government may think best in the circumstances to bring the imposition of the collective fine to the notice of the inhabitants of the said area.

(3) (a) Any person aggrieved by the imposition of the collective fine under sub-section(1) or by the order of appointment, may, within the prescribed period, file a petition before the State Government or such other authority as that Government may specify in this behalf for being exempted from such fine or for modification of the order of apportionment:

Provided that no fee shall be charged for filing such petition.

(b) The State Government or the authority specified by it shall, after giving to the petitioner a reasonable opportunity of being heard, pass such order as it may think fit:

Provided that the amount of the fine exempted or reduced under this section shall not be realisable from any person, and the total fine imposed on the inhabitants of an area under sub-section (1) shall be deemed to have been reduced to that extent.

(4) Notwithstanding anything contained in sub-section (3), the State Government may exempt the victims of any offence punishable under this Act or any person who does not, in its opinion, fall within the category of persons specified in sub-section (1), from the liability to pay the collective fine imposed under sub-section (1) or any portion thereof.

(5) The portion of collective fine payable by any person (including a Hindu undivided family) may be recovered in the manner provided by the Code of Criminal Procedure, 1973 for the recovery of fines imposed by a Court as if such portion were a fine imposed by a Magistrate.

11. Whoever having already been convicted of an offence under this Act or of an abetment of such offence is again convicted of any such offence or abetment, shall, on conviction, be punishable—

(a) for the second offence, with imprisonment for a term of not less than six months and not more than one year, and also with fine which shall be not less than two hundred rupees and not more than five hundred rupees.

(b) For the third offence or any offence subsequent to the third offence, with imprisonment for a term of not less than one year and not more than two years, and also with fine which shall be not less than five hundred rupees and not more than one thousand rupees.

12. Where any act constituting an offence under this Act is committed in relation to a member of a Scheduled Caste the court shall presume, unless the contrary is proved, that such act was committed on the ground of "untouchability".

13. (1) No civil court shall entertain or continue any suit or proceeding or shall pass any decree or order or execute

wholly or partially any decree or order if the claim involved in such suit or proceeding or if the passing of such decree or order or if such execution would in any way be contrary to the provisions of this Act.

(2) No court shall, in adjudicating any matter or executing any decree or order, recognise any custom or usage imposing any disability on any person on the ground of "untouchability"

14. (1) If the person committing an offence under this Act is a company, every person who at the time the offence was committed was incharge of, and was responsible to, the company for the conduct of the business of the company, shall be deemed to be guilty of the offence and shall be liable to be proceeded against and punished accordingly.

Provided that nothing contained in this sub-section shall render any such person liable to any punishment, if he proves that the offence was committed without his knowledge or that he exercised all due diligence to prevent the commission of such offence.

(2) Notwithstanding anything contained in sub-section (1), where an offence under this Act has been committed with the consent of any director or manager, secretary or other officer of the company, such director, manager, secretary or other officer shall also be deemed to be guilty of that offence and shall be liable to be proceeded against and punished accordingly.

Explanation— For the purposes of this section—

(a) "company" means any body, corporate and includes a firm or other association of individuals; and

(b) "director" in relation to a firm means a partner in the firm.

14A. (1) No suit, prosecution or other regal proceeding shall lie against the Central Government or a State Government for anything which is in good faith done or intended to be done under this Act.

(2) No suit or other legal proceeding shall lie against the

Central Government or a State Government for any damage caused or likely to be caused by anything which is in good faith done or intended to be done under this Act.

15. (1) Notwithstanding anything contained in the Code of Criminal Procedure, 1973, every offence punishable under this Act shall be cognizable and every such offence, except where it is punishable with imprisonment for a minimum term exceeding three months, may be tried summarily by a Judicial Magistrate of the first class or in a metropolitan area by a Metropolitan Magistrate in accordance with the procedure specified in the said code.

(2) Notwithstanding anything contained in the Code of Criminal Procedure, 1973, when any public servant is alleged to have committed the offence of abetment of an offence punishable under this Act, while acting or purporting to act in the discharge of his official duty, no court shall take cognizance of such offence of abetment except with the previous sanction—

(a) of the Central Government, in the case of a person employed in connection with the affairs of the Union; and

(b) of the State Government, in the case of a person employed in connection with the affairs of a State.

15A. (1) Subject to such rules as the Central Government may make in this behalf, the State Government shall take such measures as may be necessary for ensuring that the rights arising from the abolition of "untouchability" are made available to, and are availed of by, the persons subjected to any disability arising out of "untouchability"

(2) In particular, and without prejudice to the generality of the provisions of sub-section (1), such measures may include—

(i) the provision of adequate facilities, including legal aid, to the persons subjected to any disability arising out of "untouchability" to enable them to avail themselves of such rights;

(ii) the appointment of officers for initiating or exercising supervision over prosecutions for the contravention of the provisions of this Act;

(iii) the setting up of special courts for the trial of offences under this Act;

(iv) the setting up of Committees at such appropriate levels as the State Government may think fit to assist the State Government in formulating or implementing such measures;

(v) provision for a periodic survey of the working of the provisions of this Act with a view to suggesting measures for the better implementation of the provisions of this Act.

(vi) the identification of the areas where persons are under any disability arising out of "untouchability" and adoption of such measures as would ensure the removal of such disability from such areas.

3. The Central Government shall take such steps as may be necessary to co-ordinate the measures taken by the State Governments under sub-section (1).

4. The Central Government shall, every year, place on the Table of each House of Parliament, a report on the measures taken by itself and by the State Governments in pursuance of the provisions of this section.

16. Save as otherwise expressly provided in this Act, the provisions of this Act shall have effect notwithstanding anything inconsistent therewith contained in any other law for the time being in force, or any custom or usage or any instrument having effect by virtue of any such law or any decree or order of any court or other authority.

16A. The provisions of the Probation of Offenders Act, 1958, shall not apply to any person above the age of fourteen years who is found guilty of having committed any offence punishable under this Act.

16B. (1) The Central Government may, by notification in the Official Gazette, make rules to carry out the provisions of this Act.

(2) Every rule made by the Central Government under this Act shall be laid, as soon as may be after it is made, before each House of Parliament while it is in session for a total period of thirty days which may be comprised in one session or in two or more successive sessions, and if, before the expiry of the session immediately following the session or the successive sessions, and if, before the expiry of the session immediately following the session or the successive sessions aforesaid, both Houses agree in making any modification in the rule or both Houses agree that the rule should not be made, the rule shall thereafter have effect only in such modified form or be of no effect, as the case may be; so, however, that any such modification or annulment shall be without prejudice to the validity of anything previously done under the rule.)

17. The enactment specified in the Schedule are hereby repealed to the extent to which they or any of the provisions contained therein correspond or are repugnant to this Act or to any of the provisions contained therein.

THE SCHEDULE

(See section 17)

1. The Bihar Harijan (Removal of Civil Disabilities) Act, 1949 (Bihar Act XIX of 1949).
2. The Bombay Harijan (Removal of Social Disabilities) Act, 1946 (Bombay Act X of 1974).
3. The Bombay Harijan Temple Entry Act, 1947 (Bombay Act XXXV of 1974).
4. The Central Provinces and Berar Scheduled Castes (Removal of Civil Disabilities) Act, 1947 (Central Provinces and Berar Act XXIV of 1947).
5. The Central Provinces and Berar Temple Entry Authorisation Act, 1947 (Central Provinces and Berar Act XIII of 1947).
6. The East Punjab (Removal of Religious and Social Disabilities) Act, 1948 (East Punjab Act XVI of 1948).
7. The Madras Removal of Civil Disabilities Act, 1938 (Madras Act XXI of 1938).

8. The Orissa Removal of Civil Disabilities Act, 1946 (Orissa Act XI of 1946).
9. The Orissa Temple Entry Authorisation Act, 1948 (Orissa Act XI of 1948).
10. The United Provinces Removal of Social Disabilities Act, 1947 (U.P. Act XIV of 1947).
11. The West Bengal Hindu Social Disabilities Removal Act, 1948 (West Bengal Act XXXVII of 1948).
12. The Hyderabad Harijan Temple Entry Regulation, 1358F (No.LV of 1358F Fasli).
13. The Hyderabad Harijan (removal of Social Disabilities) Regulation, 1358F (No.LVI of 1358F Fasli).
14. The Madhya Bharat Harijan Ayogta Nivaran Vidhan, Samvat 2005 (Madhya Bharat Act No.15 of 1949).
15. The Removal of Civil Disabilities Act, 1943 (Mysore Act XLII of 1943).
16. The Mysore Temple Entry Authorisation Act, 1948 (Mysore Act XIV of 1948).
17. The Saurashtra Harijan (Removal of Social Disabilities) Ordinance (No.XL of 1948).
18. The Travancore-Cochin Removal of Social Disabilities Act,1125 (Travancore-Cochin Act VIII of 1125).
19. The Travancore-Cochin Temple Entry (Removal of Disabilities Act, 1950 (Travancore Cochin Act XXVII of 1950).
20. The Coorg Scheduled Castes (Removal of Civil and Social Disabilities) Act, 1949 (Coorg Act I of 1940).
21. The Coorg Temple Entry Authorisation Act, 1949 (Coorg Act II of 1949).

THE PROTECTION OF CIVIL RIGHTS RULES, 1977

Dated 15th September, 1977

In exercise of the powers conferred by section 16-B of the Protection of Civil Rights Act, 1955 (22 of 1955), the Central Government hereby makes the following rules namely:—

1. Short title and commencement

(1) These rules may be called the **Protection of Civil Rights Rules, 1977.**

(2) They shall come into force on the date of their publication in the Official Gazette.

2. Definition

In these rules unless the context otherwise requires—

(a) "Act" means the Protection of Civil Rights Act, 1955 (22 of 1955);

(b) "Section" means a section of the Act.

3. Manner of Inquiry under sub-section (1) of section 10-A.

(1) The State Government may appoint an officer not below the rank of a Sub-divisional Magistrate for the purpose of making an inquiry referred to in sub-section (1) of section 10-A.

(2) The Officer appointed under sub-rule (1) (hereinafter in this rule referred to as the inquiry officer) shall issue public notice specifying the date, time, place and the purpose of such inquiry and calling upon all the residents of the area in respect of which the inquiry is to be held to furnish such information and materials including documents in their possession, as may be relevant for the purposes of the enquiry, or

(3) The public notice referred to in sub-rule (2) shall be in the local language or languages of the area and the same shall be—

(i) published on the notice –board in the offices of the District Magistrate, the District Superintendent of Police, the Village Panchayat or Municipal Committee of the area and such other places as the inquiry officer deems fit and at least in one daily newspaper circulating in the area; and

(ii) proclaimed in the area by beat of drum or in such other manner as the inquiry officer may think best in the circumstances to bring the contents of the public notice to the notice of the inhabitants of the area.

(4) The inquiry officer, while making such inquiry shall follow as nearly as practicable, the procedure for summary trials including the recording of evidence as laid down in Chapter XXI of Code of Criminal Procedure, 1973,2 of 1974).

(5) The inquiry officer shall complete the inquiry as expeditiously as possible and submit his report to the State Government within such period, not exceeding six weeks as may be specified by the State Government in the order appointing the inquiry officer:

Provided that the State Government may having regard to

the nature of the inquiry, extend the period of submission of the report by such period not exceeding two months in total as it may consider necessary.

4. Period for filing a petition under sub-section (3) of section 10-A

Any person aggrieved by the imposition of a collective fine under sub-section (1) of section 10-A or by the order of apportionment, may within a period of thirty days from the date of proclamation of the notification under sub-section (2) of that section file a petition before the State Government or the authority specified by it:

Provided that where the State Government or the authority, as the case may be, may entertain the petition after the expiry of the said period if it is satisfied that the petitioner was prevented by sufficient cause from filing the petition in time.

(2) The State Government or the authority before which the petition is filed shall dispose off the petition as expeditiously as possible.

5. Report by the State Government

Every State Government shall, for the purpose of enabling the Central Government, place the report referred to in sub-section (4) of Section 15-A on the Table of each House of Parliament, furnish to the Government before the 15th day of February each year, a summary of the measures taken by it under sub-section (1) and (2) of that section during the preceding calendar year and shall also furnish such other information as may be required by the Central Government from time to time.

What is required to be done in case any atrocities is committed? What is covered under atrocities against SC & ST?

The affected person may file an First Information Report (FIR) in the Police Station of the area as per provision under Section 3 of the Scheduled Castes and the Scheduled Tribes (Prevention of Atrocities) Act, 1989.

In case a person, not being a member of a Scheduled Caste or a Scheduled Tribe, forces a member of SC/ST

(i) to drink or eat any inedible or obnoxious substance;

(ii) to cause injury, insult or annoyance by dumping excreta, waste matter, carcasses or any other obnoxious substance in his premises or neighborhood;

(iii) forcibly removes clothes or parades him naked or with painted face or body or commits any similar act which is derogatory to human dignity;

(iv) wrongfully occupies or cultivates any land owned by, or allotted to, or notified by any competent authority to be allotted to him transferred;

(v) wrongfully dispossesses from his land or premises or interferes with the enjoyment of his rights over any land, premises or water;

(vi) compels or entices to do "begar" or other similar forms of forced or bonded labour other than any compulsory service for public purposes imposed by Government;

(vii) forces or intimidates not to vote or to vote a particular candidate or to vote in a manner other than that provided by law;

(viii) institutes false, malicious or vexatious suit or criminal or other legal proceedings;

(ix) gives any false or frivolous information to any public servant and thereby causes such as public servant to use his lawful power to the injury or annoyance;

(x) intentionally insults or intimidates with intent to humiliate any place with in public view;

(xi) assaults or uses force to any woman with intent to dishonour or outrage her modesty;

(xii) being in a position to dominate the will of a woman and uses that position to exploit her sexually to which she would not have otherwise agreed;

(xiii) corrupts or fouls the water of any spring, reservoir or any other source ordinarily used so as to render it less fit for the purpose for which it is ordinarily used ;

(xiv) denies any customary right of passage to place of public resort or obstructs such member so as to prevent him from using or having access to a place of public resort to which other members of public or any section thereof have a right to use or access to;

(xv) forces or causes to leave his house, village or other place of residence.

What is the maximum punishment provided for commission of such offences under the act?

The offenders of such offences shall be punishable with imprisonment for a term which shall not be less than six months but which may extend to five years and with fine.

Relief is provided to a SC/ST person affected by atrocities:

Relief is provided as under

(a)	Murder of earning member	Rs. 2 lakhs
(b)	Murder of non- – earning member	Rs. 1 lakh
(c)	100% incapacitation	Rs. 1 lakh
(d)	Sexual exploitation of a woman	Rs. 50,000

In 1989, the Scheduled Cases and the Scheduled Tribes (Prevention of Atrocities) Act, 1989 was enacted for checking crime committed by other communities against persons belonging to Scheduled Castes and Scheduled Tribes. These special enactments seek to ensure the protection of the SCs and STs by providing more stringent penalties than provided under the Indian Penal Code (IPC) and other laws for similar offences. Comprehensive Rules were also framed under the POA Act in the year 1995, which inter-alia provide for relief and rehabilitation of the victims of the practice of untouchability and other atrocities.

Scheduled Castes and Scheduled Tribes (Prevention of Atrocities) Act, 1989,which came into force on 30 January 1990, specifies offences, which are considered as atrocities, and provides for deterrent punishments for commission of the same. It also envisages preventive measures, and states have to evolve schemes, among others, for economic and social rehabilitation of such victims. All States and Union Territories except Arunachal Pradesh and Nagaland have specified special courts for trial of offences under this Act.

The detailed text of The Scheduled Castes and Scheduled Tribes (Prevention of the Atrocities) Act, 1989 is given hereunder:

THE SCHEDULED CASTES AND THE SCHEDULED TRIBES (PREVENTION OF ATROCITIES) ACT, 1989

(11th September 1989)

THE SCHEDULED CASTES AND THE SCHEDULED TRIBES (PREVENTION OF ATROCITIES) ACT, 1989 is an Act to prevent the commission of offences of atrocities against the members of the Scheduled Castes and the Scheduled Tribes, to provide for Special Courts for the trial of such offences and for the relief and rehabilitation of the victims of such offences and for matters connected therewith or incidental thereto.

CHAPTER-1

PRELIMINARY

1. (1) This Act may be called the Scheduled Castes and the Scheduled Tribes (Prevention of Atrocities) Act, 1989.
   (2) It extends to the whole of India except the State of Jammu and Kashmir.
   (3) It shall come into force on such date as the Central Government may, by notification in the Official Gazette, appoint.
2. (1) In this Act, unless the context otherwise requires—
   (a) "Atrocity" means an offence punishable under section 3;
   (b) "Code" means the Code of Criminal Procedure, 1973;
   (c) "Scheduled Castes and Scheduled Tribes" shall have the meanings assigned to them respectively under clause (24) and clause (25) of article 366 of the Constitution;
   (d) "Special Court" means a Court of Session specified as a Special Court in section **14;**
   (e) "Special Public Prosecutor" means a Public Prosecutor specified as a Special Public Prosecutor or an advocate referred to in Section 15;
   (f) words and expressions used but not defined in this Act and defined in the Code or the Indian Penal Code shall have the meanings assigned to them respectively in the Code, or as the case may be, in the Indian Penal Code.

(2) Any reference in this Act to any enactment or any provision thereof shall, in relation to an area in which such enactment or such provision is not in force, be construed as a reference to the corresponding law, if any, in force in that area.

CHAPTER- II
OFFENCES OF ATROCITIES

3. (1) Whoever, not being a member of a Scheduled Caste or a Scheduled Tribe—

(i) forces a member of a Scheduled Caste or a Scheduled Tribe to drink or eat any inedible or obnoxious substance;

(ii) acts with intent to cause injury, insult or annoyance to any member of a Scheduled Caste or a Scheduled Tribe by dumping excreta, waste matter, carcasses or any other obnoxious substance in his premises or neighborhood;

(iii) forcibly removes clothes from the person of a member of a Scheduled Caste or a Scheduled Tribe or parades him naked or with painted face or body or commits any similar act which is derogatory to human dignity;

(iv.) wrongfully occupies or cultivates any land owned by, or allotted to, or notified by any competent authority to be allotted to, a member of a Scheduled Caste or a Scheduled Tribe or gets the land allotted to him transferred;

(v) wrongfully dispossesses a member of a Scheduled Caste or a Scheduled Tribe from his land or premises or interferes with the enjoyment of his rights over any land, premises or water;

(vi) compels or entices a member of a Scheduled Castes or a Scheduled Tribes to do 'begar' or other similar forms of forced or bonded labour other than any compulsory service for public purposes imposed by Government;

(vii) forces or intimidates a member of a Scheduled Caste or a Scheduled Tribe not to vote or to vote to a particular candidate or to vote in a manner other than that provided by law;

(viii) institutes false, malicious or vexatious suit or criminal or other legal proceedings against a member of a Scheduled Caste or a Scheduled Tribe;

(ix) gives any false or frivolous information to any public servant and thereby causes such public servant to use his lawful power to the injury or annoyance of a member of a Scheduled Caste or cheduled Tribe;

(x) intentionally insults or intimidates with intent to humiliate a member of a Scheduled Caste or a Scheduled Tribe in any place within public view;

(xi) assaults or uses force to any woman belonging to a Scheduled Caste or a Scheduled Tribe with intent to dishonour or outrage her modesty;

(xii) being in a position to dominate the will of a woman belonging to a Scheduled Caste or a Scheduled Tribe and uses that position to exploit her sexually to which she would not have otherwise agreed;

(xiii) corrupts or fouls the water of any spring, reservoir or any other source ordinarily used by members of the Scheduled Castes or the Scheduled Tribes so as to render it less fit for the purpose for which it is ordinarily used;

(xiv) denies a member of a Scheduled Caste or a Scheduled Tribe any customary right of passage to a place of public resort or obstructs such member so as to prevent him from using or having access to a place of public resort to which other members of public or any section thereof have a right to use or access to;

(xv) forces or causes a member of a Scheduled Caste or a Scheduled Tribe to leave his house, village or other place of residence;

Shall be punishable with imprisonment for a term, which shall not be less than six months but which may extend to five years and with fine.

(2) Whoever, not being a member of a Scheduled Caste or a Scheduled Tribe—

(i) gives or fabricates false evidence intending thereby to cause, or knowing it to be likely that he will thereby cause, any member of a Scheduled Caste or a Scheduled Tribe to be convicted of an offence which is capital by the law for the time being inforce shall be punished with imprisonment for life and with fine; and if an innocent member of a Scheduled Caste or a Scheduled Tribes be convicted and executed in consequence of such false or fabricated evidence, the person who gives or fabricates such false evidence, shall be punished with death;

(ii) gives or fabricates false evidence intending thereby to cause, or knowing it to be likely that he will thereby cause, any member of a Scheduled Caste or a Scheduled Tribe to be convicted of an offence which is not capital but punishable with imprisonment for a term of seven years or upwards, shall be punishable with imprisonment for a term which shall not be less than six months but which may extend to seven years or upwards and with fine;

(iii) commits mischief by fire or any explosive substance intending to cause or knowing it to be likely that he will thereby cause damage to any property belonging to a member of a Scheduled Caste or a Scheduled Tribe, shall be punishable with imprisonment for a term which shall not be less than six months but which may extend to seven years and with fine;

(iv) commits mischief by fire or any explosive substance intending to cause or knowing it to be likely that he will thereby cause destruction of any building which is ordinarily used as a place of worship or as a place for human dwelling or as a place for custody of the property by a member of Scheduled Caste or a Scheduled Tribe, shall be punishable with imprisonment for life and with fine;

(v) commits any offence under the Indian Penal Code punishable with imprisonment for a term of ten years or more against a person or property on the ground that such person is a member of a Scheduled Caste or a Scheduled Tribe or such property belongs to such member, shall be punishable with imprisonment for life and with fine;

(vi) knowingly or having reason to believe that an offence has been committed under this Chapter, causes any evidence of the commission of that offence to disappear with the intention of screening the offender from legal punishment, or with that intention gives any information respecting the offence which he knows or believes to be false shall be punishable with the punishment provided for that offence; or

(vii) being a public servant, commits any offence under this section, shall be punishable with imprisonment for a term which shall not be less than one year but which may extend to the punishment provided for that offence.

4. Whoever, being a public servant but not being a member of a Scheduled Caste or a Scheduled Tribe, willfully neglects his duties required to be performed by him under this Act, shall be punishable with imprisonment for a term which shall not be less than six months but which may extend to one year.
5. Whoever, having already been convicted of an offence under this Chapter is convicted for the second offence or any offence subsequent to the second offence, shall be punishable with imprisonment for a term which shall not be less than one year but which may extend to the punishment provided for that offence.
6. Subject to the other provisions of this Act, the provisions of

section 34, Chapter III, Chapter IV, Chapter V, Chapter VA, section 149 and Chapter XXIII of the Indian Penal Code, shall, so far as may be, apply for the purposes of this Act as they apply for the purposes of the Indian Penal Code.

7. (1) Where a person has been convicted of any offence punishable under this Chapter, the Special Court may, in addition to awarding any punishment, by order in writing, declare that any property, movable or immovable or both, belonging to the person, which has been used for the commission of that offence, shall stand forfeited to Government.

   (2) Where any person is accused of any offence under this Chapter, it shall be open to the Special Court trying him to pass an order that all or any of the properties, movable or immovable or both, belonging to him, shall, during the period of such trial, be attached, and where such trial ends in conviction, the property so attached shall be liable to forfeiture to the extent it is required for the purpose of realisation of any fine imposed under this Chapter.

8. In a prosecution for an offence under this Chapter, if it is proved that—

   (a) the accused rendered any financial assistance to a person accused of, or reasonably suspected of committing, an offence under this Chapter the, Special Court shall presume, unless the contrary is proved, that such person had abetted the offence;

   (b) a group of persons committed an offence under this Chapter and if it is proved that the offence committed was sequel to any existing dispute regarding land or any other matter, it shall be presumed that offence was committed in furtherance of the common intention or in prosecution of the common object.

9. (1) Notwithstanding anything contained in the code or in any other provision of this Act, the State Government may, if it considers it necessary or expedient so to do—

      (a) for the prevention of and for coping with any offence under this Act, or

(b) for any case or class or group of cases under this Act, in any district or part thereof, confer, by notification in the Official Gazette, on any officer of the State Government, the powers exercisable by a police officer under the Code in such district or part thereof or, as the case may be, for such case or class or group of cases, and in particular, the powers of arrest, investigation and prosecution of persons before any Special Court.

(2) All officers of police and all other officers of Government shall assist the officer refereed to in sub-section (1) in the execution of the provisions of this Act or any rule, scheme or order made thereunder.

(3) The provisions of the Code shall, so far as may be, apply to the exercise of the powers by an officer under sub-section (1)

CHAPTER III

EXTERNMENT

10. (1) Where the Special Court is satisfied, upon a complaint or a police report that a person is likely to commit an offence under Chapter II of this Act in any area included in 'Scheduled Areas' or 'tribal areas', as referred to in article 244 of the Constitution, it may, by order in writing, direct such person to remove himself beyond the limits of such area, by such route and within such time as may be specified in the order, and not to return to that area from which he was directed to remove himself for such period, not exceeding two years, as may be specified in the order.

(2) The Special Court shall, along with the order under sub-section (1), communicate to the person directed under that sub-section the grounds on which such order has been made.

(3) The Special Court may revoke or modify the order made under sub-section (1), for the reasons to be recorded in writing, on the representation made by the person against whom such order has been made or by any other person on his behalf within thirty days from the date of the order.

11. (1) If a person to whom a direction has been issued under section 10 to remove him self from any area—
   (a) fails to remove himself as directed; or
   (b) having so removed himself enters such area within the period specified in the order,

   otherwise than with the permission in writing of the Special Court under sub-section (2), the Special Court may cause him to be arrested and removed in police custody to such place outside such area as the Special Court may specify.

   (2) The Special Court may, by order in writing, permit any person in respect of whom an order under section 10 has been made, to return to the area from which he was directed to remove himself for such temporary period and subject to such conditions as may be specified in such order and may require him to execute a bond with or without surety for the due observation of the conditions imposed.

   (3) The Special Court may at any time revoke any such permission.

   (4) Any person who, with such permission, returns to the area from which he was directed to remove himself shall observe the conditions imposed, and at the expiry of the temporary period for which he was permitted to return, or an the revocation of such permission before the expiry of such temporary period, shall remove himself outside such area and shall not return thereto within the unexpired portion specified under section 10 without a fresh permission.

   (5) If a person fails to observe any of the conditions imposed or to remove himself accordingly or having so removed himself enters or returns to such area without fresh permission the Special Court may cause him to be arrested and removed in police custody to such place outside such area as the Special Court may specify.

12. (1) Every person against whom an order has been made under section 10 shall, if so required by the Special Court, allow his measurements and photographs to be taken by police officer.

(2) If any person referred to in sub-section (1), when required to allow his measurements or photographs to be taken resists or refuses to allow his taking of such measurements or photographs, it shall be lawful to use all necessary means to secure the taking thereof.

(3) Resistance to or refusal to allow the taking of measurements or photographs under sub-section (2) shall be deemed to be an offence under section 186 of the Indian Penal Code.

(4) Where an order under section 10 is revoked, all measurements and photographs (including negative) taken under sub-section (2) shall be destroyed or made over to the person against whom such order is made.

13. Any person contravening an order of the Special Court made under section 10 shall be punishable with imprisonment for a term which may extend to one year and with fine.

CHAPTER IV

SPECIAL COURTS

14. For the purpose of providing for speedy trial, the State Government shall, with the concurrence of the Chief Justice of the High Court, by notification in the Official Gazette, specify for each district a Court of Session to be a Special Court to try offences under this Act.

15. For every Special Court, the State Government shall, by notification in the Official Gazette, specify a Public Prosecutor or appoint an advocate who has been in practice as an advocate for not less than seven years, as a Special Public Prosecutor for the purpose of conducting cases in that Court.

CHAPTER-V

MISCELLANEOUS

16. The provisions of section 10A of the Protection of Civil Rights Act, 1955, shall, so far as may be, apply for the purposes of imposition and realisation of collective fine and for all other matters connected therewith under this Act.

17. (1) A District Magistrate or a Sub-divisional Magistrate or

any other Executive Magistrate or any police officer not below the rank of a Deputy Superintendent of Police may, on receiving information and after such inquiry as he may think necessary, has reason to believe that a person or a group of persons not belonging to the Scheduled Castes or the Scheduled Tribes, residing in or frequenting any place within the local limits of his jurisdiction is likely to commit an offence or has threatened to commit any offence under this Act and is of the opinion that there is sufficient ground for proceeding, declare such an area to be an area prone to atrocities and take necessary action for keeping the peace and good behavior and maintenance of public order and tranquility and may take preventive action.

(2) The provisions of Chapters VIII, X and XI of the Code shall, so far as maybe, apply for the purposes of sub-section (1)

(3) The State Government may, by notification in the Official Gazette, make one or more schemes specifying the manner in which the officers referred to in sub-section (1) shall take appropriate action specified in such scheme or schemes to prevent atrocities and to restore the feeling of security amongst the members of the Scheduled Castes and the Scheduled Tribes.

18. Nothing in section 438 of the code shall apply in relation to any case involving the arrest of any person on an accusation of having committed an offence under this Act.

19. The provisions of section 360 of the Code and the provisions of the Probation of Offenders Act, 1958 shall not apply to any person above the age of eighteen years who is found guilty of having committed an offence under this Act.

20. Save as otherwise provided in this Act, the provisions of this Act shall have effect notwithstanding anything inconsistent therewith contained in any other law for the time being in force or any custom or usage or any instrument having effect by virtue of any such law.

21. (1) Subject to such rules as the Central Government may make in this behalf, the State Government shall take

such measures as may be necessary for the effective implementation of this Act.

(2) In particular, and without prejudice to the generality of the foregoing provisions, such measures may include—

(i) the provision for adequate facilities, including legal aid, to the persons subjected to atrocities to enable them to avail themselves of justice;

(ii) the provision for travelling and maintenance expenses to witnesses, including the victims of atrocities, during investigation and trial of offences under this Act;

(iii) the provision for the economic and social rehabilitation of the victims of the atrocities;

(iv) the appointment of officers for initiating or exercising supervision over prosecutions for the contravention of the provisions of this Act;

(v) the setting up of committees at such appropriate levels as the State Government may think fit to assist that Government in formulation or implementation of such measures;

(vi) provisions for a periodic survey of the working of the provisions of this Act with a view to suggesting measures for the better implementation of the provisions of this Act;

(vii) the identification of the areas where the members of the Scheduled Castes and the Scheduled Tribes are likely to be subjected to atrocities and adoption of such measures so as to ensure safety for such members.

(3) The Central Government shall take such steps as maybe necessary to co-ordinate the measures taken by the State Governments under sub-section- (1).

(4) The Central Government shall, every year, place on the table of each House of Parliament a report on the measures taken by itself and by the State Governments in pursuance of the provisions of this section.

22. No suit, prosecution or other legal proceedings shall lie against the central Government or against the State

Government or any officer or authority of Government or any other person for anything which is in good faith done or intended to be done under this Act.

23. (1) The Central Government may, by notification in the Official Gazette, make rules for carrying out the purposes of this Act.

(2) Every rule made under this Act shall be laid, as soon as may be after it is made, before each House of Parliament, while it is in session for a total period of thirty days which may be comprised in one session or in two or more successive sessions, and if, before the expiry of the session immediately following the session or the successive sessions, aforesaid, both Houses agree in making any modification in the rule or both Houses agree that the rule should not be made, the rule shall thereafter have effect only in such modified form or be of no effect, as the case may be; show however , that any such modification annulment shall be without prejudice to the validity of anything previously done under that rule.

Empowerment of the Scheduled Castes through Statutory Commissions

The Ministry of Social Justice & Empowerment, in its nodal capacity, continued to make special efforts towards ensuring social justice to the weaker sections through enforcement of special legislations and implementation of protective programmes.

There are two statutory Commissions namely i) National Commission for Scheduled Castes and STs; ii) National Commission for Safai Karamcharis play a very important role in safeguarding the rights and interests of the Scheduled Castes.

Armed with the powers of a Civil Court, the ***National Commission for SCs and STs*** investigated individual complaints/ grievances made on-the-spot visits to the areas where the incidence of crimes/atrocities took place and placed the 'Action Taken Reports' before both Houses of Parliament. The Commission for Scheduled Castes and STs also played an effective interventionist role in reviewing the progress of the implementation of Special

Component Plan (SCP) and Tribal Sub-Plan (TSP) by the Central Ministries/Departments and the State Governments and also the utilisation of Special Central Assistance (SCA) to SCP and TSP. The outstanding contribution of the Commission was holding national-level consultations with District Development Commissioners/Collectors to develop a direct district-wise dialogue for receiving the first-hand report on the progress of the implementation of various policies and programmes in improving the status of the Target Groups.

With a major objective of accomplishing complete eradication of the obnoxious and in-human practice of manual scavenging, the National Scheme of Liberation and Rehabilitation of Scavengers and their Dependents was modified in 1998 to accommodate revised norms and involve NGOs in the efforts made for identification, liberation and rehabilitation of scavengers. Though, complete elimination of the practice of manual scavenging could not be achieved by the end of the Ninth Plan (2002) as targeted, yet around 3.84 lakh out of the 6.53 lakh identified scavengers were rehabilitated, while 1.47 lakh were imparted training to take up alternative vocations.

The National Commission for Safai Karamcharis, set up in 1994, has been playing its role in promoting as well as safeguarding the interests and rights of Safai Karamcharis, besides investigating specific grievances as well as matters relating to implementation of programmes and schemes for the welfare of the Safai Karamcharis. It also has the responsibility of over-seeing the progress of fulfilling the national commitment of Total Eradication of Manual Scavenging.

The above two statutory Commissions viz. i) National Commission for Scheduled Castes and STs; ii) National Commission for Safai Karamcharis are discussued in detail hereunder.

National Commission for Scheduled Castes and Scheduled Tribes

The Constitution of India provided for appointment of a Special Officer under Article 338 for investigation of all matters relating to the safeguards provided for the Scheduled Castes and Scheduled Tribes and to submit reports to the President. In order to oversee the implementation of various safeguards provided for Scheduled Castes and Scheduled Tribes, a Multi-Member Commission, known as the Commission for SCs & STs, came into being with effect from 21-7-78. This Commission was renamed as the National Commission for SCs & STs with effect from 1-9-87 to act as a National level Advisory Body in Scheduled Castes and Scheduled Tribes matters. The existing and erstwhile field offices of Commissioner for SCs & STs were brought under the control of the newly formed multi member Commission. In 1990, the provisions of Article 338 were amended, vide the Constitution (Sixty fifth) Amendment Act, 1990 and the Office of the Commissioner for SCs & STs was replaced by the National Commission for SCs & STs with effect from 12.3.92.

THE CONSTITUTION (SIXTY-FIFTH AMENDMENT) ACT, 1990

1. Short title and Commencement

(1) This Act may be called the Constitution (Sixty-fifth Amendment) Act, 1990.

(2) It shall come into force on such date as the Central Government may, by notification in the Official Gazette, appoint

2. Amendment of Article 338 In Article 338 of the Constitution

(a) for the marginal heading, the following marginal heading shall be substituted, namely:—

"National Commission for Scheduled Castes and Scheduled Tribes".

(b) for clauses (1) and (2), the following clauses shall be substituted, namely:—

"(1) There shall be a Commission for the Scheduled Castes and Scheduled Tribes to be known as the National Commission for the Scheduled Castes and Scheduled Tribes.

(2) Subject to the provisions of any law made in this behalf by Parliament, the Commission shall consist of a Chairperson, Vice-Chairperson and five other Members and the conditions of service and tenure of office of the Chairperson, Vice-Chairperson and other Members so appointed shall be such as the President may by rule determine.

(3) The Chairperson, Vice-Chairperson and other Members of the Commission shall be appointed by the President by warrant under his hand and seal.

(4) The Commission shall have the power to regulate its own procedure.

(5) It shall be the duty of the Commission:

(a) to investigate and monitor all matters relating to the safeguards provided for the Scheduled Castes and Scheduled Tribes under this Constitution or under any other law for the time being in force or under any order of the Government and to evaluate the working of such safeguards;

(b) to inquire into specific complaints with respect to the deprivation of rights and safeguards of the Scheduled Castes and Scheduled Tribes;

(c) to participate and advise on the planning process of socio-economic development of the Scheduled Castes and Scheduled Tribes and to evaluate the progress of their development under the Union and any State;

(d) to present to the President, annually and at such other time as the Commission may deem fit, reports upon the working of those safeguards;

(e) to make in such reports recommendations as to the measures that should be taken by the Union or any State for the effective implementation of those safeguards and other measures for the protection, welfare and socio-economic development of the Scheduled Castes and Scheduled Tribes; and

(f) to discharge such other functions in relation to the protection, welfare and development and advancement of the Scheduled Castes and Scheduled Tribes as the President may, subject to the provisions of any law made by Parliament, by rule specify.

(6) The President shall cause all such reports to be laid before each House of Parliament along with a memorandum

explaining the action taken or proposed to be taken on the recommendations relating to the Union and the reasons for the non-acceptance, if any, of any of such recommendations.

(7) Where any such report, or any part thereof, relates to any matter with which any State Government is concerned, a copy of such report shall be forwarded to the Governor of the State who shall cause it to be laid before the Legislature of the State along with a memorandum explaining the action taken or proposed to be taken on the recommendations relating to the State and the reasons for the non-acceptance, if any, of any of such recommendations.

(8) The Commission shall, while investigating any matter referred to in sub-clause (a) or inquiring into any complaint referred to in sub-clause (b) of clause (5), have all the powers of a civil court trying a suit and in particular in respect of the certain matters.

The National Commission for Scheduled Castes and Scheduled Tribes is a statutory body. It is having its Headquarters at New Delhi and its eighteen State Offices are located at Agartala, Ahmedabad, Bangalore, Bhubaneswar, Bhopal, Calcutta, Chennai, Chandigarh, Guwahati, Hyderabad, Jaipur, Lucknow, Patna, Pune, Ranchi, Raipur, Shillong and Tiruvananthapuram. A Chairman who is aided by a Vice-Chairman and five other Members heads the Commission. The present Commission, fourth in the series, was constituted in March 2002.

There are four Wings namely 1. Administration & Coordination Wing 2. Service Safeguards Wing 3. Atrocities and Protection of Civil Rights Wing and 4. Economic & Social Development Wing.

The **Administration and Co-ordination Wing** looks after personnel management of officers and staff of the Secretariat of the Commission and provides administrative support in the functioning of the Commission. The Co-ordination Cell co-ordinates various activities being performed in the Commission, including making arrangements for holding internal meetings of the Commission as well as arranging meetings with the State/UT Administrations for reviewing the implementation of constitutional safeguards.

The **Service Safeguards Wing** deals with the implementation of service safeguards provided to Scheduled Castes and Scheduled Tribes in the Central/State Government services as well as Central and State Government Public Sector Undertakings. All representations/complaints relating to Scheduled Castes and Scheduled Tribes persons about their service matters are dealt within this Wing. In addition, policy matters relating to enactment/ Government orders and instructions pertaining to representations of Scheduled Castes and Scheduled Tribes in service, evaluation studies/surveys relating to implementation of various Constitutional safeguards in respect of service matters are dealt in this Wing. Cases relating to false caste certificates and inclusion or exclusion of caste(s) in Scheduled Castes and Scheduled Tribes list are also dealt in this Wing.

The **Atrocities and Protection of Civil Rights Wing** deals with matters pertaining to atrocities caused on Scheduled Castes and Scheduled Tribes and cases relating to protection of Civil Rights Act, the Bonded Labour System (Abolition) Act, the Minimum Wages Act, etc. either on receipt of complaints from individuals or from newspaper reports. This Wing also conducts evaluation studies/surveys on these subjects.

The **Economic and Social Development Wing** deals with matters relating to development of Scheduled Castes and Scheduled Tribes particularly implementation and monitoring of plan schemes of the Central/State Governments. Some of the specific items of work handled by this Wing are:

(i) Special Component Plan for Scheduled Castes and Tribal Sub Plan for Scheduled Tribes;

(ii) National Scheduled Castes and Scheduled Tribes Finance and Development Corporation

(iii) Cooperative Marketing Federation (TRIFED)

(iv) Representations/complaints made by SC/ST persons regarding their grievances on matters other than atrocities, untouchability practices and service matters;

(v) Tribal Research Institutes and other research bodies;

(vi) Land Reforms Acts and their implementation; Education Schemes for Scheduled Castes and Scheduled Tribes, etc.

Functions and Duties of the Commission

The functions, duties and powers of the Commission have been laid down in clauses (5), (8) and (9) of the amended Article 338 of the Constitution.

Clause (5)

It shall be the duty of the Commission:—

(a) To investigate and monitor all matters relating to the safeguards provided for the Scheduled Castes and Scheduled Tribes under this Constitution or under any other law for the time being in force or under any order of the Government and to evaluate the working of such safeguards;

(b) To inquire into specific complaints with respect to the deprivation of rights and safeguards of the Scheduled Castes and Scheduled Tribes;

(c) To participate and advise on the planning process of socio-economic development of the Scheduled Castes and Scheduled Tribes and to evaluate the progress of their development under the Union and any State;

(d) To present to the President, annually and at such other times as the Commission may deem fit, reports upon the working of those safeguards;

(e) To make in such reports recommendations as to the measures that should be taken by the Union or any State for the effective implementation of those safeguards and other measures for the protection, welfare and socio-economic development of the Scheduled Castes and Scheduled Tribes; and

(f) To discharge such other functions in relation to the protection, welfare and development and advancement of the Scheduled Castes and Scheduled Tribes as the President may, subject to the provisions of any law made by Parliament, by rule specify.

Clause (8)

The Commission shall, while investigating any matter referred to in sub-clause (a) or inquiring into any complaint referred to in sub-clause (b) of clause (5), have all the powers of a civil court trying a suit and in particular in respect of the following matters, namely:—

(a) Summoning and enforcing the attendance of any person from any part of India and examining him on oath;
(b) Requiring the discovery and production of any documents;
(c) Receiving evidence on affidavits;
(d) Requisitioning any public record or copy thereof from any court or office;
(e) Issuing commissions for the examination of witnesses and documents;
(f) Any other matter, which the President may by rule, determine;

Clause (9)

The Union and every State Government shall consult the Commission on all major policy matters affecting Scheduled Castes and Scheduled Tribes.

Functions of the State Offices of the Commission

The State Offices keep a watch on the formulation of policy and issue of guidelines relating to the welfare of Scheduled Castes and Scheduled Tribes in the respective States/Union Territories under their jurisdiction and keep the Commission Headquarters informed about the developments periodically. Policy decisions taken by any State Government/ Union Territories Administration affecting the interests of the Scheduled Castes and Scheduled Tribes are brought to the notice of the concerned authorities for necessary modifications. The State officers are required to liaise with the State/ Union Territories Administration for taking up evaluation and other studies to assess the working of various development programmes implemented for the welfare of the Scheduled Castes/Scheduled Tribes and their impact on ameliorating the socio-economic conditions of the target groups. The findings of the studies are brought to the notice of the concerned State Government for taking remedial measures. The main observations are highlighted in the Commission's Report.

The State offices of the Commission interact with the State Administrations and guide them with a view to see that the interests of the Scheduled Castes and Scheduled Tribes are protected and promoted in formulating plans and policies. The State Offices also monitor the utilization of funds earmarked for plans pertaining to Scheduled Castes/Scheduled Tribes, including keeping a watch on diversion of funds from the Special Component Plan and Tribal Sub-Plan, if any.

Each of the State Offices sends Quarterly Report to the Commission headquarters on the activities undertaken by them highlighting major issues relating to welfare of Scheduled Castes/ Scheduled Tribes in each State/UT under their jurisdiction. These reports contain useful information about the developments on Scheduled Castes and Scheduled Tribes matters in a State and enable the Commission to have an overall view on various States as well as national situation for taking appropriate action.

State Offices of the National Commission for SCs & STs

Headquarters & Jurisdiction	*Address*
Agartala (Tripura)	National Commission for SCs and STs, Pragati Road, Lake Chowmohani, Agartala-799001. (Tripura West)
Ahmedabad (Gujarat and Dadra & Nagar Haveli)	National Commission for SCs and STs, 2nd Floor, Mavlankar Haveli, Vasant Chowk, Lal Darwaja, Ahmedabad-380001.
Bangalore (Karnataka)	National Commission for SCs and STs, 3rd Floor, 'D' Wing, CGO Complex, Kendriya Sadan, Koramangala, Bangalore-560034.
Bhubaneswar (Orissa)	National Commission for SCs and STs, 575, Shahid Nagar, Bhubaneswar-751007
Jaipur (Rajasthan)	National Commission for SCs and STs, C-29, Lal Kothi Scheme, Behind SMS Stadium, Pankaj Sidhri Marg, Jaipur-302015.

Lucknow (Uttar Pradesh)	National Commission for SCs and STs, C-44, Sector-F, Kapurthala Complex, Aliganj, Lucknow-226020.
Chennai (Tamil Nadu and Pondicherry)	National Commission for SCs and STs, 2nd Floor, Block-5, Shastri Bhawan, Chennai-600006.
Patna (Bihar)	National Commission for SCs and STs, 189-B, Shrikrishnapuri, Patna-800001.
Pune (Maharashtra, Goa & Daman)	National Commission for SCs and STs, Chiplunkar Bhawan, Navipeth, Shastri Marg, Pune-411030.
Shillong (Meghalaya & Mizoram)	National Commission for SCs and STs, Temple Road, Lower Lachumire, Shillong-793001.
Tiruvananthapuram (Kerala & Lakshadweep)	National Commission for SCs and STs, 15/1658, "Kandla" MP Appan Road, Vazhuthacaud Junction, Thiruvananthapuram-695014.
Bhopal (Madhya Pradesh)	National Commission for SCs and STs, E-100/50, Shivaji Nagar, Arera, Bhopal-462016.
Calcutta (West Bengal, Sikkim and Nicobar Islands)	National Commission for SCs and STs, Mayukh Bhawan, (Ground Floor), Salt Lake City, Calcutta-700091.
Chandigarh (Haryana, Punjab, Himachal Pradesh, Jammu & Kashmir & Chandigarh)	National Commission for SCs and STs, 6th Floor, Kendriya Sadan, Sector-9-A, Chandigarh-160017.
Guwahati (Assam, Arunachal Pradesh, Nagaland & Manipur)	National Commission for SCs and STs, IInd Floor, "VN Enterprises Building", Christian Basti, G.S. Road, Dispur, Guwahati-781005.
Hyderabad (Andhra Pradesh)	National Commission for SCs and STs, Flat no.103, Tejaswi Apartment, IInd Floor, Dwarka Puri Colony, Panjagutta, Hyderabad-500008

How to Approach the Commission

Any member of the Scheduled Castes and Scheduled Tribes who feels aggrieved or has been denied his rights/safeguards provided under the Constitution or under various statutes/ laws/ rules etc. can approach the Commission directly at Commission's Headquarters at New Delhi or any of its State offices.

The following guidelines may, however, be kept in view before filing any formal complaint with the Commission:—

(a) The complaint should be addressed to the Chairman/ Vice-Chairman/ Secretary, National Commission for Scheduled Castes and Scheduled Tribes, New Delhi, or the head of its State office located in the concerned State/UT;

(b) The complainant should disclose his identity and give his complete address and should also sign the representation. Absence of any of these details would make the representation infructuous;

(c) Complaints should be legibly written or neatly typed out and, wherever necessary, supported by authenticated documents;

(d) No action will be taken on matters which are sub-judice. Hence, such matters need not be referred to the Commission as complaints;

(e) Cases pending in courts or cases in which a court has already given its ruling may not be taken up afresh with the Commission

Inquiry into specific complaints

The Commission is required to inquire into specific complaints with respect to the deprivation of rights and safeguards provided to the Scheduled Castes and Scheduled Tribes. In order to enable the Commission to perform this function effectively and efficiently, the Commission would like the members of Scheduled Castes and Scheduled Tribes to know that it will be helpful to inquire into their grievances if they substantiate their complaints with supporting documents and quote relevant provisions of the Act or Rules or directions which have been violated.

Inquiry into cases of atrocities

Whenever information is received in the Commission about any incident of atrocity against a person belonging to Scheduled Castes and Scheduled Tribes, the Commission would immediately get in touch with the law enforcing agency and administrative machinery of the State and the District to ascertain details of the incident and the action taken by the District Administration.

While monitoring and issuing instructions to the concerned authorities, the Commission ensures the following:

I. Whether the scene of occurrence of the crime has been visited immediately by Collector and Superintendent of Police of the District on receipt of information;

II. Whether proper FIR has been registered in local Police Station;

III. Whether names of all the persons involved/cited by the complainant have been included in the FIR;

IV. Whether investigation has been taken up by a Senior Police Officer as per provisions of SCs & STs (POA) Act, 1989;

V. Whether culprits have been apprehended and booked without loss of time;

VI. Whether proper charge sheet has been filed mentioning the relevant sections of IPC together with the PCR Act, 1955 and SCs & STs (POA) Act, 1989 in Court;

VII. Whether the cases are tried by the Special Courts;

VIII. Whether Special Public Prosecutors are appointed to handle these cases;

IX. Whether Police assists the courts in bringing forward witnesses and see that the culprits are suitably punished by the courts.

The Commission will also monitor that

(i) the victims are provided with suitable medical assistance and on time;

(ii) adequate protection is arranged for the victims of such incidents by providing police protection by stationing a police party, patrolling, etc.;

(iii) to see that proper compensation is paid to the victims as per provisions of law.

The Commission will, wherever possible depending upon the gravity and circumstances of the case, visit the place of incident to oversee the arrangements and to console and infuse confidence among the victims.

The Commission has laid down detailed procedure for conducting such inquiries and monitoring at all levels. Such inquiries can be conduced by the Members of the Commission or Teams of Investigators from Headquarters or State offices of the Commission.

Powers of the Commission to act as a Civil Court

While investigating any matter referred to in Sub-Clause (a) or inquiring into specific complaints under Sub-Clause (b) of the Clause (5) of Article 338 of the Constitution, the Commission shall have the powers of a Civil Court trying a suit and in particular in respect of the following matters:

(a) summoning and enforcing the attendance of any person from any part of India and examining him on oath;
(b) requiring the discovery and production of any document;
(c) receiving evidence on affidavits;
(d) requisitioning of any public record or copy thereof from any court of office;
(e) issuing commissions for the examination of witnesses or the documents;
(f) any other matter which the President may , by rule, determine.

The Working of the Commission

For the overall development and mainstreaming of the Scheduled Castes and Scheduled Tribes, the present Commission, constituted in October 1998 has adopted a more vigorous approach in its functioning. The meetings of the Commission are held regularly and the implementation of decisions taken is monitored keenly.

In order to monitor and evaluate the impact of development schemes, the Commission has decided to interact with the State/ Union Territory Governments more actively by holding State level review meetings with the Chief Secretaries and other senior officers and conducting field level visits. The Commission feels that as a result of these visits and meetings, the State/ Union Territory Governments will become more conscious of the genuine problems of the Scheduled Castes and Scheduled Tribes and would take the necessary initiative in working out remedial measures and adopting appropriate strategies.

The Commission, through its Headquarters and State offices, has also conducted field level inquiries and studies. This process has been given a renewed vigour with a view to ensure prompt relief, specially in matters relating to crimes and atrocities on Scheduled Castes and Scheduled Tribes and the grant of development benefits.

The procedure for investigating into complaints, especially with reference to violation of service safeguards, has also been streamlined to ensure prompt and speedy disposal of cases and relief in genuine cases. By calling officers and concerned Liaison Officers to the Commission with all relevant records, many long pending cases are being decided in one or two sittings. The Commission has also used its powers of Civil Court to summon documents and enforcing attendance in conducting the inquiries.

The Commission is of the view that it is only through proper planning and effective implementation of appropriate schemes for development that the Scheduled Castes and Scheduled Tribes can hope to catch up with the rest of the population and realise their full potential. The Commission has, thus, made a beginning by actively associating itself and participating in the planning process at the National and State levels. Regular communication is being maintained with the Planning Commission, Ministry of Social Justice & Empowerment, Ministry of Tribal Affairs and the State/ Union Territory Governments. The Annual Plans of the Central Ministries, States and UT Governments are being analysed in the Commission to this end with the support of its State Offices.

Consultation with Commission

Under the amended Article 338 (9), it has been provided that the Union and State Governments shall consult the Commission on all major policy matters affecting the interests of the Scheduled

Castes and Scheduled Tribes. The Commission has impressed upon all concerned that this provision should be strictly enforced. As a result of this many Bills and other Policy matters affecting Scheduled Castes and Scheduled Tribes are now being received in the Commission for its views. The Commission would like to reiterate the obligatory nature of this provision and solicit the support of all concerned to bring to its notice new policies and changes in existing policy, which have a bearing on the interests of Scheduled Castes and Scheduled Tribes.

Commission's Report

Clause 5 (d) of Article 338 provides "to present to the President, annually and at such other times as the Commission may deem fit, reports upon the working of those safeguards" and Clause 5 (e) provides "to make in such reports, recommendations as to the measures that should be taken by the Union or any State for the effective implementation of those safeguards and other measures for the protection, welfare and socio-economic development of the Scheduled Castes and Scheduled Tribes."

As per provisions of these Clauses it is the duty of the Commission to present annually a report upon the working of Constitutional safeguards and measures taken by the Union and the States for the protection and welfare of the Scheduled Castes and the Scheduled Tribes. In this series the Commission has presented four Annual Reports and one Special Report during the period March 1992 to 31st March 1998 containing a number of recommendations".

Clause 6 of Article 338 provides, "The President shall cause all such reports to be laid before each House of Parliament along with a Memorandum explaining the action taken or proposed to be taken on the recommendations relating to the Union and the reasons for the non-acceptance, if any, of any of such recommendations".

Clause 7 of Article 338 provides, "Where any such report or any part thereof relates to any matter with which any State Government is concerned, a copy of such report shall be forwarded to the Governor of the State who shall cause it to be laid before the Legislature of the State along with a Memorandum explaining the action taken or proposed to be taken on the recommendations relating to the State and the reasons for non-acceptance, if any, of any of such recommendations".

One of the duties assigned to the Commission is to submit reports to the President annually or at such other time as the Commission may deem fit, upon the working of the safeguards. The Commission constituted after 65th Amendment Act has presented four Annual Reports and four Special Reports to the President containing recommendations.

NATIONAL SAFAI KARAMCHARI FINANCE & DEVELOPMENT CORPORATION

With a view to liberate the scavengers handling manually with night soil and filth, a National Scheme was launched in 1991-92. The scheme was formulated with the following components; (i) time bound survey for identification of scavengers and their dependents with their aptitudes for alternative, trades, etc., (ii) training as per TRYSEM norms in identified trades at the nearest local training institutions/centres of the State governments/Central government and semi-government and non-government organisations, and (iii) rehabilitation of scavengers in trades and occupations by providing subsidy, margin money loan and bank loan.

The scheme provides financial assistance to scavengers for their training and rehabilitation in alternate occupations. Assistance is provided for training in the training institutes run by Government, local bodies and NGOs as per TRYSEM norms. The training is given for a maximum duration of 6 months. Stipend @ Rs.200/- to Rs.500/- is paid depending upon the training institute. Cost of raw materials, allowance for tools kit etc. are provided under the scheme. The scheme also provides for funding projects costing upto Rs 50,000 per beneficiary with 50 per cent of the project cost as subsidy with a maximum of Rs 10,000, 15 per cent Margin Money Loan at four per cent rate of interest and balance loan from bank. The expenditure on subsidy and training is met by the Central government and Margin Money Loan is shared between the Central and State governments in the ratio of 49:51. During 1997-98, Rs 90 crores were released to the States for implementation of the scheme. Rs.661.99 crore has been released for assisting 1,46,840 scavengers for training and 3,84,117 for rehabilitation upto 2000-01.

The National Safai Karamchari Finance and Development Corporation was set up in January 1997 and it provides loans for higher education to students from Safai Karamchari community besides providing assistance in self-employment ventures and technical and entrepreneurial skills. During 1999-2000, the corporation disbursed Rs. 20.16 crores for 78 schemes to it various channelising agencies benefiting 5005 Safai Karamcharis.

There are about 6.76 lakh scavengers in the country. An account of State-wise figures as reported is given below:

Sl. No.	*Name of the State/UT*	*Number of Scavengers*
1	Andhra Pradesh	30921
2	Assam	40413
3	Bihar	12226
4	Gujarat	64195
5	Haryana	36362
6	Himachal Pradesh	4757
7	Jammu & Kashmir	4150
8	Karnataka	14555
9	Kerala	1339
10	Madhya Pradesh	80072
11	Maharashtra	64785
12	Orissa	35049
13	Punjab	531
14	Rajasthan	57736
15	Tamil Nadu	35561
16	Uttar Pradesh	149202
17	West Bengal	23852
18	Delhi	17420
19	Nagaland	1800
20	Meghalaya	607
21	Pondicherry	476
	TOTAL	676009

In order to liberate and rehabilitate the scavengers, the Ministry launched the concept of 'Sanitary Marts' during 1999-2000. The objective is to organize scavengers into groups/cooperatives in towns with a population of 20,000 to 1,00,000 and having sufficient number of scavengers to establish these marts cum production Centres. These marts and the production centers would cater to the common mans' sanitary needs and motivate those using dry latrines to covert to water borne flush latrines, and supply material/equipment for latrines and even construct them. Co-operatives of 25 scavengers would be formed and they would run the marts as a commercial establishment capable of sustaining the alternative occupation of the scavengers. The Sanitary Marts have been set up in the following States:—

Sl.No.	*Name of State*	*Number of Sanitary Marts set up*
1.	Andhra Pradesh	113
2.	Gujarat	5
3.	Madhya Pradesh	7
4.	Rajasthan	200
5.	Tamil Nadu	128
6.	Maharashtra	1

In order to prohibit the employment of manual scavenging and construction of dry latrines, the Govt. of India had enacted a legislation viz. "The Employment of Manual Scavengers and Construction of Dry Latrines (Prohibition) Act, 1993. As per Section 3 of the Act, no person shall construct and maintain a dry latrine. Section 14 of the Act provides fine upto Rupees two thousand and imprisonment which may extend to one year or with both. At present 15 States are implementing this Act.

The Minister for Social Justice & Empowerment, on 17th January 2003 announced two new Schemes for empowerment of Safai Karamcharis. These are the Micro Credit Finance Scheme for Safai Karamchari/Scavenger Women and their Daughters and the Interest Free Loan Scheme to NGOs for promotion of Self Help Groups. The Schemes have been formulated to reach the most vulnerable and discriminated groups amongst the downtrodden

Safai Karamchari community. The NSKFDC has also decided to enhance the term loan limit for acquiring vehicles for removal of sanitary waste and garbage to Rs.10 lakh. The lending policy of NSKFDC has also been revised for Training Schemes and Entrepreneurial Development Programmes and Education loans. The minister noted that making Safai Karamcharis to change their traditional occupations is a difficult task. Despite the programme for liberation and rehabilitation of scavengers being in operation for the last thirty years, they have not been able to totally eradicate manual scavenging work. He also noted that it is not merely an administrative problem and advocated for the schemes that work for change of social attitude towards Scavengers and Safai Karamcharis. Praising Andhra Pradesh and Karnataka governments for their programmes for wiping out manual scavenging in a mission mode.

The Micro Credit Finance Scheme is for women Safai Karamcharis/ scavengers and their dependent daughters for starting or augmenting any income generating activity to free them from their traditional occupation. These activities could be in the field of small businesses/trades, tiny/cottage industry or service activity, artisan activity, agriculture and allied activities and transport sector. The maximum loan for an individual would be 25,000/- rupees and five lakh rupees for an organisation. The NSKFDC would charge 2% interest to the State Channelising agency/NGO which in turn would charge 5% from the borrower.

The Interest Free Loan Scheme to NGOs is for promotion of Self Help Groups which would be required to conduct a socio-economic survey of the village/locality. The survey would enable the NGO to identify the target groups of the NSKFDC in villages/ localities needing economic help for crafts/ businesses of their choice which they want to start or upgrade.

Empowerment of the Scheduled Castes through Safeguards

The need for providing adequate safeguards for the weaker section like Scheduled Castes and Scheduled Tribes was very much recognised by the authors of the Indian Constitution and as a result, special provisions were made in the Constitution of India to promote their social, educational, economic and service interests.

Development and Protective Safeguards

These safeguards are contained in the Directive Principles of State Policy of the Constitution and a specific provision in Article 46 which is a comprehensive provision comprising both the developmental and regulatory aspects. It reads as follows:

Article 46 "The State shall promote with special care the educational and economic interests of the weaker sections of the people, and in particular, of the Scheduled Castes and the Scheduled Tribes, and shall protect them from social injustice and all forms of exploitation".

Social Safeguards

Article 17 "Untouchability" is abolished and its practice in any form is forbidden. The enforcement of any disability arising out of "Untouchability" shall be an offence punishable in accordance with law.

To give effect to this Article, Parliament made an enactment viz., **Untouchability (Offences) Act, 1955**. To make the provisions of this Act more stringent, the Act was amended in 1976 and was also renamed as the **Protection of Civil Rights Act, 1955**. As provided under the Act, the Government of India also notified the Rules, viz., the PCR Rules, 1977, to carry out the provisions of this Act. As cases of atrocities on SCs/STs were not covered under the provisions of PCR Act, 1955, Parliament passed another important Act in 1989 for taking specific measures to prevent the atrocities. This Act known as the **Scheduled Castes and Scheduled Tribes (Prevention of Atrocities) Act, 1989,** became effective from 30-1-1990. For carrying out the provisions of this Act the Govt. of India have notified the SCs and STs (Prevention of Atrocities) Rules, 1995 on 31-3-1995.

Article 23 prohibits traffic in human beings and begar and other similar forms of forced labour and provides that any contravention of this provision shall be an offence punishable in accordance with law. It does not specifically mention SCs and STs but since majority of bonded labour belong to SCs/STs this Article has a special significance for these communities. In pursuance of this Article, Parliament has enacted the Bonded Labour System (Abolition) Act, 1976. For effective implementation of this Act, the

Ministry of Labour is running a Centrally Sponsored Scheme for identification, liberation and rehabilitation of bonded labour.

Article 24 provides that no child below the age of 14 years shall be employed to work in any factory or mine or engaged in any other hazardous employment. There are Central and State laws to prevent child labour. This Article is also significant for SCs and STs as a substantial portion of child labour engaged in hazardous jobs belong to these groups.

Article 25(2) (b) provides that Hindu religious institutions of a public character shall be thrown open to all classes and sections of Hindus. This provision is relevant as some sects of Hindus used to claim that only members of the concerned sects had a right to enter their temples. This was only a subterfuge to prevent entry of SC persons in such temples. For the purpose of this provision the term Hindu includes Sikh, Jain and Buddhist.

Educational and Cultural Safeguards

Article 15(4) empowers the State to make any special provision for the advancement of any socially and educationally backward classes of citizens or for SCs and STs. This provision was added to the Constitution through the Constitution (First Amendment) Act, 1951, which amended several Articles. This provision has enabled the State to reserve seats for SCs and STs in educational institutions including technical, engineering and medical colleges and in Scientific & Specialized Courses. In this Article as well as in Article 16(4) the term 'backward classes' is used as a generic term and comprises various categories of backward classes, viz., Scheduled Castes, Scheduled Tribes, Other Backward Classes, Denotified Communities (Vimukta Jatiyan) and Nomadic/Seminomadic communities.

Article 29(1) provides "any section of the citizens residing in the territory of India or any part thereof having a distinct language, script or culture of its own shall have the right to conserve the same". This Article has special significance for all the Scheduled Tribes. Santhals have a script of their own, viz., Olchiki. But this provision need not be understood to educate Tribals only in their language and thereby making them isolated. Tribals should be educated in the language of the State as well as National Language to expose them to the outside knowledge.

Article 350 A: "It shall be the endeavour of every State and of every local authority within the State to provide adequate facilities for instructions in the mother-tongue at the primary stage of education to children belonging to linguistic minority groups, and the President may issue such directions to any State as he considers necessary or proper for securing the provision of such facilities". Most of the tribal communities have their own languages or dialects, which usually belong to a different family of languages than the one to which the State's official language belongs.

Political Safeguards

Article 164(1) provides that in the States of Bihar, Madhya Pradesh and Orissa there shall be a Minister in charge of tribal welfare who may in addition be in charge of the welfare of the Scheduled Castes and backward classes or any other work.

Article 330 provides for reservation of seats for Scheduled Castes and Scheduled Tribes in the Lok Sabha.

Article 332 provides for reservation of seats for Scheduled Castes and Scheduled Tribes in the State Vidhan Sabhas (Legislative Assemblies).

Article 334 originally laid down that the provisions relating to the reservation of seats for Scheduled Castes and Scheduled Tribes in the Lok Sabha and State Vidhan Sabhas (and the representation of the Anglo-Indian community in the Lok Sabha and the State Vidhan Sabhas by nomination) would cease to have effect on the expiration of a period of ten years from the commencement of the Constitution. This Article has been amended five times, extending the said period by ten years on each occasion. This provision will now expire in January 2010.

Service Safeguards

Article 16(4) empowers the State to make "any provision for the reservation in appointments or posts in favour of any backward class of citizens which, in the opinion of the State, is not adequately represented in the services under the State".

Article 16(4A) Specific that nothing in this Article shall prevent the State from making any provision for reservation in matters of promotion to any class or classes of posts in the services under the State in favour of the Scheduled Castes and the Scheduled Tribes which, in the opinion of the State, are not adequately represented in the services under the State".

Article 16(4B) Nothing in this article shall prevent the State from considering any unfilled vacancies of a year which are reserved for being filled up in that year in accordance with any provision for reservation made under clause (4) or clause (4A) as a separate class of vacancies to be filled up in any succeeding year or years and such class of vacancies shall not be considered together with the vacancies of the year in which they are being filled up for determining the ceiling of fifty percent, reservation on total number of vacancies of the year.

Article 335 mentions that the claims of the members of the Scheduled Castes and the Scheduled Tribes shall be taken into consideration, consistently with the maintenance of efficiency of administration, in the making of appointments to services and posts in connection with the affairs of the Union or of a State.

Provided that nothing in this article shall prevent in making of any provision in favour of the members of the Scheduled Castes and the Scheduled Tribes for relaxation in qualifying marks in any examination or lowering the standards of evaluation, for reservation in matters of promotion to any class or classes of services or posts in connection with the affairs of the Union or of a State.

Article 320 (4) provides that nothing in clause (3) shall require a Public Service Commission to be consulted as respects the manner in which any provision under Article 16(4A) may be made or the manner in which effect may be given to the provisions of Article 335

Articles 341 and 342 of the Constitution define as to who would be the SCs and STs with respect to any State or Union Territory. The inter-state area restrictions have been imposed so that the people belonging to the specific community residing in a specific area which has been assessed to qualify for SCs and STs status only benefit from the facilities provided for them. The main objective for providing the reservation for SC/ST in civil posts and services of the Government is not just to give jobs to some persons belonging to these communities and thereby increase their representation in the services (though that constituted an important, immediate aim) but to uplift these people socially and educationally and make some place for them in the society. The quantum of reservation to Scheduled Castes recruitment on all-India basis by open competition is 15 per cent. In direct recruitment on all-India basis otherwise than by open competition, the reservation is 16.2/3 per cent for the Scheduled Castes. Post-based rosters have replaced vacancy-based rosters earlier prescribed by an order dated 2 July 1997 consequent upon judgment of the Supreme Court in R.K.Sabharwal's case.

To facilitate adequate representation of SCs/STs and OBCs in services, certain relaxations and concessions are given. A few of these are as follows:

1. Relaxation of five years in upper age-limit for SC candidates;
2. Relaxation of qualification regarding experience in the case of direct recruitment wherever necessary for SC candidates; and
3. Exemption from the payment of application fee for SC candidates.

The scheme of reservation is also being followed by public-sector undertakings including nationalised public-sector banks. State governments have also framed rules under the powers given to them by item 41 of the state list of the Seventh Schedule to the Constitution for reservation of posts for these classes, and have taken steps to increase their representation in state services. Reservation in State government services, however, is under the exclusive jurisdiction of State government. For ensuring implementation of reservation orders, liaison officers have been appointed for Scheduled Castes/Scheduled Tribes and Other Backward Classes in each department under different Ministries/Departments. Annual statements are required to be submitted by recruiting authorities for scrutiny by Government.

Socio-Economic Development

Clause (9) of the Article 338 of the Constitution reads as follows:

"The Union and every State Government shall consult the

National Commission on SCs & STs on all major policy matters affecting Scheduled Castes and Scheduled Tribes."

The Constitution has made it mandatory for the Union and every State government to consult the Commission on all major Policy matters affecting Scheduled Castes and Scheduled Tribes. This is very important function of the Commission, which has to keep track of all the major policy decisions, Legislative or Executive action taken by the Government of India or any State Government.

As per the provisions of Clause 5 (c) of Article 338, the Commission is required to participate and advise on the planning process of socio-economic development of Scheduled Castes and Scheduled Tribes and evaluate the progress of their development under Union and any State. The role of the Commission in these areas involves interaction at various levels, i.e., with the Planning Commission, with the Central Ministries and with the State Governments. The Commission and its officers both at Headquarters and the State offices participate in formulation of policies and the developmental programmes for Scheduled Castes and Scheduled Tribes including Special Component Plan for Scheduled Castes and Tribal Sub-Plan for Scheduled Tribes.

Empowerment of the Scheduled Castes through Five Year Plans: (Especially the Ninth and Tenth Plans)

The Ninth Five-year plan was unlike the early five year plans in terms of empowerment of the Scheduled Castes. The plan was completed in the year 2002 and as such is discussed in detail hereunder.

Different from the early plans the Ninth Plan commits to empower the Scheduled Castes, as the agents of socio-economic change and development. Therefore, a major shift is visualised in the approach as it envisages advancement of these socially disadvantaged groups through a process of 'empowerment', wherein efforts will be made to create an enabling environment that is conducive for them to exercise their rights freely, enjoy their privileges and be able to lead a life of self confidence and dignity along with the other citizens of the country. Policies and programmes directed towards empowering the Socially Disadvantaged Groups to be the active partners and partakers of the country's development rather than continuing as passive recipients of various developmental benefits.

THE NINTH PLAN (1997-2002)

Ninth Plan Commits to

Objective

- Empower the Socially Disadvantaged Groups viz., the Scheduled Castes (SCs), the Scheduled Tribes (STs), the Other Backward Classes (OBCs) and Minorities as the Agents of Social Change and Development

Strategies

- Create an enabling environment that is conducive for the Scheduled Castes, STs, OBCs and Minorities to exercise their rights freely, enjoy their privileges and be able to lead a life with confidence and dignity
- Adopt a three-pronged strategy of – i) Social Empowerment; ii) Economic Empowerment; and iii) Social Justice, in empowering these disadvantaged groups
- Ensure removal of disparities; eliminate exploitation and suppression and provide protection to the disadvantaged groups
- Ensure the developmental benefits to 'Reach the Unreached' through equitable distribution and with social justice
- Ensure participation of the Socially Disadvantaged Groups in the process of planning not merely as the beneficiaries but to take part effectively in the formulation of the need-based programmes/projects, their implementation, supervision and monitoring

Accelerate the on-going process of improving the socio-economic status of the disadvantaged groups through effective implementation of various policies and programmes and thus bring them on par with the rest of the society

The approach towards empowering these Groups in the Ninth Plan will be holistic in nature so as to accomplish all-round development of these weaker sections with an inter-sectoral approach and inputs from both the governmental and the non-governmental agencies. In the Ninth Plan, efforts will continue to extend all assistance to Scheduled Castes, STs and OBCs to ensure speedy socio-economic development through qualitative concern and quantitative substance in every measure undertaken, especially in removing the disparities, eliminating exploitation and suppression. Thus, these vulnerable groups, particularly the Scheduled Castes and the STs will not only be protected, but will be ensured of the developmental benefits reaching the unreached, bringing about equitable distribution and growth with social justice.

For this, the most effective instrument, which provides a special cushion for these categories in meeting their basic needs, is the Special Plan of Action of 1998. In this direction, efforts are being initiated to fill the critical gaps in providing the basic minimum services to those living below the poverty line. These special efforts are expected to ensure that every habitation with concentration of these Groups will have access to potable drinking water, nutrition supplements with both macro and micro nutrients, primary health care services, primary education facilities, sanitation and housing for the shelter less poor.

While formulating/implementing programmes for these Groups, the Ninth Plan will strive to ensure 'People-Centered Development' and 'People's Participation' with effective involvement of Panchayati Raj Institutions, in pursuance of the recent Constitutional (73rd and 74th) Amendments. Immediate steps will also be taken for the devolution of financial as well as administrative powers to the local self-governments, so that the marginalised groups will also get the opportunities to participate not only in formulating the need-based programmes but also in their effective implementation, supervision and monitoring. This will not only go a long way in empowering these Groups but will also ensure that the implementation of various developmental programmes is carried out in the true sense of co-operative federalism.

In the context of adopting the special strategy of 'Women's Component Plan' in the Ninth Plan, action will be taken by the nodal Ministry of Social Justice and Empowerment to earmark funds/benefits under all its programmes exclusively for women belonging to these socially disadvantaged groups who are the worst affected as they are generally living in extreme poverty.

In the Ninth Plan, the vital ongoing programmes for the advancement of these socially disadvantaged groups will be streamlined, strengthened and enriched to accomplish the unfinished task of bringing these sections on par with the rest of the society. Simultaneously, new measures, wherever necessary, will be initiated to accelerate the process of empowering these weaker sections. Empowerment of these groups will, therefore, be attempted in an integrated manner, essentially encompassing the three vital and inter-related components viz., i) Social Empowerment; ii) Economic Empowerment; and iii) Social Justice.

I. Social Empowerment

The National Agenda of Governance clearly spells out the commitment of the Government to safeguard adequately the interests of Scheduled Castes, STs and OBCs through appropriate legal, executive and societal efforts and by large-scale education and empowerment.

Education, being the most effective instrument for socio-economic empowerment, high priority will be accorded to improving the educational status of Scheduled Castes and STs, particularly that of the women and the girl children. In fact, the educational backwardness, prevalent amongst these Groups, necessitates an added thrust on their education, training and skill up gradation, as it will bring forth not only social empowerment but also economic empowerment. Therefore, the endeavour in the Ninth Plan will be to provide suitable education keeping in view, their cultural milieu, their genius and their special needs.

Social Empowerment through Education

Social Empowerment through Education being the most effective instrument of empowering the Socially Disadvantaged Groups, all-out efforts will be made to improve the educational status of these Groups, especially that of the Women and the Girl Child, through:

- Universalisation of primary education by 2005 A.D. with a special focus on low-literacy pockets and on the educationally backward communities like SC, ST, OBCs and Minorities
- 'Reaching the Unreached' through removal of the existing problem of inaccessibility by providing residential schools in the remote and the far-flung tribal areas, hostel facilities etc.

- Extending special concessions like free education; free supply of books; uniforms/stationery; scholarships/fellowships for both within and outside country
- Special efforts to vocationalise education both at the middle/ high school levels which can equip the Disadvantaged Groups either for wage/self-employment
- Encouraging higher and technical/professional education amongst these, through effective implementation of Post-Matric Scholarships with an added thrust and wider coverage
- Promoting education amongst children whose parents are engaged in unclean occupation and thus divert the future generation away from the practice of scavenging through incentives like Pre-Matric Scholarships
- Providing more opportunities for these Groups to appear in the competitive examinations and get into the stream of planning and decision making process through expansion of pre-examination coaching services
- Complete eradication of the practice of Untouchability and thus provide a rightful place and status for these socially disadvantaged groups
- Achieving complete eradication of the practice of Manual Scavenging by the end of the Ninth Plan (2002) and thus liberate and rehabilitate the Scavengers and those engaged in Unclean Occupations through a time-bound programme
- Introducing the concept of Mini-Anganwadis with relaxed norms in the remote areas and thus ensure children and mothers belonging to these Groups are taken care of with basic health and nutrition services through National Programmes like Integrated Child Development Services (ICDS), Special Nutrition Programme (SNP) and Nutrition Support to Primary Education popularly known as Mid-day Meals Programme

Encouraging the participation of the disadvantaged groups/ in the planning and developmental process at every level through ensuring their adequate representation in various Democratic/ decision-making Institutions like Panchayati Raj/Local Bodies, State Assemblies/Parliament etc.

The need for a time-bound programme to improve the educational status of the Socially Disadvantaged Groups has been identified as one of the immediate tasks to be fulfilled during the Ninth Plan as part of the total commitment of making the country fully literate by the year 2005 A.D. Efforts will, therefore, be made to fulfill this commitment through Universalisation of primary education with a special focus on low literacy pockets and on the Scheduled Castes, STs, OBCs and Minorities whose literacy rates are very low compared to the rest of the population.

In view of the low enrolment/retention rates and high drop-out rates amongst these groups, special measures will be taken not only to strengthen the ongoing programmes but also to launch new initiatives for ensuring easy access through residential schools; minimum standards with trained teachers, preferably local women; appropriate and adequate support services like hostels and crèches; other infra-structural facilities and special incentives to poor students and their families through scholarships/financial assistance, free books, free uniforms etc. In this context, the earlier initiative of the Government to start crèche facilities within the school campus or nearer to the school will be revived/intensified to ensure that the girl children are not deprived of education as they have to play the role of a mother-substitute in many respects, when the mothers go out for work to supplement the family income.

The spread of literacy through the efforts of the National Literacy Mission will be ensured so as to reach the backward rural, tribal and urban slums where the incidence of illiteracy especially amongst women and girl children belonging to these weaker sections is very high. Residential schools and schools with attached hostel facilities right upto the block-level will be encouraged in the Ninth Plan to solve the present problem of inaccessibility of schools being faced by the girls in the backward rural and tribal areas. The recent launching of Kasturba Gandhi Swatantrata Vidyalayas in 1997 is one of such initiatives exclusively meant for the educational improvement of girl children belonging to Scheduled Castes and STs.

Employment-oriented education and diversified vocational training, which has been recognised as the need of the day, will be given top priority. Special efforts will be made to vocationalise education both at the middle/high school levels, depending upon the need and demand. Also, job-oriented condensed courses will be accorded priority in the Ninth Plan to extend functionally viable and productive education to these Groups, especially in tribal areas. Monitoring of the working of these institutions will be taken up through PRIs to ensure un-interrupted and smooth imparting of education to the target population, especially those living below the poverty line.

To ensure educational development amongst the Scheduled Castes and the STs, the vital ongoing programme of Post-Matric Scholarships, which was modified in 1995-96 by lifting all the restrictive clauses during the Eighth Plan, will be implemented with added thrust and wider coverage to encourage these groups to enter into higher/technical streams of education. To promote school education amongst children whose parents are engaged in unclean occupations and to divert the future generations away from the practice of scavenging, the recently revised scheme of Pre-Matric Scholarships will be expanded to reach these facilities to all those who are in need. The scheme of Pre-examination Coaching Centers will be further expanded to benefit the rural candidates also. Intensified efforts will be made through effective expansion of Education Complexes in low literacy pockets for development of SC and ST women and girls as they lag much behind their counterparts. Hostels for SC and ST Girls and Boys will also be strengthened/expanded to ensure that the demand for those hostels is completely met as the hostels solve the problem of inaccessibility. Also, other programmes like Book Banks, Merit Scholarships and Fellowships for studies abroad, will be put into action effectively to act as special incentives.

Elimination of the most inhuman practice of manual carrying of night soil is yet to be accomplished. During the Ninth Plan, complete eradication of this practice of manual scavenging will be achieved as a time-bound commitment by ensuring occupational mobility and breaking the nexus between the traditional occupations and social and economic disabilities. Total liberation and full rehabilitation of the scavengers, especially focusing on the women and girl children, will be taken up intensively in the Ninth Plan after accomplishing the total identification of the scavengers.

Rehabilitation programmes with vocational training for alternative jobs with sustainable income will be taken up. Loans and other financial and technical assistance will be extended to the scavengers to start self-employment with income generating activities to keep themselves gainfully engaged. Simultaneous efforts, in close collaboration with the agencies of Local Self Governments, will be put into action to ensure that all the dry latrines are changed into wet latrines so as to wipe off this inhuman practice completely from the present day list of professions. With a view to freeing the future generations from the traditional occupation of scavenging, all encouragement for promotion of education by providing hostel facilities, scholarships, mid-day meals, free books and uniforms etc. will be given, on priority basis, to the children belonging to these communities. To keep a close vigil on the progress of this programme with national commitment, the term of the National Safai Karamchari Commission has also been extended till the end of the Ninth Plan period. The National Safai Karamcharis Finance and Development Corporation will be strengthened/activated to act as a catalytic agent in rehabilitating the scavengers on a time-bound basis through extending alternative jobs/ employment for those who want to start self-employment-cum-entrepreneurial ventures.

II. Economic Empowerment

As there exists a sizeable population belonging to the Socially Disadvantaged Groups of Scheduled Castes, STs, OBCs and Minorities living under extreme conditions of poverty, mobilisation of adequate financial and social support to free them from the clutches of poverty, will be taken up on a priority basis. To this effect, economic empowerment through employment and income generation programmes will be given special emphasis in the Ninth Plan to ensure that at least their basic needs are met.

ECONOMIC EMPOWERMENT

- A special thrust will be given on employment and income generation programmes with an ultimate objective of making these groups economically independent and self-reliant and thus raise them above the poverty line

- All the 5 National and other State Level Finance and Development Corporations will be strengthened to play a catalytic role in promoting employment-cum-income generation activities through 'Backward' and 'Forward' linkages
- Special efforts through various training programmes to upgrade the traditional skills, equip them with modern technology so as to meet the market demands
- To enforce special legislative measures to ensure payment of minimum wages and equal wages, with no gender discrimination in the informal/unorganised sector
- The private and the corporate sectors will be motivated to invest on the welfare and development of the weaker sections as they form a potential force in the country's human resources
- To endow every landless SC and ST family with a minimum piece of land; restoration/preservation of land ownership and effective implementation of protective legislation
- Involvement of NGOs in the promotion of small and lift irrigation projects, especially in the drought prone, dry and hilly areas to ensure food security at the village level
- To sensitise/motivate the Financial Institutions to pay special attention to these priority groups and extend loans on differential rates of interest

The national and State level Apex bodies viz., the National SC and the ST Finance Development Corporations (NSFDC) and State Scheduled Castes Development Corporations (SCDCs) will be strengthened to play a leading and a catalytic role in promoting employment-cum-income generation opportunities. As most of the Scheduled Castes, STs, OBCs and Minorities living in rural areas, continue to depend upon the low-income and less-productive informal/unorganised sectors of agriculture, dairying, animal husbandry, fisheries, handlooms, handicrafts including other craftsmanship/artisanship, special efforts will be made through various training programmes to upgrade their traditional skills, equip them with modern technology and extend both 'backward' and 'forward' linkages of credit and marketing facilities with the ultimate objective of making them economically independent and self-reliant. Special legislative measures will also be taken to ensure payment of minimum wages and equal wages, with no gender discrimination in the informal/unorganised sector.

The adoption and implementation of the New Economic Policies warrant watchful and protective attention towards the weaker sections so that the commitment to bring about comprehensive improvement in their living conditions does not get diluted and more importantly they are neither displaced nor marginalised. Therefore, the efforts in the Ninth Plan will be to synchronise empowerment of these weaker sections with the national developmental policies and programmes. The private and the corporate sectors will be motivated to invest on the welfare and development of the weaker sections as they form a potential force in the country's human resources.

Prominent amongst the various Action Points to be taken up in the Ninth Plan are endowing every landless SC and ST family with a minimum piece of land, restoration and preservation of land ownership and effective implementation of the protective legislation. As most of the SC and ST families depend upon the cultivation of small land holdings, steps will be taken to ensure revision of irrigation facilities.

Special measures will also be taken to sensitise and motivate the financial institutions to pay special attention to these priority groups and extend loans to them on differential rates of interest. Sensitisation programmes to inculcate a positive attitude towards these disadvantaged and neglected sections will also form part of the economic development package. The youth and women amongst these Groups will be given special attention as they are the most important potential and productive 'human resource', by setting up small scale and cottage industries, village crafts, weaving and other occupations/enterprises with effective market linkages.

Efforts will also be made to simplify the lending and other procedures of banks and other financial institutions as the procedures followed by them appear to be too complicated for the poor illiterate, ignorant and desperate weaker sections to avail of the loan. Since the majority of the population belonging to these Groups depend upon agriculture and allied activities for their livelihood, steps will be taken to ensure that loans are given on a priority basis to these Groups for agricultural purposes viz., purchase of seeds, Fertilisers, pesticides and training in farming and application of advance technology.

Measures will be initiated to ensure effective implementation including earmarking and utilisation of funds under the special strategies of Special Component Plan (SCP), both at the Central and State levels, and the Special Central Assistance (SCA) to SCP and TSP to States/UTs. Special efforts will be made to impress upon those Ministries/ Departments, who are not earmarking funds, so far, under SCP and TSP in the name of non-divisibility of the programmes of their Ministries/Departments. The Centre will also pursue with the State Governments for developing effective mechanisms on the lines of the Maharashtra Model to pool the funds of SCP/TSP from all the concerned Ministries/Departments and authorise the State nodal Departments in charge of the welfare of Scheduled Castes and STs to take the responsibility in allocating the funds as per the local needs of both the target areas and the target population. This system is expected to prevent/control diversion of SCP, TSP and SCA funds and ensures effective utilisation of the same for the purpose they are meant for. While a close vigil, in close collaboration with all the concerned, will be kept at various levels for effective monitoring of the utilisation of these special funds, the ongoing regular reviews at the Central level will continue to assess as to how effective are these instruments in supplementing/ complementing the efforts of the nodal Ministry of Social Justice and Empowerment in empowering these Socially Disadvantaged Groups. To this effect, efforts will be made to install an effective monitoring mechanism with adequate manpower at various levels starting from the Centre to the Block levels.

III. Social Justice

Affirmative action and legislative measures being the most powerful instruments to ensure social justice to the Socially Disadvantaged Groups, the Government commits to bring forth into action a 'National Charter for Social Justice' based on the principle of social harmony, besides extending legal protection to existing percentages of reservation in educational institutions at the State level. To this effect, implementation of the reservation policy in both educational institutions and services for Scheduled Castes and STs and for OBCs in the Services will be strictly adhered to by filling up all the reserved posts promptly, arrangement will also be made simultaneously for quick judicial adjudication of complaints and grievances in the matters related thereto.

To prevent/curb the persistent problems of social discrimination, prevalence of social evils like untouchability, and the increasing exploitation and atrocities against these disadvantaged groups, collaborative efforts by all concerned will be made towards effective implementation of the Indian Penal Code and the other two special legislations viz., The Protection of Civil Rights Act, 1955 and the SC and ST (Prevention of Atrocities) Act, 1989. To remove the last vestiges of untouchability, special efforts with commitment will be put into action to change the mind-set of the people through societal re-orientation. In this context, immediate measures will be undertaken to ensure that adequate number of Special/Mobile Courts are set up with adequate staff in each district to provide both speedy and on-the-spot settlement/redressal of grievances. As an important measure of social justice, special efforts will be made to extend timely and adequate financial support, as per the provisions, to compensate/rehabilitate the SC/ST victims and make them self-reliant. In this direction, efforts will also be made to enhance the compensation through necessary amendments in the Act. Simultaneously, efforts will be made to develop a community-based defence mechanism by empowering the institutions of local governance and NGOs. As part of these measures, a few selected local NGOs will be identified to act as authorised informants to the enforcement authorities or file papers on behalf of the victims or assist them in the legal proceedings.

TOWARDS SOCIAL JUSTICE

- To institute a 'National Charter for Social Justice' for ensuring equity and social justice to the socially disadvantaged groups viz., Scheduled Castes, STs, OBCs and Minorities

- To implement Reservation Policy strictly in educational institutions and in services for Scheduled Castes, STs and OBCs
- To curb social discrimination, untouchability, exploitation and atrocities on these Groups through effective implementation of:
  — The Indian Penal Code
  — The Protection of Civil Rights Act, 1955
  — The SCs and STs (Prevention of Atrocities) Act, 1989
- To set up adequate number of Special / Mobile Courts in each district for speedy settlement/redressal of grievances of the Scheduled Castes/STs
- To extend timely and adequate financial support, as a measure of social justice, to compensate/rehabilitate the SC/ST victims
- To develop a community-based defence mechanism by empowering the institutions of local governance and NGOs
- To change the mind-set and attitudes of the people towards these Groups through awareness generation campaigns and media, both print and electronic
- To equip these Groups with necessary information and thus conscientise them to exercise their rights, privileges and also make the best use of the Governmental support to overcome various social disabilities
- To sensitise all those working for the well-being of these Disadvantaged Groups through special training programmes for ensuring social justice to them

To make all the three existing National Commissions as effective instruments to ensure that the rights and interests of these Disadvantaged Groups are well protected

Awareness generation, conscientization and sensitization programmes are yet other means to work towards social justice. Special efforts will be made to put this three-pronged approach into action simultaneously for holistic effect. The first being awareness generation, efforts will be made to change the mindset and the attitudes of the people towards these Groups as the same is very crucial in creating an enabling environment for empowering these Groups. To this effect, awareness generation programmes/ special campaigns will be taken up on a continuing basis all over the country especially in rural areas involving effectively both the governmental and the non-governmental organisations and the media towards erasing the long-standing social biases/stigmas like untouchability and thus create the feeling of all being equal. The second being, conscientization of the target groups, simultaneous efforts will be made to make the target groups conscious of their own rights, privileges and the governmental support available for them besides making them realise their own potentials to be self-confident and self-reliant. The third being, sensitizing both officials and non-officials, special training programmes, both pre-service and in-service, will be undertaken from time to time to sensitize all those working for these Groups so that they can work with right perspectives in meeting/handling the special needs and problems of these marginalised groups and thus ensure social justice. To encourage/reward those officials and non-officials, who are working for the good of these deprived lot by living in the most backward and difficult tribal areas, efforts will be made to impress upon the State Governments to revive the earlier practice of extending incentives, both in kind and cash.

PLAN OUTLAYS

While a total outlay of Rs.5399.50 crore has been earmarked for both Central and Centrally Sponsored Schemes including Special Central Assistance (SCA) to Special Component Plan (SCP) for Scheduled Castes, an amount of Rs. 9568.68 crore (Provisional) has been allocated for State Sector Schemes for empowering the Socially Disadvantaged Groups viz, Scheduled Castes, STs, OBCs and Minorities in the Ninth Five Year Plan (1997-2002).

PERSISTING PROBLEMS

After the completion of the Ninth Plan, the Tenth plan has recognised the following problems as persisting problems of the Scheduled Castes.

Notwithstanding the improvements accomplished in the overall living conditions through various welfare and developmental efforts made so far, the disadvantaged groups continue to remain backward due to certain persisting problems that they have been facing. In fact, these problems, which are of considerable complexity and magnitude, are standing as major hurdles in empowering these Groups with social justice. The following paragraphs enlist some of those problems which have emerged as critical areas of concern:

Amongst the disadvantaged groups, Scheduled Castes remain the most backward, as they continue to suffer from various forms of social disabilities as well as economic deprivation, as discussed below:

Educational Backwardness

The educational status of Scheduled Castes continues to be much lower than that of the rest of society, as figures given earlier show, as they hold very low literacy rates (37.4 per cent for Scheduled Castes against 52.21 per cent for total population in 1991), enrolment ratios (92.4 per cent for Scheduled Castes against 94.9 per cent for total population at primary level in 1999-2000) and high drop-out rates (44.27 per cent at primary level, 63.58 per cent at middle level and 76.63 per cent at the secondary level against 39.74 per cent, 56.83 per cent and 67.44 per cent respectively for total population in 1998-99) besides the ever increasing gap between the educational status of Scheduled Castes and that of the general population. Adding to this are the Region/State and caste-wise variations which are quite disturbing as they continue to persist on very unequal terms. Further, the educational status of SC women is also very depressing as it continues to be very low at 23.8 per cent in 1991 when compared to the total female literacy of 39.3 per cent indicating a very wide gap. Owing to their social and economic disability, and inaccessibility to educational facilities, the educational backwardness of Scheduled Castes continues to persist as a major handicap in the process of empowering them socially.

Economic Backwardness

Economic conditions of Scheduled Castes continue to remain very depressing as 36.3 per cent of Scheduled Castes in rural areas and 38.5 per cent in urban areas still live below the poverty line, while it was only 27.1 per cent in rural areas and 23.6 per cent in urban areas in respect of total population as per the Poverty Estimates of the Planning Commission in 1999-2000. The reason being Scheduled Castes still continue to depend upon those very stereo-typed occupations which do not provide any scope or opportunity either for any occupational shift or for upward mobility. Also, the economic backwardness of Scheduled Castes when compared to others is depressingly obvious as they continue to derive their livelihood from such occupations as could provide neither continuity of work nor minimum subsistence for their survival, including those menial occupations like scavenging, flaying, tanning etc. While the economic scenario of the country has taken striking strides registering change, growth and development, the situation of Scheduled Castes continued with not much of a change, as reflected in their high poverty rates when compared to the general population, as pointed out in the previous section. Ultimately, unless there is a dramatic change in the economic occupation of Scheduled Castes, their participation in the other productive sectors of economy will continue to be negligible, implying that the gap between the percentage of SC population and the total population will widen further as they continue to remain in the cycle of deprivation.

Lower Rates of Work Participation

The work participation amongst Scheduled Castes, as per the 1991 Census, reveals that more than 76 per cent of them are engaged in the primary sector of the economy. Of these, nearly half of them (48.2 per cent) are agricultural labourers and a little more than one-fourth (28.2 per cent) are cultivators. The employment pattern amongst Scheduled Castes indicates no significant shift during the 1990s. However, there has been a decrease in the number of SC cultivators from 28.17 per cent in 1981 to 25.44 percent in 1991 and an increase in the percentage of agricultural labourers from 48.22 per cent in 1981 to 49.06 per cent in 1991. It is also likely that some of the Scheduled Castes who have lost their lands may have also joined the ranks of labourers. Evidently, their hold on agrarian economy has also been declining as the number of cultivators has declined from 38 per cent in 1961 to 25.44 percent in 1991.

Participation of SC workers in the other upcoming sectors of economy also continues to be negligible, as Scheduled Castes can neither compete nor sustain in the liberalised market economy, wherein the national/multi-national companies with their cost effective products are causing a serious threat to the tradition-based economy of Scheduled Castes. In the absence of backward and forward linkages, Scheduled Castes are being further marginalised in the new economic regime.

Social Exploitation

Letting certain communities do the job of manual scavenging, especially carrying the night soil as head-loads is no less than any crime that any civilised society can ill-afford to commit. In fact, it was the commitment of the Government to eliminate the practice of manual scavenging totally by the end of the Eighth Plan (1997) and to rehabilitate those liberated scavengers with alternative and viable occupations. This could not be achieved even at the end of the Ninth Plan (2002). Reasons for no accomplishment of this commitment include tardy progress in the identification of scavengers as well as their rehabilitation; failure to convert the dry latrines into wet; demand for manual scavenging in those areas where the dry latrines still exist; lack of coordination between the State Welfare Departments and the Local bodies in respect of conversion of dry latrines; absence of follow-up on the rehabilitated persons etc. So far, out of the total of 6.53 lakh scavengers identified, only 3.84 lakh could be rehabilitated and 1.47 lakh could be trained. Thus, the most inhuman practice of manual scavenging continues to persist as a complex problem of serious concern even today. As a matter of fact, the perpetuation of manual scavenging is also adding to the otherwise existing practice of social segregation and the age-old social evil of untouchability.

Segregation and Deprivation

The SC dwellings, which are located outside the main settlements in rural areas due to social segregation, continue to be deprived and denied of basic amenities and services. The conditions of Scheduled Castes living in urban slums are no better as they also lack access to basic minimum services of connecting roads, supply of drinking water, primary health care, sanitation, housing etc. Non-availability of these basic services not only denies these deprived classes the right to lead a minimum standard of living but also has a negative impact on their capabilities, capacity, confidence and efforts to join the mainstream. With the growing population of Scheduled Castes and the large influx of rural SC population into towns/cities, the problem is getting further compounded through emergence of a large number of SC-concentrated slums in and around the urban cities/urban agglomeration. This, in turn, has given birth to various social problems including resettlement and rehabilitation of migratory SC population.

Crimes and Atrocities

Closely related to the problem of inequalities and low status, are the increasing incidence of crimes and atrocities against Scheduled Castes.

As per the National Crimes Record Bureau (Crime in India – 1999), although the number of crimes against Scheduled Castes has declined from 27,944 in 1997 to 25,093 in 1999, yet their share of 0.5 per cent in the total incidence of crime in the country remained almost the same in 1999. Some of the major states, which had the dubious distinction of higher incidence of crime against Scheduled Castes, include Uttar Pradesh (24.4 per cent); Rajasthan (22.4 per cent); Himachal Pradesh (18.6 per cent); Gujarat (7.1 per cent); Andhra Pradesh (7 per cent) and Tamil Nadu (3.5 per cent). Further, the number of crimes committed under the Special Laws of PCR Act of 1955 and the Prevention of Atrocities Act of 1989, enforced exclusively for Scheduled Castes and STs, has also shown a declining trend by coming down from 9,286 in 1997 to 7,979 in 1999, but continues to be very high.

Further, of the total crimes of 25,093 registered in 1999, the number of cases registered under the two Special Legislations account for 7,979 (31.8 per cent) having the biggest share and followed by the cases of hurt 3,241 (12.92 per cent); rape numbering 1,000 (3.98 per cent); murder 506 (2.02 per cent); arson 337 (1.34 per cent); kidnap and abduction 228 (0.9 per cent); robbery 109 (0.4 per cent); dacoity 36 (0.1 per cent) and others 11,657 (46.46 per cent) etc. To this effect, the National Commission for Scheduled Castes and Scheduled Tribes has also been documenting in their Annual Reports about several recurring pathologies, such as delays in reporting, refusal to register complaints, half-hearted investigations, poor quality of prosecution, protracted pendency, procedural delays of the Courts etc. Offences committed against the Scheduled Castes not only reinforce the problem of tyranny and fear psychosis in them, but also further weakens their struggle and aspirations to achieve better quality of life.

THE TENTH PLAN (2002-2007)

APPROACH

The long-drawn process of empowering the socially and economically Disadvantaged Groups launched during the Ninth Plan has, no doubt, enabled them to develop their capacities and capabilities to be the active partners and partakers of the country's development, rather than continuing as passive recipients of various developmental benefits. Therefore, the very process of empowering these Disadvantaged Groups will continue as the major approach in the Tenth Plan and beyond till the Constitutional commitment of raising their status to that of the rest of the society is fulfilled.

The first step in this direction will be to initiate action with a holistic approach to alter the harsh conditions in which these Groups live and work so as to accomplish all round development of these weaker sections with an effective intersectoral co-ordination inputs from both the governmental and non-governmental organisations. Improvement in the socio-economic conditions of these vulnerable groups will be made possible only by removing the disparities and eliminating exploitation and suppression. To this effect, due weightage and priority will be given to programmes catering to educational and economic development by taking into consideration the varying status of each target groups. Also, every effort will be made to reach the developmental benefits to all the needy persons belonging to these Groups and thus ensure equitable distribution and growth with social justice.

In these efforts, the major focus will be to accomplish the task of providing basic needs to one and all as an essential measure for realizing empowerment amongst these weaker sections. Accordingly, the fulfillment of basic needs viz. food and nutrition, safe drinking water, primary health care, primary education, shelter, sanitation, good environment etc. becomes a priority. To this effect, special attention will, therefore, be paid to attend to the problems of resettlement and rehabilitation of the large influx of rural population belonging to the Socially Disadvantaged Groups congregating into urban slums. Efforts will, therefore, be made through the on-going programme of Pradhan Mantri Gramodaya Yojana to ensure that the above said basic minimum services reach every habitation with concentration of these groups.

Further, while formulating/implementing programmes for these Groups, the Tenth Plan will strive to ensure 'People-Centred Development' and 'People's Participation' with effective involvement of PRIs in pursuance of the 73rd and 74th Constitutional Amendments. Immediate steps will also be taken for the devolution of financial as well as administrative powers to PRIs and Local Bodies so that these marginalised groups will get opportunity to participate in the formulation of the need-based programmes, as well as in their effective implementation, supervision and monitoring. This will not only go a long way in empowering these Groups, but will also ensure that implementation of various developmental programmes is taken care of in the true sense of decentralised planning.

While Scheduled Castes, OBCs and Minorities, in general, occupy a lower status in the society in the case of their women and children and especially in the case of the girl child, there persists a gap between the literacy rates of Scheduled Castes and the general population, even till today. represent the weakest link. Though there has been a perceptible improvement in the overall situation of these women, yet the development indicators that reflect their status imply that they are the most deprived and discriminated, when compared to their counterpart women belonging to other communities. While taking note of their plight, the Tenth Plan proposes to adopt a comprehensive strategy towards ensuring their protection, welfare, development and empowerment through extending special educational, health, nutrition, employment, legal and other services. The nodal Ministry of Social Justice & Empowerment, in collaboration with the Department of Women and Child Development, will ensure that SC women receive their rightful share, both funds and benefits, from all the other developmental sectors under the Women's Component Plan.

While the above paragraphs outline the general approach towards empowering the Socially Disadvantaged Groups during the Tenth Plan, details of the Group-wise strategy in achieving the much wanted – 'Social Empowerment' through removal of the still existing inequalities, disparities and other persisting problems; 'Economic Empowerment' through various employment-cum-income generation activities with an ultimate objective of making them economically independent and self reliant; and 'Social Justice' through elimination of all types of discrimination against these Groups with the strength and support of legislative measures, awareness generation and change in the mind-set of the people, are discussed below:

I. Social Empowerment

Education being the best means not only to empower the disadvantaged, but also to provide the essential base for all developmental pursuits, the Tenth Plan will work out special effective interventions to 'reach the un-reached' and thus fill the existing gaps between the Scheduled Castes and the general population, with a focus on SC women and the girl children.

Further, the Tenth Plan will endeavour to improve the educational status of Scheduled Castes on a time bound basis, in close collaboration with the Department of Elementary Education, as part of the total commitment of making the country fully literate by the year 2007. The Tenth Plan will make special efforts to fulfill this commitment through universalisation of elementary education with a special focus on low-literacy pockets and on the educationally backward Scheduled Castes, whose literacy rates are very low compared to the rest of the population. The on going programmes of the Department of Elementary Education viz. Sarva Shiksha Abhiyan, DPEP, Shiksha Karmi, NFE, Mid-Day Meals etc. are going to play a major role in this endeavour.

In fact, the recent directive of the Supreme Court to treat education as a fundamental right imposes an ultimatum on the Tenth Plan to act rigorously to improve the educational status of Scheduled Castes and thus accomplish social empowerment. The first step in this direction will be to arrest the problem of school drop-outs, and improve enrolment/retention rates by ensuring easy access; and provision of adequate support facilities like hostels, crèches and special incentives to poor students like scholarships, free books, free uniforms, transport charges, besides compensation to families etc. In this context, the earlier initiatives of starting crèches/ Anganwadis within the school campus or near to the school will be revived to ensure that the girl children are not deprived of education, while substituting for their mothers when the latter go out to work. To this effect, the scheme of Balika Samriddhi Yojana, an exclusive programme for girl children living below the poverty line and the much wanted nutritional support through the popular scheme of Mid-Day Meals will be expanded/ universalised to improve both enrolment/retention rates.

Further, steps will also be taken to ensure provision of quality education to equip the educationally backward Scheduled Castes to enhance their employment prospects with competitive ability and thus mitigate the problems of their marginalisation and deprivation in the employment market. Along with the general education, efforts will also be made to vocationalise education both at the middle and high school levels to enable SC students to enhance their technical and productive capabilities in those vocations that have a direct bearing/relevance to their local needs and market demands. To this effect, job-oriented condensed courses of education and training will be given priority. In all these efforts, the ultimate objective will be to fulfill the Tenth Plan commitment of minimising the gap between the educational status of Scheduled Castes and that of the general population.

II. Economic Empowerment

Towards the economic upliftment of Scheduled Castes, the Tenth Plan will prioritise those activities that ensure employment and income generation which can provide them sustainable income to meet their basic needs. Recognising their traditional ability and skills in the agriculture production, efforts will be made not only to endow every landless SC family with a minimum piece of land with ownership rights but also to maximise their productive capacities through upgradation of their skills, modernisation of methods and equipment and supply of seeds and pesticides etc. Also, the State Departments will be persuaded to ensure that irrigation facilities are extended to the small land holdings of SC farmers, collectively so as to reduce the relative costs. Special legislative measures will also be taken to ensure payment of minimum wages and equal wages for women, with no gender discrimination, especially in the informal/un-organised sector.

The on-going efforts made for uplifting Scheduled Castes above the poverty line will be further intensified/ expanded, with an ultimate objective of enhancing their income levels at a higher pace so that they could be brought above the poverty line on a priority basis. To this effect, all the poverty alleviation programmes would be reinvigorated and expanded to make a better impact on the economic conditions of Scheduled Castes leading to qualitative betterment in their overall living conditions. Thus, the strategy in the Tenth Plan will be to implement the on-going nation-wide poverty alleviation programmes, with enriched components, best suited to the specific needs and poverty situation of the Scheduled Castes. This will include organising landless and agricultural labourers to constitute the largest occupational segments amongst Scheduled Castes on the pattern of swarozgaris of the SGSY with special focus on women.

In the changing economic scenario wherein the private sector is being consciously promoted to take up all production and commercial activities and the role of government sector is getting restricted to core activities, the Tenth Plan will endeavour to reorient Scheduled Castes to face the challenges arising out of the inevitable economic reforms. Further, as the services sector today represents the fastest growing sector of the economy whose contribution is going to increase manifold in providing new employment opportunities in the coming years, the strategy to be adopted for empowering Scheduled Castes will be in consonance with this changing phenomenon.

With the globalisation and liberalisation of economy, new opportunities and avenues, both at the national and international levels, are being opened up substantially. The Tenth Plan will, therefore, endeavour to, in collaboration with the concerned Ministries/Departments, equip Scheduled Castes with technical knowledge and ability to cope with the upcoming trades and trends in the employment market. Interventions with appropriate training, technology, capacity-building, development of entrepreneurship, either individually or collectively through formation of Co-operatives/Self-Help Groups (SHGs) along with both 'forward and backward' linkages will be made to produce quality goods, as per the demand, and thus exploit the market to the extent possible. To this end, the Tenth Plan will initiate action to tie up with the concerned Ministries dealing with agriculture, fisheries, dairying, animal husbandry, handlooms and handicrafts to open up avenues for exports.

The exclusive Financial Institution working for the economic empowerment of Scheduled Castes viz. the NSFDC and State-level Corporations will be geared to function as catalytic agents for accomplishing economic development of respective weaker sections by making them self-reliant and self-sustaining mechanisms. For this purpose, the functioning of this Apex Corporation will be reviewed and necessary reforms be brought into with the strength of professional expertise in marketing and business management to ensure that this exclusive Corporation proves its worth as an effective financial institution in improving the economic status of Scheduled Castes.

Simultaneous efforts will also be made to ensure effective earmarking and utilisation of funds under the special strategy of SCP, both at the central and state levels, besides the funds released under SCA to SCP to ensure optimum benefit to improve the economic status of Scheduled Castes through family-oriented income-generation activities. Special efforts will also be made by both Central and State Standing Tripartite Committees (CSSTC) to impress upon those Ministries/Departments, which are not earmarking funds, under SCP in the name of nondivisibility of the programmes of their Ministries/ Departments to do the needful. While the nodal Ministry of Social Justice & Empowerment will keep a close vigil on the utilisation of these special funds, the on-going reviews at the Centre both by the CSSTC and the National Commission for Scheduled Castes and STs will continue on a regular basis to assess how effective are these instruments in supplementing/ complementing the efforts of the nodal Ministry in empowering these disadvantaged groups economically.

III. Social Justice

A conscious shift in the name and role of the nodal Ministry from 'Welfare' to 'Social Justice and Empowerment' in 1998 is not only to re-affirm the governmental commitment of ensuring social justice, but also to extend a focused attention to these Groups.

Affirmative action and legislative measures being the most powerful instruments to ensure social justice to the Disadvantaged Groups, the Government renews its earlier commitment of instituting a 'National Charter for Social Justice' based on the principles of social harmony with social and gender justice and necessary legal measures to protect their interests. To this effect, implementation of the reservation policy both in the educational institutions and services for Scheduled Castes, and in services for OBCs will be strictly adhered to by filling up all the reserved posts promptly. Arrangements will also be made simultaneously for quick judicial disposals of complaints and grievances in matters related thereof.

As the most inhuman practice of carrying the night soil manually continues to be a matter of national concern, the Tenth Plan will embark upon a nation-wide programme for total eradication of manual scavenging on a time-bound basis by 2007. To this effect, the Tenth Plan will emphasise preparation of State-specific Plans of Action to initiate time-bound programmes in respect of - conversion of dry latrines into wet ones; identification of scavengers; wean them away from this profession; and rehabilitate them with training and alternative jobs; keep a follow-up of the rehabilitated persons; and bring forth an effective co-ordination between the Welfare Departments of the States and the Local Bodies. In these national endeavours, the National Commission for Safai Karamcharis is going to play a lead role.

Taking note of the urgent need for upholding the Civil Rights on the one hand and preventing/curbing the persistent problems of social discrimination, exploitation, untouchability, and atrocities against these disadvantaged groups, on the other, the Tenth Plan will initiate collaborative efforts with all the concerned for effective implementation of the Indian Penal Code, 1860 and the other two Special Legislations viz. the PCR Act, 1955 and the SC & ST (Prevention of Atrocities) Act, 1989. To this effect, efforts will also be made to prepare state /district-specific Programmes of Action ensuring preventive, investigative and rehabilitative measures in those districts/areas where the incidence of crime/ atrocities/ violence against these weaker sections is high. Measures will also be undertaken to ensure that adequate number of Special/ Mobile Courts are set up with adequate staff in each district to provide both speedy and on-the-spot settlement/redressal of grievances.

Further, the problem relating to the practice of untouchability, which is still in vogue in certain pockets, will be addressed squarely towards total elimination of the same from the face of the society. As an important measure of social justice, special efforts will be made to extend timely and adequate financial support, as per the provisions, to compensate/ rehabilitate the victims. Simultaneously, efforts will also be made to develop a community-based defence mechanism by empowering the institutions of local governance and NGOs. As part of these, a few selected local NGOs will also be identified to help assist the victims besides acting as the authorised informants to the Enforcement Authorities.

Simultaneously, the Tenth Plan will also endeavour to reinforce the implementation of both the mechanisms viz. SCP for Scheduled Castes and SCA to SCP which was launched specially in support of social justice to ensure that adequate funds flow for the development of Scheduled Castes through various sources. While SCP ensures that additional funds, in proportion to the population of Scheduled Castes, are earmarked for implementation of various programmes for their development, the SCA to SCP extends additional funds to fill the critical gaps in the family-based income-generation activities being implemented under State SCP. Taking note of the fact that the implementation of these mechanisms is becoming routinised, the Tenth Plan will activate all the concerned, especially the Central Tripartite Committee as well as the nodal Ministry of Social Justice & Empowerment and the State Planning and Welfare Departments to keep continuous monitoring towards more effective implementation of these two mechanisms. In this context, the State Governments which are yet to set up State Tripartite Committees will be involved to initiate necessary action for setting up of these Committees and start the detailed reviews with regard to earmarking of funds under SCP and the utilization of SCA to SCP. Also, the Tenth Plan will take special measures to ensure effective implementation and monitoring of the other two Special Mechanism viz. the '20-Point.

Thus, the Tenth Plan will ensure that these special mechanisms justify the purpose for which they were launched by keeping a special vigil on the effectiveness of their implementation.

Further, the Tenth Plan will invoke the statutory Commissions viz. National Commission for SCs and STs (1992) and National Commission for Safai Karamcharis (1994) to make a detailed review of their work since their inception and revitalise themselves to be able to play their role as Custodians and Public Defenders and thus, ensure Social Justice to the deprived lot.

Special efforts will be made to put into action simultaneously the three-pronged strategy of 'Awareness Generation, Conscientisation and Sensitisation', towards achieving a holistic impact. The first being awareness generation, efforts will be made to change the mind-set and the attitudes of the people towards these Groups as the same is very crucial in creating an enabling environment for empowering them. To this effect, awareness generation programmes/special campaigns will be taken up on a continuing basis all over the country, especially in rural areas by involving effectively both the governmental and the non-governmental organisations and the media towards erasing the longstanding social biases/stigmas like untouchability and thus create the feeling of all being equal. The second being conscientisation of the target groups, simultaneous efforts will be made to make the target groups conscious of their own rights, privileges and the governmental support available for them besides making them realise their own potentials to be self confident and self-reliant. The third being sensitising both officials and non-officials, special training programmes, both pre-service and in-service, will be undertaken from time to time to sensitise all those working for these Groups so that they can work with right perspectives in handling/meeting the special needs and problems of these marginalised groups and thus ensure social justice. To encourage/reward those officials and non-officials, who are working for the good of these deprived lot by living in the most backward areas, efforts will be made to impress upon the State Governments the urgent need to revive the earlier practice of extending incentives, both in kind and cash.

In this context, the supporting institutional structures of the Ministry of Social Justice & Empowerment, such as the National

Commissions for SCs and Safai Karamacharis, will be invoked to probe into and take necessary action to ensure that not only the interest of the concerned sections are protected but also to maximise their role of a watch-dog especially on effective implementation of various welfare and developmental programmes of the Government. Similarly, functioning of the support Financial Institutions, viz. NSFDC, NSKDC, NBCFDC working for the economic upliftment of these sections will be streamlined/ optimised by bringing forth necessary modifications/revisions in their modus operandi and thus ensure that they not only perform their due role of being viable and sustainable financial institutions, but also accomplish the task of providing all the necessary inputs to the target groups to achieve their economic upliftment through employment and income generating activities. In this context, the need for re-establishing an independent Division in the Planning Commission to deal exclusively with the welfare and development of Scheduled Castes, OBCs and Minorities comes up very strongly as an Action Point towards ensuring social justice and empowerment of these disadvantaged groups.

PLAN OUTLAYS

A total outlay of Rs. 6,526 crore (which includes Rs. 2313.40 crore for SCA to SCP) has been earmarked in the Central Budget of the Ministry of Social Justice & Empowerment (SCs, OBCs and Minorities) in the Tenth Plan. Also, this sector receives plan financial support from the state sector.

In preparation to the Tenth Plan, special efforts were made to ensure effective distribution of the otherwise limited resources through the application of Zero Based Budgeting (ZBB). This has brought down the number of 31 on-going schemes of the Ninth Plan to 13 (4 Central Sector and 9 Centrally Sponsored Schemes) for empowering the Socially Disadvantaged Groups in the Tenth Plan.

Note: Chapter 2: The setting, Chapter 3: Education, Chapter 4: Occupation, Chapter 5: Political Participation, Chapter 6: Social status, were the outcome of extensive fieldwork. For writing the Chapter 7: The Empowerment of Scheduled Castes, the author, to a large extent has used the information provided by the Planning Commission, Ministry of Social Justice and Empowerment and other Government departments and the author gratefully acknowledges the same.

Eight

Summary and Conclusions

The major thrust of the present study is to explore the trends of social change and development occurring among the Scheduled Castes in semi-urban research setting of Gooty in Anantapur district of Andhra Pradesh. In pursuit of this aim the disparities in educational attainment, persistence and change of occupation, trends and patterns of political participation and leadership over three generations, namely grandfather, father and respondent, and change of social status within the present generation of respondents have been examined.

The universe of the study consists of all the 320 households in Gooty. Because of the manageable size of the universe all the 320 households were approached for collection of data. The data were collected by the use of a standardised schedule. The work is being presented in eight chapters.

The socio-economic profile of the respondents reveals that the Scheduled Castes represent two cultural groups namely Mala and Madiga. The Madigas are numerically dominant. Majority of the respondents is in the age group of 40 years and above, with almost 90 per cent of them being returned as married. Less than 50 per cent of them are literates with minimal educational attainments. As much as 70 per cent of the respondents are in low income fetching occupational categories of manual worker and menial services. The female favourable sex ratio of the Scheduled Castes under study is contrary to the district and all India census. Leaving aside the respondents in the 320 households the other members constitute the population. The population of the Scheduled Castes under study has a large percentage of young members. Even in the population a majority of them are illiterates, and among the literates majority have minimal educational attainment. A significant percentage of population is returned as unmarried. Of thc total workforce in the population, a majority is in the lowly paid occupational categories of manual workers and menial services. Majority of the families is nuclear families and lives in their own houses. The average size of family is 5.2.

Considering the education among the Scheduled Castes of Gooty, it is clear that throughout all the three generations, illiteracy is high. However the illiteracy over generations has come down; more so in case of fourth generation, the children of the respondents. Among the literates' majority have only minimal educational attainment and this is clear from the findings such as;

That the illiteracy among the Scheduled castes is very high and this holds good throughout the three generations considered for the study, the semi urban area of Gooty;

That at the same time, the illiteracy over generations is on the decline and this is clear from the figures of illiteracy that stand 93.1, 86 and 60.6 per cent for respondents' grandfather, respondents' father and respondent generations respectively in the semi urban place of Gooty;

That the levels of achievement in terms of education are low among the Scheduled Castes as about 50 per cent of them have only the lowest level of achievement, the primary education, and this holds good for all the three generations. At the same time less than one per cent of the Scheduled Castes only could achieve the highest level of educational attainment, the post graduation;

That among the literate respondents about 50 per cent of them could achieve more than primary education *and they are distributed in all the levels of education;*

Taking into consideration educational mobility, the immobility is more pronounced than mobility. Of the immobile, majority is illiterates throughout. In case of the mobility a substantial majority have shown upward mobility in all the cases. Except in the case of mobility between father and respondent generations, the downward mobility is very insignificant. This is clear from the observations such as;

> that compared to the grand father as many as 267 fathers have remained immobile, with a staggering majority of them being illiterate;
>
> that compared to the respondents' grandfathers 30 fathers

have shown upward mobility whereas only five fathers have shown downward mobility;

of the upwardly mobile respondents' fathers, a majority have shown only minimal upward mobility;

In terms of steps taken, the total mobility, positive mobility, negative mobility and net mobility is more in mobility analysis between the grandfather and respondent, than in the mobility analysis between grand father and father and father and respondent. It is clear from the analysis that a staggering majority of the wives of respondents are illiterates. The educational attainment in the fourth generation is very encouraging; with boys having an edge over the girls. The educational attainment is satisfactory in the generation of the children of the respondents both in terms of the number taking up the education and quality of education and this is clear from the observations such as;

that, of the children of Scheduled Castes more than 60 per cent are educated and are in different levels of education which is an encouraging phenomena;

that of the children of the respondents more boys are taking to education than girls;

that speaking in terms of families, as many as 78.43 per cent of families that have school going age group children are pursuing the education of their children;

that of the 200 families where the highest educated child's education was collected, in 78.5 percent of families the children are still pursuing their education which shows the education levels of the children are still to improve;

The persistence and change of the occupation among the Scheduled Castes under study is considered in the chapter, Occupation. Among the Scheduled Castes under study, as the study reveals, as much as 75 per cent of them are in the occupational categories of manual workers and menial services, in all the three generations, which are considered to be their traditional agricultural and non-agricultural occupations. However the number of persons in these occupational categories has remained more are less same in the first two generations but come down in the respondents generation which indicates more change than persistence in the respondents generation. Taking into consideration the menial services alone the concentration of Scheduled castes has steadily decreased over generations.

Taking into consideration the mobility, in all the cases of the mobility analysis that is between the generations of grandfather and father, father and respondent and grandfather and respondent immobility is more pronounced than mobility. Again in all the three cases, wherever there is change of occupation, in majority cases the change is from the occupational categories of manual workers and menial services to others. In majority cases the occupational shift is upward in nature and this is clear from the findings such as;

that compared to the grandfather's , about 80 per cent of the fathers had remained in the same occupations, whereas only 20 per cent of them have moved away from the occupations of grandfather;

That majority of the fathers who moved away from the occupations of the grandfather, and here the occupational categories of grandfathers were Manual workers and Menial services;

That majority of fathers, who changed occupations compared to the grandfathers, have moved up in occupational categories, and they amount to as much as 71 per cent. As many as 35 of the fathers have given up Menial services compared to the grandfathers;

That compared to the fathers about 64 per cent of the respondents have remained in the occupations of their fathers. Only about 36 per cent of the respondents have moved into different occupations;

That again the majority of the respondents who have moved into other occupations have their fathers in the occupational categories of Manual workers and Menial services;

That compared to the fathers, the respondents who moved into other occupations, a majority— which is about 77 per cent have moved into higher occupational categories;

That compared to the grandfathers about 56 percent of the respondents have remained in the occupations of the grandfathers, which is a small per cent compared to the two other cases(grand father to father, father to respondent) and about 44 per cent of them have moved into different occupations;

That even in this case the majority of the mobile respondents have their grandfathers in the occupational categories of Manual workers and Menial services;

The political participation, mobilisation and emergence of leadership among the Scheduled Castes under study are presented in the chapter, Political Participation. From the analysis it is clear that the caste associations are present in all the three generations but never had any firm grip over its members. The caste associations are now being replaced by the formal associations, which are taking over the roles of the traditional caste associations. The Scheduled Castes under study are organising themselves into powerful organizations and associations to achieve the desired goals. The Madigas compared to the Malas are better organised and are in the forefront in case of organizations and associations. The Scheduled Castes of the present generation in the locale are actively involved in the political participation and this is evident as a sizeable number of them are reported to be members or supporters of one political party or the other. A few among the members of the political parties are holding official positions in the party. Two individuals among the Scheduled Castes of Gooty could rise to the position of the Member of the Legislative Assembly and of them one was the minister in the former State cabinet and the other was the Government whip. To the Scheduled Castes of Gooty, besides the formal leadership informal leadership is also available in the form of elders, educated youth, and educated well placed employees among them.

There is considerable change in the social status of the Scheduled Castes under study, which is evident from the analysis. The Scheduled Castes though are living apart in their exclusive colonies; do not indicate the ecological segregation being enforced on them. The Scheduled Castes of Gooty feel they are free to construct house wherever they like. The Scheduled Castes in the locale can make use of all the civic amenities, if they are so desirous, without discrimination. There is perceptible improvement in their social status, as untouchability is no longer practised. The improvement is further in evidence as the Scheduled Castes in Gooty are more and more being accepted in social interaction situations such as interdining, common gatherings etc. To some extent, a small number of the Scheduled Castes who are still in the low-income fetching occupations of manual work and menial services, still feel discriminated. It was also observed such discrimination more often than not, is self-construed discrimination. The Scheduled Castes of Gooty are free to enter into any temples of Gooty. Majority of them opined that they do not feel discrimination. Those who reported of feeling being discriminated have given unclean occupation, food habits and fear of pollution as the major reasons, for the upper castes to keep them at a distance. Some of the respondents have given better education and employment as effective remedies to ward off whatever little discrimination that is present.

The findings of the study reveal that the status of the Scheduled Castes of Gooty is changing with reference to education, occupation, political participation and the overall social status as evident from the intergenerational variations. The changes are due to mutually complementary supportive forces like urbanisation, economic development and progressive legislation.

Analysing the situation at Gooty, the semi urban setting thus presents a unique feature.

Since Gooty is a semi-urban place it is provided better educational infrastructure than the villages and hence the increased literacy attainment. Similarly since it is not a city or industrial centre it did not encourage need for higher educational attainment for the lack of opportunities.

Relatively larger population and diversity has enabled the Scheduled Castes to diversify their occupational base and thus become relatively free from the bias of occupational pollution and the consequent discrimination. The other sections of the population more apparently felt the larger concentration of Scheduled Castes in Gooty, as it happens to be only a semi-urban place that is neither a village (small population) nor a city (very large population)

The relative location advantage enabled the Scheduled Castes to act as an effective political pressure group and thus avail the benefits of constitutional guarantees and also ward off social resistance and discrimination to an extent.

Being a semi-urban place Gooty still retains the rural characteristics. Hence polarisation of Scheduled Castes into separate community colonies and demand for exclusive civic amenities as there is enough scope for provision and expansion in this regard. Further the overt discrimination on the basis of nature of occupation is also primarily due to its semi-urban nature where members can immediately recognise each other.

On the strength of the above findings it may be concluded that the status of the Scheduled Castes is under transition for the better. This change is being realised and experienced in general by the respondents and more particularly by the younger generation, subject to the extent of economic development supported by the process of politicisation and modern education.

Annexure

About List of Scheduled Castes

Who can be included?

The criteria for inclusion of any community in the list of Scheduled Castes is as under:

> "Extreme social, education and economic backwardness arising out of the traditional practice of untouchability".

Getting a Caste certificate

A person belonging to Scheduled Castes has to apply to the designated authority, i.e., Sub-Divisional Officer of the area where the applicant resides permanently. The Designated Authority will issue the certificate after verification of the claim of the applicant. It can be obtained from State Government/Union Territory Administration.

The status of Scheduled Caste with regard to religion

As per orders issued, only persons professing either Hindu or Sikh or Buddhist religion are deemed to be members of Scheduled Caste. A person of Scheduled Caste origin who has embraced Christian religion or Islam will not be treated as Scheduled Caste.

Can a non-Scheduled Caste person who marries a Scheduled Caste person will get the benefits meant for the Scheduled Caste?

The guiding principle is that no person who was not a Scheduled Caste by birth will be deemed to be a member of a Scheduled Caste merely because he or she had married a person belonging to a Scheduled Caste. However, a Scheduled Caste person who marries non-Scheduled Castes person will continue to get benefits of Scheduled Castes.

The status of the child of a couple one of whom is a Scheduled Caste

To decide the status of an off-spring of a couple where one of the spouses is a member of Scheduled Caste, the crucial test followed is to determine whether the child has been accepted by the Scheduled Caste as a member of their community and has been brought up in that surrounding and in that community or not. If the child has been accepted by the Scheduled Caste Community and has been brought up in the surrounding of Scheduled Caste spouse then, the child would be treated as Scheduled Caste. However, each case is to be examined on its merit, each case will be decided on case-to-case basis but in general, the following illustrations are made:

Example I

Father	Scheduled Caste
Mother	non-Scheduled Caste
Child	shall be Scheduled Caste

Example II

Mother	Scheduled Caste
Father	non-Scheduled Caste
Child	shall be non-Scheduled Caste

Is a member of Scheduled Caste listed in the list of one State eligible for benefits as Scheduled Caste in another State / Union Territory?

The list of Scheduled Castes is State/ Union Territory specific. As such a member of Scheduled Caste is eligible for benefits in his State of origin only. A member of Scheduled Caste Community, who migrates to other State/ Union Territory, is not entitled to get Scheduled Caste benefits, from the state of migration.

Example— A Scheduled Caste person who migrates from State of Punjab to Rajasthan will not get the benefits extended to the Scheduled Castes of Rajasthan but he will continue to get benefits of the State of his origin, i.e., Punjab. But he will be eligible for benefits available under Central Government and its agencies in the State of Rajasthan also.

Whether the courts have powers to list a Community as Scheduled Castes?

In the Pankaj Kumar Saha Vs. the Sub-Divisional Officer, Islampur in SLP© No. 4680 of 1996 the Supreme Court has observed as under:

> "It is now settled law that though evidence may be admissible to the limited extent of finding out whether a caste which claims the status as Scheduled Caste or Tribe was in fact included in the Presidential notification as amended under 1976 Act, the court is devoid of power to include in or exclude from or substitute or declare synonyms to be a Scheduled Caste or Scheduled Tribe. The courts would only look into the notification issued by the President to see whether the name finds place in the notification?"

LIST OF SCHEDULED CASTES

ANDHRA PRADESH

1 Adi Andhra
2 Adi Dravida
3 Anamuk
4 Aray Mala
5 Arundhatiya
6 Arwa Mala
7 Bariki
8 Bavuri
9 Beda Jangam, Budga Jangam
10 Bindla
11 Byagara
12 Chachati
13 Chalavadi
14 Chamar, Mochi, Muchi
15 Chambhar
16 Chandala
17 Dakkal, Dokkalwar
18 Dandasi
19 Dhor
20 Dom, Dombara, Paidi, Pano
21 Ellamalawar, Yellammala-wandlu
22 Ghasi, Haddi, Relli Chachandi
23 Godagali
24 Godari
25 Gosangi
26 Holeya
27 Holeya Dasari
28 Jaggali
29 Jambuvulu
30 Kolupulvandlu
31 Madasi Kuruva, Madari Kuruva
32 Madiga
33 Madiga Dasu, Mashteen
34 Mahar
35 Mala
36 Mala Dasari
37 Mala Dasu
38 Mala Hannai
39 Malajangam
40 Mala Masti
41 Mala Sale, Netkani
42 Mala Sanyasi
43 Mang
44 Mang Garodi
45 Manne

46 Mashti
47 Matangi
48 Mehtar
49 Mitha Ayyalvar
50 Mundala
51 Paky, Moti, Thoti
52 Pambada, Pambanda
53 Pamidi
54 Panchama, Pariah
55 Relli
56 Samagara
57 Samban
58 Sapru
59 Sindhollu, Chindollu

ARUNACHAL PRADESH

1 Bansphor
2 Bhuinmali or Mali
3 Brittial-Bania or Bania
4 Dhupi or Dhobi
5 Dugla or Dholi
6 Hira
7 Jalkeot
8 Jhalo, Malo or Jhalo-Malo
9 Kaibartta or Jaliya
10 Lalbegi
11 Mahara
12 Mehtar or Bhangi
13 Muchi or Rishi
14 Namasudra
15 Patni
16 Sutradhar

Assam

1 Bansphor
2 Bhuinmali, Mali
3 Brittial Bania, Bania
4 Dhupi, Dhobi
5 Dugla, Dholi
6 Hira
7 Jalkeot
8 Jhalo, Malo, Jhalo-Malo
9 Kaibartta, Jaliya
10 Lalbegi
11 Mahara
12 Mehtar, Bhangi
13 Muchi, Rishi
14 Namasudra
15 Patni
16 Sutradhar

BIHAR

1 Bantar
2 Bauri
3 Bhogta
4 Bhuiya
5 Bhumij (excluding North Chotanagpur and South Chotanagpur divisions and Santal Parganas district)a
6 Chamar, Mochi
7 Chaupal
8 Dabgar
9 Dhobi
10 Dom, Dhangad
11 Dusadh, Dhari, Dharhi
12 Ghasi
13 Halalkhor
14 Hari, Mehtar, Bhangi
15 Kanjar
16 Kurariar
17 Lalbegi
18 Musahar
19 Nat
20 Pan, Sawasi
21 Pasi
22 Rajwar
23 Turi

CHHATISGARH

1 Audhelia
2 Bagri, Bagdi
3 Bahna, Bahana
4 Balahi, Balai
5 Banchada
6 Barahar, Basod
7 Bargunda

8 Basor, Burud, Bansor, Bansodi, Bansphor, Basar
9 Bedia
10 Beldar, Sunkar
11 Bhangi, Mehtar, Balmiki, Lalbegi, Dharkar
12 Bhanumati
13 Chadar
14 Chamar, Chamari, Bairwa, Bhambhi, Jatav, Mochi, Regar, Nona, Rohidas, Ramnami, Satnami, Surjyabanshi, Surjyaramnami, Ahirwar, Chamar, Mangan, Raidas
15 Chidar
16 Chikwa, Chikvi
17 Chitar
18 Dahait, Dahayat, Dahat
19 Dewar
20 Dhanuk
21 Dhed, Dher
22 Dohor
23 Dom, Dumar, Dome, Domar, Doris
24 Ganda, Gandi
25 Ghasi, Ghasia
26 Holiya
27 Kanjar
28 Katia, Patharia
29 Khatik
30 Koli, Kori
31 Khangar, Kanera, Mirdha
32 Kuchbandhia
33 Mahar, Mehra, Mehar
34 Mang, Mang Garodi, Mang Garudi, Dankhni Mang, Mang Mahasi, Madari, Garudi, Radhe Mang
35 Meghwal
36 Moghia
37 Muskhan
38 Nat, Kalbelia, Sapera, Navdigar, Kubutar
39 Pasi
40 Rujjhar
41 Sansi, Sansia
42 Silawat
43 Zamral

CHANDIGARH

1 Ad Dharmi
2 Bangali
3 Barar, Burar or Berar
4 Batwal
5 Bauria or Bawaria
6 Bazigar
7 Balmiki, Chura or Bhangi
8 Bhanjra
9 Chamar, Jatia Chamar, Rehgar, Raigar, Ramdasi or Ravidasi
10 Chanal
11 Dagi
12 Darain
13 Dhanak
14 Dhogri, Dhangri or Siggi
15 Dumna, Mahasha or Doom
16 Gagra
17 Gandhila or Gandil Gondola
18 Kabirpanthi or Julaha
19 Khatik
20 Kori or Koli
21 Marija or Marecha
22 Mazhabi
23 Megh
24 Nat
25 Od
26 Pasi
27 Perna
28 Pherera
29 Sanhai
30 Sanhal
31 Sansi, Bhedkut or Manesh
32 Sansoi
33 Sapela
34 Sarera

35 Sikligar
36 Sirkiband

DADRA & NAGAR HAVELI
1 Bhangi
2 Chamar
3 Mahar
4 Mahyavanshi, Dhed

DAMAN & DIU
1 Bhangi (Hadi)
2 Chambhar
3 Mahar
4 Mahyavanshi (Vankar)
5 Mang

DELHI
1 Adi-Dharmi
2 Agria
3 Aheria
4 Balai
5 Banjara
6 Bawaria
7 Bazigar
8 Bhangi
9 Bhil
10 Chamar, Chanwar Chamar, Jatya or Jatav Chamar, Mochi, amdasia, Ravidasi, Raidasi, Rehgarh or Raigar
11 Chohra (Sweeper)
12 Chuhra (Balmiki)
13 Dhanak or Dhanuk
14 Dhobi
15 Dom
16 Gharrami
17 Julaha (Weaver)
18 Kabirpanthi
19 Kachhandha
20 Kanjar or Giarah
21 Khatik
22 Koli
23 Lalbegi
24 Madari
25 Mallah
26 Mazhabi
27 Meghwal
28 Naribut
29 Nat (Rana)
30 Pasi
31 Perna
32 Sansi or Bhedkut
33 Sapera
34 Sikligar
35 Singiwala or Kalbelia
36 Sirkiband

GOA
1 Bhangi (Hadi)
2 Chambhar
3 Mahar
4 Mahyavanshi (Vankar)
5 Mang

GUJARAT
1 Ager
2 Bakad, Bant
3 Bawa-Dedh, Dedh-Sadhu
4 Bhambi, Bhambhi, Asadaru, Asodi, Chamadia, Chamar, Chambhar, Chamgar, Haralayya, Harali, Khalpa, Machigar, Mochigar, Madar, Madig, Mochi, Nalia, Telegu Mochi, Kamati Mochi, Ranigar, Rohidas, Rohit, Samgar
5 Bhangi, Mehtar, Olgana, Rukhi, Malkana, Halalkhor, Lalbegi, Balmiki, Korar, Zadmalli
6 Chalvadi, Channayya
7 Chenna Dasar, Holaya Dasar
8 Dangashia
9 Dhor, Kakkayya, Kankayya
10 Garmatang

11 Garoda, Garo
12 Halleer
13 Halsar, Haslar, Hulasvar, Halasvar
14 Holar, Valhar
15 Holaya, Holer
16 Lingader
17 Mahar, Taral, Dhegu Megu
18 Mahyavansi, Dhed, Dhedh, Vankar, Maru Vankar, Antyaj
19 Mang, Matang, Minimadig
20 Mang-Garudi
21 Meghval, Meghwal, Menghvar
22 Mukri
23 Nadia, Hadi
24 Pasi
25 Senva, Shenva, Chenva, Sedma, Rawat
26 Shemalia
27 Thori
28 Tirgar, Tirbanda
29 Turi
30 Turi Barot, Dedh Barot

HARYANA

1 Ad Dharmi
2 Balmiki, Chura, Bhangi
3 Bangali
4 Barar, Burar, Berar
5 Batwal
6 Bauria, Bawaria
7 Bazigar
8 Bhanjra
9 Chamar, Jatia Chamar, Rehgar, Raigar, Ramdasi, Ravidasi
10 Chanal
11 Dagi
12 Darain
13 Deha, Dhaya, Dhea
14 Dhanak
15 Dhogri, Dhangri, Siggi
16 Dumna, Mahasha, Doom
17 Gagra
18 Gandhila, Gandil Gondola
19 Kabirpanthi, Julaha
20 Khatik
21 Kori, Koli
22 Marija, Marecha
23 Mazhabi
24 Megh
25 Nat
26 Od
27 Pasi
28 Perna
29 Pherera
30 Sanhai
31 Sanhal
32 Sansi, Bhedkut, Manesh
33 Sansoi
34 Sapela
35 Sarera
36 Sikligar
37 Sirkiband

HIMACHAL PRADESH

1 Ad Dharmi
2 Badhi, Nagalu
3 Balmiki, Bhangi, Chuhra, Chura, Chuhre
4 Bandhela
5 Bangali
6 Banjara
7 Bansi
8 Barad
9 Barar, Burar, Berar
10 Batwal
11 Bauria, Bawaria
12 Bazigar
13 Bhanjra, Bhanjre
14 Chamar, Jatia Chamar, Rehgar, Raigar, Ramdasi, Ravidasi, Ramdasia, Mochi
15 Chanal
16 Chhimbe, Dhobi

17 Dagi
18 Darain
19 Darai, Daryai
20 Daule, Daole
21 Dhaki, Toori
22 Dhanak
23 Dhaogri, Dhuai
24 Dhogri, Dhangri, Siggi
25 Doom, Doomna, Dumna, Dumne, Mahasha
26 Gagra
27 Gandhila, Gandil Gondola
28 Hali
29 Hesi
30 Jogi
31 Julaha, Julahe, Kabirpanthi, Keer
32 Kamoh, Dagoli
33 Karoack
34 Khatik
35 Kori, Koli
36 Lohar
37 Marija, Marecha
38 Mazhabi
39 Megh
40 Nat
41 Od
42 Pasi
43 Perna
44 Phrera, Pherera
45 Rehar, Rehara
46 Sanhai
47 Sanhal
48 Sansi, Bhedkut, Manesh
49 Sansoi
50 Sapela
51 Sarde, Sarera, Sarare, Siryare, Sarehde
52 Sikligar
53 Sipi
54 Sirkiband
55 Teli
56 Thathiar, Thathera

JAMMU & KASHMIR

1 Barwala
2 Basith
3 Batwal
4 Chamar or Ramdasia
5 Chura
6 Dhyar
7 Doom or Mahasha
8 Gardi
9 Jolaha
10 Megh or Kabirpanthi
11 Ratal
12 Saryara
13 Watal

JHARKHAND

1 Bantar
2 Baurri
3 Bhogta
4 Bhuiya
5 Chamar, Mochi
6 Chaupal
7 Dabajar
8 Dhobi
9 Dom, Dhangad
10 Dusadh, Dhari, Dharhi
11 Ghasi
12 Halalkhor
13 Hari, Mehtar, Bhangi
14 Kanjar
15 Kurariar
16 Lalbegi
17 Musahar
18 Nat
19 Pan, Sawasi
20 Pasi
21 Rajwar
22 Turi

KARNATAKA

1 Adi Andhra
2 Adi Dravida
3 Adi Karnataka

4 Adiya (in Coorg district)a
5 Ager
6 Ajila
7 Anamuk
8 Aray Mala
9 Arunthathiyar
10 Arwa Mala
11 Baira
12 Bakad
13 Bant (in Belgaum, Bijapur, Dharwar and North Kanara districts)b
14 Bakuda
15 Balagai
16 Bandi
17 Banjara, Lambani
18 Bathada
19 Beda Jangam, Budga Jangam
20 Bellara
21 Bhangi, Mehtar, Olgana, Rukhi, Malkana, Halalkhor, Lalbegi, Balmiki, Korar, Zadmalli
22 Bhambi, Bhambhi, Asadaru, Asodi, Chamadia, Chamar, Chambhar, Chamgar, Haralayya, Harali, Khalpa, Machigar, Mochigar, Madar, Madig, Mochi, Muchi, Telegu Mochi, Kamati Mochi, Ranigar, Rohidas, Rohit, Samgar
23 Bhovi
24 Bindla
25 Byagara
26 Chakkiliyan
27 Chalavadi, Chalvadi, Channayya
28 Chandala
29 Chenna Dasar, Holaya Dasar
30 Dakkal, Dokkalwar
31 Dakkaliga
32 Dhor, Kakkayya, Kankayya
33 Dom, Dombara, Paidi, Pano
34 Ellamalwar, Yellammalawandlu
35 Ganti Chores
36 Garoda, Garo
37 Godda
38 Gosangi
39 Halleer
40 Halsar, Haslar, Hulasvar, Halasvar
41 Handi Jogis
42 Hasla
43 Holar, Valhar
44 Holaya, Holer, Holeya
45 Holeya Dasari
46 Jaggali
47 Jambuvulu
48 Kadaiyan
49 Kalladi
50 Kepmaris
51 Kolupulvandlu
52 Koosa
53 Koracha
54 Korama
55 Kotegar, Metri
56 Kudumban
57 Kuravan
58 Lingader
59 Machala
60 Madari
61 Madiga
62 Mahar, Taral, Dhegu Megu
63 Mahyavanshi, Dhed, Vankar, Maru Vankar
64 Maila
65 Mala
66 Mala Dasari
67 Mala Hannai
68 Mala Jangam
69 Mala Masti
70 Mala Sale, Netkani
71 Mala Sanyasi
72 Mang, Matang, Minimadig

73 Mang Garudi, Mang Garodi
74 Manne
75 Masthi
76 Mavilan
77 Meghval, Menghvar
78 Moger
79 Mukri
80 Mundala
81 Nadia, Hadi
82 Nalkadaya
83 Nalakeyava
84 Nayadi
85 Pale
86 Pallan
87 Pambada
88 Panchama
89 Panniandi
90 Paraiyan, Paraya
91 Paravan
92 Raneyar
93 Samagara
94 Samban
95 Sapari
96 Sillekyathas
97 Sindhollu, Chindollu
98 Sudugadu Siddha
99 Thoti
100 Tirgar, Tirbanda
101 Valluvan

KERALA

1 Adi Andhra
2 Adi Dravida
3 Adi Karnataka
4 Ajila
5 Arunthathiyar
6 Ayyanavar
7 Baira
8 Bakuda
9 Bandi
10 Bathada
11 Bellara
12 Bharatar
13 Boyan [excluding the areas comprising the Malabar district as specified by sub-section (2) of section 5 of the States Reorganisation Act, 1956 (37of 1956)]a
14 Chakkiliyan
15 Chamar, Muchi
16 Chandala
17 Cheruman
18 Domban
19 Gavara
20 Godagali
21 Godda
22 Gosangi
23 Hasla
24 Holeya
25 Kadaiyan
26 Kakkalan
27 Kalladi
28 Kanakkan, Padanna
29 Karimpalan
30 Kavara
31 Koosa
32 Kootan, Koodan
33 Kudumban
34 Kuravan, Sidhanar
35 Maila
36 Malayan [in the areas comprising the Malabar district as specified by sub-section (2) of section 5 of the States Reorganisation Act, 1956 (37of 1956)]a
37 Mannan
38 Mavilan
39 Moger
40 Mundala
41 Nalakeyava
42 Nalkadaya
43 Nayadi
44 Padannan
45 Pallan

46 Palluvan
47 Pambada
48 Panan
49 Panchama
50 Paraiyan, Parayan, Sambavar
51 Paravan
52 Pathiyan
53 Perumannan
54 Pulayan, Cheramar
55 Pulaya Vettuvan
56 Puthirai Vannan
57 Raneyar
58 Samagara
59 Samban
60 Semman
61 Thandan
62 Thoti
63 Vallon
64 Valluvan
65 Vannan
66 Velan
67 Vetan
68 Vettuvan

MADHYA PRADESH

1 Audhelia
2 Bagri, Bagdi
3 Bahna, Bahana
4 Balahi, Balai
5 Banchada
6 Barahar, Basod
7 Bargunda
8 Basor, Burud, Bansor, Bansodi, Bansphor, Basar
9 Bedia
10 Beldar, Sunkar
11 Bhangi, Mehtar, Balmik, Lalbegi, Dharkar
12 Bhanumati
13 Chadar
14 Chamar, Chamari, Bairwa, Bhambi, Jatav, Mochi, Regar, Nona, Rohidas, Ramnami, Satnami, Surjyabanshi, Surjyaramnami, Ahirwar, Chamar Mangan, Raidas
15 Chidar
16 Chikwa, Chikvi
17 Chitar
18 Dahait, Dahayat, Dahat
19 Dewar
20 Dhanuk
21 Dhed, Dher
22 Dhobi (in Bhopal , Raisen and Sehore districts)
23 Dohor
24 Dom, Dumar, Dome, Domar, Doris
25 Ganda, Gandi
26 Ghasi, Ghasia
27 Holiya
28 Kanjar
29 Katia, Patharia
30 Khatik
31 Koli, Kori
32 Kotwal (in Bhind, Dhar, Dewas, Guna, Gwalior, Indore, Jhabua, Khargone, Mandsaur, Morena, Rajgarh, Ratlam, Shajapur, Shivpuri, Ujjain and Vidisha districts)a
33 Khangar, Kanera, Mirdha
34 Kuchbandhia
35 Kumhar (in Chhatarpur, Datia, Panna, Rewa, Satna, Shahdol, Sidhi and Tikamgarh districts)
36 Mahar, Mehra, Mehar
37 Mang, Mang Garodi, Mang Garudi, Dankhni Mang, Mang Mahasi, Madari, Garudi, Radhe Mang
38 Meghwal
39 Moghia
40 Muskhan
41 Nat, Kalbelia, Sapera, Navdigar, Kubutar

42 Pardhi (in Bhind, Dhar, Dewas, Guna, Gwalior, Indore, Jhabua, Khargone, Mandsaur, Morena, Rajgarh, Ratlam, Shajapur, Shivpuri, Ujjain and Vidisha districts)a
43 Pasi
44 Rujjhar
45 Sansi, Sansia
46 Silawat
47 Zamral

MAHARASHTRA

1 Ager
2 Anamuk
3 Aray Mala
4 Arwa Mala
5 Bahna, Bahana
6 Bakad, Bant
7 Balahi, Balai
8 Basor, Burud, Bansor, Bansodi
9 Beda Jangam, Budga Jangam
10 Bedar
11 Bhambi, Bhambhi, Asadaru, Asodi, Chamadia, Chamar, Chamari, Chambhar, Chamgar, Haralayya, Harali, Khalpa, Machigar, Mochigar, Madar, Madig, Mochi, Telegu Mochi, Kamati Mochi, Ranigar, Rohidas, Nona, Ramnami, Rohit, Samgar, Samagara, Satnami, Surjyabanshi, Surjyaramnami
12 Bhangi, Mehtar, Olgana, Rukhi, Malkana, Halalkhor, Lalbegi, Balmiki, Korar, Zadmalli
13 Bindla
14 Byagara
15 Chalvadi, Channayya
16 Chenna Dasar, Holaya Dasar, Holeya Dasari
17 Dakkal, Dokkalwar
18 Dhor, Kakkayya, Kankayya, Dohor
19 Dom, Dumar
20 Ellamalvar, Yellammalawandlu
21 Ganda, Gandi
22 Garoda, Garo
23 Ghasi, Ghasia
24 Halleer
25 Halsar, Haslar, Hulasvar, Halasvar
26 Holar, Valhar
27 Holaya, Holer, Holeya, Holiya
28 Kaikadi (in Akola, Amravati, Bhandara, Buldana, Nagpur, Wardha and Yavatmal districts and Chandrapur district, other than Rajura tahsil)a
29 Katia, Patharia
30 Khangar, Kanera, Mirdha
31 Khatik, Chikwa, Chikvi
32 Kolupulvandlu
33 Kori
34 Lingader
35 Madgi
36 Madiga
37 Mahar, Mehra, Taral, Dhegu Megu
38 Mahyavanshi, Dhed, Vankar, Maru Vankar
39 Mala
40 Mala Dasari
41 Mala Hannai
42 Mala Jangam
43 Mala Masti
44 Mala Sale, Netkani
45 Mala Sanyasi
46 Mang, Matang, Minimadig, Dankhni Mang, Mang Mahashi, Madari, Garudi, Radhe Mang
47 Mang Garodi, Mang Garudi
48 Manne

49 Mashti
50 Meghval, Menghvar
51 Mitha Ayyalvar
52 Mukri
53 Nadia, Hadi
54 Pasi
55 Sansi
56 Shenva, Chenva, Sedma, Ravat
57 Sindhollu, Chindollu
58 Tirgar, Tirbanda
59 Turi

MANIPUR

1 Dhupi, Dhobi
2 Lois
3 Muchi, Ravidas
4 Namasudra
5 Patni
6 Sutradhar
7 Yaithibi

MEGHALAYA

1 Bansphor
2 Bhuinmali, Mali
3 Brittial Bania, Bania
4 Dhupi, Dhobi
5 Dugla, Dholi
6 Hira
7 Jalkeot
8 Jhalo, Malo, Jhalo-Malo
9 Kaibartta, Jaliya
10 Lalbegi
11 Mahara
12 Mehtar, Bhangi
13 Muchi, Rishi
14 Namasudra
15 Patni
16 Sutradhar

MIZORAM

1 Bansphor
2 Bhuinmali, Mali
3 Brittial Bania, Bania
4 Dhupi, Dhobi
5 Dugla, Dholi
6 Hira
7 Jalkeot
8 Jhalo, Malo, Jhalo-Malo
9 Kaibartta, Jaliya
10 Lalbegi
11 Mahara
12 Mehtar, Bhangi
13 Muchi, Rishi
14 Namasudra
15 Patni
16 Sutradhar

ORISSA

1 Adi Andhra
2 Amant, Amat
3 Audhelia
4 Badaik
5 Bagheti, Baghuti
6 Bajikar
7 Bari
8 Bariki
9 Basor, Burud
10 Bauri
11 Bauti
12 Bavuri
13 Bedia, Bejia
14 Beldar
15 Bhata
16 Bhoi
17 Chachati
18 Chakali
19 Chamar, Mochi, Muchi, Satnami
20 Chandala
21 Chandhai Maru
22 Cherua, Chhelia
23 Dandasi
24 Dewar
25 Dhanwar
26 Dhoba, Dhobi

27 Dom, Dombo, Duria Dom
28 Dosadha
29 Ganda
30 Ghantarghada, Ghantra
31 Ghasi, Ghasia
32 Ghogia
33 Ghusuria
34 Godagali
35 Godari
36 Godra
37 Gokha
38 Gorait, Korait
39 Haddi, Hadi, Hari
40 Irika
41 Jaggali
42 Kandra, Kandara
43 Karua
44 Katia
45 Kela
46 Khadala
47 Kodalo, Khodalo
48 Kori
49 Kummari
50 Kurunga
51 Laban
52 Laheri
53 Madari
54 Madiga
55 Mahuria
56 Mala, Jhala, Malo, Zala
57 Mang
58 Mangan
59 Mehra, Mahar
60 Mehtar, Bhangi
61 Mewar
62 Mundapotta
63 Musahar
64 Nagarchi
65 Namasudra
66 Paidi
67 Painda
68 Pamidi
69 Pan, Pano
70 Panchama
71 Panika
72 Panka
73 Pantanti
74 Pap
75 Pasi
76 Patial, Patikar, Patratanti, Patua
77 Rajna
78 Relli
79 Sabakhia
80 Samasi
81 Sanei
82 Sapari
83 Sauntia, Santia
84 Sidhria
85 Sinduria
86 Siyal
87 Tamadia
88 Tamudia
89 Tanla
90 Tiar, Tior
91 Turi
92 Ujia
93 Valamiki, Valmiki

PONDICHERRY

1 Adi Andhra
2 Adi Dravida
3 Chakkiliyan
4 Jambuvulu
5 Kuravan
6 Madiga
7 Mala, Mala Masti
8 Paky
9 Pallan
10 Parayan, Sambavar
11 Samban
12 Thoti
13 Valluvan
14 Vetan
15 Vettiyan

PUNJAB

1 Ad Dharmi
2 Balmiki, Chuhra, Bhangi
3 Bangali
4 Barar, Burar, Berar
5 Batwal
6 Bauria, Bawaria
7 Bazigar
8 Bhanjra
9 Chamar, Jatia Chamar, Rehgar, Raigar, Ramdasi, Ravidasi
10 Chanal
11 Dagi
12 Darain
13 Deha, Dhaya, Dhea
14 Dhanak
15 Dhogri, Dhangri, Siggi
16 Dumna, Mahasha, Doom
17 Gagra
18 Gandhila, Gandil Gondola
19 Kabirpanthi, Julaha
20 Khatik
21 Kori, Koli
22 Marija, Marecha
23 Mazhabi
24 Megh
25 Nat
26 Od
27 Pasi
28 Perna
29 Pherera
30 Sanhai
31 Sanhal
32 Sansi, Bhedkut, Manesh
33 Sansoi
34 Sapela
35 Sarera
36 Sikligar
37 Sirkiband

RAJASTHAN

1 Adi Dharmi
2 Aheri
3 Badi
4 Bagri, Bagdi
5 Bairwa, Berwa
6 Bajgar
7 Balai
8 Bansphor, Bansphod
9 Baori
10 Bargi, Vargi, Birgi
11 Bawaria
12 Bedia, Beria
13 Bhand
14 Bhangi, Chura, Mehtar, Olgana, Rukhi, Malkana, Halalkhor, Lalbegi, Balmiki, Valmiki, Korar, Zadmalli
15 Bidakia
16 Bola
17 Chamar, Bhambhi, Bambhi, Bhambi, Jatia, Jatav, Jatava, Mochi, Raidas, Rohidas, Regar, Raigar, Ramdasia, Asadaru, Asodi, Chamadia, Chambhar, Chamgar, Haralayya, Harali, Khalpa, Machigar, Mochigar, Madar, Madig, Telegu Mochi, Kamati Mochi, Ranigar, Rohit, Samgar
18 Chandal
19 Dabgar
20 Dhanak, Dhanuk
21 Dhankia
22 Dhobi
23 Dholi
24 Dome, Dom
25 Gandia
26 Garancha, Gancha
27 Garo, Garura, Gurda, Garoda
28 Gavaria
29 Godhi
30 Jingar
31 Kalbelia, Sapera
32 Kamad, Kamadia
33 Kanjar, Kunjar
34 Kapadia Sansi

35 Khangar
36 Khatik
37 Koli, Kori
38 Kooch Band, Kuchband
39 Koria
40 Madari, Bazigar
41 Mahar, Taral, Dhegumegu
42 Mahyavanshi, Dhed, Dheda, Vankar, Maru Vankar
43 Majhabi
44 Mang, Matang, Minimadig
45 Mang Garodi, Mang Garudi
46 Megh, Meghval, Meghwal, Menghvar
47 Mehar
48 Nat, Nut
49 Pasi
50 Rawal
51 Salvi
52 Sansi
53 Santia, Satia
54 Sarbhangi
55 Sargara
56 Singiwala
57 Thori, Nayak
58 Tirgar, Tirbanda
59 Turi

SIKKIM

1 Damai (Nepali)
2 Kami (Nepali), Lohar (Nepali)
3 Majhi (Nepali)
4 Sarki (Nepali)

TAMIL NADU

1 Adi Andhra
2 Adi Dravida
3 Adi Karnataka
4 Ajila
5 Arunthathiyar
6 Ayyanavar (in Kanyakumari district and Shenkottah taluk of Tirunelveli district).
7 Baira
8 Bakuda
9 Bandi
10 Bellara
11 Bharatar (in Kanyakumari district and Shenkottah taluk of Tirunelveli district).
12 Chakkiliyan
13 Chalavadi
14 Chamar, Muchi
15 Chandala
16 Cheruman
17 Devendrakulathan
18 Dom, Dombara, Paidi, Pano
19 Domban
20 Godagali
21 Godda
22 Gosangi
23 Holeya
24 Jaggali
25 Jambuvulu
26 Kadaiyan
27 Kakkalan (in Kanyakumari district and Shenkottah taluk of Tirunelveli district)a
28 Kalladi
29 Kanakkan, Padanna (in the Nilgiris district)b
30 Karimpalan
31 Kavara (in Kanyakumari district and Shenkottah taluk of Tirunelveli district).
32 Koliyan
33 Koosa
34 Kootan, Koodan (in Kanyakumari district and Shenkottah taluk of Tirunelveli district)
35 Kudumban
36 Kuravan, Sidhanar
37 Madari
38 Madiga
39 Maila

40 Mala
41 Mannan (in Kanyakumari district and Shenkottah taluk of Tirunelveli district)
42 Mavilan
43 Moger
44 Mundala
45 Nalakeyava
46 Nayadi
47 Padannan (in Kanyakumari district and Shenkottah taluk of Tirunelveli district)
48 Pagadai
49 Pallan
50 Palluvan
51 Pambada
52 Panan (in Kanyakumari district and Shenkottah taluk of Tirunelveli district)
53 Panchama
54 Pannadi
55 Panniandi
56 Paraiyan, Parayan, Sambavar
57 Paravan (in Kanyakumari district and Shenkottah taluk of Tirunelveli district) 58 Pathiyan (in Kanyakumari district and Shenkottah taluk of Tirunelveli district)
59 Pulayan, Cheramar
60 Puthirai Vannan
61 Raneyar
62 Samagara
63 Samban
64 Sapari
65 Semman
66 Thandan (in Kanyakumari district and Shenkottah taluk of Tirunelveli district)
67 Thoti
68 Tiruvalluvar
69 Vallon
70 Valluvan
71 Vannan (in Kanyakumari district and Shenkottah taluk of Tirunelveli district)
72 Vathiriyan
73 Velan
74 Vetan (in Kanyakumari district and Shenkottah taluk of Tirunelveli district)
75 Vettiyan
76 Vettuvan (in Kanyakumari district and Shenkottah taluk of Tirunelveli district)

TRIPURA

1 Bagdi
2 Bhuimali
3 Bhunar
4 Chamar, Muchi
5 Dandasi
6 Dhenuar
7 Dhoba
8 Dum
9 Ghasi
10 Gour
11 Gur
12 Jalia Kaibarta
13 Kahar
14 Kalindi
15 Kan
16 Kanda
17 Kanugh
18 Keot
19 Khadit
20 Kharia
21 Koch
22 Koir
23 Kol
24 Kora
25 Kotal
26 Mahisyadas
27 Mali
28 Mehtor
29 Musahar

30 Namasudra
31 Patni
32 Sabar

UTTARANCHAL

1 Agariya
2 Badhik
3 Badi
4 Baheliya
5 Baiga
6 Baiswar
7 Bajaniya
8 Bajgi
9 Balhar
10 Balai
11 Balmiki
12 Bangali
13 Banmanus
14 Bansphor
15 Barwar
16 Basor
17 Bawariya
18 Beldar
19 Beriya
20 Bhantu
21 Bhuiya
22 Bhuyiar
23 Boria
24 Chamar, Dhusia, Jhusia, Jatava
25 Chero
26 Dabgar
27 Dhangar
28 Dhanuk
29 Dharkar
30 Dhobi
31 Dom
32 Domar
33 Dusadh
34 Dharmi
35 Dhariya
36 Gond
37 Gwal
38 Habura
39 Hari
40 Hela
41 Kalabaz
42 Kanjar
43 Kapariya
44 Karwal
45 Kharaita
46 Kharwar (excluding Vanwasi)
47 Khatik
48 Kharot
49 Kol
50 Kori
51 Korwa
52 Lalbegi
53 Majhwar
54 Mazhabi
55 Musahar
56 Nat
57 Pankha
58 Parahiya
59 Pasi, Tarmali
60 Patari
61 Sahariya
62 Sanaurhiya
63 Sansiya
64 Shilpkar
65 Turaiha

UTTAR PRADESH

1 Agariya
2 Badhik
3 Badi
4 Baheliya
5 Baiga
6 Baiswar
7 Bajaniya
8 Bajgi
9 Balahar
10 Balai
11 Balmiki
12 Bangali
13 Banmanus

14 Bansphor
15 Barwar
16 Basor
17 Bawariya
18 Beldar
19 Beriya
20 Bhantu
21 Bhuiya
22 Bhuyiar
23 Boria
24 Chamar, Dhusia, Jhusia, Jatava
25 Chero
26 Dabgar
27 Dhangar
28 Dhanuk
29 Dharkar
30 Dhobi
31 Dom
32 Domar
33 Dusadh
34 Gharami
35 Ghasiya
36 Gond
37 Gual
38 Habura
39 Hari
40 Hela
41 Kalabaz
42 Kanjar
43 Kapariya
44 Karwal
45 Khairaha
46 Kharwar (excluding Benbansi)
47 Khatik
48 Khorot
49 Kol
50 Kori
51 Korwa
52 Lalbegi
53 Majhwar
54 Mazhabi
55 Musahar
56 Nat
57 Pankha
58 Parahiya
59 Pasi, Tarmali
60 Patari
61 Rawat
62 Saharya
63 Sanaurhiya
64 Sansiya
65 Shilpkar
66 Turaiha

WEST BENGAL

1 Bagdi, Duley
2 Bahelia
3 Baiti
4 Bantar
5 Bauri
6 Beldar
7 Bhogta
8 Bhuimali
9 Bhuiya
10 Bind
11 Chamar, Charmakar, Mochi, Muchi, Rabidas, Ruidas, Rishi
12 Chaupal
13 Dabgar
14 Damai (Nepali)
15 Dhoba, Dhobi
16 Doai
17 Dom, Dhangad
18 Dosadh, Dusadh, Dhari, Dharhi
19 Ghasi
20 Gonrhi
21 Halalkhor
22 Hari, Mehtar, Mehtor, Bhangi
23 Jalia Kaibartta
24 Jhalo Malo, Malo
25 Kadar
26 Kami (Nepali)
27 Kandra
28 Kanjar

29 Kaora
30 Karenga, Koranga
31 Kaur
32 Keot, Keyot
33 Khaira
34 Khatik
35 Koch
36 Konai
37 Konwar
38 Kotal
39 Kurariar
40 Lalbegi
41 Lohar
42 Mahar
43 Mal
44 Mallah
45 Musahar
46 Namasudra
47 Nat
48 Nuniya
49 Paliya
50 Pan, Sawasi
51 Pasi
52 Patni
53 Pod, Poundra
54 Rajbanshi
55 Rajwar
56 Sarki (Nepali)
57 Sunri (Excluding Saha)
58 Tiyar
59 Turi

Select Bibliography

Abbasayulu, Y.B.: 'Scheduled Castes Elite' Book Links Corporation, Hyderabad, 1978.

Abraham, C.M.: 'A review of trends in the Caste System', Seminar Paper presented at the Research Methodology Workshop, June, 1979.

Agarwal Pratap, C. and Mohamad, S.A.: 'Equality through privilege' Sri Ram Centre for Industrial Relations and Human resources, New Delhi, 1976.

Ainapur, L.S.: 'The Dynamics of Caste Relations in Rural India' Rawat Publications, Jaipur, 1986.

Alexander, K.C.: 'A study of Changing pattern of Behaviour: The Pullaya Untouchables of the Kerala', Unpublished Doctoral Theses, 1966.

Amarnath, R. Das: 'Comprehensive Institutional Care and School Education of Scheduled Caste of Andhra Pradesh', Unpublished Doctoral Thesis,1990.

Ambedkar, B.R.: 'The Untouchables - Who are they? Why they have become Untouchable', Amrit Book Company, New Delhi, 1948.

Anant, S.S.: 'The Changing concept of Caste in India', Vikas Publishers, Banglore, 1972.

Atal, Yogesh.: 'The Changing Frontiers of Castes', National Publishers, Delhi, 1968.

Bailey, C.: 'Caste and Economic Frontiers', Manchester University Press, Manchester, 1958 (Reprint, 1959)

Bailey, C.: 'Politics and Social Change in High Lands of Orissa in 1959', University of California Press, Berckley, 1963.

Barber, Bernard.: 'Social Mobility in Hindu India', in James Silverberg (ed) Social Mobility in the Caste System in India, Mouton Publishers, The Hague, 1968.

Barth, F.: 'The System of Social Stratification in Swat, North West Pakistan' in E.R. Leach (ed) Aspect of Caste in South India Ceylone and North West Pakistan, 1987.

Beteille, Andre.: Caste, Class and Power', University of California Press, Bombay, 1965, reprint 1966.

———: 'Caste Old and New', Asia Publishing House, Bombay, 1969.

Beals, A.R.: 'Leadership in Mysore Village', in Park R.L. and Tinker, I. (eds) Leadership and Political Institutions in India, Princeton University Press, Princeton, 1965.

Benerjee, A.: 'India: Social Forces in a Sunned Polity', in Mukhopadhayay (ed) Society and Politics in Contemporary India, Council for Political Studies, Calcutta, 1974.

Bendix, R.: 'Nation Building and Citizenship', Studies of Changing Social order', John Witney and Sons, New York, 1964.

Benjamin, Joseph.: 'Scheduled Caste in India Politics and Society', Ess Ess Publications, New Delhi, 1989.

Bennis, Waren et.al.: 'The Planning of Change', Holt Rineharr and Wiston, New York, 1969.

Berreman, Gerald.: 'Stratification and Pluralism and Interaction: A comparative analysis of Caste' in Rouck and Knight Foundations 1967.

Bhatt, A.: 'Caste, Class, and Politics', Monohar Book Service, Delhi, 1975.

Bhattacharya, B.N.: 'Hindu Castes and Sects' Editions India, Calcutta, reprint, 1968.

Blunt, E.A.H.: 'Caste System of Northern India', S. Chand and Company, New Delhi, 1931 reprint: 1969.

Borala, P.T.: 'Segregation and desegregation in India', Popular Prakasan, Bombay, 1968.

Bose, N.K.: 'Calcutta: A social survey' Lavani Publishing House, Bombay, 1969.

Bottomore, T.B.: 'Sociology', George Allen and Unwin London, 1962.

British Paramountacy: 'British Paramountacy and Indian Renaissance', PartII, Bharathiya Vidya Bhavan, Bombay.

Bougle, Calestine.: 'Essays on the Caste system', Cambridge University Press, Cambridge, 1971.

Chaplin, Susan E.: Scavengers: Still Marginalised in Ghanshyam Shah (ed) 'Dalits and the State', Concept Publishing Company', New Delhi, 2001.

Chouhan, B.R.: 'Leadership in Rajasthan Village' in Vidyathi (ed) Leadership in India, Asia Publishing House, Bombay, 1967.

———: 'Special Problems of the Education of the Scheduled Castes', N.C.E.R.T, New Delhi, 1967.

Cohn, Beranard, S.: 'The Changing status of a Depressed Caste', in Mc Kim Marriot (ed) Village India, Chicago, 1955.

Dahendorf, R.: 'Class and Class conflict in Industrial Society', Stanford University Press, Stanford, 1966.

Dallord, John.: 'Caste and Class in a southern town', Doubleday, New York, 1937. .

Damle, Y.B.: 'Reference Group theory and Mobility in Indian Caste system', in James Silverberg (ed) Social Mobility in Caste System in India, Moutan Publishers, The Hague, 1968

Davis, Kingsley: 'The Population of India and Pakistan', Princeton University Press, Princeton, 1951.

Desai, A.R.: 'Social Background of Indian Nationalism', Popular Prakasan Bombay, 1966.

Desai, A.R. and Damle, Y.B.: 'A Note on the change in Rural Gujarat', in Kapadia (ed) Ghurye Facilitation Volume, Popular Book Depot, Bombay, 1954.

Dhillon, S.C.: 'Leadership and Group in a Souch Indian Village', Project Evolutionary Organisation, Delhi, 1955.

D'Souza, V.S.: 'Educational inequalities among Scheduled Castes' Punjab University Press, Chandigarh, 1980.

Dube, S.C.: 'Indian Village', Toutledge and Kegan Paul Ltd., London, 1960.

———: 'The study of complex cultures' in T.K.N. Unnithan et. al (ed) Towards a Sociological of Cultures in India, Prentice Hall, New Delhi, 1965.

Dumint, Louis.: 'Homo Heirarchiaus', Vikas Publications, Delhi, 1970.

Duskis, Lelah.: 'The Policy of Indian National Congress Towards the Depressed Classes: A Historical Study', Unpublished thesis, 1957.

Einsentadt, S.N.: 'Prologue: Some remarks on patterns of change in traditional and Modern India' in Iswaran (ed) Villages Columbia University Press, New York, 1970.

Elayaperumal.: 'Report of the Committee on Untouchability, 1969.

Eranda, M.: 'Small is Politics: Organizational Alternative in Indian Rural Development', Willey Eastern, Delhi, 1979.

Eriedman, John.; 'Retraking America: A Theory of Transitional Planning' Anchor Press, New York, 1974.

Frunivell, J.S. Netherlands: 'India: A Study of plural economy' Cambridge University Press, Cambridge, 1909.

Fuchs, Stphen: 'At the Bottom of the India Society', Bombay, 1981.

Ghanshyam Shah: Dalits and State: An Overview in Ghanshyam Shah (ed) 'Dalits and the State', Concept Publishing Company', New Delhi, 2001.

Ghanshyam Shah: Untouchability in Rural Gujarat: Revisited in Ghanshyam Shah (ed) 'Dalits and the State', Concept Publishing Company', New Delhi, 2001.

Gallanter, Mark.: 'The abolition of disabilities: Untouchability and Law', In Micheal Mahar (ed) The Untouchability in Contemporary India. University of Arizona Press, Tuscon, 1972.

Girridhar Gomanog: 'Constitutional Provisions for the Scheduled Castes and The Scheduled Tribes', Himalaya Publishing House, Bombay, 1992.

Gnana Prakasam: 'Social Separatism ', Rawat Publication, Jaipur, 1998.

Gough, Katheleen: 'Caste in Tanjore Village' in E.R. Leach (ed) Aspect of Caste in South India, Ceylone and Northwest Pakishthan, Cambridge University Press, Cambridge, 1960.

Ghurye, G.S.: 'Caste and Class in India' Popular Book Depot, Bombay, 1950.

Gill.: 'Unraveling Social Policy; Schenkman Publishing Company, Cambridge, 1973.

Glen, M. and Sipra Bose: 'Social Mobility among untouchables' in Giri Raj Gupta (ed) Cohesion and Conflict in Modern India, Vikas Publishing House, New Delhi, 1978.

Gould, Harold, A.: 'Time dimension and structural change' in Milton Singer, Cohn (ed) Indian Kinship System: A Problem of conceptual refinement, Aldine Publishing Company, Chicago, 1958.

Gupta, B.N.: 'The Dynamics of Caste ranking and Intercaste relations in a village community of North West India with Particulars reference to Social Change', The Sociological Congress, 1958.

Harper, Edward. B.: 'Social Consequence of an unsuccessful Low Caste Movement', in James Silverberg (ed) Social Mobility in India, Mouton, The Hague, 1968.

Harsh Mander: Status of Dalits and Agenda for State Intervention in Ghanshyam Shah (ed) 'Dalits and the State', Concept Publishing Company', New Delhi, 2001.

Havelock, Ronald, G. and Mary, C.: 'Training for Change Aspects Centre for Utilization of Scientific Knowledge', University of Mkichigan, Amn Arber, 1973.

Hazara, C.F.: 'Studies in Puranik Records on Rights and Customs', 1940.

Hitochcock, John.: 'The idea of Martial Rajput', in Milton and Singh (ed) Traditional India: Structure and Change, American Folklore Society, Philadelphia, 1960

Hocort, A.M.: 'Caste', Methuen and Company, London, 1950.

Hunter, G.: 'Modernizing Present Societies' Oxford University Press, London, 1964.

Hutton, J.H.: 'Caste in India' Cambridge Press, Cambridge, 1946.

Issac, Harold.R.: 'India's Ex-untouchables' Asia Publishing House, Bombay, 1965.

Iswaran, K.: 'Instruction' in K. Iswaran (ed) Change and Continuty in India Villages, Columbia University Press, New York, 1970.

Jackson, J.K.: 'Social Stratification, Cambridge Press, Cambridge, 1968.

Jatava, D.R.: 'The Social Philosophy of D.R. Ambedkar, Phonoix Publishers, 1965.

Jayaraman, R.: 'Caste and Clall: Dynamics of Inequality in Indian Society' Ambedkar, Phonix Publishers, 1965.

Jha, M.L.: 'Untouchability and Education' Namitha Publication, Meerut, 1973.

Jose, Kenankil.: 'The Scheduled Castes and their status in India' in inequality its bases and search for sollution (ed) Walter Fernandaes, Indian Social Institute, 180.

Joshi, R.P.: 'Constitutionalization of Panchayati Raj', Rawat Publication, Jaipur, 1998.

Kamble, N.D.: 'Atrocities on Schedules Castes in Post Independence India' Ashish Publishing House, Delhi, 1981.

Kamble, Ramesh: Untouchability in Urban Setting: Everyday Social Experience of Ex-Untouchables in Bombay in Ghanshyam Shah (ed) 'Dalits and the State', Concept Publishing Company', New Delhi, 2001.

Keer, D.: 'Dr. Ambedkar: Life and Mission', Popular Prakasan, Bombay, 1962.

Krishnan, P.S.: Untouchables and Atrocities in Ghanshyam Shah (ed) 'Dalits and the State', Concept Publishing Company', New Delhi, 2001.

Ketkar, Sridhar, V.: 'The history of Caste in India' Taylor and Carpenter, New York, 1909.

Khan, Mumthaz Ali.: 'Scheduled Castes and their status in India' Uppal Publishing House, New Delhi, 1980.

Lenski, Gerhard. E.: 'Power and Privilege: A theory of Social Stratification' Mc Graw Hill Book Company, New Delhi, 1966.

Lewis, Oscar.: 'Village life in Northern India' University of Illinois Press, Urbaba, 1958.

Lynch, Owen. M.: 'The Politics of Untouchability ' Columbia University Press, New York, 1969.

Mac Iver, R.M. and Page, C.M.: 'Society' The Mac Milan Press, London, 1953.

Mine, Sir Henry Summer: 'Village Communities in the East and West', John Murray, London, 1890.

Majundar, D.N.: 'Social Contours of an Industrial City: Social Survey of Kanpur', Asia Publishing House, Bombay, 1960.

Malik, Sunila: 'Social Integration of Schedules Caste, Abhinav Publications, New Delhi, 1979.

Madelbaum, D.G.: 'Society in India' Popular Prakasan, Bombay, 1972.

Manju Kumar.: 'Social Inequality Sultan Chand and Company, Nee Delhi, 1982.

Marriot, Mckim: 'Caste ranking an community Structure in Five Regions of India and Pakistan', Poona, 1965.

Marx, Karl: 'Capital', 3 Vols. Kerr, Chicago, 1909.

Mathew, Joseph: 'Ideology Protest and Social Mobility', Inter India Publishers, New Delhi, 1986.

Mayer, Adrian, C.: 'Caste and Kinship in Central India', London, 1960.

Miller, D.B.: 'Hierarchy to Stratification: Changing pattern of Social inequality in North India village', Oxford University Press, Delhi, 1975.

Michael Mahar, J.: 'The Untouchables in Contemporary India', Rawat Publications, Jaipur, 1998.

Milton Singer.: 'Traditional India: Structure and Change', University of California Press, Berkely, 1959.

Mohinder Singh.: 'The Depressed Classes', Hind Kitab Limited, Bombay, 1947.

Mukhopadhayay. A.K.: 'Society and politics in Contemparary India' Council for Political Studies, Calcutta, 1960.

Muralidharadu, P: Political Power and Conflict' Andhra University, Waltair, 1982 (unpublished Ph.D. thesis).

Myers, A.C.: 'Caste and Kinship in Central India', University of California Press, Berkeley, 1960.

Myrdal.: 'The American Delema' Harper and Brothers Publications, New York, 1944.

Naik, J.P.: Education of the Schedules Castes', I.C.S.S.R., 1971.

Nambissan, Geetha. B.: Equity in Education? The Schooling of Dalit Children in India in Ghanshyam Shah (ed) 'Dalits and the State', Concept Publishing Company', New Delhi, 2001.

Nanduram.: 'The Mobile Scheduled Castes', Hindustan Publishing Corporation, New Delhi, 1988.

Nandu Ram: Equality Trough Legislation: Social Consequences of Gradual Change in Ghanshyam Shah (ed) 'Dalits and the State', Concept Publishing Company', New Delhi, 2001.

Narayan, I.: 'Rural Elite and Elections in Indian State', National Publishers, New Delhi. 1976.

Neele, W.E.: 'The search for Unity, Democracy and Progress', Princeton Press, Princeton, 1965.

Omprakash, S.: Castes and Politics in Indian Education', Deep and Deep Publications, New Delhi, 1986.

Omprakash, S. and Sen, A.K.: 'Caste Hindu and Scheduled Caste Children in Rural, Ess Ess Publication, New Delhi, 1985.

Oomen, T.K.:'Scheduled Caste and Schedules Tribes in India Since Independence' (ed) S.C. Dube, Vikas Publishing House, New Delhi, 1977.

Opler, M.: 'Factors of Tradition and Change in Local Elections in Rural India' Oxford University Press, London, 1959.

Orienstein, Henry.: 'Gaon: Conflict and Cohesion in an Indian Villages', Princeton University Press, London, 1959.

Pandey, P.N.: 'Protective Discrimination and Social Uplift among the Scheduled Castes and Scheduled Tribes in India: A Socio-Economic Profile' (ed) Upadhy. Anmol Publications, New Delhi, 1991.

Pannikar, K.M.: 'Hindu Society at the Cross-Roads', Asia Publishing House, Bombay, 1955.

Parmar, Y.A.: 'The Mahyavanshi' Mittal Publications, New Delhi, 1981.

Parsons, Talcott: 'A revised analytical approach to the theory of Social stratification' in Bendix and Lipset (eds) Class, Status and Power, The Freepress, New York, 1954.

Fatwardhan, Sunanda: A Study of Scheduled Castes in Urban Setting' Unpublished Doctoral thesis, Poona University, 1965.

Pimpley, P.N. and Sharma, S.K.: 'Struggle for Status' B. R. Publishing Corporation, Delhi, 1985.

Punit, A.E.: 'Structural Determinants in Rural Leadership' Unpublished Doctoral Thesis, Karnataka University, 1969.

Rangari, A.D.: 'Indian Caste System and Education' Deep and Deep Publications, New Delhi, 1984.

Rao, P.K. and Rao, M.C.: 'Critique on group prejudice in India', in Nanavathi M.B. and C.N. Vakil (ed) Group Prejudice in India, Vora Publications, Bombay, 1951.

Rathod, P.V. and Vijay Kumar: The working of the Scheduled Castes and Scheduled Tribes (Prevention of Atrocities) Act 1989 in Gujarat in Ghanshyam Shah (ed) 'Dalits and the State', Concept Publishing Company', New Delhi, 2001.

Revankar, Ratna.: 'The Indian Constitution: A case study of Backward Class', Dixon University Press, Faridabad, 1973.

Risley, H.H.: 'Tribes and Castes of Bengal Ethnographic Glossary', Calcutta, 1891.

Rowe, William. K.: 'Mobility in the Nineteenth Century Caste system', in Milton Singer and Cohn (eds) Structure and Change in Indian Society, Aldine Publishers, Chigago, 1963.

Rudolph, C.I. and Rudolph, S.H.: 'The modernity of tradition' Orient Longman, New Delhi, 1969.

Ryan, Bruce.: Caste in Modern Ceylone' Rudgers University Press, New Brunswick, 1953.

Sabarwa, Stasish,: 'Status, Mobility and Network in Pubjabi Industrial Town' (ed) Beyond Village, Indian Institute of Advanced Study, Simla, 1972.

Sachidananda: 'The Harijan Elite', Thomson Press (India) Ltd., Faridabad, 1977.

Sagar, S.L.: 'Hindu Culture and Caste System in India', Uppal Book House, Delhi, 1974.

Sankaran, S.R.: Dalits and State: An Overview in Ghanshyam Shah (ed) 'Dalits and the State', Concept Publishing Company', New Delhi, 2001.

Santhakumari, R.: 'Impact of Welfare measure on Backward Classes, A study on Scheduled Castes of Kerala', University of Trivendrum, 1976.

Selvanathan.: 'Status of Scheduled Caste', Asiah Publishing House, New Delhi, 1989.

Senart, Emile.: 'Caste in India' Mathuen & Co. London, 1930.

Sheshadri, K.: 'Political Linkages and Rural Development' National Publishers, New Delhi, 1976.

Shah, A.M. and Shorff, R.G.: 'Hindu Castes and Tribes', Cosmo Publications, New Delhi, 1974.

Simon R. Charsley & G.K. Karanth.: 'Challenging Untouchability', Sage Publication, New Delhi, 1998.

Singh, Yogendra.: 'Chanukhera – Cultural Change in Eastern Uttar Pradesh' in Iswaran (ed) Change and Continuity in Indias Vilalges, Columbia University Press, New York, 1970.

———: 'Modernization of Indian Traditions', Thomson Press, New Delhi, 1973.

———: Social Stratification and Change in India', Monohar, New Delhi, 1977.

Silverberg, James: 'Social Mobility in the Caste System in India', (ed) Mounton Publishers, The Hague, 1968.

Sivakumar, C.: 'Higher Educational: Social Stratification and Social change in Mysore in 1960's in Dimensions of Social Change (eds) Srinivas, M.N., Sheshaiah, and Partha Sarathy, Allied Publishers, New Delhi, 1977.

Soran Singh.: 'Abstract of Thesis', Indian Dissertation Abstracts. (C.S.S.R.) Delhi, 1976.

Sorokin, Pitrim. A.: 'Social and Cultural Dynamics' American Book Company, New York, 1976.

Sovani.: 'Poona: A resurvey' Gokhale Institute of Politics and Publications No. 34.

Srinivas, M.N.: 'Religion and Society among Coorgs of south India', Oxford, Bombay, 1952.

———: 'Caste in Modern India' in Srinivas Essays, Asia Publishing House, London, 1962.

———: 'Mobility in Caste System' in Milton Singer and Cohn (eds) Structure and change in Indian Society. Aldine Publishing Company, Chicago, 1969.

Stein, Burton.: 'Social Mobility and medieval South Indian Sects' in James Silverberg (ed) Social Mobility in the Caste System in India, Mouton, The Hague 1968.

Thangaraj, M.: Access to Land by Scheduled Castes and Schedules Tribes in India in Ghanshyam Shah (ed) 'Dalits and the State', Concept Publishing Company', New Delhi, 2001.

Thekkamallai S.S.: 'Educational Mobility: A study of the Perception of the Harijans on the role Structural Elements' XIX All India Sociological Conference, Harayan Agl. College, Hissar, 1989.

Tumin, Melvin.: 'Social Stratification: The forms and Functions of Equality' Englewood Cliffs, New Jersey.

Umamohan, Ch.: 'Occupational Mobility in Two Villages of Andhra Pradesh' Unpublished Doctoral Thesis, Osmania University, Hyderabad.

Usha Rao, N.J.: 'Deprived Caste in India' Chugh Publications, Allahabad, 1981.

Vagheswari, Alladi: 'Income earning trends and Social status of Harijan Community in Tamil Nadu', Sangham, Madras, 1972.

Vanaja S. Kumar.: Political process in Rayalaseema Villages', Unpublished Doctoral Thesis, Anantapur, 1991.

Velblen, T.: 'The theory of Leisure Class' Viking Press, New York, 1953.

Venkateshwarlu, G.: 'Perceptions by Scheduled Castes and Attitudes of Caste Hindus on forms of untouchability in Andhra Pradesh', in Upadhy (ed) Scheduled Castes and Scheduled Tribes, Anmol Publications, New Delhi, 1977.

Vidyarthi, L.P. and Mishra, N.: 'Harijan Today', Classical Publications, New Delhi, 1977.

Vya, N.N. and Chowdary, N.D.: 'The Frontier Bhils and Meghwalas', Udaipur, 1970.

Wankhede, G.G.: 'Social Mobility & Schedluled Castes', Rawaat Publication, Jaipur, 1999.

Water, Neal. C.: 'India: The Search for unity, democracy, and power', D. Van Nostrand Company, Princeton, 1965.

Weber, Mad.: 'Class Status and Party' in Gerth and Mills (Eds) from Max Weber: Essays in Sociology, New York, Oxford University Press, 1940.

Weslowskim, W.: 'Some notes on the Functional theory of Stratification' in Bendix and Lipset (eds) Class, Status and Power, New York, 1966.

William, Jr. Robin.: 'American Society' Alfred Knopf, New York, 1960

Zelliot: 'Dr. Ambedkar and the Mahar Movement, Unpublished Doctoral Thesis, Pensylvania.

Articles

Adams, E.M.: 'The Logic of Planning, *Social Forces,* Vol.28, 1950.

Alexander, K.C.: 'The problems of neo Christians of Kerala', *Man in India,* Vol. 47, 1967.

Bada, C.R.: 'Urbanization of Scheduled Castes' *Inter-discipline.* Vol. 12, 1975.

Bailey, C.: 'For a Sociology of India', *Contributions to Indian Sociology,* Vol. III, 1959.

Bennur, C.S. and Abraham, D.: 'A study of the relation between Socio-economic Status and Academic Achievement of Pupils in Rural and Urban High School, *Journal of Karnataka University,* No. 90, 1973.

Berreman, Gerald.: 'Caste in India and United States', *American Journal of Sociology,* Vol. IXVI, No.2, 1960.

———: "Race caste other indiduous Distinctions in Social Stratification', *Race* Vol. XIII NO.4, 1972.

Bhatt, A.: 'Politics and Social Mobility in India', *Contributions to Indian Sociology,* 1971.

Bhattacharya, B.N., Yadav, R.C. and Pandey, G.D.: 'Some Characteristics of Households in Rural Varanasi" *Society and Culture,* No. 7, 1966.

Boite, U. and Boite, A.: 'The Dalit Shitya Movement in Maharastra: A Sociological Analysis' *Sociological Bulletin,* No. 26, 1966.

Bhowmkick, P.K.: 'Occupational changes in two Villages in Bengal', *Man in India,* No. 48, 1968.

Bopegamage, A.: 'Caste and Poverty', *Sociology and Social Research,* Vol. 57, 1972.

Freema, J.M.: 'Occupational Change in an Urbanizing Hindu Temple Village', *Man in India,* No. 51, 1973.

Gandhi, P.C.: 'Caste Distinction' *Times of India,* (July 14) 1973.

Gangrade, K.D.: 'Social Mobility in India: A Study Depressed Class' *Man in India,* Vol. 55, 1975.

Garg, B.B.: 'A study on occupational mobility' *Inter-discipline,* Vol. 10, 1973.

Ghough, Kathleen.: 'Criteria of Caste ranking in South India', *Man in India,* Vol. 39, 1965.

Habid, Ifran.: 'An Examination of Wiltigogal's Theory of Oriental Despotism' *Enquiry,* 1963.

Harddgrave, R.L. (Jr.): 'Caste fission and fussion', *Economic and Political Weekly,* July, 1968.

Hasan, Amir.: 'The Occupational pattern in Teroy Village', *Eastern Anthropologist* Vol. 1968.

———: 'Harijan Welfare in Uttar Pradesh', *Social Welfare,* Vol. XVIII, 1972.

Jain, S.P.: 'Occupational differentiation in North Indian Community' *Man in India,* Vol. 47, 1967.

Jaiswa, N.K. and Ambastha, C.K.: 'Caste and Occupational Mobility in east Bihar Village', *Indian Journal of Social Research,* Vol. 3, 1967.

Jetley.: 'Transfer of Power to a Low Caste', *Inter-discipline,* Vol. 5, 1969.

Jorapur, P.B.: 'Intergenerational Occupational Mobility', *The Indian Journal of Social Work,* Vol. No. XXXI, 1971.

Jyothirmayee Sharma.: 'The Secular Status of Caste', *Eastern Anthropologist,* Vol.7, 1958.

Kamat, A.R.: 'Primary Education: Participation and Wastage', *Economic and Political Weekly,* Vol. 18, 1972.

Kassambaum, G. and Vidya Sagar N.E.C.: 'A Survey of Caste and Occupational Mobility in a Small city of India', *Man in India,* 1974.

Kemper, T.D.: 'Marxist and Functionalist Theories of Social Stratification: Common Elements that Lead to a Test' *Social Forces,* Vol. 54. (3), 1976.

Kochole, D.D.: 'Marriage and family life in Mongs', *Indian Journal of Social Research,* Vol. 3, 1980.

Kothurkar, V.K. and Pendise, V.V.: 'Study of Social Prejudice in Three Indian Villages: The Problem of Nav Bhudda', *Journal of University of Poona,* 1962.

Kuppuswamy, B.: 'A statistical study of attitude to the Caste system in South India' *Journal of Psychology,* Vol. 1942m 1956.

La Touche, T.W.: 'Citadel of Untouchability Shaken but not taken', *Social Welfare,* January 1958.

Mandal, B.B.: 'Social Mobility: An appraisal in Indian Context', *Journal of Social Research,* Vol. XVIII, 1975.

Mankdy, A.: 'Intergenerational Occupational Mobility among the Scheduled Caste', *Social Change,* March-June, 1979.

Mohapatra, M. and Mohapatra, S.: 'Untouchability and Untouchables in an India State', *Journal of Social Research,* Vol. XXII, 1979.

Moore, Wilbert. E.: 'Comment', *American Sociological Review,* Vol. No. 18, 1953.

Muralidharudu P.: 'Political Power Structure in Rural India', *Man and Life,* Vol. 7, 1981.

Nadel: 'Caste and Government in Primitive Society', *Journal of the Anthropological Society of Bombay,* 1954.

Nandi, S.K.: 'Impact of Christinanity on the Chamars of Majwari: A Bajpuri Village', *Journal of Social Research,* Vol. 1, 1976.

Parasons, Talcot: 'An Analytical approach to the Theory of Social Stratification', *American Journal of Sociology,* Vol. 45, 1945.

Paratamma.: 'Ambedkar and after: The Position and future of Scheduled Caste masses and class', *Eastern Anthropology,* Vol. 26, 1954.

———: 'The Weaker Sections of the Society the Scheduled Castes of India', *Sociological Bulletin,* Vol.30 1981.

Patrudu, B.V.S.: 'Scheduled Caste in India: Social progress and Social Legislation', *Social Welfare,* Vol. 10, 1971.

Philips, W.S.K.: 'Occupational Mobility: Pattern in Urban India' *The Indian Journal of Social Work,* Vol. 13, 1957.

Pocock, D.: 'Inclusion and Exclusion: A Process in the Caste System of Gujarat', *SouthWestern Journal of Anthropology,* Vol. 13, 1957.

Ramu, G.N.: 'Untouchability in rural areas' *The Indian Journal of Social Work,* Vol. 2, 1968.

Ramu, G.N. and Weibe, Paul.: 'Occupational and Educational Mobility in relation to caste in Urban India, *Sociology and Social Research,* Vol. 5, 1975.

Rao, K.R.: 'Intergenerational Social and occupational mobility', *The Indian Journal of Social Research,* Vol. 7, 1966.

Rath, R.: 'From Social Isolation to Stagnation A Study of Schedule Caste Group', *Social Action,* Vol. 24, 1974.

Reddy, G.P.: 'Caste and change of Occupation in a village in Andhra Pradesh', *The Eastern Anthropologist,* Vol.1, 1968.

Redfield, R.: 'The Social Organisation of Tradition', *Far Eastern Quarterly,* Vol. 15, 1955.

Riemer, Svend.: 'Social Planning and Social Organisation', *American Journal of Sociology,* Vol. 52, 1947.

Sarkar, J.: 'Occupational Mobility among the Kumbars of Mysore City', *Man in India,* Vol. 53, 1973.

Shah, A.M.: 'Basic terms and concepts in the study of Family in India', *Economic and Social History View,* Vol. 1, 1964.

Shakir, M.: 'Scheduled Castes: Beyond the System', *Economic and Political Weekly,* Vol.18, 1975.

Shamalal: 'Caste and Occupational Mobility in a Jodhpur Bhangi Basti', *Journal of Social Research,* Vol. 18, 1975.

Shrama, K.L.: 'Stresses in Caste stratification: A Study of six Villages in Rajasthan', *Economic and Political Weekly,* Vol. VI, 1969.

Shrama, H.P.: 'Caste and Occupational Mobility in A Delhi Village', *The Eastern Anthropology,* Vol. XXIV, 1971.

Sinha, A.K.P and: 'A study of prejudice among university students', *Indian Journal of Psychology,* Vol. 35, 1960.

Soundarajan, K.R.: 'The Great Betrayal' *The Illustrated Weekly,* (Sept) 1973.

Srinivastava, S.P.: 'Educated Harijans Should show the way', *Social Welfare,* Vol. 11, 1973.

Stinch Combe, A.L.: 'Some Empirical consequences of Davis and Moore Theory of Stratification', *American Sociological Review,* Vol. 18, 1953.

Troisi, J.: 'Social Movements among the Santhals', *Social Action,* Vol. 26, 1976.

Tumin, Melvin.: 'Some Principle of Stratification', *American Sociological Review,* Vol. 18, 1953.

———: 'Rewards and Task Orientation' *American Sociological Review,* Vol. XX, 1955.

———: 'On Inequality', *American Sociological Review,* Vol. 28, 1953.

Uma, Ramaswamy,: 'Scheduled Castes of Andhra Pradesh some aspect of Challenge', *Economic and Political Weekly,* 1974.

———: 'Preference and Progress: The Scheduled Caste', *Economic and Political Weekly,* Vol. 19, 1984.

Vanaja, S.K. and Venkateswarulu, G.: 'Socio-economic Structure of Harijans of Kalyanadurg town of Anantapur District. A Survey Study', *Indian journal of Social Research,* Vol. XXI, 1980.

Viswanadham.: 'Functional Theory of Stratification and Social inequalities in India', *Indian Journal of Comparative Sociology,* Vol. 1, 1975.

Weibe, P.D. and Peter, J.: 'The Catholic Church and Caste in Rural Tamil Nadu', *Eastern Anthropologist,* Vol. XXV (1), 1972.

Wrong, Dennis. H.: The Functional theory of Stratification: Some neglected Considerations', *American Sociological Review,* Vol. 24, 1959.

Index